HEIRS OF AN AMBIVALENT EMPIRE

McGILL-QUEEN'S STUDIES IN EARLY CANADA / AVANT LE CANADA

Series Editors / Directeurs de la collection:
Allan Greer and Carolyn Podruchny

This series features studies of the history of the northern half of North America – a vast expanse that would eventually be known as Canada – in the era before extensive European settlement and extending into the nineteenth century. Long neglected, Canada-before-Canada is a fascinating area of study experiencing an intellectual renaissance as researchers in a range of disciplines, including history, geography, archeology, anthropology, literary studies, and law, contribute to a new and enriched understanding of the distant past. The editors welcome manuscripts in English or French on all aspects of the period, including work on Indigenous history, the Atlantic fisheries, the fur trade, exploration, French or British imperial expansion, colonial life, culture, language, law, science, religion, and the environment.

Cette série de monographies est consacrée à l'histoire de la partie septentrionale du continent de l'Amérique du nord, autrement dit le grand espace qui deviendra le Canada, dans les siècles qui s'étendent jusqu'au début du 19e. Longtemps négligé par les chercheurs, ce Canada-avant-le-Canada suscite beaucoup d'intérêt de la part de spécialistes dans plusieurs disciplines, entre autres, l'histoire, la géographie, l'archéologie, l'anthropologie, les études littéraires et le droit. Nous assistons à une renaissance intellectuelle dans ce champ d'étude axé sur l'interaction de premières nations, d'empires européens et de colonies. Les directeurs de cette série sollicitent des manuscrits, en français ou en anglais, qui portent sur tout aspect de cette période, y compris l'histoire des autochtones, celle des pêcheries de l'atlantique, de la traite des fourrures, de l'exploration, de l'expansion de l'empire français ou britannique, de la vie coloniale (Nouvelle-France, l'Acadie, Terre-Neuve, les provinces maritimes, etc.), de la culture, la langue, le droit, les sciences, la religion ou l'environnement.

1 A Touch of Fire
Marie-André Duplessis, the Hôtel-Dieu of Quebec, and the Writing of New France
Thomas M. Carr, Jr

2 Entangling the Quebec Act
Transnational Contexts, Meanings, and Legacies in North America and the British Empire
Edited by Ollivier Hubert and François Furstenberg

3 Listening to the Fur Trade
Soundways and Music in the British North American Fur Trade, 1760–1840
Daniel Robert Laxer

4 Heirs of an Ambivalent Empire
French-Indigenous Relations and the Rise of the Métis in the Hudson Bay Watershed
Scott Berthelette

Heirs of an Ambivalent Empire

French-Indigenous Relations and the Rise of the Métis in the Hudson Bay Watershed

SCOTT BERTHELETTE

McGill-Queen's University Press
Montreal & Kingston • London • Chicago

ISBN 978-0-2280-1058-6 (cloth)
ISBN 978-0-2280-1059-3 (paper)
ISBN 978-0-2280-1249-8 (ePDF)
ISBN 978-0-2280-1250-4 (ePUB)

Legal deposit third quarter 2022
Bibliothèque nationale du Québec

Reprinted 2024

Printed in Canada on acid-free paper that is 100% ancient forest free (100% post-consumer recycled), processed chlorine free

This book has been published with the help of a grant from the Canadian Federation for the Humanities and Social Sciences, through the Awards to Scholarly Publications Program, using funds provided by the Social Sciences and Humanities Research Council of Canada.

Funded by the Government of Canada | Financé par le gouvernement du Canada | Canada | Canada Council for the Arts | Conseil des arts du Canada

We acknowledge the support of the Canada Council for the Arts.

Nous remercions le Conseil des arts du Canada de son soutien.

McGill-Queen's University Press in Montreal is on land which long served as a site of meeting and exchange amongst Indigenous Peoples, including the Haudenosaunee and Anishinabeg nations. In Kingston it is situated on the territory of the Haudenosaunee and Anishinaabek. We acknowledge and thank the diverse Indigenous Peoples whose footsteps have marked these territories on which peoples of the world now gather.

Library and Archives Canada Cataloguing in Publication

Title: Heirs of an ambivalent empire: French-Indigenous relations and the rise of the Métis in the Hudson Bay watershed / Scott Berthelette.

Names: Berthelette, Scott, author.

Series: McGill-Queen's studies in early Canada; 4.

Description: Series statement: McGill-Queen's studies in early Canada; 4 | Includes bibliographical references and index.

Identifiers: Canadiana (print) 20220161534 | Canadiana (ebook) 20220171475 | ISBN 9780228010593 (softcover) | ISBN 9780228010586 (hardcover) | ISBN 9780228012498 (PDF) | ISBN 9780228012504 (ePUB)

Subjects: LCSH: Canada—History—To 1763 (New France) | CSH: French Canadians—Hudson Bay Region—History. | CSH: Canadians, French-speaking—Hudson Bay Region—History. | LCSH: Métis—Hudson Bay Region—History. | LCSH: Fur trade—Hudson Bay Region—History. | LCSH: Canada—Race relations—History. | LCSH: Canada—Ethnic relations—History.

Classification: LCC FC3211.9.16 B47 2022 | DDC 971.01/8—dc23

This book was typeset by Marquis Interscript in 10.5/13 Sabon.

Contents

Figures

PREFACE

La Vérendrye and the Roots of the Métis People

When I was an MA student at the University of Manitoba, not so many years ago in 2013, I attended my first ever academic conference in Ottawa. The conference was the ninth annual Pierre Savard Conference, a graduate student colloquium hosted by the University of Ottawa. I was presenting some of my early research on Pierre Gaultier de Varennes, sieur de La Vérendrye (1685–1749), a French explorer and key figure in the French-Indigenous history of western North America. To my delight, Dr Nicole St-Onge, a renowned historian in the field of Métis history, was chairing our after-lunch session, which was titled "Les Autochtones et les Métis en Amérique du Nord/North American Aboriginal and Métis History." Upon arriving at the conference room, I was surprised to see that Dr St-Onge recognized my surname immediately, even though we had never met and I was just a graduate student from an out-of-province university. Since I was only at the beginning of my academic journey, I had no reputation worth recognizing.

Dr St-Onge is known for her work with the Métis community of Saint-Laurent, on the shores of Lake Manitoba, but from the outset she seemed to know a lot about my own Métis family's history from St Vital, in Winnipeg, Manitoba. Dr St-Onge pointed me to an article that she had written in 1985 about Métis families at Pointe-à-Grouette (Sainte-Agathe, Manitoba), including the Berthelettes, who were dispossessed of their agricultural landholdings by francophone settlers from Quebec. Members of the Berthelette family who lost their river lots and were displaced from Pointe-à-Grouette included my great-great-great-great grandfather Joseph Berthelet (*père*, 1809–1894) and my great-great-great grandfather Joseph Berthelet (*fils*, 1835–1916).

Following the Manitoba Act of 1870, agrarian settlers from Ontario and Quebec transformed and supplanted the Métis landholdings of the Red River Valley, a process of dispossession that transformed Pointe-à-Grouette, a Métis settlement of farmers and hunters, into Sainte-Agathe du Manitoba, a French-Canadian village.[1] The loss of land experienced by many Métis families has led to poverty, rootlessness, and the displacement of identity and language that are still being experienced by many Métis people today.

As interesting as the history of the Métis and my family was, I was in Ottawa to present my research on La Vérendrye's relations with the Indigenous peoples of the Hudson Bay watershed, which seemed chronologically quite distant from my late nineteenth-century ancestors at Pointe-à-Grouette. When I first began my MA in 2013, my aim was to disprove that La Vérendrye was a French explorer and fur trader worthy of commendation and commemoration, or that he was someone who had entertained "good relations with the First Nations by respecting their way of life," or, even worse, that he should be mythologized as some sort of "founding father" of the Franco-Manitobans.[2] Rather than being an emblematic figure of western Canada, La Vérendrye was an ethnocentric imperial agent, a lackluster explorer, and a war profiteer who trafficked in Indigenous slaves in the 1730s and '40s. While I still explore some of these themes in chapter 3 of this book, I realize now that La Vérendrye's relations with the Indigenous peoples of the Northwest was part of a much more expansive story of Indigenous-French relations in the Hudson Bay watershed. Indeed, more important than La Vérendrye's character or aptitude was the fact that his explorations and attempted imperial projects set in motion a series of cultural processes whose ultimate outcome was unintended: the birth of a new people. The prolonged history of Indigenous-French trade, diplomacy, and cultural exchange in the Northwest would see the emergence of a brand-new Indigenous culture, language, people, and nation – namely, the Métis.

The Métis connection that Dr St-Onge located at the conference in Ottawa through the recognition of my family name would, in the end, draw me to a much more interesting history, one that lies beneath the veneer of La Vérendrye's French imperialism in the Northwest. Following the completion of my master's thesis, and upon receiving much invaluable advice from mentors, colleagues, and friends, I was determined to write a history that told the story of Indigenous-French relations in the Hudson Bay watershed over the *longue durée*, one that led to and accounted for the birth of the Métis people. This forced me to seek out and uncover the salient Indigenous-French history that unfolded concurrently with La Vérendyre's explorations; this was, in essence, a history of the forebearers of the Métis. This Indigenous-French world of the Hudson Bay watershed was just waiting to be reconstructed from what I was able to unearth in French colonial correspondence, Hudson's Bay Company post journals, voyageur contracts, parish registers, historical maps, Očhéthi Šakówiŋ winter counts, and even in the landscape itself. I was not the first historian to observe that the deep roots of the Métis people extended into the imperial period of New France (1608–1760). The first historian of the Métis, August-Henri de Trémaudan (1874–1929), writing in collaboration with the Union Nationale Métisse Saint-Joseph du Manitoba, posited that the voyageurs that accompanied La Vérendrye's expedition "married Indian women in this immense region from the Red River to the Pacific Ocean [and] were among the first ancestors of a new people: the Métis."[3] Although Trémaudan drew on archival sources to write his *Histoire de la nation métisse dans l'Ouest Canadien*, the old Métis leaders and elders, who had been with Louis Riel at the Red River Resistance of 1869–70 and the Northwest Resistance of 1885, also shared their community traditions with Trémaudan, whom they had commissioned to write down their history. Trémaudan's assessment that Métis origins were tied to the La Vérendrye expedition might therefore have been derived from the oral history of the Red River Métis. More recently, historians like Heather Devine, Ruth Swan, and Edward A. Jerome, who have probed more deeply into French colonial archives than Trémaudan ever could, have traced the genealogical roots of the Métis to voyageurs and coureurs de bois who ventured into the Hudson Bay watershed during the era of New France. However, most historians of the Métis have been either unwilling or unable to accept the fact (or are uninterested altogether) that the history of the Métis people extends far back into the eighteenth century, instead preferring to frame events, such as the Battle of Seven Oaks in 1816 or the Sayer trial in 1849, as the fundamental moments that crystalized Métis group identity. I envision an alternative trajectory for Métis peoplehood in the Northwest, one that recognizes that the preceding relations between Indigenous women and French men in the eighteenth century were a salient part of the Métis story.

I always knew that my family had deep roots in the vast territory variously called the Northwest, Rupert's Land, or the Hudson Bay watershed. Growing up in St Vital, a neighbourhood in Winnipeg, I learned at school and at home about the voyageurs, the fur trade, the Métis, and the Red River Resistance. For better or for worse, figures like La Vérendrye, Cuthbert Grant, and Louis Riel loomed large and were commemorated as pivotal and foundational figures in our provincial and personal histories. My family lived and my parents continue to live near the Seine River, just south of the land grant (Lot 51) belonging to Julie Riel, Louis Riel's mother, in the old parish of St Vital. Although I claim Jean-Baptiste Lagimodière and Marie-Anne Gaboury (Louis Riel's grandparents) as my ancestors, the majority of my Métis forebears, like Joseph Huppé, Josephte Cyr, Marie Fortin, Simon Bérard, and the aforementioned Berthelets, were ordinary men and women who were often employed or self-employed as voyageurs, buffalo hunters, farmers, freighters, and merchants.[4] I think this positioned me to write the history of the ordinary Canadiens that preceded the Métis. Growing up in Manitoba also offered me the opportunity to live and breathe this history. While researching and writing, I often explored these landscapes of encounter and visited many of the sites discussed in the book – including the locations of Fort La Reine, Fort Paskoya, Fort Saint-Charles, Kaministiquia, and the Saskatchewan River Forks – which, in turn, helped me to imagine the fur trade world of the Hudson Bay watershed more concretely. This ended up being a deeply personal story, especially as it concludes with the rise of the Métis people and occurs largely within the landscape where my family and our Métis ancestors have resided for the past two hundred years. I can only hope that the following pages do justice to my ancestors, both the ordinary and the extraordinary, whose stories are deeply rooted and buried in the proverbial soil of the Hudson Bay watershed, often just waiting to be uncovered.

Acknowledgments

This book is the result of many years of research, writing, conversation, and reflection, and ultimately came to fruition thanks to an immense network of both professional and personal support. Acknowledging the support and encouragement of all these people is never an easy or straightforward task. Since this monograph is derived from a PhD dissertation, I want to especially highlight the role that my former supervisor, Robert Englebert, played in making this project possible over the past seven years. His considerable mentorship, guidance, and expertise contributed enormously to helping me refine my arguments and improve my writing style. His profound belief in my work and my abilities brought me much confidence and reassurance throughout the project. Now that I am a professor, I hope that I can be as helpful and supportive a mentor to my own graduate students as Robert has been for me. I would also like to thank committee members Kathryn Magee Labelle, Benjamin Hoy, Paul Hackett, and Paul Mapp for their advice, questions, and feedback, all of which pushed me and the project in interesting and unexpected directions, ultimately greatly benefiting the manuscript.

Many scholars have acted as sounding boards and offered invaluable critiques over the last few years. In addition to the aforementioned PhD committee members, I would also like to thank Allan Greer, Nicole St-Onge, Andrew Jainchill, Samuel Derksen, and Michael Davis for reading earlier drafts of chapters and offering very useful insights and suggestions. I would also like to thank a great number of colleagues who engaged in stimulating and thought-provoking conversations, including Catherine Desbarats, Helen Dewar, Guillaume Teasdale, Timothy Foran, Jean-François Lozier, José Brandão, Carolyn

Podruchny, Max Hamon, Joseph Gagné, Émilie Pigeon, Daniel Meister, and Michael Borsk, to name only a few. Over the years, I have also received invaluable advice from colleagues, kind listeners, and fellow conference attendees. The annual meetings/conferences for the American Society for Ethnohistory, the French Colonial Historical Society, and the Omohundro Institute were particularly fertile and vibrant spaces for sharing, thinking about, and discussing preliminary research related to this project. I would also like to thank Paul C. Thistle, David Meyer, Heather Devine, and Laura Peers, who had never met me in person but who nevertheless generously took the time to answer some of my esoteric questions over email.

I would like to single out Donald B. Smith, professor emeritus of history at the University of Calgary, who generously donated a sizeable collection of books to me on the histories of the Métis, the fur trade, Indigenous peoples, and New France. My office's bookshelves look far less bare because of your generous gift. Your charity is enormously appreciated, and I owe you several beers.

I also think it would be appropriate to thank a number of professors from the University of Winnipeg and the University of Manitoba, including Robin Jarvis Brownlie, Mark Meuwese, Roland Bohr, Alexander Freund, Jorge Nállim, and Gerry Bowler, who provided invaluable feedback and support during my master's program, which ultimately led me to pursue a PhD program at the University of Saskatchewan.

I would like to thank friend and neighbour Tom Kean for teaching me so much about the Lake of the Woods and the surrounding waterways and for actually taking me to visit Fort Saint-Charles, Massacre Island, and the Reed River, where we literally retraced the canoe routes of La Vérendrye and his voyageurs.

Throughout this project I held several short-term research fellowships, and I would like to thank those individuals who made those periods of my life more productive, intellectually engaging, and generally more enjoyable. First, thanks to Cathrine Davis for driving out on Michigan's snowy highways to meet me and show me around Kalamazoo while I was a research fellow at Western Michigan University in January 2018. I would like to thank Maddison Jane, Ryan Langton, and Daniella Bassi for including me in beers, sharing local history, and generally making me feel at home in Williamsburg, Virginia, when I was a visiting research fellow at the Omohundro Institute during the summer of 2018. I would also like to thank my John Carter Brown Library pals at Fiering House – Sebastián Gómez,

Megan McDonie, Pablo Hernández Sau, Elizabeth Montañez-Sanabria, Myron McShane, Peter Jakob Olsen-Harbich, Beatriz Marín-Aguilera, Stefan Hanß, and Fabrício Prado – with whom I enjoyed many stimulating conversations, research presentations, and social engagements during the summer of 2019.

I would like to thank the anonymous readers for their time and generous feedback, which was overwhelmingly positive, constructive, and encouraging, and which recognized the scholarly potential of the project. Their comments helped to make this monograph stronger. I would also like to thank Kyla Madden, Elli Stylianou, Kathleen Fraser, Ryan Perks, and the entire team at McGill-Queen's University Press for their tireless support in seeing this manuscript to fruition. Lastly, I would like to thank series editors Allan Greer and Carolyn Podruchny for accepting this book in the "McGill-Queen's Studies in Early Canada/Avant le Canada" series, a new and exciting endeavour that I am delighted to be a part of.

This project was made possible by financial support from the University of Saskatchewan, the Social Sciences and Humanities Research Council of Canada, Queen's University's Pre-Doctoral Fellowship for Indigenous Students, the Joseph L. Peyser Endowment for the Study of New France (Western Michigan University), the Omohundro Institute of Early American History and Culture Short-Term Visiting Fellowship (College of William and Mary), and the Jane L. Keddy Memorial Fellowship (John Carter Brown Library). A portion of chapter 2 was previously published as an article in the *Canadian Historical Review*; thank you to the University of Toronto Press for permission to reprint that material here.

Thank you to all my friends, who greatly enriched my life in a non-academic capacity throughout the duration of this project. They helped me take my obsessive mind off history and my PhD research, and our time together was always well-spent and enjoyable. I want to thank my family for their unmatched support throughout my undergraduate and graduate studies. I am forever grateful to my parents, Allan and Yvonne, for encouraging me to continue to pursue university degrees as my love for history flourished. I also want to thank my sister Michele and my brother-in-law Jonathan Berrington for their support and our engaging conversations – despite our largely disparate academic interests. Lastly, I want to thank my wife, Kathryn Lauvstad, for her enduring support, loving encouragement, and delicious home-cooked meals, all of which sustained me over the course of this project. Although a Manitoban like myself, Kathryn uprooted herself and moved five times within or between three different cities/provinces over the last seven years, which I want to recognize. Her flexibility and patience were and still are much appreciated. I love you, Kathryn, and am looking forward to continuing our life together in Kingston, Ontario.

HEIRS OF AN AMBIVALENT EMPIRE

Introduction

In the summer of 1767, William Tomison, a Hudson's Bay Company (HBC) servant, journeyed inland from Severn House, on Hudson Bay, to Lake Winnipeg.[1] After three months of hard travelling, Tomison finally arrived at the eastern shore of Lake Winnipeg, where the rapidly flowing Winnipeg River discharges into the great lake that HBC servants often referred to as "Frenchman's Lake" or the "Little Sea." The moniker "Frenchman's Lake" was telling, for Tomison, an Orcadian himself, dreaded encountering the Canadiens (French Canadians) who dominated commerce throughout the Lake Winnipeg basin. At the windblown sandy beaches of Lake Winnipeg's southeastern shore, Tomison was disappointed to find that he could do little to dissuade a Cree band from selling their best furs to Canadien traders at well-established posts along the Red River.[2] The Crees, though they had once traded with the HBC, were now all "cloathed in french cloth, blankets, printed callicoes and other stuffs."[3] Disappointed yet undeterred, Tomison continued his journey in an effort to entice Indigenous customers around the Lake Winnipeg basin to come and trade at the company's distant bayside posts. By Tomison's day, the HBC had been trading guns, copper kettles, porcelain beads, cloth blankets, iron axes and knives, and Brazil tobacco with the region's Indigenous peoples in exchange for beaver pelts for almost a century.

Despite its longevity, the company had learned remarkably little about the human and physical geography of the Northwest, largely because of its reluctance to move inland from the secure posts that dotted the shorelines of Hudson and James Bays. Now, Tomison and a few other HBC officers and servants were beginning to move inland because successful and entrepreneurial Canadien traders had severely hamstrung the company's operations by siphoning off fur trade revenue at the bay.

A month later, Tomison encountered a Canadien trader and his entourage of ten voyageurs (fur trade labourers) and fourteen Crees in six large canoes on their way to Opāskweyāw, or "narrows between woods," a seasonal Cree gathering site on the lower reaches of the Saskatchewan River (present-day The Pas, Manitoba).[4] The Canadien trader's name was François Jérôme *dit* Latour. Tomison wrote that Jérôme wore a loose-hanging ruffled shirt, a capote (a long coat with a hood), and a long pair of trousers without stockings or shoes. Like his Cree partners, Jérôme was dressed for practicality and travel. Although Tomison described him as "a poor looking small man about 50 years of age," Jérôme still seemed to command great respect from his French and Cree travelling companions. Not only did he manage a large flotilla of six trade canoes, but he sat in the middle of the lead canoe with his family without paddling, indicating that he maintained a position of some significance within his kinship group. Tomison also remarked that Jérôme travelled with his Cree wife and their son.[5] Jérôme's clothing, travel companions, and his wife and child reflected processes of *métissage* (cultural hybridity) that were at work in the Hudson Bay watershed throughout the eighteenth century.

In 1773, Matthew Cocking, another HBC fur trader, also encountered Jérôme and about twenty Canadien voyageurs at a trading post at the Forks of the Saskatchewan River. Upon arriving at the post, Jérôme invited Cocking to come dine with him in his cabin. During dinner, Cocking noticed that Jérôme did not keep a proper and formal distance from his men, and he later complained that the voyageurs kept "coming into his apartment & talking with him [Jérôme] as one of themselves."[6] Cocking also marvelled at how the French kept "no watch in the night; even when the Natives are lying on their plantation," and he dismissed Jérôme as "an old ignorant Frenchman" in his journal.[7] What Cocking and many other HBC observers failed to understand, however, was that Jérôme had resided and traded along the Saskatchewan River for many years prior to the British conquest of Canada in 1760. In the intervening years, Jérôme had built up an expansive kinship network, strong trade connections, and had married and fathered children with a Cree woman. He was a successful trader and leader who got along as well with Canadien voyageurs as he did with his Indigenous customers and relatives.

Jérôme began his career in 1743 as a voyageur in the employ of colonial officers and merchants from New France. As a voyageur bound to a legal contract, Jérôme's duties had included paddling the canoes that transported commercial cargoes to and from the Northwest, as well as carrying out labouring jobs at the posts where he and his fellow voyageurs wintered. During these formative years in the Northwest, he had acquired knowledge of local Indigenous customs and the Cree language and its local dialects, which later helped him pursue a successful career as an independent trader in charge of his own men.[8] Newly arrived English and Scottish merchants, operating out of Montreal after the British conquest, recognized Jérôme's position as a crucial intermediary in the Northwest. Bourgeois traders like Alexander Baxter, James Finlay, Charles Paterson, and William Holmes financed Jérôme as a partner in their fur trading outfits throughout the 1760s and '70s. This meant that Jérôme did not have to make regular trips back to Montreal and could manage his affairs from the Hudson Bay watershed on a more or less permanent basis.

Jérôme was not the only Canadien intimately tied to Indigenous kinship networks in the Hudson Bay watershed. HBC observers reported that other "French inland masters" enjoyed the financial backing of Montreal merchants and were actively engaged in the lower Saskatchewan River fur trade, where they were firmly entrenched in Indigenous kinship networks.[9] Through prolonged contact, Indigenous peoples of the region had incorporated Canadiens into their own networks of reciprocity, rituals of trade and alliance, and quotidian patterns of existence. French and later Canadien traders, like Jérôme, had been trading and forming kinship ties with Native communities in the Hudson Bay watershed since the 1660s. The region was a dynamic contact zone where Indigenous, French, and British politics, cultures, and economies both clashed and intermingled.

Many of the key works analyzing French-Indigenous relations have traditionally focused on contact zones in other parts of North America, such as the *pays d'en haut* (the Great Lakes region), the Illinois Country, and Louisiana; few studies, however, have dealt specifically with the Hudson Bay watershed.[10] Those scholars who have turned their attention toward the Hudson Bay watershed have largely fixated on either ethnohistories of Indigenous peoples, commercial and social histories of the British-run HBC, or later national and cultural histories of the Métis people.[11] This book seeks to reorient that historical gaze by reintegrating the Hudson Bay watershed into French colonial and French Atlantic history. Because of the promise of a prospective Northwest Passage and the lucrative northern fur trade, the Hudson Bay watershed was a key asset of the French Empire rather than a peripheral share of its imperial holdings.

The main subjects of this book are a specific segment of New France's Canadien settler population – coureurs de bois (illicit fur traders), company clerks, runaway soldiers, and veteran voyageurs – who acted as intermediaries and cultural brokers between Indigenous peoples and the French colonial government. I employ the term "Canadiens" in opposition to colonial elites – governors, intendants, bishops, seigneurs (landholders), magistrates, members of the Sovereign Council, and Troupes de la Marine officers – who dominated New France's military and social hierarchy. I use the term less to designate birthplace than to articulate perspective and familial networks. Although by the eighteenth century, many of the colony's "elite" were born in Canada, they were still embedded in court politics at Versailles, the promotional hierarchy of the Ministry of the Marine, and merchant credit systems operating out of French port cities like La Rochelle, Bordeaux, and Le Havre. Unlike colonial elites, Canadiens did not look across the Atlantic Ocean, but rather forged their own lives and household production economies in the Saint Lawrence valley and the pays d'en haut, inhabited their own parish-based social hierarchies, and many looked west – toward the continental interior of North America – for economic and social opportunities. Unsurprisingly, then, most colonial elites returned to France after the British conquest of Canada in 1760, whereas "non-elite" Canadiens had no such choice, nor such an attachment to metropolitan France. Few, if any, Canadien coureurs de bois, voyageurs, and rank-and-file soldiers ever ventured eastward across the Atlantic before or after the 1763 Treaty of Paris.

In 1725, about 200 leading seigneurial families, occupying an officer corps totalling around 130 commissions, with an additional 56 cadetships, ostensibly dominated a Canadien settler population of around 35,000 in the Saint Lawrence valley.[12] One historian of New France estimated that this dominant class comprised only 1 per cent of the total settler population.[13] Excluded from the officer corps and seigneurial class, the mass of Canadiens were farmers, artisans, shopkeepers, urban labourers, voyageurs, and militiamen.[14] Despite their subordinate status in colonial society, this study argues that a small subsection of Canadiens involved in the Hudson Bay watershed fur trade (which ranged from a few dozen to a few hundred men at any given time) were key figures who allowed the French to gain a commercial and imperial foothold in the region. Alongside the lack of scholarly attention on the Hudson Bay watershed as a French aspirational imperial space, many scholars (with a few notable exceptions) have also neglected Canadien voyageurs and coureurs de bois during the period of the French regime (1608–1763).[15] While Nicole St-Onge, Robert Englebert, Carolyn Podruchny, Jean Barman, and others, have examined the "voyageur world" in recent years, these works have largely focused on the period after 1760.[16] Gilles Havard's recent contribution to the literature on the fur trade, *Histoire des coureurs de bois*, is an impressive and sweeping study of coureurs de bois and is the single largest detailed work on illicit fur traders in North America. Ranging widely in terms of both chronology and geography, Havard nonetheless leaves substantial room for an analysis and re-interpretation of the roles played by voyageurs and coureurs de bois in the Hudson Bay watershed specifically.[17] Currently, there is no comprehensive pre–1760 study of voyageurs and coureurs de bois in the Hudson Bay watershed, a geographic region where French-Indigenous relations have been largely understated in both French colonial and fur trade literature. This book seeks to remedy this oversight.

Accordingly, in what follows I tackle questions about Indigenous and French sovereignty, empire, and agency. The narrative is organized chronologically in order to analyze and expound on the evolving role and position of Canadiens vis-à-vis the French colonial government, Indigenous peoples, and each other. French colonial usage of Canadien voyageurs and coureurs de bois to drive western imperial expansion and to secure effective state control over the Hudson Bay watershed was never a straightforward process. Since colonial authorities were for the most part unable to command these Canadiens outright, there was a certain ebb and flow to the relationship between the architects of empire in colonial and imperial centres and Canadiens in the Hudson Bay watershed. Simply put, these voyageurs and coureurs de bois were not unwavering agents of imperial power, but rather ambivalent agents of empire. Their own agendas and interests often ensured that western expansion and French imperial designs advanced at an erratic, haphazard, and oscillating pace. This demonstrates that French imperialism in western North America was not a monolithic, top-down process but rather a multifaceted one, with competing visions, perspectives, and agendas. The result was an ambivalent empire that grew in fits and starts – guided by ambiguous or imperfect information, built upon a contested Indigenous borderland, fragmented by local interests, periodically neglected by government administrators; and yet, at critical junctures, still perceived as immensely valuable by French ministers and bureaucrats. Over time, the ambivalent relationship between colonial authorities and local actors led, unpredictably and unexpectedly, to the development of a new culture, language, people, and nation – the Métis.

Because sovereign Indigenous peoples and autonomous Canadiens interacted and intermingled in a region where kinship ties represented the main social structure and avenues of power, the Métis would emerge as a new Indigenous people, one whose community and kinship structures were rooted culturally in the local landscape and world views of Indigenous women. Certainly, at the end of the day, Indigenous power in the Northwest was predominant, but French empire (however tenuous) and imperial projects (however poorly executed) still profoundly affected the social, cultural, political, and demographic landscapes of the Hudson Bay watershed. Even where state power was limited, French Atlantic imperialism introduced trade goods, technologies, global markets, disease epidemics, military alliances, new cultural and religious practices, and, perhaps most importantly, prospective French husbands. By this measure, the changes wrought by the French Empire in North America were remarkable. In the Hudson Bay watershed, it was ultimately the tension between localized Indigenous sovereignty and French imperial ambitions that formed the crucible in which Métis identity was forged.

SOVEREIGNTY AND EMPIRE

Throughout the French regime in the Hudson Bay watershed there was a constant tension between localized Indigenous sovereignty and French statecraft, governance, and imperial ambition. In fact, many historians have used the dialectics of order/disorder or imperial success/failure as a paradigm to analyze the French Empire in the Atlantic world. The ordered vision of imperial control belied a disordered reality in many parts of France's overseas empire. In Atlantic imperial spaces like Louisiana, French Guiana, and Acadia, the failure of idealistic visions of empire gave way to local exigencies, such as the clash of colonial interest groups, the rivalry between European powers, and Indigenous hegemony.[18] Indeed, scholars such as James Pritchard, Philip P. Boucher, and Shannon Lee Dawdy have articulated the overwhelming weakness of metropolitan authority within the French Atlantic world by emphasizing the agency of independent colonial actors to interpret, shape, and sometimes reconfigure metropolitan policies and directives.[19] This general lack of imperial cohesion has led historian Kenneth J. Banks to conclude that "the French empire was always in the making but never made."[20]

From metropolitan centres of power, French ministers and imperial planners attempted to shape policies to justify conquest, draw imperial borders, extract wealth, and to claim sovereignty over Indigenous peoples.[21] The French state attempted to make colonial spaces and peoples "legible," often by visually representing demographic and geographic information on maps.[22] James C. Scott sees "legibility" as the state's attempt to simplify, organize, and rationalize a complex social reality, a process that early modern theorists thought was integral to controlling and exploiting wealth from overseas colonies.[23] Despite careful imperial planning through a constant centripetal flow of information – letters, reports, dispatches, censuses, balance sheets, surveys, and maps – French ministers and imperial planners still failed to understand the complexity of their overseas colonies. Even when the French state did produce topographically and hydrographically accurate maps of their North American empire, thus improving its "legibility" for imperial eyes to gaze upon, they still failed to understand how to fully put that into effect to extract wealth. Historian S. Max Edelson argues that early modern maps reflected the technocratic aspirations of the early modern state, which ultimately lacked the capacity to put such information to proper use.[24] Kenneth J. Banks has called this phenomenon "imperial overstretch," a term he uses to describe the "information overload" that inundated the Bureau des Colonies in the early eighteenth century, preventing French ministers from absorbing and effectively using the knowledge generated by the colonies to make imperial decisions.[25] The French government's attempts to make western North America "legible" through the collection of information betrayed its own imperial fantasies and vain aspirations when it came to controlling the peoples and resources of the Hudson Bay watershed.

In New France's colonial spaces, suggests historian Brett Rushforth, it was "independent Natives and defiant colonists, not wigged royals, [who] defined the day-to-day realities."[26] Likewise, Richard White argues that "minor agents, allies, and even subjects at the periphery often guide the course of empire" in the pays d'en haut.[27] In colonial Louisiana, Shannon Lee Dawdy similarly posits that explorers, entrepreneurs, and rogues "sweet-talked, lobbied, bullshitted, bullied, and wheedled their way into the chambers of power, either directly or through letter writing, to sway European power-holders to value their colonial enterprise."[28] Canadien voyageurs and coureurs de bois were the rogue agents of empire who pushed the colonial frontiers of New France, not simply to extend Catholicism, empire, and the glory of the king, but also in pursuit of their own personal interests, ambitions, and fortunes. In other words, colonial development was driven by individuals on the ground who acted with or without metropolitan consent or approval. Realizing that their empire was rapidly spinning out of their control, French kings, ministers, and bureaucrats of the late seventeenth and early eighteenth centuries tried to co-opt this unique class of "backcountry specialists" as agents of empire, often embedding them within transatlantic patronage networks and appointing them as representatives of the French Crown in order to gain some semblance of control over the far reaches of North America. Of course, in this context, I employ the term "backcountry" merely to articulate the westward-facing positionality of French government officials and bureaucrats, who perceived western North America as sparsely inhabited, remote, undeveloped, and difficult to access – which in turn helps to explain the unique skill set and political leverage that voyageurs and coureurs de bois possessed in the French Atlantic world.[29] Later, in the mid-eighteenth century, the French state would sideline these backcountry specialists in favour of noble Troupes de la Marine officers, a policy that divested Canadiens from imperial projects while ultimately contributing to the French Empire's collapse in the Hudson Bay watershed.

Faced with French imperial expansion, the Indigenous peoples of the region asserted sovereignty and dictated the terms of encounter. Although the effects of colonialism were certainly disruptive and destabilizing, many Indigenous peoples were nevertheless able to adapt and even thrive under these changing circumstances. Historians like Pekka Hämäläinen, Michael Witgen, Robert Michael Morrissey, and Jacob F. Lee have recognized that many Indigenous peoples in western North America formed powerful confederacies, leagues, and even empires in the wake of their encounters with European powers.[30] In fact, as the French pushed into the Hudson Bay watershed, they encountered strong Indigenous societies and coalitions. For example, the Očhéthi Šakówiŋ (Dakota, Yankton, Yanktonai, and Lakota) had benefited from the Columbian Exchange and were a major obstacle to French imperial expansion west of the Mississippi River. Native-newcomer exchange economies facilitated Siouan western territorial and diplomatic expansion in the late seventeenth and early eighteenth centuries, helping them to reorient themselves toward the interior. Aided by horses (a European introduction), the pursuit of bison herds provided sustenance to fuel the Očhéthi Šakówiŋ's demographic growth, which also facilitated their western military expansion.[31] Throughout the period analyzed here (1663–1782), Indigenous sovereignty – albeit adapted to the conditions and circumstances of encroaching European colonialism – ruled the day in the Hudson Bay watershed.

The presence of powerful autonomous Indigenous polities, coupled with the sometimes haphazard actions of backcountry specialists, compelled colonial officials, chartered companies, and the French Crown to recalibrate and reconsider already established overseas policy.[32] In the mid-seventeenth century, Canadien adventurers, fur traders, and entrepreneurs began to push into the Hudson Bay watershed. Independent of colonial and metropolitan authority, these backcountry specialists formed alliances with Indigenous peoples, established fur trade networks, and seized HBC posts, pillaging their provisions, trade goods, and furs. These Canadiens shaped the destiny of French empire in North America and set the tone for the development of the fur trade in the Hudson Bay watershed. When the French colonial government did take initiative to extend the French Empire westward by dispatching Troupes de la Marine officers to the region, Canadiens became the backbone of broadly conceived French imperial projects, often working as general labourers, voyageurs, soldiers, and provisioners. Over time, as Canadiens became more enmeshed in Indigenous social structures and more knowledgeable about the human and physical geography of the Hudson Bay watershed, imperial planners and colonial officials realized their crucial role as cultural brokers and employed them as guides, interpreters, and diplomats.

Notwithstanding the role that Canadiens played in pursuit of imperial projects, the lofty ambitions of the French state never came to fruition because the peoples of the Hudson Bay watershed were effectively beyond imperial control. Viewed through James C. Scott's theoretical framework, the Hudson Bay watershed could be construed as a vast hinterland whose "friction of terrain" allowed non-state peoples (Natives and Canadiens) to evade state control.[33] Scott argues that for the last two thousand years of human history, various stateless peoples have fled from fertile alluvial valleys to "non-state spaces" to escape coercive state-making projects – slavery, conscription, taxes, corvée labour, sedentary agriculture, and warfare – and enacted strategic cultural practices and social organizations "designed to keep the state at arm's length."[34] Indeed, at the edge of empire, local Native and Canadien actors had the power to resist and repel metropolitan and colonial authorities, and within that space to join together to experiment, shape, and create their own worlds and fulfill their own destinies. Localized Indigenous sovereignty and French imperial ambitions in the Hudson Bay watershed resulted in a prolonged history of French-Indigenous trade, diplomacy, and cultural exchange, which in turn led to the ultimate (albeit completely unintentional) act of creation, which no French imperial architect or colonial official could have foreseen: the emergence of a new Indigenous people in the Métis.

SOCIAL HIERARCHY IN NEW FRANCE

Canadien backcountry specialists had immense power and agency in the Hudson Bay watershed because they were beyond effective imperial control. But at the same time, the colonial social hierarchy played an important role in this history because Canadiens maintained a complicated, contested, and negotiated relationship with the French Empire and New France's colonial administration. Unlike James C. Scott's Southeast Asian "hill people" of Zomia, who wanted nothing to do with valley states, Canadiens frequently navigated various avenues of power back east within the social hierarchy of New France.[35] To understand the historical relationship between Canadien backcountry specialists and the French state, we therefore need to look to the social hierarchy as it developed and operated in New France. Wielding power as influential cultural brokers on the margins of empire, metropolitan ministers and colonial officials sometimes feared that Canadien voyageurs and coureurs de bois challenged the mandated social, economic, and religious order of New France.[36] During the first generation of settlement, exceptional circumstances of warfare, threats of invasion, and imperial expansion occasionally rendered the colonial hierarchy more elastic and porous, which offered opportunities for upward social mobility. In the first half of the seventeenth century, the governor general of New France granted commissions, promotions, lands, and letters patent of nobility for exceptional service to the embattled French colony.[37] Charles Le Moyne and Pierre Boucher, for instance, are two key examples of ordinary settlers who rose through the colony's hierarchy during this period. Both arrived in the colony around the same time as indentured servants to the Jesuits, but through successful military careers defending New France against the Haudenosaunee, they received promotions, land grants, commissions, seigneuries, and eventually ennoblement.[38] Such extreme social mobility was, however, rare. The colonial elite mostly emanated from newly arrived French migrants who had been part of the provincial *noblesse d'épée* and *noblesse de robe* in France and were granted seigneurial holdings upon arriving in the colony. New France's seigneurial system reflected Old World feudal structures of economic exploitation and social hierarchy.[39]

Men of the seigneurial class showed a predilection for military service, where the noble profession of arms in defence of the colony reinforced their worth as nobility and prominent seigneurs.[40] By the eighteenth century, seigneurs and their male offspring were the dominant military elite of the colony. Several leading families – Le Moyne, Boucher, Legardeur, Marin, and La Corne, among others – came to occupy the highest military and administrative positions in New France and thus became the colony's de facto elite.[41] Several historians have identified New France's "military establishment" as the crucible in which the colony's nobility was forged. In other words, the military officers from the Compagnies Franches de la Marine and their families comprised New France's ruling class.[42] These officers and seigneurs intermarried with wealthy Montreal and Quebec merchants with ties to French markets and port cities such as La Rochelle, Bordeaux, and Le Havre in order to improve their material circumstances and to build powerful family alliances.[43]

Within this military establishment, a great social gulf existed between rank-and-file soldiers and more senior leaders, with most junior positions in the Troupes de la Marine reserved for the sons and grandsons of serving officers. The rank-and-file soldiers recruited for the Compagnies Franches de la Marine came mostly from lower-class families, whereas the officers were mostly from families with hereditary ties to the noblesse d'épée or noblesse de robe.[44] Since rank-and-file soldiers were not plugged into the patronage networks of elite military families, with their stronger ties to metropolitan France, promotion to the officers corps was virtually impossible for these men. The colonial elite, by contrast, vied for advancement in either the Troupes de la Marine or in the colonial administration through patronage appointments that connected them to New France's governor general or intendant. The governor and intendant were themselves intimately bound to the Bureau des Colonies and the French court at Versailles through marriage and patronage.[45] In other words, New France's military elite were stakeholders in the imperial project, embedded in transatlantic patronage networks and invested in the symbolic culture of divine-right monarchy, linking king and colonial elites to a shared process of state formation.

Despite the power and wealth that colonial elites derived from seigneurial holdings and dominance of the military establishment, they still relied heavily on Canadiens to help assert French claims of sovereignty in western North America. Unlike colonial elites – seigneurs and Troupes de la Marine officers – whose Atlantic networks tied them to urban colonial and metropolitan spaces, certain Canadiens in the fur trade were deeply embedded within Indigenous informational, commercial, and kinship networks. Colonial officers usually divided their time between brief sojourns to military or trading posts in the pays d'en haut and visits to colonial council chambers and royal courts. In other words, they spent much of their lives vying for promotion and securing patronage within elite colonial and metropolitan circles. Canadiens, on the other hand, often resided year-round in the interior of North America and frequently became backcountry specialists with direct kinship ties to Indigenous peoples.[46]

Canadiens parlayed their experience and relationships in the Hudson Bay watershed into key roles as intermediaries between the French colonial government and Indigenous polities. French imperial planners and colonial administrators relied heavily upon Canadiens to provide ethnographic, geographic, and strategic knowledge, which then informed and shaped imperial projects and policies in western North America. This detailed and long-term study of French-Indigenous relations in the Hudson Bay watershed reveals that Canadiens, predominately coureurs de bois and voyageurs, emerged as salient intermediaries between Indigenous peoples and the French state at the edge of empire. The Hudson Bay watershed became a place where the rules, protocols, and social order of the *ancien régime* were stretched, bent, and at times even broken.

EURO-INDIGENOUS RELATIONS AND THE "MIDDLE GROUND"

While New France's social hierarchy is key to understanding the relationship between French elites and Canadiens, Euro-Indigenous relations and the "middle ground" are crucial for understanding Indigenous sovereignty and the limits of French imperial control in western North America. Historians cannot analyze Euro-Indigenous relations in colonial North America without first considering Richard White's seminal book *The Middle Ground: Indians, Empires, and Republics in the Great Lakes Region, 1650–1815*, which has been one of most influential works in the field of North American history.[47] First, *The Middle Ground* transformed the field of "new Indian history" by countering tired and dated narratives of Native declension and dependency with the argument that Euro-Indigenous encounters entailed processes of creative misunderstanding, cultural accommodation, mutual invention, and social experimentation, thereby painting a fresh portrait of a shared and improvised cultural space that was neither entirely Native nor entirely French.[48] White employed the phrase "middle ground" to define both a process and a particular historical space (the pays d'en haut). The "middle ground" described creative and expedient mutual misunderstandings from which arose new shared meanings and cultural practices that characterized Euro-Indigenous encounters in the Great Lakes basin. But the space of the middle ground was only made possible through an equal balance of power in which neither Natives nor newcomers could impose their will on one another but instead had to at least attempt cross-cultural accommodation or adaption (but not acculturation).[49] White argued that the middle ground emerged in the pays d'en haut because the Great Lakes region was a "shatter zone" where the French and their Algonquian-speaking allies pieced together a world from fragments; it was a world that had been sundered by virulent disease and the endemic violence of the "Beaver Wars."[50]

In the past decade, however, *The Middle Ground* has been hotly contested by several French colonial and early American scholars who have pushed beyond White's thesis to contribute to a growing body of literature pertaining to Indigenous power, sovereignty, and empire. These scholars have reinterpreted the role of Indigenous power and agency, delved into the complexity of Euro-Indigenous relations and métissage, and overturned assumptions about imperial power and control in North America. Employing an ethnohistorical approach and building upon decades of previous scholarship, they have reinterpreted the landscapes of encounter to show that the interior of North America remained an almost overwhelmingly Native political space in which Europeans often played only minor roles in much broader Indigenous narratives.[51] Moving beyond the middle ground framework, many scholars have argued that Great Lakes Indigenous peoples were not "shattered peoples" or "refugees," nor did they abandon their pre-existing collective identities (such as the clan, or *doodem*) to form a middle ground with French and British newcomers. Rather, Indigenous peoples maintained distinct political and cultural identities even under the mounting pressures of French, British, and Haudenosaunee imperial expansion into the Great Lakes.[52] These "post–middle grounders" have also challenged historians who "have tended to assume that [all] Native Americans *wanted* to construct middle grounds with Europeans."[53] Historian Michael McDonnell has even stated outright that, "as more and more histories are written that face east, rather than west, the evidence is mounting that White was simply wrong."[54] My own research contributes to this post–middle ground literature by framing the Hudson Bay watershed as a largely Indigenous space where kinship ties, not monarchs or empires, represented the main social structure and avenues of power.

Euro-Indigenous intermediaries deftly navigated these social structures and avenues of power in contact zones and borderlands. The literature on cultural brokers, intermediaries, and "go-betweens" in these spaces is vast, and is certainly not limited to the field of French colonial history. For example, many scholars of colonial Latin America have shown how Indigenous elites with knowledge of Spanish language, law, and literacy acted as intermediaries, not only in the interest of their communities, but also to carve out power for themselves vis-à-vis the colonial state apparatus.[55] Historians have emphasized the important role that slaves (particularly female slaves) played as cultural intermediaries between different groups in the Spanish borderlands of the Southwest.[56] In the Atlantic world, Ira Berlin painted African "Atlantic creoles" in the seventeenth century as "cosmopolitan cultural brokers, familiar with the languages, religions, jurisprudence, and trading etiquette of the Atlantic."[57] Along the Anglo-American frontier, early Americanists have examined the role of cultural brokers between Anglo-American settlements and various Indigenous polities in the Appalachian and Allegheny Mountains as well as in the Ohio

Valley.[58] My own research contributes to the literature on Euro-Indigenous cultural intermediaries by demonstrating the pivotal role that Canadiens played in contact zones as ambivalent agents of empire. Canadiens sometimes promoted imperial projects and other times limited and fragmented French influence, thereby demonstrating that European colonialism was not a homogeneous process, but rather a messy and multifarious one, with competing voices and visions.

MÉTISSAGE AND THE MÉTIS

Prolonged French-Indigenous relations in the Hudson Bay watershed invariably led to extensive métissage, or cultural and ethnic mixing, in Euro-Indigenous contact zones; we saw this with the example of François Jérôme *dit* Latour in the vignette with which I opened this introduction. French colonial historian Gilles Havard defines métissage as a dynamic and creative process of cultural exchange and borrowing that generated cultural traits and behaviours that were both hybrid and unprecedented.[59] In the Hudson Bay watershed, French-Indigenous métissage was centred on many processes, including material culture and sartorial expression, religion and spiritual ceremonies (as diverse as Catholic baptism or Native ceremonial tattooing, for example), and even participation in and adoption of different modes of warfare.[60]

Scholars who have examined métissage in other parts of North America, such as the Saint Lawrence valley, the pays d'en haut, the Lower Missouri, the Ohio Valley, the Illinois Country, and Louisiana, have all demonstrated that métissage did not always or necessarily lead to the emergence of distinct hybrid peoples with a shared sense of collective identity or national consciousness.[61] Acknowledging the complexity of French-Indigenous métissage and the fluidity of identities in the Great Lakes, historian Susan Sleeper-Smith argues that the inhabitants of fur-trading communities like Detroit, Michilimackinac, and Fort Saint-Joseph predominantly identified themselves through family and kin networks, whereas Anglo-American observers attempted to categorize them in binary terms as either French or Indigenous.[62] French colonial historian Robert Englebert has cautioned that métissage was "more than the creation of some sort of static mixed identity" – it was "a process whereby one could navigate fluid ethnic boundaries without abandoning other notions or expressions of self."[63] Within the specific context of the Hudson Bay watershed fur trade, however, ongoing processes of métissage between Indigenous peoples and Canadien voyageurs and coureurs de bois eventually did give rise to a distinct Indigenous people – the Métis. Appearing in historical records as "Bois-Brûlés," "Otipemisiwak," "gens libres," or "half-breeds," the Métis were a new people who emerged as a salient cultural and political force that asserted their sovereignty and a group identity in western North America.

Not all offspring of mixed marriages became Métis, of course; many "mixed" individuals occupied a liminal cultural space and moved freely between their mother's and father's respective communities. French-Indigenous intermarriage, cultural exchange, and religious syncretism in Acadia, the Saint Lawrence valley, and the Great Lakes did not always lead to the creation of distinct peoples and nations possessing their own unique histories, cultures, and territorial boundaries.[64] Many scholars have mistakenly referred to any mixed-ancestry individual or any culturally hybrid fur trade society as "métis." However, scholar of Métis history Jacqueline Peterson argues that we should only describe as Métis those historical communities that understood themselves as such; in her view, this means that the Red River Valley is the site of Métis emergence, as opposed to either the Great Lakes or locations even further east like Quebec or Acadia. Peterson argues that the present-day usage of the term "Métis" from the Great Lakes eastward is a misappropriation partially resulting from scholars' projection of the terms "Métis" or "métis" backward in time to relabel those once known in archival records only as "half-breeds" or "mixed-bloods," or by no distinct term at all.[65] Similarly, Métis scholar Chris Andersen suggests that ethnohistorians have "retrofitted" or "imagined" mixed populations of the Great Lakes as "Métis" or "métis" even though there is little documentation confirming this historical self-ascription.[66] Furthermore, Andersen argues against the "Métis-as-mixed" paradigm, positing that scholars should not recognize Métis for their "mixedness," but rather for their own "Métisness" as a distinct Indigenous people and nation with its own history and culture.[67] Andersen explains that the genesis of the Métis Nation was in the Red River Valley in the nineteenth century:

> Red River Métis collectively created, borrowed and combined elements to form a distinctive culture and lifestyle separate from both their Euro-Canadian and First Nations neighbours, including a new language, form of land tenure, laws, a distinctive

> form of dress, music, a national flag and, in 1869–70, distinctive political institutions. Indeed, by Canada's formal establishment in 1867 the Métis constituted an indigenous nation of nearly 10,000 people possessing a history, culture, imagined territorial boundaries, national anthem and, perhaps most importantly, a sense of self-consciousness as Métis.[68]

Darryl Leroux and Adam Gaudry also argue that Métis identity, kinship, and collective self-consciousness were and are rooted in western North America within an extensive alliance of Indigenous peoples – Cree, Ojibwe, Nakoda, and Dene.[69] Peterson, Andersen, Leroux, and Gaudry have reoriented the discussion of Métis identity around historical self-ascription and political consciousness rather than biological descent from a mixture of Indigenous and European ancestors.

By historicizing and analysing French-Indigenous patterns of métissage in the Hudson Bay watershed we can more clearly pinpoint developments that led to the eventual emergence of the Métis people as *la nouvelle nation*. An examination of Indigenous-French relations in the Hudson Bay watershed over a 150-year period paints an alternative trajectory for Métis peoplehood in the Northwest, one that still reserves a salient role for the French Empire and its imperial projects in the emergence of a "new" Indigenous people in the West. While the buffalo hunt, pemmican trade, and the Battle of Seven Oaks were important moments in Métis history, helping to crystalize group identity and political expressions of self-determination, it is also important to take into account the Indigenous-French relations in the Hudson Bay watershed that preceded these events – namely, the relations that stemmed from French imperial ambitions earlier in the eighteenth century. These earlier relations between Indigenous women and French men were a salient part of the story of Métis people- and nationhood, though they are mostly ignored in conventional Métis historiography.

THE HUDSON BAY WATERSHED

The Hudson Bay watershed is vast, but for the purposes of this study it can be divided into four broadly defined physiographic regions: the Hudson Bay Lowlands, the Canadian Shield, the aspen parkland, and the northern Great Plains. The Hudson Bay Lowlands are a vast wetland located between the Canadian Shield and the southern shores of Hudson and James Bays. The gently sloping lowlands are marked by turbid muskegs, a few sparse stands of stunted trees, and brackish estuaries at the mouths of a few major rivers that drain into Hudson Bay – the Churchill, Nelson, Hayes, Severn, and Albany. To the south, the Canadian Shield is an expanse of Precambrian rock that encircles the bay. Its crab-like pincers reach out toward the Mackenzie basin to the northwest and to Cape Wolstenholme on the Hudson Strait to the northeast. The shield's rocky grey granite landscape is punctuated by tall and crowded forests of black and white spruce, larches, poplars, aspens, and white birches. Many fur-bearing mammals – marten, muskrat, mink, and beaver – call the boreal forest, which covers much of the ancient bedrock of the Canadian Shield, home.

Where the Canadian Shield ends, along the eastern shores of Lake Winnipeg, there is a transitional biome of aspen parkland between open grasslands and boreal forest. This intermediate zone is marked by an uneven topography of steep hills, wooded groves, and ravines. Because the aspen parkland is an ecological borderland that marked the transition between the woodlands of the Northeast and the grasslands of the Southwest, its occupants benefited from a combination of ecological opportunities, from the rich presence of aquatic fur-bearing animals along the region's many lakes, rivers, and streams, to broad clearings where herds of bison and elk grazed. Many animals, too, like the white-tailed deer or mule deer, exploited the parkland environment, finding seasonal shelter in the aspen groves and grazing on the abundant grasslands.

On the other side of the transitional aspen parkland, the northern Great Plains, a sea of grasses in the heart of North America, stretches as far west as the Rocky Mountains. The plains were as important to the fur trade as were the Canadian Shield's northern boreal forests, as bison (numbering in the tens of millions) were hunted and processed into pemmican, which literally fuelled the muscle power of the fur trade. While bison herds tended to remain on the grasslands during warm and relatively snow-free winters, they sought refuge from particularly harsh winters in the island forests of Turtle Mountain, Touchwood Hills, Wood Mountain, and Cypress Hills, along the northern margins of the plains. Bison herds similarly sought sanctuary in the broad, deep, and sheltered valleys of the meandering prairie rivers of the Poplar, Milk, Red Deer, and Bow. Naturally, Indigenous (and later Canadien and Métis) plains hunters founded wintering camps among the grassy hills, wooded coulees, and streams favoured by their prey.[70] The tributaries of the rivers that eventually flow into

Hudson Bay reach out across the northern Great Plains like tendrils weaving between the buttes and plateaus of the Prairies and carving deep valleys into the undulating landscape.

Lake Winnipeg, a descendant of the ancient Lake Agassiz, is the beating heart of the Hudson Bay watershed, and through it about half of Canada's mainland waters pump into Hudson Bay through the major arteries of the Nelson-Saskatchewan River system, which originates 1,900 kilometres away on the eastern slopes of the Rocky Mountains. The drainage basins of the Red and Winnipeg Rivers also pulse through Lake Winnipeg before discharging into Hudson Bay. Lake Manitoba and Lake Winnipegosis, which Crees described as the younger siblings of Lake Winnipeg, also drain northeast into Hudson Bay via Lake Winnipeg. Circumventing Lake Winnipeg entirely, the Churchill, Hayes, Severn, Albany, Missinaibi-Moose, Nottaway, Rupert, and Eastmain Rivers also flow into Hudson Bay. In addition to physiographic regions, this study conceptualizes the geography of the Northwest into three distinct watersheds, which form another important backdrop for this narrative.

Starting at the height of land northwest of Lake Superior, the Winnipeg River drains the entire Rainy Lake–Lake of the Woods system northwest into Lake Winnipeg. By navigating numerous and strenuous portages to cross from the Great Lakes basin into the Hudson Bay watershed via the Kaministiquia or Pigeon River systems, Canadiens first encountered the turbulent and convoluted waterways that cut through the ancient granite of the Precambrian shield and eventually drain into southeastern Lake Winnipeg. The Red River basin and its major tributaries – the Assiniboine, Qu'Appelle, Souris, Pembina, and Roseau – flow north before draining into Lake Winnipeg at Netley Creek, which then drains through the Nelson River into Hudson Bay. The Saskatchewan River system originates in meltwater from glaciers locked in the peaks along the main ranges of the Rocky Mountains and stretches across the western plains toward Hudson Bay. The Saskatchewan River system formed the backbone of the fur trade economy during the period under study. The North and South Saskatchewan Rivers, along with their major tributaries the Battle, Red Deer, Bow, and Oldman Rivers, drain much of Canada's western Prairies.

The Rocky Mountains, located within the North American Cordillera, rise dramatically above the Great Plains. The ancient spine of the Rockies, comprised of metamorphic and igneous rock, marks the hydrological boundary known as the Continental Divide, where

0.1 The present study focuses on the Hudson Bay drainage basin, a vast territory whose lakes, rivers, and streams flow into Hudson Bay. The region encompasses roughly one-third of modern-day Canada.

watersheds either drain east to the Atlantic Ocean or west to the Pacific Ocean. Just as the Rocky Mountains acted as a barrier for eighteenth-century French explorers reconnoitring the heart of North America, so, too, does it act as the western barrier for this study, which remains firmly rooted within the boundaries of the Hudson Bay watershed.

TERMINOLOGY

In the past twenty years, historians have increasingly discarded antiquated names for Native groups in favour of the names by which Indigenous peoples and communities refer to themselves. By embracing

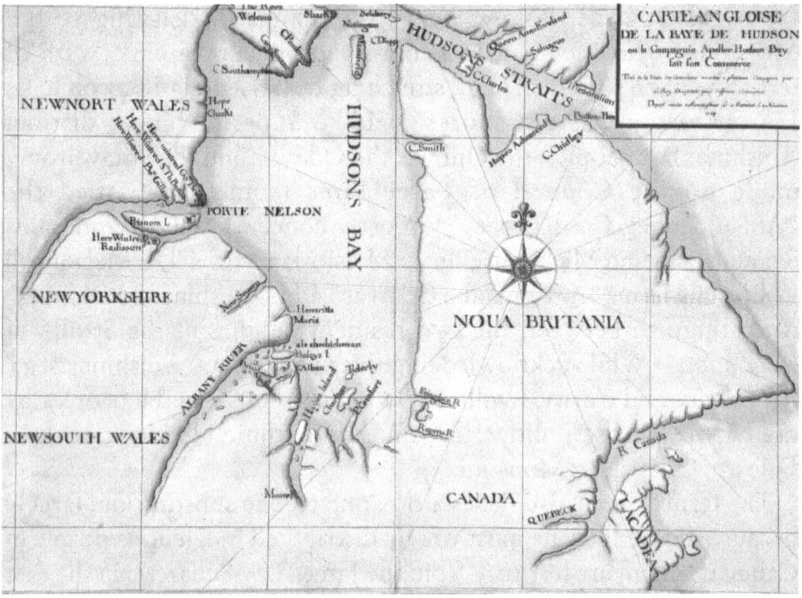

0.2 The Hudson Bay watershed represented myriad imperial opportunities for both France and Britain, including prime northern furs, valuable Indigenous alliances, and the promise of a Northwest Passage to the Pacific Ocean.

these self-designations, historians can represent Indigenous peoples in the way they choose to represent themselves, and therefore honour the rights of Indigenous peoples to self-determination. Wherever possible, I have discarded older labels like "Iroquois" in favour of more appropriate names like "Haudenosaunee." Similar examples include "Wendat" replacing "Huron," "Ho-Chunk" for "Winnebago," and "Mesquakie" instead of "Fox." However, terms like "Iroquoian," "Algonquian," and "Siouan" will still be employed as broad linguistic and cultural labels wherever appropriate. For example, "Algonquian" encompasses various peoples belonging to the same linguistic family from the east coast of North America (Mi'kmaq and Abenaki) to the Great Lakes heartland (Menominee and Potawatomi), and finally westward to the northern Great Plains and the Rocky Mountains (Crees and Niitsítapi).

Unfortunately, not all terms have easy, one-to-one replacements. For example, many scholars have taken to replacing the name "Ojibwe" (for a people featured prominently in this study) with "Anishinaabe" (singular) or "Anishinaabeg" (plural). However, the latter refers to a much larger group of interrelated peoples, such as

Ojibwes, Odawas, Potawatomis, Nipissings, Mississaugas, and Monsonis, who occupied and continue to occupy a vast swath of territory in the pays d'en haut, stretching from Georgian Bay on Lake Huron to the western shores of Lake Superior. Three distinct Anishinaabeg peoples, the Ojibwe, the Odawa, and the Potawatomi, made up the Council of Three Fires (sometimes called the "Anishinaabeg Confederacy"), mostly concentrated around Sault Sainte-Marie and Michilimackinac.[71] Historian Michael A. McDonnell utilizes the terms "Anishinaabe Odawas" and "Anishinaabe Ojibwes" to distinguish between the two resident peoples at the Straits of Mackinac.[72] While acknowledging their identity as "Anishinaabeg," for brevity and clarity, I will simply refer to Anishinaabe peoples by their more precise political divisions and ethnic identities, such as Ojibwe, Odawa, or Monsoni.

The term "Cree" also defies a tidy one-to-one substitution, largely because it describes the most widely distributed Indigenous people in Canada, occupying territory from the James Bay Subarctic in the east to the northern Great Plains in the west. Linguists and anthropologists have recognized the linguistic subdivisions in the Western Cree based primarily on the spoken dialects of /y/, /n/, and /th/, as well as geographic boundaries. Western woodland Cree (and later Plains Cree), who speak the /y/ dialect, refer to themselves as "Nêhiyaw" (singular) and "Nêhiyawak" (plural), which translates to "those who speak the same language." The Swampy (Lowland) Cree refer to themselves as "Omushkego" (singular) and "Omushkegowak" (plural), which translate to "people of the muskeg." Because the Omushkego speak the /n/ dialect, they also refer to themselves as "Nehinuw" (singular) and "Nehinuwak" (plural). The Rocky Cree of the Churchill River drainage basin speak the /th/ dialect and refer to themselves as "Asiniskaw Īthiniwak," which translates to "people of the place where there is an abundance of rock." The range of Cree self-designations has made it difficult to ascertain which Cree group is being referenced in the historical record, for French observers referred to any Crees they encountered as either "Kilistinon," "Kiristinon," "Knisteneaux," or "Christinaux." For simplicity and clarity, I will employ the term "Cree," a generic and very common self-designation, to refer broadly to Cree-speaking groups, unless a specific group identity can be ascertained with certainty.[73]

The Crees forged a powerful military alliance and a long-distance trading network through intermarriage with the Siouan-speaking

Assiniboine. The Assiniboine call themselves "Nakoda," which translates to "allies," but Great Lakes Anishinaabeg had introduced them to French fur traders as "asinii-bwaan," which meant "stone enemy" or "stone Sioux." As a result, European newcomers occasionally referred to the Nakoda as "Assiniboine," "Stone Indians," "Stony Sioux," or "Stonies."[74] Because of the negative connotation of "Assiniboine," this book uses the Nakoda self-designation when discussing this group.

Lastly, the label "Sioux" describes three principal divisions – the Dakota to the east, the Nakota in the centre, and the Lakota to the west. In the east, there were four Dakota subdivisions of Mdewakanton, Sisseton, Wahpeton, Whapekute. Not to be confused with the Nakoda (Assiniboine), the central Nakota of the "Sioux" subdivided between the Yankton and Yanktonai ("Little Yankton"). The Lakota subdivisions were more nebulous, but they divided themselves into smaller political units at the regional level, like the Oglala and Hunkpapa. These seven "Sioux" *oyáte* (people) referred to themselves collectively as "Očhéthi Šakówiŋ," or the Seven Council Fires, and controlled a territory that stretched from the Upper Mississippi River to the Missouri River.[75] This study rejects "Sioux" in favour of names like Očhéthi Šakówiŋ, Dakota, Yankton, Yanktonai, and Lakota, which more accurately reflect the cultural and linguistic heritage of these peoples.

Despite my best efforts, seemingly outdated terms have occasionally forced their way into the text due to both widespread usage in the literature as well as a current lack of suitable alternative terminology. For example, with some reluctance, I maintain the term "Iroquois Wars" to describe the series of conflicts fought primarily among Iroquoian peoples (Haudenosaunee, Wendat, Tionnontaté, Neutral, Erie, Wenrohronon, and Susquehannock) in northeastern North America throughout the latter half of the seventeenth century. Similarly, I have retained the term "Fox Wars" to designate the two consecutive early eighteenth-century conflicts between New France, Great Lakes peoples, and the peoples of the Fox-Wisconsin watershed (Mesquakie, Sauk, Kickapoo, and Mascouten). In the seventeenth and early eighteenth centuries, the French referred to the homeland of the Dakota (Mdewakanton, Sisseton, Wahpeton, Whapekute) in the Upper Mississippi valley as the *pays des Sioux*, or "Sioux Country," a term which I retain to designate this westerly territory situated outside of both the pays d'en haut and the Hudson Bay watershed.

CHAPTER OUTLINE

Chapter 1 explores New France and the Hudson Bay watershed from 1663 to 1714. During this period, the French state learned an indispensable lesson in governance and adopted a largely informal policy of co-opting fur traders already operating within the Hudson Bay watershed. Canadiens such as Pierre-Esprit Radisson, Daniel Greysolon Du Lhut, and Nicolas Jérémie *dit* Lamontagne, became key figures in New France's western diplomacy with the Cree, Nakoda, Ojibwe, and Dakota. These men were successful not because they annexed the Hudson Bay watershed as an imperial space, but because they were capable of forging on-the-ground relationships with local Indigenous communities, a technical and cultural challenge that eluded the inexperienced governors and officers of the French colonial administration. Thus, in the period prior to the Treaty of Utrecht, France gained a commercial and imperial foothold in the Hudson Bay watershed by harnessing the local knowledge, experience, and expertise of French (later Canadien) backcountry specialists.

Chapter 2 begins with the surrender of Hudson Bay, Newfoundland, and Acadia to England under the Treaty of Utrecht in 1713. Despite these territorial losses and the subsequent death of Louis XIV, the treaty ushered in an unprecedented era of peace, both at home and abroad. A reinvigorated French state was led by a capable regent, the Duke of Orléans (1715–23), who recognized information gathering as an essential precursor to empire building and thus pursued scientifically minded inquiries into the geography and peoples of western North America. During this period, the question of the Mer de l'Ouest, or "Western Sea," became particularly salient in driving the French imperial imagination westward. Under the auspices of Philippe de Rigaud, Marquis de Vaudreuil, governor general of New France, backcountry Canadiens became essential purveyors of intelligence, however ambiguous or imperfect, for the expansion of French imperialism into the Hudson Bay watershed.

Following this period of extensive reconnaissance and information gathering, chapter 3 examines France's big push into the Hudson Bay watershed (1731–43) with the establishment of les postes de la Mer de l'Ouest (the posts of the Western Sea) under the command of nobleman and member of the colonial elite Pierre Gaultier de Varennes, sieur de La Vérendrye. This chapter argues that French colonial policy under the new governor general, Charles de la Boische, Marquis de

Beauharnois, deviated from the precedents set by the previous government of Vaudreuil. Beauharnois largely refused to promote capable Canadiens over noble Troupes de la Marine officers. As the French colonial government was to discover, however, the more they tried to impose the hierarchy of the ancien régime, the more they suffered setbacks in terms of effective imperial expansion and control. While the Hudson Bay watershed had always been a "Native ground," the more overt French imperial posturing encountered serious Indigenous resistance. This was indeed a step back for the French, who, thanks largely to La Vérendrye's mismanagement of Indigenous geopolitics and the prevalence commercial misconduct, became entangled in a protracted war between the Cree, Monsoni, Nakoda, Ojibwe, and Dakota.

Chapter 4 demonstrates that, even while Beauharnois tried to enforce social order and hierarchy, Canadiens like Louis Galloudek and René Bourassa *dit* La Ronde continued to play salient roles as cultural and political intermediaries in the Hudson Bay watershed. Because of their kinship connections with Cree, Monsoni, Nakoda, Ojibwe, and Dakota communities, Beauharnois and La Vérendrye were forced to rely on Canadiens to acquire information and to maintain a French presence within the geographic, political, and cultural landscapes of the Hudson Bay watershed. Chapter 4 also shows the role that Canadiens played as labourers, interpreters, diplomats, provisioners, and surveyors of precious metals and other resources.

Chapter 5 marks the beginning of the end for French imperial plans in the Hudson Bay watershed. The War of the Austrian Succession (1740–48) checked French imperial ambitions in a substantial way. This imperial setback was the beginning of Canadien ascendency and the formation of a genuine French-Indigenous community, a process that occurred largely outside the purview of the French colonial government. During this period, it became clear that Canadiens had all along been successful cultural brokers, not because they had turned the Hudson Bay watershed into an imperial space, or its Indigenous residents into imperial subjects, but because they worked to integrate themselves into an Indigenous social world. As a result, many Canadiens broke away from the weakly garrisoned and poorly managed Western Posts, which resulted both in the fragmentation of an official French imperial presence in the Hudson Bay watershed as well as the initiation of significant patterns of métissage; understood within a particular demographic and political context, this ultimately prefigured the rise of the Métis people in the coming generations.

The final chapter challenges previous scholars who maintained that the French presence in the Hudson Bay watershed vanished during the Seven Years' War (1754–63). The Hudson Bay watershed remained a French-Indigenous social space even after Troupes de la Marine officers withdrew to the battlefields in the East. Through Indigenous kinship networks, many Canadiens, such as François Jérôme *dit* Latour and Louis Primeau gained knowledge of the region's physical, political, and cultural landscapes, which allowed them to carve out a salient socio-cultural space for themselves and their families, even once the hierarchy of the ancien régime had collapsed at the Western Posts. As this chapter demonstrates, the story of French-Indigenous relations in the Hudson Bay watershed did not conclude with the British conquest of Canada, but rather continued with the emergence of the Métis people and the Métis Nation, the result of *longue durée* processes of métissage manifested in the context of late eighteenth-century political and demographic reorganization in the Northwest.

Over the course of the seventeenth and eighteenth centuries, a motley assortment of voyageurs, soldiers, and coureurs de bois incorporated themselves into expansive Indigenous kinship networks extending from the shores of Lake Winnipeg to the Mississippi, Missouri, and Saskatchewan Rivers, and finally over the Great Plains to the foothills of the Rocky Mountains. Through consecutive generations, Canadiens and Indigenous peoples together shaped the cultural, demographic, and environmental landscapes of the Northwest. In the eighteenth century, Canadiens formed the cornerstone of New France's fur trade empire, but, following the British conquest of 1760, they, along with their Indigenous wives and kinsmen, fashioned their own social world in the Hudson Bay watershed – that of the Métis Nation.

1

The Battle for the Hudson Bay Watershed, 1663–1714

The Iroquois Wars of the mid-seventeenth century had a profound effect on Indigenous and imperial geopolitics from the Saint Lawrence valley and Iroquoia to the Great Lakes, disrupting, and at times displacing, Algonquian and Iroquoian societies. Throughout the conflict, the Haudenosaunee fractured and dispersed several large confederacies – including the Wendat, Neutral, Erie, Wenrohronon, and Susquehannock – and became a dominant political force in the eastern Great Lakes. Historians have provided a number of economic, geopolitical, and cultural rationales to explain the eruption of violence and warfare in the Saint Lawrence valley and the pays d'en haut in the mid-seventeenth century.[1] Even though several scholars have recently questioned the destructiveness of the Iroquois Wars, the conflict nonetheless had a significant impact on the geopolitical makeup of the pays d'en haut.[2] Samuel de Champlain, the so-called Father of New France, had staked the future of the colony on an alliance with Wendat, Innu, and Anishinaabe-Algonquin peoples almost half a century earlier, inciting the enmity of the Haudenosaunee.[3] The Wendat dispersal in 1649 weakened Canada's western flank and made the colony along the Saint Lawrence River increasingly vulnerable to attack.[4]

The geopolitical upheaval of the Iroquois Wars exposed a series of demographic, economic, military, and organizational deficiencies that beset the early French colony.[5] Realizing that New France was on the brink of collapse due to these internal shortcomings as well as external threats, Louis XIV and Jean-Baptiste Colbert, his chief minister, introduced a series of reforms rescinding the Compagnie des Cent-Associés's charter and incorporating New France as a royal colony in 1663. These reforms had the effect of introducing the institutions of metropolitan France to the colony, thereby establishing the militaristic authority of a governor general, an intendant (chief civil and legal official), a bishop, and a high court – the Sovereign Council.[6] In the early summer of 1665, twelve hundred men of the Carignan-Salières Regiment landed in Canada with orders to safeguard New France against the Haudenosaunee and to consolidate royal authority.[7] Although early Canadian historiography has largely credited the arrival of the Carignan-Salières Regiment under the leadership of Alexandre de Prouville de Tracy for turning the tide of the Iroquois Wars, ethnohistorians of the period have pointed to the role that Anishinaabe and Wendat warriors played in pushing back the Haudenosaunee by themselves, without French help and largely outside the purview of European observers.[8]

The French Crown worked toward exerting royal control over New France throughout the remainder of the seventeenth century, which made it more difficult for everyday Frenchmen – voyageurs, soldiers, and coureurs de bois – to acquire influence, wealth, and prestige in colonial society. Unlike noblesse d'épée and noblesse de robe, whose rank in society was derived from hereditary ties to military, judicial, or administrative services, a small number of ordinary French settlers had managed to rise to prominence in both Indigenous and French colonial society in the early seventeenth century due to their natural aptitudes and talents.[9] Samuel de Champlain had recognized the potential of many disenfranchised youths, such as Étienne Brûlé, Jean Nicolet, Jean Godefroy de Lintot, and Nicolas Marsolet, whose skills in language, diplomacy, and exploration were of great service to the young colony.[10] These "interpreters" (*truchements* in seventeenth-century French) became an asset to New France's early fur trade and diplomacy with Indigenous peoples.[11] In the early days of the colony, opportunities for promotion and social advancement were intrinsically tied to one's ability to gain knowledge of Indigenous societies and to work with Indigenous peoples in the fur trade.

Under the new colonial structure established in 1663, however, rank outweighed ability, and the governor general regulated traders' access to the Great Lakes region (pays d'en haut) – moves that favoured the colonial elite. High-ranking military officers from the Compagnies Franches de la Marine (initially from the Carignan-Salières Regiment but soon followed by others) obtained a *congé* (fur trade licence) and then went about hiring *habitants* (peasant farmers) as *engagés* (indentured servants) to paddle canoes and carry out trade in the pays d'en haut.[12] And yet even with restrictions in place, the French Crown grew increasingly concerned that the allure of the western fur trade would prompt habitants to abandon their farms and undermine one of the colony's most precious resources – namely, people. In 1681, Louis XIV and Colbert declared by royal edict that "it is forbidden for all habitants from our country of New France to trade furs in the villages of the Natives in the depths of the woods without our permission."[13] The royal decree did little to halt a growing clandestine trade of coureurs de bois (illicit fur traders), who travelled throughout the North American interior, flaunting the hierarchy of the ancien régime.

The French state feared that these itinerant and illicit traders would bring about the moral and economic collapse of colonial society, and yet they ultimately proved to be indispensable to the economic prosperity, geopolitical stability, and even expansion of the colony in the late seventeenth century. For example, Governor General Joseph-Antoine Le Febvre de La Barre appointed Daniel Greysolon Du Lhut, a clandestine fur trader, as the principal ambassador and peacemaker between New France's Great Lakes allies and the Dakota.[14] Nicolas Perrot, a fur trader and former Jesuit lay servant (*donné*), served as chief interpreter for royal official Simon-François Daumont de Saint-Lusson at Sault Sainte-Marie in 1671, and again for Governor General Louis-Hector de Callière at the Great Peace of Montreal in 1701.[15] The French Crown even ennobled and awarded the Croix de Saint-Louis (France's highest military honour) to Étienne de Veniard, sieur de Bourgmont, a military deserter and coureur de bois, for his explorations of the Missouri River and the Great Plains.[16] Throughout the latter half of the seventeenth century, the French colonial government learned an indispensable lesson about governing the nascent royal colony. When colonial officials ignored or repressed the local knowledge and expertise of voyageurs and coureurs de bois, imperial projects often failed at the edge of empire. However, when the state harnessed their talents, the colony was able to pursue truly ambitious imperial projects in colonial hinterlands. In this early period, runaway soldiers and illicit fur traders became key figures in French western diplomacy with the Indigenous peoples of the Hudson Bay watershed, such as the Ojibwes, Crees, and Dakota.

The first section of the chapter gives a broad overview of the seventeenth-century French state and explores the relationship between colonial and metropolitan governments. The second section examines the ecclesiastical diffusion of knowledge, and particularly how the Society of Jesus informed and shaped French imperial aspirations in the Hudson Bay watershed. The third and final section focuses on ordinary French habitants in the Hudson Bay watershed through an examination of three case studies. After some initial missteps with coureurs de bois Pierre-Esprit Radisson and Médard Chouart des Groseilliers, French colonial officials began to harness the local knowledge and expertise of other rogue agents of empire, such as Daniel Greysolon Du Lhut, who became a prominent figure in seventeenth-century French imperial policy in the Great Lakes and the Hudson Bay watershed. In these places, where empire was more imagined than real, imperial coercion gave way to kinship as a means of extending French interests. Following suit, other fur traders, such as company clerk Nicolas Jérémie *dit* Lamontagne, established salient kinship relations with the local Cree population, which helped the French to establish a commercial foothold in the Hudson Bay watershed.

Between 1686 and 1714, the French were able to maintain a consistent presence in the Hudson Bay watershed due to the tireless work of voyageurs and coureurs de bois who developed on-the-ground connections with various Indigenous polities. The region, however, remained a Native space. Any notion of French influence should therefore be understood not as a displacement of Indigenous sovereignty, but rather as an attempt to make commercial inroads vis-à-vis France's English colonial rivals. In other words, the two European powers battled less for "control" of the Hudson Bay watershed than for a preferential position in commercial and military alliances; the victor would have the prospect of trading with the region's Indigenous inhabitants. Throughout this conflict, a variety of voyageurs, coureurs de bois, soldiers, and interpreters were crucial to guaranteeing a steady French presence in the Hudson Bay watershed.

FRANCE AND EMPIRE

France did not participate in the first wave of colonialism in the Americas prompted by Christopher Columbus's four voyages to the so-called New World in 1492, 1493, 1498, and 1502.[17] In the early sixteenth century, the Kingdoms of Castile, Aragon, and Portugal conquered and colonized vast swaths of territory in the Caribbean, Mesoamerica, Brazil, and Peru.[18] The Iberian powers ratified their conquests through a papal bull, *Aeterni regis*, and by signing the

Treaty of Tordesillas (1494), according to which they divided the newly discovered hemisphere between themselves.[19] All this prompted an irate King Francis I of France to declare to a Spanish ambassador that the "sun shines for me as it does for others. I would very much like to see the clause of Adam's will by which I should be denied my share of the world."[20] Defying the papacy and disregarding the Treaty of Tordesillas, Francis I launched France onto the colonial stage in 1524 when he commissioned Florentine navigator Giovanni Verrazzano to survey the Atlantic coast of North America between Florida and the Maritimes.[21]

Despite Francis's bravado, French interest and success in the colonization of the Americas waxed and waned due to tumultuous wars fought in Europe over dynastic ambitions and religious discord.[22] Between 1534 and 1604, France experienced numerous false starts in its colonial ventures in the Saint Lawrence valley, the Maritimes, Brazil, and Florida.[23] By the early seventeenth century, however, Samuel de Champlain, Pierre Dugua de Mons, François Gravé Du Pont, and Jean de Poutrincourt had finally achieved some promising progress in colonizing the regions around the Bay of Fundy and the Saint Lawrence valley, with the establishments, respectively, of Port-Royal (1605) and Quebec (1608). Shortly thereafter, English privateers began raiding France's seaboard settlements and trading stations, which culminated in the seizure of Quebec by David Kirke in 1629.[24] Unwilling to see years of labour undone, Champlain hounded royal officials, urging them to hasten the restitution of New France and arguing that Kirke's privateers had unlawfully captured the colony only two months after the signing of a peace treaty between England and France. Following the restoration of Quebec and Port-Royal to the French under the Treaty of Saint-Germain-en-Laye (1632), settlement of the Saint Lawrence valley and of Acadia began to stabilize, in part thanks to the tireless efforts of Champlain, who henceforth enjoyed the full support of Louis XIII and Cardinal Richelieu, his chief minister.[25]

In this early period of colonization, trade companies administered the colony, securing monopolies in exchange for an annual royalty and an obligation to populate the fledgling settlement. The French Crown maintained a stake in the administration of New France through Richelieu, who founded the Compagnie des Cent-Associés in 1627. After the restoration of the colony to France in 1632, the new company, which had acquired seigneurial rights over New France, committed to transporting four thousand Catholic settlers to the colony within fifteen years, as well as converting Indigenous peoples to Catholicism.[26] Moreover, the French king appointed a governor general to represent him in New France, just as he did in the provinces of the metropole.[27]

Following the French Wars of Religion of the sixteenth century, the French state worked to centralize its bureaucracy and wrest power away from the old provincial noble families.[28] Under the competent stewardship of a succession of monarchs and their chief ministers, such as Louis XIII and Louis XIV, Cardinal Richelieu, Cardinal Mazarin, and Jean-Baptiste Colbert, a centralized French state essentially came into being in the seventeenth century. When Cardinal Mazarin crushed the rebellion of nobles and parliamentarians known as the Fronde (1648–53), he and young Louis XIV moved to subjugate the *parlements* to royal authority.[29] Although such authority was centralized at Paris and later Versailles, most historians of early modern France have sought to add nuance to Alexis de Tocqueville's early interpretation that "the Bourbon monarchs had laid the foundations for the modern state by reducing the nobility to obedience and beginning a process of national unification."[30] Most historians now recognize that, in practice, French absolutism (or more accurately, governance) was characterized by compromise and negotiation with socially powerful elites – at court, in Paris, and in the provinces.[31] In this more flexible understanding, absolutism represented a shared process of state formation whereby kings and rulers bound particularistic sites of power and authority to the success of the emerging state through personal relationships, finance and debt networks, circuits of knowledge, and symbolic culture.[32] While acknowledging the collaborationist view of governance, some historians, like John C. Rule and Jacob Soll, have nevertheless argued that the French monarchy's accumulation of information and centralization of decision-making and administration translated more directly into state power and control.[33]

Jacob Soll has described the ancien régime as "a government born of myriad ancient and often disparate traditions, knotted together like ivy so old it is impossible to discern the original root."[34] Jean-Baptiste Colbert (1661–83) helped young Louis XIV untangle the "knotted ivy" of the French state, advising and guiding the young monarch through the labyrinth of medieval customs, ancient constitutions, the Catholic Church, and the emerging bureaucracy of a centralized administrative government.[35] Cardinal Mazarin had brought Colbert into the royal inner circle to manage his personal finances and household. Within a year, Colbert had become indispensable.[36] Colbert, with his financial savvy and obsession with information and its instrumentalization, made it increasingly clear that a humanist education in the Neoplatonist tradition was on its own insufficient for a monarch to rule a state effectively.[37] A generation earlier, Cardinal Richelieu had recognized that money comprised the "sinews of power," but he had not bothered to study the mercantile traditions that flourished in the banks and workshops of the great Italian city states.[38] By the late seventeenth century, it was becoming ever more apparent that Plato's "philosopher-kings" could not manage "a large, industrial, colonial, and militarized state."[39] Colbert would help Louis XIV control the finances of his kingdom and growing overseas empire.

More than his predecessors, Colbert associated state power with a strong navy that tightly controlled overseas colonies. To this end, he centred his attention on the port of Rochefort, launching a massive project to overhaul shipbuilding, improve colonial transportation, and build an intricate information-management system.[40] In 1663, Louis XIV revoked the royal charter of the Compagnie des Cent-Associés and placed New France in the exclusive *domaine du roi*, arguing that the company was unable to administer the colony and that it had not honoured its obligation to colonize the settlement.[41] Louis and Colbert encouraged the colony's demographic growth with a more concerted immigration plan and by transplanting a feudal social order to the colony resembling that of the mother country.[42] Louis and Colbert's larger colonial strategy in North America centred on the transplantation of French feudal agrarian society to the Saint Lawrence valley and growing a favourable, or internal, balance of trade throughout the French Atlantic world.[43] Leading economic theorists of the day believed that there was a finite amount of gold and other precious metals in the world, and that possession of this limited supply of wealth was the basis of state power.[44] With the absence of gold and silver mines in France's overseas colonies, however, mercantilism promised to at least keep specie within imperial borders. Colbert organized mercantile companies and granted state-sponsored monopolies to exploit the French Empire in the "New World," which he hoped would challenge Dutch and English economic prowess.[45]

Colbert and other theorists of mercantilism argued that a country must sell more goods abroad than it bought in order to accumulate gold. A French economy that sold abroad and purchased domestically would create a favourable balance of trade because French goods would be exported to foreign nations for gold, which would increase France's national wealth and royal revenues.[46] Colbertism (Colbert's economic doctrine, a variant of mercantilism) was a closed economic system designed to ensure that French colonies bought only metropolitan manufactured goods and traded commodities exclusively with France and other French colonies. By severely regulating what came in and out of French colonial markets, Colbertism commercially disadvantaged French colonists, who until 1670 had enjoyed free trade with other European nations and colonies.[47] Although trade between English, Dutch, and French colonies continued in the form of smuggling,[48] Colbert attempted to regulate the French Atlantic economy by promoting an internal triangular trade between Canada, the Caribbean, and France.[49] In addition to Colbert's mercantilist policies, territorial expansion, glory, and dynastic politics were also important considerations in formulating French colonial agendas in the Americas.[50] This was especially evident in Canada, where the financial dividends of the fur trade were paltry compared to the fabulously bountiful sugar islands of the West Indies.[51] The total value of New France's fur exports amounted to less than 7 per cent of the total value of West Indian exports to France during this period.[52] By the eighteenth century, the value of French Caribbean exports of sugar, tobacco, cotton, indigo, and coffee to France amounted to an average of 100 million livres per year, whereas New France's fur exports fluctuated from about 100,000 to 600,000 livres annually.[53] In other words, when comparing Canadian and Antillean commerce, the difference in both profitability and volume of trade was staggering.

Compared with Atlantic trade, Colbert showed little interest in the early reports documenting the Indigenous peoples who dominated the western interior of North America and who contested France's claims of sovereignty. Indeed, what little attention Colbert did pay to the Hudson Bay watershed consisted primarily of his attempts to strategically thwart the English-backed HBC. In 1682, Colbert begrudgingly offered government support to the Compagnie du Nord to challenge the English fur trade, but strictly maintained that the fur trade alone could not economically sustain New France.[54] Recognizing the economic instability of the fur trade, Colbert rightly reasoned that unregulated commercial overexpansion would result in peltries exceeding European demand. He feared, moreover, that the fur trade would strain New France's limited labour and capital resources. In other words, the trade would pull colonists and funds away from the centralized colony and market of the Saint Lawrence valley. Rather than building up village economies, population densities, and agricultural surpluses in Canada, labour and capital would be dispersed, as traders went off to the pays d'en haut to pursue a resource whose market value was dubious and ever-fluctuating. Colbert advised colonial officials to "crowd [settlers] together, and group them and settle them in towns and villages, and so give them the greater possibility of protecting themselves well."[55] He also worried that the unregulated pursuit of the fur trade would leave posts and forts scattered throughout the pays d'en haut and the Hudson Bay watershed, making them difficult to defend and vulnerable to attacks by Indigenous peoples and European rivals.[56]

Merely sending more settlers from France to Canada was also out of the question as pre-Enlightenment French scholastics had a perennial fear that France was undergoing a demographic crisis.[57] Although France's population was surprisingly healthy, standing at about twenty million in the seventeenth century, Colbert argued against mass emigration to North America, noting that "it would not be prudent to depopulate his [Louis XIV's] kingdom … in order to populate Canada."[58] Many French observers posited that the religious wars fought in Europe in the wake of the Protestant Reformations of the early sixteenth century, such as the destructive French Wars of Religion (1562–98), the Huguenot Rebellions (1620–29), and the Thirty Years' War (1618–48), had culled the peasant population of Western Europe, and had thus diminished the potential settler pool for France's overseas colonies. A Récollet traveller in North America echoed this view, noting that "the more bloody Wars which have rag'd so long in all parts of Europe, have hinder'd the sending [of] Christian Colonies to [North America]."[59] Colbert strove instead to convert the subsistence economy of New France, largely dependent on the exportation of furs, into a diversified pre-industrial economy that would be capable of supporting natural population growth from the initial small nucleus of French settlers. Intendant Jean Talon attempted to implement Colbert's policies by establishing a shipyard and a lumber industry, as well as promoting mineral surveying.[60] The activities of fur traders, merchants, corrupt government officials, and coureurs de bois clashed with Colbert's vision of a compact colony.[61] By the end of the late seventeenth century, New France maintained fortified posts over a vast territory, from Fort Frontenac on Lake Ontario in the east to Fort Saint-Louis on the Illinois River in the west. Regardless of Louis and

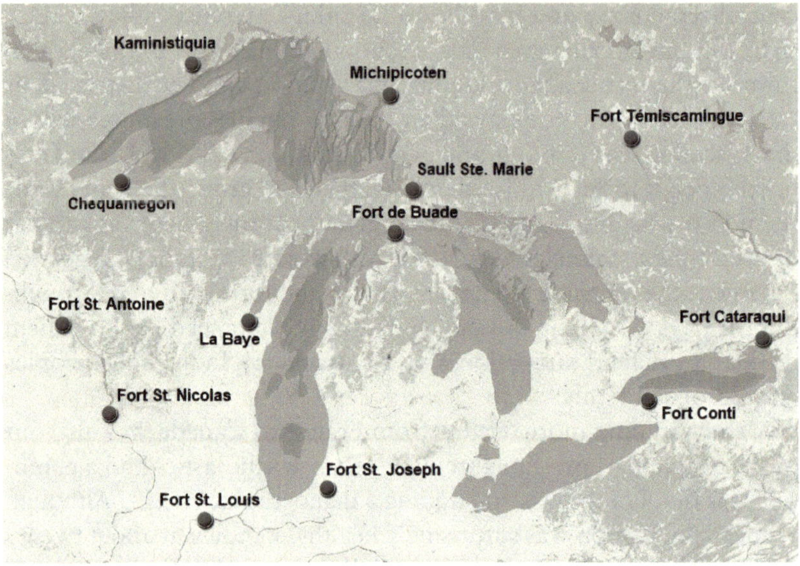

1.1 Much to the chagrin of Louis XIV and Jean-Baptiste Colbert, colonial officials, Troupes de la Marine officers, and backcountry specialists (voyageurs and coureurs de bois) had independently expanded New France far into the interior, often against the designs of metropolitan planners.

Colbert's designs, Indigenous alliances and the fur trade had drawn colonial officials, officers of the Troupes de la Marine, and habitants away from the Saint Lawrence valley and toward the western interior.[62] As we shall see, there were limits to the metropole's ability to maintain coercive control over its colonies.

Historian James Pritchard has posited that colonies did best when left alone to forge commercial ties with other colonies or nations in Europe, thereby integrating themselves into the wider Atlantic economy. In Pritchard's view, the French government's intervention (particularly Colbert's mercantilist policies) in colonial affairs usually bore negative consequences for the colonies and were at odds with the Crown's expressed desire to build an empire in the Americas.[63] Moreover, as many historians have argued, distance and isolation, as well as the intersection and interchange of French, Indigenous, and African cultures, created unique and dynamic colonial societies – a condition that put them at odds with the metropolitan government and pushed them to negotiate and pursue their own agendas.[64] In other words, governance in the French colonies "did not proceed by absolute command and unqualified obedience, but by negotiation and accommodation."[65] When the goals and agendas of metropolitan ministers and colonial elites aligned, however, this facilitated overseas expressions of empire, even if it was negotiated haphazardly at times. Though Louis XIV and Colbert favoured a compact colony, they reluctantly backed colonial efforts to seize HBC posts in the seventeenth century, an endeavour that promised to provide some financial return, but more importantly to deprive England of territory and trade, thus preventing the envelopment of French colonization efforts in North America. As Jacob Soll argues, "Colbert spoke of the New World as connected to England, Holland, Spain, France, and their colonial holdings and concessions."[66] For Colbert, then, the colonies mattered only insofar as they would contribute to Louis XIV's state power and glory within a European context.

THE SOCIETY OF JESUS

In the seventeenth century, the Jesuits were at the forefront of French western imperial expansion in North America. Historian Bronwen McShea has helpfully framed the Jesuits as "Apostles of Empire," who from "the reign of King Louis XIII through the era of the Seven Years' War were enthusiastic, enterprising empire-builders for the Bourbon state."[67] The association between religious conversion and alliance was initially an important aspect of the Indigenous reception of Christianity.[68] Conversion was also a vehicle for extending French claims of sovereignty in North America.[69] Many Indigenous peoples understood that having a Jesuit, or "black robe," among them was often an essential prerequisite for the establishment of official trade relations with the French. This had been especially pertinent during the Iroquois Wars, when the French staunchly refused to trade firearms with their non-Christian Native allies.[70] In certain instances, Indigenous peoples perceived baptism as a sacred pledge of friendship and alliance with the French, without necessarily understanding the theological tenets of Christianity.[71] Despite being primarily motivated by their Christian faith and a profound desire to convert Indigenous peoples, Jesuits were also adept at discussing secular policies connected to trade and politics, as well as acting as interpreters and middlemen between French administrators and Indigenous civil headmen and war chiefs.[72] McShea has more firmly argued for the inextricable entanglement of French empire and religion, highlighting how Jesuits were tied to the project of empire building for the Bourbon state as colonial lobbyists, military advisers, army chaplains, wartime propagandists, emissaries, interpreters, go-betweens, and spies.[73] In other words, Jesuits like Paul Le Jeune, Isaac Jogues, and Jean de Brébeuf were not just apostles of Christ, but also apostles of French empire.

The Jesuit order still sat awkwardly within the absolutist hierarchy of the ancien régime; priests answered first and foremost to the superior general of the Society of Jesus and the papacy, not the French Crown. This circumvention of absolutist royal authority represented an affront to the principles of Gallicanism, which posited that the French king and government should have greater authority in appointing bishops and approving papal decrees.[74] Notwithstanding the hierarchy of the Roman Catholic Church, the Society of Jesus organized and operated their missions within a largely national framework, attempting as much as possible to co-operate with the imperial projects of the Bourbon state.[75] And yet, despite this metropolitan tension, Jesuit activity in the western Great Lakes and the Hudson Bay watershed often aligned with the interests of French colonial officials.[76] As previously mentioned, the fur trade in general, and coureurs de bois in particular, were seen to operate counter to, and at the expense of, mercantilist imperial policies. The illicit fur trade smuggled pelts to Dutch and English markets, which drove down French metropolitan profits and pulled colonists away from their farms.[77] Coureurs de bois were also a thorn in the side of Jesuit missions in the Saint Lawrence valley and the pays d'en haut, but for different reasons altogether. Morally panicked Jesuits argued that coureurs de bois exposed Indigenous peoples to what they considered lax morals, as well as "that detestable traffic" of the liquor trade, which contradicted their teachings and undermined their spiritual authority.[78] In the *Relation* of 1672–73 from the mission of Saint-François Xavier des Prés (La Prairie), Father Jean de Lamberville opined that "brandy has ruined the Algonquin missions; and it still prevents many Savages from being converted. The insatiable avarice of the French is the cause of it. They go as far as two and three hundred leagues to seek the Savages in the woods, for the purpose of getting their furs by making them intoxicated."[79] Similarly, Father François de Crespieul argued that "the less one employs coureurs de bois, the better it is for the Mission and for the trade."[80] Jesuit missions in the Saint Lawrence valley and the pays d'en haut reported on the behaviour of coureurs de bois, and colonial authorities occasionally used that information in their efforts to curb these illicit trade activities and prevent the loss of fur trade profits among colonial elites.[81]

The Jesuits were just one of many religious orders in seventeenth-century New France; Récollet, Capuchin, Sulpician, Ursuline, Congrégation de Notre-Dame, and Hospitaller missions and schools also dotted the Saint Lawrence valley. By 1640, Jesuits ran missions and schools at Quebec and Trois-Rivières at which they attempted to convert the early allies of New France, the Wendat, Innu, and Anishinaabe-Algonquin. By the eighteenth century, Jesuits operated missions at Lorette (1674), Kahnawake (1680), Odanak (1701), and Kanesatake (1717), where they harboured displaced Christian congregations of Wendats, Haudenosaunees, and Abenakis.[82] While many Jesuits remained among their missionary settlements in the Saint Lawrence valley, others travelled far into the interior, taking their proselytizing message to the Indigenous peoples of the pays d'en haut. Jesuits were often skilled rhetoricians, excellent teachers, and seasoned missionaries. Great Lakes Indigenous peoples regularly perceived Jesuits as official political emissaries from France and welcomed them because they valued the French as suppliers of goods and as allies in their wars against the Haudenosaunee.[83]

Jesuits not only preached Catholicism, but also imparted French culture. Jesuit activities aligned with Colbert's seventeenth-century policy of *francisation*, or "Frenchification," a colonial strategy aimed at assimilating New France's Indigenous allies through religious instruction, cultural integration, intermarriage, and procreation.[84] Pre-Enlightenment French notions of blood purity and intermarriage between social classes (*mésalliance*) meant that women were viewed as mere vessels for male bloodlines. Transposed to a North American context, it was thought that if Frenchmen married Native women, the qualities transmitted through blood from one generation to the next would be solely French, which would lead to the dilution of Native blood and achieve both cultural and biological assimilation.[85]

Historian Gilles Havard argues that métissage in New France was deeply rooted in notions of European supremacy, arguing that "the children of a French father and a Christianized Aboriginal mother [did] not become 'Métis' in the sense of a new category with particular characteristics ... but [instead became] obedient, Catholic, and Frenchified subjects."[86] Adam Gaudry and Darryl Leroux likewise argue that "French policy in New France was an attempt at Frenchification and not *métissage* … French colonists sought to assimilate Indigenous peoples rather than produce a culturally hybrid Indigenous society."[87] In other words, French ministers and officials did not recognize métissage as an equal mixture between two peoples, but rather as a process meant to displace the Indigenous element in favour of its French or European element. The French colonial government believed that Jesuits and other religious orders would be effective intermediaries in overseeing this policy of francisation in North America.

On a macro-imperial level, Jesuits also contributed to Colbert's growing state intelligence system. Colbert envisioned a virtual panopticon that would allow him to govern the kingdom of France and its colonial empire from his desk at Versailles through state paperwork and an intricate system of information exchange and circulation.[88] In other words, Colbert's blueprint for statecraft constituted and necessitated a constant centripetal flow of information – letters, reports, dispatches, censuses, balance sheets, surveys, and maps – toward the metropole.[89] Emerging from the Renaissance humanist tradition, Jesuits were encyclopedic learners who had mastered the travel narrative (*récit de voyage*) and ethnographic description. They meticulously composed empirical "relations" of their voyages, describing peoples, plants, animals, places, buildings, navigation, and geography, which they sent back to their headquarters in Paris and Rome.[90] Colbert admired the Society of Jesus's system of knowledge management and their information-handling techniques, and sought to make Versailles the nerve centre of a world empire by integrating economic, historical, legal, natural, political, and religious data into the internal system of the state apparatus.[91] And yet, while this information was crucial to imperial planning, all intelligence had its limits. Even in the most conducive scenario of information transmission, there was still a large disconnect between the halls of Versailles and overseas colonial and Indigenous spaces.

In the seventeenth century, the Jesuit mission at Sault Sainte-Marie was the veritable gateway to the Hudson Bay watershed. In 1642, the Ojibwe of Sault Sainte-Marie were the Jesuits' chief informers. The Ojibwe people formed part of an Anishinaabe collective called the Council of Three Fires, which also included the Odawa and Potawatomi.[92] The Ojibwe advised visiting Jesuits at Sault Sainte-Marie that the Dakota, who were "situated to the Northwest or West of the Sault," made "continual wars" against the Crees and Nakoda, "and other great Nations who inhabit the same Country."[93] While the

Jesuits still did not precisely understand the intricacies of fluctuating Indigenous alliances, coalitions, and conflicts, they still wrote many of the first European accounts to make it into the hands of metropolitan ministers and imperial planners at Versailles.[94] The Jesuits published annual *Relations* for the benefit of a small but dedicated audience back home in France: "pious well-wishers, potential donors, and simply curious readers."[95]

The Jesuits had been on the front line of the Iroquois Wars, which saw the devastation of their mission at Sainte-Marie and the dispersal of the Wendat.[96] Now, Jesuits watched as Wendats and Anishinaabeg (Ojibwes, Odawas, and Potawatomis), driven from their own homelands by the Haudenosaunee, in turn made war on the eastern woodland Dakota in the Fox-Wisconsin watershed and Upper Mississippi valley. Wendats and Anishinaabeg recognized the strategic advantage they held over the Dakota, who did not yet have access to European iron weapons and firearms, and thus conspired "to drive the Scioux [Dakota] from their own country in order that they themselves might thus secure a greater territory in which to seek their living."[97] Anishinaabe oral histories recorded by William W. Warren in the Wisconsin Territory in the nineteenth century reveal that, once the Ojibwes of Zhaagawaamikong (La Pointe) gained a steady supply of French firearms, they pushed inland from Lake Superior to hunt valuable fur-bearing animals. The Ojibwes waged a war against the Dakota in order to gain access to these rich hunting grounds of the Wisconsin, Chippewa, and St Croix Rivers.[98]

The Wendats, Ojibwes, Odawas, and Potawatomis began raiding the eastern woodland Dakota of the upper Mississippi valley but failed to realize the sheer enormity of the confederation of people who identified as "Sioux." The Dakota (encompassing the Mdewakanton, Sisseton, Wahpeton, Whapekute oyáte) and their Yankton, Yanktonai, and Lakota allies referred to themselves collectively as "Očhéthi Šakówiŋ," or the Seven Council Fires, and claimed a homeland that spanned from the Upper Mississippi River to the Missouri River.[99] The combined strength of the Očhéthi Šakówiŋ repulsed the Anishinaabe and Wendat coalition back to the southwestern shores of Lake Superior.[100] Jesuit priest Jacques Marquette wrote that Očhéthi Šakówiŋ warriors, lacking firearms, nonetheless handled bows and arrows "with such skill and readiness as to fill the air with shafts in an instant," and when in retreat were still able to "discharge their arrows so rapidly as to render themselves not less formidable when fleeing than when attacking."[101] Even with a technological disadvantage, the Dakota, Yankton, Yanktonai, and Lakota were still able to defend themselves and their territory.

Realizing the magnitude and martial prowess of the Očhéthi Šakówiŋ, Wendat, Odawa, Potawatomi, and Ojibwe withdrew to consolidate their mutual alliance and to establish polyethnic villages centred around *doodemag* (clans) at La Pointe (Ashland, Wisconsin), Green Bay, Michilimackinac (Mackinaw City, Michigan), and Sault Sainte-Marie. Reflecting on the conflict, Father Marquette described the Očhéthi Šakówiŋ as "the Iroquois of this country, beyond la Pointe," noting that "all the nations of the Lake make war on them, but with little success."[102] Such a statement would have strongly resonated with the French readership of the *Jesuit Relations*, who were familiar with the Iroquois Wars of a few decades earlier, especially the martyrdoms of Jean de Brébeuf, Isaac Jogues, and Gabriel Lalemant.[103] However, given the fact that the Očhéthi Šakówiŋ were defending a homeland that was being invaded by Wendats and Anishinaabeg armed by the French, the employment of the "Iroquois" analogy seems especially perplexing, and only serves to demonstrate how French colonial discourse perceived Indigenous peoples in essentializing and binary categories – either as allies or enemies.

The Dakota and their Yankton, Yanktonai, and Lakota allies emerged victorious against the Great Lakes peoples by using their traditional weapons, but the protracted conflict nevertheless showed them the tactical importance of acquiring iron weapons and firearms. Father Marquette thought European technology was a pivotal factor in Indigenous warfare, saying that the Dakota "fear the Frenchman because he brings iron into this country."[104] In colonial and Indigenous historiography, there is an ongoing debate over the importance that Indigenous peoples placed on firearms.[105] Despite contrasting viewpoints, it is clear that firearms had a much greater capacity for carnage and killing in warfare than traditional Native weaponry. For example, the kinetic energy of the lead ball could travel through bone and sinew, sending fragments of deadly shrapnel into muscles and organs. Compared to an arrow, which left a relatively clean puncture wound, a lead ball had a much higher chance of splintering into pieces and pushing scraps of cloth into the body, which turned an initially survivable injury into a potentially deadly gangrenous infection.[106] In the end, firearms would reconfigure the battlefields of North America.[107]

The apparent advantages of iron weapons and firearms compelled all Great Lakes peoples to seek valuable alliances and commercial connections with the French at Sault Sainte-Marie. Realizing they had reached a stalemate with the Dakota, the Ojibwe opted to extend peace overtures to them, believing that an alliance would allow them to access the abundant hunting grounds of the Upper Mississippi valley. The Jesuits were anxious for peace and the prospect of extending their proselytizing efforts to more westerly Indigenous peoples like the Cree and Nakoda.[108] By 1670, the Jesuits had had some contact with both groups, two demographically significant but loosely associated polities who lived to the northwest of Lake Superior in the Hudson Bay watershed, but were beginning to make their own trading forays to Sault Sainte-Marie and Michilimackinac.[109] Many Jesuits were optimistic that a mission among the Cree and Nakoda would be a great spiritual and commercial success. Father Marquette relished the thought of not only the innumerable souls to convert and beaver pelts to trade, but also of the potential access to "a great River leading to the Western Sea," an imperial triumph that would have transformed New France from a colonial backwater into the crown jewel of Louis XIV's overseas empire.[110]

In 1674, the Ojibwe of Sault Sainte-Marie invited a delegation of Mdewakanton Dakota to negotiate the release of eighty Dakota prisoners from the previous war. The meeting was an opportunity for the Ojibwe and Očhéthi Šakówiŋ to form an alliance that would extend from the pays d'en haut to the headwaters of the Mississippi River, and onto the northern Great Plains. Fearing that a peace between the Ojibwe and Dakota would cut them out of the Great Lakes trade network, northern Crees visiting at Sault Sainte-Marie endeavoured to sabotage the peace conference. The Jesuit superior Claude Dablon recorded that the Crees "not only expressed their dissatisfaction in the matter, but resolved moreover to prevent the peace from being concluded," thereafter conspiring to kill the Dakota ambassadors.[111] Concealing their knives to enter the French chapel where the meeting had assembled, the Cree conspirators threatened and then assaulted the Dakota emissaries. The Dakota defended themselves, "and struck with their Knives at all the assembled savages, without making any distinction between" Crees or Ojibwes, "believing that they had all equally Conspired in the design to assassinate them."[112] When the fighting ended, ten Dakota ambassadors and over forty Ojibwes and Crees lay dead. Consumed by a great conflagration, the Jesuit mission at Sault Sainte-Marie burned to the ground.[113]

What became known as the "Sault Sainte-Marie massacre" brought about a renewed general conflict to the region northwest of Lake Superior. A Jesuit observer noted that the Dakota now "gave all their attention to waging war against the Kiristinons [Crees], the Assiniboüles [Nakoda], and all the nations to the north."[114] As stalwart Cree allies, the Nakoda, who lived further to the west, were drawn into the renewed war against the Očhéthi Šakówiŋ. Some Ojibwe bands also participated in this renewed conflict, but to a lesser extent as they sought to conciliate these warring peoples, as had been their initial intention at the meeting at Sault Sainte-Marie before it turned into a massacre. The war between the Cree and Nakoda on one side and the Očhéthi Šakówiŋ on the other presented too great a danger for the Jesuits to proselytize to the Indigenous peoples of the Hudson Bay watershed. For the time being, the Jesuits would have to wait at Sault Sainte-Marie and content themselves with the few Crees and Nakoda who ventured inland to come trade and fish at the Sault.[115] The Sault Sainte-Marie massacre marked not only the beginning of an intense conflict between the Cree-Nakoda and the Očhéthi Šakówiŋ, but also highlighted the powerlessness of the Jesuits as "apostles of empire" in the West. In this period of initial Native-newcomer interactions, French imperial agents, like the Jesuits, commanded little authority among the shifting Indigenous alliances in the western Great Lakes and the Hudson Bay watershed. Powerless to control or influence the unfolding events, Jesuits observed, chronicled, and commented upon the conflicts and geopolitical reconstitutions taking place in the region.

VOYAGEURS AND COUREURS DE BOIS IN THE HUDSON BAY WATERSHED

Amid the power struggle between calculating ministers, avaricious governors, bellicose Troupes de la Marine officers, and zealous missionaries over the fate of New France, a distinct group of ambitious Frenchmen emerged in the late seventeenth century – ordinary traders, soldiers, explorers, and adventurers who sought to carve out a space for themselves in the social hierarchy of New France. These voyageurs and coureurs de bois pushed westward into the Hudson Bay watershed, a region that was hitherto peripheral to the French imperial gaze. As one French chronicler put it, for these ambitious settlers of New France, Western North America "was a Peru for them," equating the profitability of the western fur trade with riches of the Incan Empire.[116]

Eventually, realizing the power vested in them, metropolitan ministers and the governors and intendants of New France would co-opt these French (later Canadien) backcountry specialists as agents of empire. Voyageurs and coureurs de bois in the Hudson Bay watershed moved successfully between Indigenous and French worlds. They became adopted sons to Indigenous fathers and mothers while simultaneously becoming clients of powerful patrons, and eventually even travelled overseas to visit royal courts to vie for promotion and patronage within these elite colonial and metropolitan circles.

Pierre-Esprit Radisson and Médard Chouart des Groseilliers – Coureurs de bois

About a decade before the disastrous negotiations at Sault Sainte-Marie and the eruption of warfare between the Cree and Dakota, two coureurs de bois – Pierre-Esprit Radisson and Médard Chouart des Groseilliers – successfully rendezvoused with Cree bands west of Lake Superior. Unlike their Jesuit counterparts, Radisson and Des Groseilliers journeyed to the pays d'en haut without the permission of the French colonial government. They visited and traded directly with the Ojibwe, Cree, Menominee, and Dakota. Since this was fourteen years before the Sault Sainte-Marie massacre of 1674, it was still possible for these disparate peoples to come together peaceably, although intermittent raiding still occurred. In his 1659–60 travel narrative, Radisson described how he and Des Groseilliers, his brother-in-law, utilized deception, rhetoric, and cross-cultural understandings to try to convince their newfound Indigenous allies that they commanded a powerful spirit, or *manidoo*. Radisson and Des Groseilliers purportedly held bountiful feasts and generously bestowed firearms, iron weapons, and other European trade goods upon their Indigenous hosts, which they claimed imbued them with significant prestige and influence in these communities.[117]

Some historians have interpreted Radisson's famous quote – "We weare Cesars, being no body to contradict us" – as a reflection on the life of a coureur de bois, who seemed to enjoy the liberty and freedom to come and go as they pleased in the North American wilderness. Given the context in which his narrative was constructed, however, Radisson likely meant to imply the mastery that he and Des Groseilliers believed they had achieved over Indigenous peoples west of Lake Superior.[118] Radisson also provided a vivid description of a great diplomatic and spiritual ceremony, called the Feast of the Dead (sometimes called the Feast of Souls), which took place in the winter of 1659–60 at Lac Courte Oreilles. Eighteen different Indigenous groups came to participate in this religious and political ceremony, to ratify an alliance with each other, and to trade with the French.[119] Radisson took credit for orchestrating the Feast of the Dead and the subsequent peace ceremony concluded between the Ojibwe, Wendat, Menominee, Cree, and Dakota. In reality, he and Des Groseilliers were peripheral to these events of inter-Indigenous diplomacy; the Ojibwe from Sault Sainte-Marie had organized the Feast of the Dead.[120]

There is a vital alternative narrative – one in which Radisson and Des Groseilliers were not the central actors, but mere witnesses and bystanders to what took place west of Lake Superior in the winter of 1659–60. In fact, Ojibwe oral history records that the first visit by "two white men," presumably Radisson and Des Groseilliers, to the region began with them being nursed back to health from a state of starvation in the Ojibwe village at Zhaagawaamikong (La Pointe).[121] Some young Ojibwes discovered Radisson and Des Groseilliers in such a state of malnourishment that "they had been reduced to the extremity of roasting and eating their woollen cloth and blankets as the last means of sustaining life." The young Ojibwes were "filled with compassion," and "carefully conveyed [the Frenchmen] to their village, where, being nourished with great kindness, their lives were preserved."[122] Radisson and Des Groseilliers spent the winter in the Ojibwe village, where they traded their merchandise brought from Montreal for beaver skins. In the spring, according to both Radisson's account and Ojibwe oral tradition, many Ojibwes accompanied them on their voyage home to the Saint Lawrence valley.[123]

Despite the apparent discrepancies between Radisson's written account and the Ojibwe oral tradition, one important element that both narratives have in common is the claim that Radisson and Des Groseilliers spent the entire winter in the Ojibwe village. During that time, they learned a great deal about the complex alliance system west of the Great Lakes, and they even used European goods during the negotiations at the important Feast of the Dead ceremony, which helped them establish a Euro-Indigenous trade alliance. While far from dictating Indigenous geopolitics, Radisson and Des Groseilliers fortuitously found themselves at the heart of Indigenous diplomacy and alliance-making northwest of Lake Superior.

The 1659–60 Feast of the Dead and the peace treaty between the various Indigenous peoples west of the Great Lakes allowed Radisson and Des Groseilliers to abscond with a vast quantity of furs and return home to the Saint Lawrence valley. Disappointment, however, was ultimately in store for these triumphant cultural brokers. Upon their return home, Governor Pierre de Voyer d'Argenson arrested Radisson and Des Groseilliers for illegally trading furs in the pays d'en haut.[124] Had d'Argenson pardoned them, rather than confiscate their furs and cargo, New France might have gained unparalleled geographic knowledge of western Lake Superior and the Hudson Bay watershed, as well as vital insight into the Indigenous geopolitics of those western regions. But because of d'Argenson bullheadedness, many of these western Indigenous peoples, like the Cree and Dakota, would for the time being remain outside the diplomatic and commercial purview of the French colonial government.

The two spurned coureurs de bois subsequently defected to England, where they helped Prince Rupert of the Rhine, the Duke of Cumberland, Sir James Hayes, and a group of wealthy London investors establish the "Governor and Company of Adventurers of England trading into Hudson's Bay," better known as the Hudson's Bay Company. A royal charter issued by King Charles II incorporated the HBC on 2 May 1670 and granted the new company a presumptive monopoly over the territory whose rivers and streams flowed into Hudson Bay – an area that became known as "Rupert's Land." Radisson and Des Groseilliers's knowledge of the flora, fauna, geography, and peoples of the vast territories northwest of Lake Superior set the foundation for English claims to the Hudson Bay watershed. The HBC would remain an impediment to French western imperial expansion until the final British conquest of New France in 1760.

Realizing their crucial mistake, French ministers and colonial officials sought to lure Radisson and Des Groseilliers back into the service of Louis XIV. When a financial dispute arose between the two coureurs de bois and some of the members of the HBC's London Committee, French officials enticed them briefly back into the service of the French Crown.[125] In 1682, Radisson and Des Groseilliers returned to Hudson Bay to establish a trading post at the mouth of the Hayes River. They were now in the employ of a French company, the Compagnie du Nord, under the direction of French merchant and financier Charles Aubert de La Chesnaye.[126] The HBC's charter had sanctioned the deployment of military and naval expeditions to assert sovereignty over Hudson Bay. To compete with the HBC, Philip Gaultier de Comporté, a founding member of the Compagnie du Nord, journeyed to France and petitioned Louis XIV to formally recognize the company and allow them the same privilege of organizing military and naval expeditions. Comporté's mission was a success, the French court granting the Compagnie du Nord sovereignty (by force if necessary) over the Hayes-Nelson watershed for a thirty-year period.[127]

Colbert had not built up a strong French state by gambling state revenue on risky and somewhat dubious foreign ventures. While Louis XIV's government lurched toward centralization, Colbert continued to authorize non-state actors – mercantile companies, proprietorships, and occasionally even privateers – to extend French political, territorial, and economic goals overseas.[128] Throughout the seventeenth century, overwhelmed and debt-ridden early modern states continued to employ and depend upon a patchwork of private individuals and non-state entities to assert sovereignty and to maintain order in overseas localities.[129] Not only did this allow these states to avoid the expenses associated with foreign ventures, but it also gave them the cover of plausible deniability should a colonial venture go awry.[130]

The careers of Radisson and Des Groseilliers illustrate the importance of localized knowledge and Indigenous connections in establishing imperial roots in colonial hinterlands. Radisson and Des Groseilliers, who started out as ruffians and illicit traders in the eyes of the state, became salient figures in European imperial expansion into the Hudson Bay watershed, at least from the standpoint of Versailles and Whitehall. Radisson and Des Groseilliers were successful not because they annexed the Hudson Bay watershed as an imperial space, but rather because they were the only ones capable of forging on-the-ground relationships with local Indigenous communities, a technical and cultural challenge that eluded the inexperienced shareholders, governors, captains, soldiers, and merchants of both the HBC and the Compagnie du Nord. Radisson and Des Groseilliers enjoyed a major advantage in an Indigenous space, where family ties, not monarchs or empires, represented the main social structures and avenues of power.[131] Any notion of imperial control under these chartered companies was tenuous and illusory at best, and the Hudson Bay watershed steadfastly remained a "Native ground" or "Indian Country" until at least the late nineteenth century.[132]

Radisson, who spoke various Cree and Ojibwe languages and had considerable trading experience, was able to deftly navigate the Indigenous geopolitics of the Hudson Bay watershed. Radisson explained in his journal how he formed proper kinship relations with the Cree of the Nelson River estuary. Professing a mastery of Indigenous languages and the accompanying rhetoric of trade and kinship, Radisson quickly laid the groundwork for an alliance with a local Cree elder when they met for the first time at the mouth of the Hayes River. Radisson declared to the elder, "I know the whole land. Your friends will be my friends, and I have come here to bring you weapons to destroy your enemies. You will not die of hunger, neither your wife, nor your children, for I am bringing you merchandise. Take courage. I want to be your son."[133] Following his speech, Radisson distributed tobacco, pipes, and small knives to each one of the Natives. While they smoked, Radisson wept, dried his tears, and told his new companions that he grieved to see his "brothers so undone and bereft of all things," assuring them that while he was among them "they would no longer lack anything."[134] Radisson then circulated more gifts of guns, shot, and powder to his newfound allies.

The Cree elder accepted Radisson's terms of kinship; and there, on the windswept shores of Hudson Bay, an adoption ceremony took place. Radisson later described how the Cree elder "adopted me for his son by covering me with his robe. I also gave him my blanket which I told him to carry to his wife for me, as I wished to take her for my mother."[135] Radisson's adopted father urged his followers to hand over their beaver robes and then they went to their canoes to find other skins and furs to give to the Frenchmen. By weeping and employing a discourse of pity, Radisson had placed himself in a subordinate position as an adopted son before the Cree band's leader. In short, he acted in an appropriate fashion for someone who wanted to establish proper kinship relations.[136] Because imperial control was illusory in an Indigenous space, the Hudson Bay watershed remained a place where almost anyone, regardless of their rank or status in European society, could rise to prominence and exert a profound impact, so long as they were willing to play by the rules of their Indigenous hosts. Radisson exercised influence, not because he turned the Hudson Bay watershed into an imperial space and its Indigenous residents into imperial subjects, but because he worked to integrate European traders into an Indigenous social world.[137]

After a successful sojourn at Hudson Bay, Radisson and Des Groseilliers returned to France to find out that Jean-Baptiste Colbert, their benefactor and the pre-eminent supporter of the Compagnie du Nord, had died in 1683. Radisson and Des Groseilliers, discovering that there was little chance for advancement or patronage at Versailles without Colbert, departed France in 1684.[138] Des Groseilliers returned to Canada and died in obscurity, whereas Radisson returned to the employ of the HBC. The significance of Radisson's decision was felt almost immediately. Using his local French and Indigenous connections in the Hudson Bay watershed, Radisson seized the Compagnie du Nord's trading posts on the Hayes River for the HBC; he even managed to recruit his former cohort of Frenchmen to join the company.[139] Radisson's adopted Cree father had established a trade alliance based on kinship, not monarchs or empires, and thus his allegiance was always to his adopted son. The Cree elder honoured the trade and kinship relationship with Radisson, regardless of whether he was backed by French or English chartered companies. Radisson's return to the HBC cost the Compagnie du Nord a valuable northern fur market and over 20,000 livres in stolen trade goods.[140] In the late seventeenth century, the fortunes of chartered companies and empires in the Hudson Bay watershed seemed to wax and wane in accordance with whichever company or nation Radisson and Des Groseilliers aligned themselves with.

Daniel Greysolon Du Lhut – Rogue Agent of Empire

Daniel Greysolon Du Lhut was a captain in the colonial regular troops and a petty nobleman (an *écuyer*, or esquire) whose family had only recently entered the lowest rungs of French nobility. In ancien régime France, it was possible to purchase titles, state offices, or military ranks. A member of the Third Estate with noble aspirations had to amass a large fortune, then purchase a government office that had noble status attached, often at an exorbitant price.[141] Of course, that which the Crown granted, it could also take away. In 1678–79, Du Lhut risked his status in colonial society by carrying out a clandestine trade voyage to the Upper Mississippi valley in contravention of a royal ordinance forbidding colonists from travelling and trading without a congé (fur trade licence).[142] In this sense, Du Lhut was a non-traditional coureur de bois, one who occupied a liminal space between the Second and Third Estates of the ancien régime. Even though Du Lhut was nominally an elite, he still followed in the tradition of Radisson and Des Groseilliers by pushing the boundaries of acceptable conduct and profiting from trade and Indigenous relationships at the edge of empire.

Spending the winter of 1678–79 near Sault Sainte-Marie, Du Lhut familiarized himself with Native and imperial geopolitics in the western Great Lakes and the Hudson Bay watershed. In particular, Du Lhut's Ojibwe interlocuters assured him that the Indigenous peoples of the Hudson Bay watershed – Cree, Monsoni, and Nakoda – were seeking Great Lakes alliances and European technology for their war against the seven oyáte of the Očhéthi Šakówiŋ – Mdewakanton, Sisseton, Wahpeton, Whapekute, Yankton, Yanktonai, and Lakota. The Ojibwe of Sault Sainte-Marie decided to send a peace delegation to reconcile the Cree and the Očhéthi Šakówiŋ, who had been warring since the 1674 Sault Sainte-Marie massacre. The Ojibwe stood to benefit substantially from mediating a peace between the two groups; a successful rapprochement would see the Ojibwe occupy a prominent position in both trade and geopolitics west of the Great Lakes.

Perceiving an opportunity for glory and advancement in colonial society, Du Lhut asked to accompany the Ojibwe peace delegation. The Ojibwe accepted Du Lhut's offer, knowing that his presence would indicate that they had access to French firearms, iron weapons, and other manufactured goods. Du Lhut stated that the purpose of his voyage was "to attempt the exploration of the Nadouecioux [Dakota] and the Assenipoualaks [Nakoda] who were unknown to us, and to cause them to make peace with all the nations around Lake Superior who dwell in the dominion of our invincible monarch."[143] Similar to Radisson and Des Groseilliers before him, Du Lhut journeyed to "Sioux Country," a region analogous to the Upper Mississippi valley that straddled three watersheds – that of the Saint Lawrence, the Mississippi, and Hudson Bay.

In 1679, Du Lhut planted Louis XIV's standard in the Dakota village of Issati (Mille Lacs, Minnesota). Du Lhut wrote, "I had the honour to set up the arms of his Majesty in the great village of the Nadouecioux called Izatys, where no Frenchmen had ever been."[144] Du Lhut failed to realize, however, that Radisson and Des Grossillers had probably visited the same Dakota village at Mille Lacs almost twenty years earlier. Later that summer, Du Lhut claimed that he organized a peace conference between the Cree, Nakoda, Ojibwe, and Dakota at the "extremity of Lake Superior," where the city of Duluth,

Minnesota, now stands, and where French fur traders would later establish a post called Fond-du-Lac. Du Lhut reported to the Marquis de Seignelay (Colbert's son and the newly appointed minister of the marine and colonies) that he had cemented these frail new bonds of alliance and friendship by arranging several marriages between members of different Indigenous groups.[145] Believing that he had successfully brokered a regional peace in the name of the French, Du Lhut moved on to exploring and searching for riches in the Upper Mississippi valley. Following Ojibwe and Dakota guides, he ascended the Bois Brulé River and reached Lake Saint Croix, which empties into the Mississippi. At Lake Saint Croix, Du Lhut learned that a Očhéthi Šakówiŋ war party had captured a Récollet priest, Father Louis Hennepin, and two of his companions at the junction of the Illinois and Mississippi Rivers.[146] Du Lhut feared that the French reputation among the Očhéthi Šakówiŋ would collapse if the captives remained unredeemed, believing that the Očhéthi Šakówiŋ would either take the French for cowards or so lacking in material goods that they could not treat with them in order to recover their own subjects. Recognizing another moment for prospective glory and commendation, Du Lhut departed to liberate the Frenchmen.[147] Du Lhut caught up with the trio on 14 August 1680 along the Wisconsin River, where he secured the release of the French captives and safely escorted them back to Michilimackinac for the winter.[148]

Despite Du Lhut's service to the French state, the colonial government reprimanded him for having illegally travelled and traded in the pays d'en haut. Intendant Jacques Duchesneau de la Doussinière et d'Ambault denounced Du Lhut to the Ministry of the Marine, describing him as the chief of the renegade coureurs de bois operating in the pays d'en haut. In addition, Duchesneau accused Governor Louis de Buade, Comte de Frontenac, of "favouring the disobedience of the King's ordinances concerning coureurs de bois," and surmised that his misconduct had filled the woods of North America with, by his estimates, between five and eight hundred coureurs de bois.[149] The intendant concluded that Canadiens were so "accustomed to libertinism and debauchery that all of the families in Canada found themselves committed to coureurs de bois."[150] In response to Duchesneau's accusations, Frontenac found an ally in Du Lhut and dispatched him to Versailles to plead their mutual innocence before the French court. Du Lhut ultimately succeeded in clearing his and the governor's good names, but the Marquis de Seignelay turned down

Du Lhut's specific requests for permission to continue exploring the Upper Mississippi valley and for the grant of a seigneury in these newly discovered lands.[151] Notwithstanding the initial disapproval of the French court, Du Lhut consistently maintained that his clandestine expedition to the Sioux Country had served the interests of France. Du Lhut continued to find favour with select French colonial officials, including the incoming governor, Joseph-Antoine Le Febvre de La Barre (1682–85).

Starting in 1683, La Barre appointed Du Lhut as the principal ambassador and peacemaker between New France's Great Lakes allies and the Očhéthi Šakówiŋ. Du Lhut returned to the western Great Lakes and the Upper Mississippi valley with a convoy of fifteen canoes in the hopes of rallying various Indigenous peoples of the pays d'en haut – Ojibwe, Odawa, Wendat, Menominee, Potawatomi, Mesquakie, Sauk, and Ho-Chunk – to the French military alliance against the Haudenosaunee. In 1684, when Governor La Barre went to war against the Haudenosaunee, Du Lhut persuaded five hundred Great Lakes warriors to journey to Niagara to lend support to La Barre's army.[152] Louis Armand de Lom d'Arce, Baron de Lahontan, a contemporary observer, described the size of the army composed of Indigenous peoples and coureurs de bois that Du Lhut had assembled: "he had ingag'd the Hurons [Wendats], Outaouas [Odawas], and some other People, to joyn his Army; in which he had above two hundred brave Forest Rangers [coureurs de bois]."[153] In 1687, when Governor Jacques-René de Brisay de Denonville (1685–89) organized a great military campaign against the Senecas, Du Lhut and other French cultural brokers in the west helped coordinate the perfectly timed arrival of four hundred Native warriors to join with the main army at Lake Ontario.[154] Du Lhut did not have coercive control of New France's Great Lakes allies and could not call them to action, but he did help organize and coordinate an attack against their mutual enemy the Haudenosaunee by using his knowledge of Indigenous diplomacy, language, and customs.[155]

After fighting against the Haudenosaunee in the eastern Great Lakes, Du Lhut returned to the Lake Superior region, where Governor La Barre ordered him to prevent the northern nations from trading their furs with the English at Hudson Bay.[156] The new intendant, Jacques de Meulles (1682–86), was suspicious of Du Lhut, who he worried had gone to the northern shore of Lake Superior only to line his own pockets from the fur trade. De Meulles was also suspicious that Du

Lhut's two posts at Lake Nipigon were far too distant from Hudson Bay to prevent Indigenous peoples from going there to trade with the HBC.[157] Writing to the Ministry of the Marine in 1683, La Barre defended Du Lhut, noting that his two posts at Lake Nipigon diverted trade away from the HBC and explained that "the English at the bay excite the Natives against us and only the Sieur Du Lhut alone can bring them calm."[158] The following year, Du Lhut reported back to La Barre and expounded on his success. Framing his ventures in glowing terms clearly meant to appease his patron, Du Lhut egotistically proclaimed that all the Crees had confidence in him, and that within less than two years "not one native will go to the English at Hudson Bay" instead of the post that he had established at Lake Nipigon. In a final exaggeration, Du Lhut assured La Barre that he would sooner die than see the Natives trade with the English.[159]

In a map of New France, cartographer and geographer Nicolas de Fer depicted Du Lhut's post at the mouth of the Nipigon River, and a second, Fort La Tourette, at the northeastern end of Lake Nipigon, near Ombabika Bay. De Fer overemphasized the geographic saliency of Lake Nipigon by portraying it as the source of both the Hayes and the Albany Rivers.[160] Another contemporary map by Alexis-Hubert Jaillot did the same for Du Lhut's posts at Lake Nipigon, and described Fort La Tourette in inflated terms as preventing "Assiniboels [Nakoda] and other Natives from descending to Hudson Bay."[161] Du Lhut's posts at Lake Nipigon were located so as to discourage only those Indigenous peoples from the Lake Superior region, such as Ojibwes from Michipicoten and Sault Sainte-Marie or Crees from Kaministiquia, from travelling to Hudson Bay via the various tributaries of the Albany River to trade with the English. De Fer, Jaillot, and even Du Lhut himself all claimed that Fort La Tourette on Lake Nipigon prevented *all* Nakoda and Crees from going to trade at Hudson Bay. This was a complete distortion of North American geography, as the majority of Native traders reached Hudson Bay via Lake Winnipeg and the Hayes and Nelson Rivers, which flow nowhere near Lake Nipigon.

Du Lhut either failed to understand the geography of the region or wantonly exaggerated the importance of his Lake Nipigon posts. Canadian fur trade historians Arthur J. Ray and Donald Freeman have demonstrated that the most important Cree and Nakoda fur trade routes to Hudson Bay were via the Hayes-Nelson watershed.[162] Ethnohistorian Michael Witgen has further argued that the Hayes-Nelson watershed was "a gateway to the Native peoples of the western

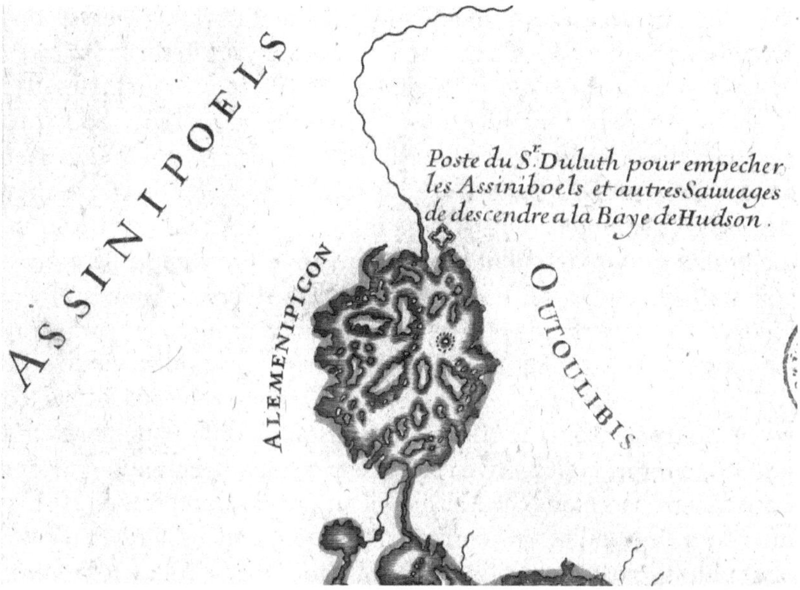

1.2 This map by Alexis-Hubert Jaillot, Parisian cartographer and publisher, shows the location of Fort La Tourette, on the northeast side of Lake Nipigon, which, according to Du Lhut, "prevented the Assiniboels [Nakoda] and other Natives from descending to Hudson Bay."

interior," connecting Hudson Bay to Lake Winnipeg, the Red River Valley, the Saskatchewan River, and the northern Great Plains.[163] Peoples, furs, and goods flowed from the interior of North America toward Hudson Bay along these vital waterways. Du Lhut did not control this important artery, and as a result would not have intercepted most of the Hudson Bay traffic. In fact, Du Lhut did not even possess enough merchandise to trade with the Indigenous peoples who did come to his posts. In the summer of 1687, Du Lhut's brother and business associate, Claude Greysolon de La Tourette, lamented that more than thirteen hundred Natives had visited the post at Lake Nipigon to trade with him and that "they were very angry to find not enough goods to satisfy them."[164]

This is not to say that Du Lhut's Lake Nipigon posts were not profitable; they unquestionably were, and Du Lhut still engaged in commerce on an extensive scale. In a letter written to his creditor Charles Aubert de La Chesnaye in 1684, in which he asked for an advance of money, Du Lhut stated that he had more than eight hundred used beaver robes at Michilimackinac with which to make the repayment the following year.[165] Although Du Lhut might have exaggerated his inventory to appease his creditor, used beaver robes still constituted the most sought-after type of beaver pelt. *Castor gras*, or greasy beaver, refers to pelts worn fur side in by Natives, whose natural body oils detached the outer guard hairs of the pelt, exposing the soft underfur beneath; these used pelts were especially desirable because they enabled furriers and hatters to more easily ply their trades.[166] Realizing the profitability of Du Lhut's operation, other Frenchmen petitioned colonial officials to set up posts along the rivers and lakes of the Hudson Bay watershed with the purpose of diverting some furs away from the HBC. In 1684, two Canadien merchants along the Moose River by the names of Saint-Germain and Argenteuil "diverted 70 canoes away from the English of Hudson Bay."[167] Both de Fer and Jaillot's maps list at least five fur trade entrepôts operated by various Canadien traders along the Abitibi, Albany, Moose, and Rupert Rivers. Intendant de Meulles was correct in suspecting that the real purpose of Du Lhut's posts, which were too far from Hudson Bay to prevent Natives from going there to trade, was indeed to promote his private commercial interests in the Lake Superior fur trade. Du Lhut had utilized the threat of the HBC to persuade French colonial officials to grant him access to the Lake Superior market.

Historian Shannon Lee Dawdy's concept of rogue colonialism, which she applied to the study of colonial New Orleans, is useful in examining Du Lhut's career. Dawdy defines rogue colonialism as "the influence of those individuals on the ground who pushed colonial frontiers in their own self-interest ... Colonialism was as much a creation of rogues and independent agents as it was the project of imperial states."[168] Dawdy describes "rogue agents" as explorers, entrepreneurs, adventurers, and con artists who appealed to European patrons and powerholders to value their colonial enterprises.[169] Some of Du Lhut's contemporaries occasionally scoffed at his self-aggrandizing accounts of his adventures. In the scornful estimation of René-Robert Cavelier, sieur de La Salle, Du Lhut "will not fail to exaggerate everything. It is his character ... He speaks more in keeping with what he wishes than what he knows."[170] In Canada, opportunists like Radisson and Des Groseilliers, and especially Du Lhut, were the rogue agents of empire that pushed the colonial frontiers of New France in pursuit of their own personal interests, ambitions, and fortunes. All three men worked their patronage networks within European states to get ships, supplies, and military backing for their various colonial ventures.[171]

Du Lhut may have been motivated by financial gain, but he was no fool. For example, while fleeing Sioux Country with Father Louis Hennepin and some French voyageurs, the group discovered some used beaver robes, which festooned the trees "as a sort of Sacrifice," below Saint-Anthony Falls on the Upper Mississippi River (present-day Minneapolis, Minnesota), a sacred site for the Mdewakanton Dakota. When some of the voyageurs avariciously plucked the *castor gras* from the consecrated branches, Du Lhut reprimanded them, telling the men "that they ought to have let the things alone in that place where they were, for that the Savages wou'd not fail to revenge the Affront which we had put upon them by this Action, and that it was to be fear'd they shou'd pursue and insult us by the Way." When one voyageur replied bluntly that "the things fitted them, and therefore shou'd not trouble their Heads about the Savages," Du Lhut fell into a violent harangue and almost came to blows with them. Before Du Lhut struck the brazen voyageur, Father Hennepin came between them and tried to calm the situation.[172] In "Indian Country," self-preservation was Du Lhut's mandate: What good were *castor gras* if he was to lose his head to the Dakota before making it back to Montreal to cash them in?

Du Lhut's career demonstrates how a minor noble turned coureur de bois could fall from grace and then rise to prominence as a diplomat, fur trader, and war leader in the western Great Lakes. Du Lhut had entered colonial service as a member of the lesser nobility, but in the hierarchical and stratified society of ancien régime New France, someone of his station may have been little better off than an average artisan in Montreal. Du Lhut appealed directly to the French court to defend himself and Governor Frontenac, his benefactor, against Intendant Duchesneau's charges of corruption. Although Duchesneau had implicated Du Lhut with the accusations against Frontenac, subsequent governors La Barre and Denonville recognized Du Lhut's utility in managing Indigenous alliances in the pays d'en haut, as well as his potential to undermine the English fur trade in the Hudson Bay watershed.

After Duchesneau, the intendants of New France begrudgingly followed the lead of the governors and accepted Du Lhut's position as an intermediary between the French colonial government and Indigenous peoples. Du Lhut, much like his predecessors Radisson and Des Groseilliers, was a veritable shaper of empire, but not because he was fiercely loyal to the French Crown and metropolitan conceptions of empire. Rather, he shaped colonial policy through his own pursuit of wealth and status. He had taken the initiative to establish relations with the Očhéthi Šakówiŋ, journeyed to Versailles to convince metropolitan ministers of the correctness of his decisions, and forged for himself a rôle as one of the most important cultural intermediaries and diplomats in the western Great Lakes and the Hudson Bay watershed. Despite all the time spent in the West, Du Lhut, his brother La Tourette, and the Frenchmen they travelled with would not make their homes there. In 1697, Du Lhut, suffering greatly from gout, retired into private life in Montreal at the age of fifty-eight. He lived in the home of Montreal tanner Charles Delaunay, also a former coureur de bois, to whom Du Lhut eventually left the majority of his estate. Although Du Lhut died in relative obscurity in 1710, he was fondly remembered as an exceptional backcountry specialist of the seventeenth century. For example, the Baron de Lahontan described "Mr. Dulhut, a *Lions* [Lyonnais] Gentleman," as "a Person of great Merit ... [who] has done his King and his Country very considerable Services."[173] Récollet father Christian Le Clercq referred to Du Lhut as "a man of talent and experience" who opened the West "to the missionaries and the Gospel."[174] Ultimately, Du Lhut, a coureur de bois and agent of empire par excellence, left an indelible footprint on French-Indigenous relations in the pays d'en haut and the Hudson Bay watershed.

Nicolas Jérémie dit *Lamontagne – a Clerk and Interpreter Becomes Governor of Fort Bourbon*

French mercantile companies and colonial officials learned from their previous mistake of spurning Radisson and Des Groseilliers and slowly came to value ability over nobility, at least for a time, in the Hudson Bay watershed. One of the most salient examples of this is the career of Nicolas Jérémie *dit* Lamontagne, an interpreter and clerk for the Compagnie du Castor (the French Crown revoked the Compagnie du Nord's monopoly in 1700).[175] Jérémie first arrived in the Hudson Bay region in 1694 when Pierre Le Moyne d'Iberville, a French privateer (who later founded Louisiana), seized York Factory from the HBC, renaming it Fort Bourbon. Jérémie described his responsibilities at Fort Bourbon as "ensign and interpreter of the languages of the Indians, and commercial director."[176] In the early days of his posting, Jérémie served in a quasi-military capacity. When HBC ships with four hundred sailors appeared off the coast at the end of the summer of 1696, the commandant of Fort Bourbon gave Jérémie the task of opposing the English landing with only fourteen company men. Jérémie wrote that "as we were lying in ambush in dense thickets ... I took care to have my men fire at the right moment, one after another ... the English promptly returned aboard their ship, not daring to risk forcing us [from our position], because they did not know the number that we were in ambush."[177] Jérémie described how company employees played an integral role in the skirmishes that took place in the surrounding woods and marshlands around Fort Bourbon.[178]

Jérémie also played a pivotal role gathering intelligence and information about the Hudson Bay watershed for the French state. He produced a succinct account of the geography, flora, fauna, and ethnology of the Hudson Bay watershed, which was written for an unnamed patron in Canada (possibly Antoine-Denis Raudot, co-intendant of New France from 1705 to 1710 and a director of the Compagnie des Indes). The purpose of Jérémie's account was to give his patron an assessment of the economic potential of the Hudson Bay watershed. Jérémie emphasized the commercial profitability of the region, positing that "this post, in my opinion, would be one of the best in America, even if a very small amount were spent on it."[179] Rather than describing walruses, muskox, belugas, and beavers for their own sake, or even for the sake of scientific inquiry, Jérémie was assessing the economic viability of the Hudson Bay watershed. When describing the large walrus population of Mansel Island, Jérémie remarked that "the teeth of these walrus are a cubit in length, and they are as thick as a man's arm, and the ivory is almost as fine as that of an elephant ... Much profit could probably be made from such a venture."[180] Jérémie also described the muskox northwest of Hudson Bay, writing that there was "a kind of ox ... which we call musk-ox on account of their musk-like odour which is so strong at a certain season of the year that their flesh cannot be eaten."[181] Despite the undesirability of muskox as a food, Jérémie was still optimistic that they could be commercially exploited by the French because of their "very beautiful wool, longer than that of Barbary sheep."[182] Jérémie even took a sample of muskox wool to France in 1708 to have stockings made of it, noting that "they were finer than those made of silk."[183] Lastly, Jérémie also noted that establishing a whaling station near French Creek, a tributary of the Hayes River where many cetaceans (particularly beluga whales) entered at high tide, would be highly profitable. He informed his patron, "if this fishery were once well established more than six hundred barrels of oils could be made every year ... This would yield a large profit as oils are always worth money in France."[184] Jérémie framed his new knowledge of the Hudson Bay watershed in mercantilist terms, emphasizing the economic benefit for French metropolitan and colonial markets.

Beyond the diversification of commercial activities, encyclopedic knowledge in the Enlightenment tradition was becoming an integral part of French statecraft in the seventeenth century. The European desire to categorize and classify the flora, fauna, peoples, and geographies of North America arose not only from a mercantile interest in commercial exploitation, but also from the intellectual and discursive need to incorporate a hitherto unknown "New World" into Europeans' pre-existing cosmographical, geographical, and anthropological understanding. In the so-called Age of Discovery, European observers invented imperial fictions and "polemics of possession" to assert hegemony over unfamiliar landscapes and previously unknown peoples.[185] More often than not, however, France's imagined imperial authority rested on the intricate negotiations and relationships between French fur traders and sovereign Indigenous peoples.

Jérémie's value to the French state extended far beyond the laconic descriptions of the Hudson Bay watershed found in his account. Jérémie's importance when it came to asserting French imperial claims in the Hudson Bay watershed during the early eighteenth century cannot be overstated. When he briefly returned to France in 1707, the Swampy Crees refused to work with other French officials, for they had not established kin relations with them. A metropolitan report stated that "the natives insist on the return of Jérémie with incredible enthusiasm."[186] Indigenous peoples dictated who they would interact with, and Jérémie had meticulously cultivated kinship relations with Cree bands during his tenure as interpreter at Fort Bourbon. The Ministry of the Marine appreciated Jérémie's value to the French state; indeed, he had already served at Fort Bourbon for a decade, where he had a better working relationship with Cree communities than anyone else working for the Compagnie du Castor.[187]

Colonial officials worried that, should Jérémie defect to the HBC, he would bring with him all the Crees from Fort Bourbon.[188] Whether there was any real possibility that Jérémie would defect, the memory of Radisson and Des Groseilliers was seemingly still on the mind of some French ministers. As soon as Jérémie returned to France, the Ministry of the Marine rushed orders to La Rochelle hoping to secure his services at Fort Bourbon. In Jérémie's telling, "Once I arrived at

La Rochelle, the Court proposed that I go and relieve the one who commanded at Fort Bourbon ... In 1708, we left La Rochelle where I had raised a new Garrison."[189] Jérémie governed Fort Bourbon for six years, until the 1713 Treaty of Utrecht surrendered the bayside posts to Great Britain.

By 1708, Jérémie, at the age of thirty-nine, had proven that he could foster good relations with Indigenous peoples. Jérémie's aptitude and proficiency as a cultural broker could possibly date back to a tragic story of his youth, which might in part help to explain his understanding of Algonquian peoples and cultures. In 1693, the Jesuit father François de Crespieul solemnized a marriage between a then twenty-four-year-old Jérémie and Marie-Madeleine Tetaouiskoué, an Innu woman, at Chicoutimi, much to the chagrin of Jérémie's father Noël.[190] Since 1676, Noël Jérémie had traded with the Innu at Tadoussac, Chicoutimi, and Lac Saint-Jean. Young Nicolas joined his father in the trade in 1690. Indeed, the epithet "*dit* Lamontagne" may have been derived from the close relationship the Jérémie family had with Innu people, who the French called "Montagnais" because they inhabited the rugged Saint Lawrence shoreline near the mouth the Saguenay River. Displeased with his son's choice of marriage partner, Noël appealed the marriage to the Sovereign Council of New France, arguing that Nicolas had been under the age of twenty-five, the legal age of majority, when the marriage occurred.[191] The Sovereign Council acceded to Noël's request and annulled the marriage in 1694, but required Noël to provide for Tetaouiskoué and appointed fur trade merchants Jacques Gourdeau and Louis Jolliet as her legal guardians.[192] Shortly after this episode, Nicolas Jérémie departed for Hudson Bay with Iberville's expedition, never to see his father again. Noël Jérémie died sometime between July 1694 and July 1697, during his son's prolonged sojourn at the bay.

Unlike Nicolas Jérémie, who had once been married to an Innu woman and grasped the precepts of Algonquian culture and society, not all Frenchmen in the Hudson Bay watershed were conversant in the cultural axioms of their Cree neighbours. In the summer of 1712, eight Frenchmen hunting caribou rested near a Cree camp whose members were "starving and who had no powder."[193] The Frenchmen refused to trade and were "feasting before their eyes without sharing anything."[194] As a result, the Crees made a plot to kill the Frenchmen and rob them for their selfishness, which they judged contrary to proper kin behaviour. To this end, they invited two of the Frenchmen to a feast in their cabin, where they hoped to kill them more easily. After some revelry, they assassinated their guests with knives before falling upon the six remaining and unsuspecting targets. One man survived the attack by pretending to be dead and made his way back to the fort through brambles and thorns, arriving at Fort Bourbon "covered with blood, and with his poor body all lacerated."[195] The episode is illustrative: In Cree society, trade encompassed more than a mere economic exchange; it also was an expression of kinship that mandated reciprocity and social obligations. Generosity was the cornerstone of all kinship relationships. The Frenchmen's failure to demonstrate generosity in times of need – whether through provisions, firearms, or gunpowder – severed their kinship ties with the Crees. In many Algonquian societies, there were only two categories of people: relatives or foreigners, insiders or outsiders, friends or enemies. If the French broke their kinship obligations, the Crees had no qualms in treating them as enemies.[196]

Thirty years later, HBC governor James Isham also recalled this incident, but he attributed the massacre to slightly different causes. Isham recounted how a group of Frenchmen from Fort Phélipeaux (an outpost on the Severn River) had forced some Cree women into the fort against their will with the intent to rape them.[197] This act enraged the husbands, brothers, and fathers of these women, who slew the predatory Frenchman in revenge. Fur trade historian Sylvia Van Kirk posits that French and English "traders who sought to side-step the formalities of marriage *à la façon du pays* [in the custom of the country] or offended Indian customs ran the risk of serious reprisal … Custom had to be observed in the Indian Country; one could not just grab any woman one pleased."[198] Both accounts of this violent episode underscore one key commonality – namely, that the Crees sought to slay the eight Frenchmen because they had violated kinship protocols and the custom of the country. Their retaliation against the violators affirmed, moreover, the tenuous grasp that the French had over the Hudson Bay watershed. Despite French colonial discourse and imperial grand design, Indigenous peoples asserted their sovereignty within their territories. Demographically, this made sense; along the Hudson Bay littoral, the Crees numbered in the thousands, whereas French newcomers numbered only in the dozens.

Another example highlights the precariousness of the French imperial position in the Hudson Bay watershed. The man Jérémie replaced as commandant in 1704 was Jean-Baptiste Le Moyne de Martigny, who had struggled to build relations with the Crees. During one Cree visit to the fort, Martigny, having recklessly shot at one of the visitors' dogs for chasing after the company's chickens, missed and accidently killed the child of a Cree chief, who was hiding in the nearby brushwood. The Ministry of the Marine reported that this "accident has removed the Natives goodwill for this Commandant; they cannot forgive him."[199] The tragedy probably heightened Jérémie's esteem among the Crees because, as the interpreter at Fort Bourbon, he would have been responsible for making the speeches and distributing the presents by which the French sought to re-establish their alliance. Martigny's reckless conduct had caused an accidental death, which Jérémie worked to rectify utilizing cross-cultural conventions of gift giving and ceremonies of mourning and condolence. In Cree society, a murder could be rectified through gifts, persuasion, and calumet ceremonies.[200]

Jérémie himself did not write much on kinship, other than observing that the Crees and French at Fort Bourbon used the language of kinship to address each other.[201] There is no direct evidence that Jérémie married a Cree woman *à la façon du pays* to secure a political alliance during his long tenure at the bay, but we know from HBC records that the Crees often imposed their own conceptions of kinship through marriage alliances in order to create reciprocal social connections with European newcomers.[202] In the Hudson Bay watershed, Euro-Indigenous nuptials occurred outside the bounds of the church, so no marriage records exist, but on the northern fringes of the boreal forest these relationships were, for all intents and purposes, just as real as those consecrated in London, Paris, or Quebec. As the master of the post, Jérémie had greater control over the trade and access to merchandise; Crees would therefore have been particularly eager to buttress their social ties with him so as to secure access to Fort Bourbon's warehouse. Jérémie, for his part, would have valued the presence of Indigenous women at Fort Bourbon since they could fulfill crucial roles as cultural go-betweens and as conduits for small furs and goods such as toboggans, snowshoes, and canoes.[203] While the sources remain silent on whether or not Jérémie married a Native woman to bridge social ties with the Crees, he was clearly well versed in the culture of Indigenous diplomacy and understood the centrality of kinship in the Hudson Bay watershed.

Jérémie's ascent from clerk and interpreter to eventual governor of Fort Bourbon, the sole French post in the Hudson Bay watershed and a maritime gateway to the peoples and resources of western North America, was truly remarkable. Jérémie's career hinged on the good relations he forged with the Indigenous peoples of the Hudson Bay watershed, particularly the Swampy Crees who dominated the littoral. The French state recognized that Jérémie was able to exert influence on trade relations in a space where most European imperialists failed to comprehend the rules governing "Indian Country." Martigny's mismanagement of Fort Bourbon and the death of the French violators demonstrates that productive intercultural relations between the Crees and the French in the Hudson Bay watershed could by no means be taken for granted, and that they required a certain degree of experience and expertise, which Jérémie possessed in droves. Learning from previous mistakes made by repudiating Radisson and Des Groseilliers, French metropolitan and colonial officials promoted Jérémie to governor, fearing that a man with his linguistic and diplomatic skills would have no trouble finding work with the rival HBC.

CONCLUSION

Starting in 1663, Louis XIV and his chief minister Jean-Baptiste Colbert favoured a compact colony restricted to the Saint Lawrence valley. However, mercantile aspirations, fear of a strong English transatlantic commerce, and the unregulated expansion of the French fur trade combined to drag France into a conflict with England for control of the Hudson Bay watershed. In the late seventeenth century, Troupes de la Marine officers and soldiers, voyageurs, coureurs de bois, HBC servants, and Indigenous peoples all vied for the upper hand within this contested space. For the English and the French, the battle for the Hudson Bay watershed was fought over access to Indigenous fur trade networks. Voyageurs and coureurs de bois played a salient role in New France's western imperial expansion in the seventeenth century because they were able to access Indigenous kinship networks through their knowledge of and experience with Native languages and protocols in the region.

Between 1663 and 1713, the French learned a harsh but valuable lesson in governance. The loss of Pierre-Esprit Radisson and Médard Chouart des Groseilliers to the HBC taught metropolitan ministers and colonial officials that coureurs de bois and other backcountry specialists who possessed local knowledge, experience, and expertise were valuable assets of empire. These backcountry specialists had a vastly different vision for North America than that of metropolitan ministers, colonial elites, and Jesuit missionaries. Colbert's meticulous planning for a compact, self-sufficient colony and "Frenchified" Indigenous subjects clashed with the goals of the actual agents of colonialism – coureurs de bois, voyageurs, interpreters, merchants, and soldiers. This alternative vision of empire was predicated upon individualism, fortune, kinship, and negotiation with sovereign Indigenous nations, all meant to effectuate a vast empire of fur. Beyond the confines of the Saint Lawrence valley, these backcountry specialists pushed the frontiers of empire in creative and unexpected ways. In so doing, they not only dashed the meticulous preparations of metropolitan planners, but also allowed French influence to extend into the hyperborean regions of North America. Radisson, Des Groseilliers, Du Lhut, and Jérémie played integral roles in staking France's claim to these northerly territories. Seeing the successful colonial project unfold before their eyes, colonial officials and administrators appointed them as key ambassadors, peacemakers, and diplomats in the Hudson Bay watershed.

Although the first generation of backcountry specialists after the 1663 royal takeover of New France found adopted fathers, mothers, brothers, sisters, and perhaps even wives among Anishinaabe, Cree, Nakoda, and Dakota peoples, with whom they interacted on their military expeditions and commercial ventures, none would find a new home in the West. And thus, the intergenerational presence of métissage and mixed marriages was negligible – for the time being at least. At the end of the day, in the seventeenth century, coureurs de bois, voyageurs, and company clerks allowed the French to make great inroads in developing imperial projects in the Hudson Bay watershed. Yet events far beyond the reach or influence of on-the-ground agents meant that French colonial activities in the region were cut short. The Treaty of Utrecht brought an end to the War of the Spanish Succession (1701–14) in Europe, and stipulated that France return all of its territories in the Hudson Bay region to England. On 5 September 1714, a British frigate, the *Union*, arrived at the mouth of the Hayes River, within sight of Fort Bourbon. Captain James Knight and Henry Kelsey, his deputy, presented a letter from the French government ordering the garrison to surrender Fort Bourbon in accordance with the terms of the treaty.[204] The remaining Compagnie du Castor employees and soldiers evacuated Fort Bourbon and returned with HBC vessels to England, where they were subsequently ferried across the English Channel to France.[205] The absolutist French state had demonstrated once again that the vast northwestern interior of North America was at best of peripheral strategic interest. In an instant, decision-makers and imperial planners at Versailles undid decades of progress toward an imperial foothold in the Hudson Bay watershed in exchange for peace closer to home.

2

Transatlantic Networks, Backcountry Specialists, and French Imperial Projects in Post-Utrecht North America, 1715–1729

The Treaty of Utrecht in 1713 and the death of King Louis XIV in 1715 marked a decisive political shift for France. The affairs of the French state passed to Louis XIV's nephew Philippe, the Duke of Orléans, as regent because the man next in line for the throne, the Sun King's great-grandson, Louis XV, had not yet attained his age of majority. The Duke of Orléans moved the French court from the magnificent and decadent palace at Versailles to the more pragmatically located Palais-Royal in Paris (the ancestral home of the House of Orléans).[1] The Conseil de Régence (1715–23) reorganized the old ministries as councils, which served to decentralize the power previously vested in individual ministers.[2] Under Louis XIV, Minister of the Marine Jean-Baptiste Colbert (1661–83) had showed little interest in expansion into North America's colonial hinterlands, preferring instead to concentrate on Atlantic trade and settlement in the Saint Lawrence valley.[3] Following the death of the Sun King, however, a Marine Council replaced the old Ministry of the Marine and vigorously debated how to redefine France's role in North America following the Peace of Utrecht.[4]

By mere happenstance, Philippe de Rigaud, Marquis de Vaudreuil and governor general of New France, was in France during this transformative period in order to lobby for a reorganization of the fur trade in Canada and to re-garrison the posts and forts of the pays d'en haut.[5] Vaudreuil found himself in the role of an expert adviser to the new Marine Council, which was short on experience but bent on imperial expansion, and which was engaged in debates over the existence and location of the Western Sea. Discovery and control of such a passage would have given France strategic access to the Pacific Ocean and trade in the Far East. With New France's riverine corridors serving as a door to the Western Sea, the colony would enjoy a geographic advantage comparable to the Strait of Gibraltar or the Danish Sound, and a commercial edge as a vital imperial hub for global trade.[6] With these aims in mind, following Louis XIV's exhaustive and costly European wars with England, Austria, and the Netherlands, a redefined French Empire, with the assistance of Vaudreuil, pursued lofty goals in the heart of North America, particularly in the Hudson Bay watershed – the vast territory of streams, rivers, and lakes that flowed into Hudson Bay.

Metropolitan ministers, colonial officials, and royal cartographers recognized intelligence and information gathering as an essential precursor to imperial expansion in North America. During Vaudreuil's tenure as governor, coureurs de bois and voyageurs provided local information obtained through their Indigenous networks, which proved essential for French imperial expansion into the Hudson Bay watershed. Many of these Frenchmen were backcountry specialists; they understood Indigenous politics, customs, languages, and protocols better than any other Europeans in North America. As a result, the Marine Council recognized their importance as cross-cultural mediators in the heart of North America and aspired to harness them as agents of empire. Various *récits de voyage*, *mémoires*, and cartographic surveys reveal how the French state absorbed and disseminated information as instruments of empire during the Régence. Voyageurs and coureurs de bois collected information from Native informants, which they provided to Troupes de la Marine officers, Jesuit missionaries, and colonial officials. Subsequently, these manuscripts were published in the metropole and circulated for ministerial use and public consumption. Within the Palais-Royal, members of royal councils synthesized and summarized these travel narratives, ethnographic writings, and cartographic surveys of North America.[7] Geography and cartography were salient imperial tools, and European monarchs asserted sovereignty and possession in the Americas by surveying territories and issuing printed maps, which avowed and reinforced royal claims of authority over, and familiarity with, the New World.[8]

Recognizing that cartography played a central role in sovereignty and empire building in post-Utrecht North America, this chapter begins by examining how backcountry specialists operating within Indigenous and transatlantic networks provided information that fuelled the French geographic fantasy of the Western Sea to the Pacific

Ocean. While this knowledge was never perfect, even somewhat ambiguous information could still fundamentally drive the imperial imagination westward away from the geographic core of the Atlantic Basin and toward a more expansive global vision of empire. In other words, whether or not the Western Sea existed in the middle latitudes of North America was largely irrelevant; a hypothetical sea was enough to fuel the French dream of a global empire spanning the North American Far West to the Pacific Rim, which made the Hudson Bay watershed an enticing and potentially lucrative imperial asset in post-Utrecht North America.

As members of ministerial councils began to ask questions about the Western Sea in the Hudson Bay watershed, French intermediaries and cultural brokers, already deeply embedded in informational networks, became pivotal informants in what Atlantic historian Kenneth J. Banks has called a "reporting hierarchy" that provided the French sate with overseas intelligence. Information became the medium of exchange among an eclectic array of administrators, explorers, fur traders, privateers, geographers, hydrographers, lawyers, diplomats, and spies, who traded it for promotions and honours in the ancien régime hierarchy. This "reporting hierarchy" formed the primary basis upon which the Ministry of the Marine, whose members never actually crossed the Atlantic themselves, managed all of France's overseas possessions.[9] Although metropolitan decision-makers drew from a diverse spectrum of colonial informants – governors, intendants, members of the Superior Council, Ursuline nuns, Jesuit missionaries, military officers, wealthy merchants – my focus is primarily on the individuals at the lower rungs of New France's social hierarchy.[10] These men – coureurs de bois and voyageurs, as well as a miscellany of interpreters, diplomats, and negotiators operating on the fringes of empire – formed a unique class of backcountry specialists.

The second part of this chapter analyzes how the French colonial government attempted to utilize backcountry specialists, particularly coureurs de bois, to assert imperial control over the geographic, political, and cultural landscapes of the Hudson Bay watershed. Vaudreuil framed coureurs de bois as potential linchpins of French-Indigenous alliances who would facilitate western imperial expansion into the Hudson Bay watershed. He ultimately discovered, however, that they pursued their own agendas and interests in the region at the expense of French colonial policy. Even though Vaudreuil failed to co-opt coureurs de bois as loyal agents of empire, they still succeeded – albeit indirectly and unofficially – in extending some French influence into the Hudson Bay watershed. In other words, coureurs de bois and other backcountry specialists occupied a liminal space between imperial service and imperial subversion. This position comports with the recent work of some French Atlantic historians who have discarded the success-versus-failure paradigm in favour of a new imperial history that examines how French colonists, Natives, and Africans creatively engaged with the French state, producing dynamic tensions that reshaped the metropole even as they reshaped the worlds that were colonized.[11] Shannon Lee Dawdy contends that "colonialism is fundamentally experimental and usually poorly controlled," meaning that even when colonies failed to meet imperial expectations, they still served imperial ends.[12] Therefore, even a failure to locate the Western Sea could still strengthen the larger French imperial vision by sustaining a French presence in the Hudson Bay watershed at the expense of France's British rivals. Similarly, Robert Michael Morrissey posits that historians of French empire should discard traditional themes of "failure" or "dysfunction" and instead seek to understand "the nature of colonialism itself as a complicated system mutually created by diverse, entangled peoples."[13] In other words, French empire rested on a series of collaborations among French settlers, Natives, and Africans, which fostered social arrangements that simultaneously frustrated and fulfilled imperial designs throughout France's overseas empire.

The Hudson Bay watershed offers a unique vantage point from which to examine the complexity of the advancement of French imperialism into the North American interior. It was neither an imperial success nor a failure, but rather something in between; backcountry specialists fragmented imperial authority, but they also simultaneously ensured that French influence came to permeate the western interior – even if this was achieved at an erratic, haphazard, and oscillating pace – which in turn facilitated overseas expressions of empire. Through an examination of intersecting channels of information exchange and communication, both within the North American interior and the Atlantic world more broadly, it becomes clear that voyageurs and coureurs de bois were crucial but sometimes unwitting and ambivalent intermediaries between the French state and Indigenous peoples. In other words, the information regarding Indigenous and colonial spaces procured by backcountry specialists, as well as their subsequent actions on the ground, did not necessarily or easily translate into French sovereignty in western North America.

THE TREATY OF UTRECHT, THE CONSEIL DE RÉGENCE, AND THE WESTERN SEA

Louis XIV's Conseil d'État had overseen a remarkable period of prosperity in France during his long reign. Throughout the seventeenth century, proficient ministers, such as Cardinal Mazarin, Jean-Baptiste Colbert, François-Michel le Tellier, Marquis de Louvois, and military engineer Sébastien Le Prestre de Vauban, overhauled France's judicial, military, and financial infrastructure. Compared to its European rivals in the latter half of the seventeenth century, France possessed a large and growing population, a coherent national territory, a comparatively modern state apparatus with unparalleled ability to raise state revenue, and a powerful army, all governed by a strong king and council.[14]

Despite these advantages, however, England was beginning to mobilize resources to challenge French political and economic hegemony in Europe by the beginning of the eighteenth century.[15] The War of the Spanish Succession (1701–14) and a severe famine brought on by the particularly harsh winter of 1709–10 brought the French state to the brink of collapse. French military victories in Flanders, the Rhineland, and the Iberian Peninsula the following year, however, secured the ratification of a peace treaty at Utrecht in 1713, which provided a much-needed reprieve at home and drastically altered the political landscape of colonial North America.[16] From this perspective, the treaty seemed to be a humiliating defeat for Louis XIV, who surrendered territorial claims to Hudson Bay, Newfoundland, and peninsular Acadia in North America.[17] He did so in exchange for his rivals' political concessions in Europe. By the terms of the treaty, France retained Lille and Strasbourg, but perhaps most importantly, Britain, the Netherlands, and Austria recognized Louis XIV's grandson Philippe, the Duke of Anjou, as Felipe V, king of Spain.[18]

Across the sea, creative colonial policies allowed France to minimize the disaster of its concessions in North America. France retained fishing rights on the north coast of Newfoundland, for example, which allowed it to maintain a large fishing fleet to harvest cod off the Grand Banks. Because the fishery also served as a training school for naval seaman, the French Crown considered the Grand Banks fishery paramount to the maintenance of a strong navy.[19] The French also cleverly interpreted the phrase "ancient boundaries," used in the treaty to imply only the peninsula of what is now Nova Scotia, so as to maintain their claims to other portions of Acadia (New Brunswick), Île Saint-Jean

(Prince Edward Island), and Île Royale (Cape Breton).[20] Starting in 1716, New France also re-garrisoned posts throughout the pays d'en haut to prevent the incursion of Anglo-American traders, whose presence they feared would disrupt and destabilize French-Indigenous alliances in the interior. The tenth article of the Treaty of Utrecht pertained directly to the territories of the Hudson Bay watershed: "The said most Christian King [Louis XIV] shall restore to the kingdom and Queen of Great Britain, to be possessed in full right for ever, the bay and the straights of Hudson, together with all lands, seas, seacoasts, rivers, and places situated in the said bay and straights."[21] Somewhat ambiguous in its phrasing, the treaty was construed by the French as having only restored the Hudson Bay shoreline and the Hudson Strait to England, and not the entire drainage basin. French officials reasoned, therefore, that their empire could still expand into the Hudson Bay watershed via the western Great Lakes and Lake Winnipeg without breaching the articles of the treaty.

Despite sustained periods of continuous warfare near the end of his reign, Louis XIV had managed to create a French state that was cohesive, centralized, and that commanded a great deal of influence both abroad and at home.[22] On his deathbed, Louis XIV purportedly told the young dauphin, Louis XV (1715–74), "I am dying, but the State will always remain."[23] The Treaty of Utrecht and the death of the Sun King two years later ushered in a new era of peace and prosperity in both Europe and North America, what some Canadian historians have described as New France's "Golden Age."[24] Kenneth J. Banks has labelled the peace between France and Great Britain as a *Pax Atlanticum* – an era marked by commercial prosperity, a dramatic rise in Atlantic commerce, a bourgeoning slave trade, and the beginnings of mass consumerism. The Duke of Orléans led the Conseil de Régence until Louis XV attained his legal majority in 1723, and it was during this time that France emerged as economically buoyant and politically stable.[25]

The "Long Peace" (1713–40) provided a respite for both Britain and France, whose manpower and resources had been drained from decades of warfare in the Americas and Europe.[26] This period of recovery allowed France to re-establish oceanic trade routes, to season a new maritime fleet off the Grand Banks, to consolidate control over its new colony of Louisiana, and to expand the fur trade beyond the pays d'en haut. The Marine Council approved colonial policies to pursue the fur trade and Indigenous alliances in the Hudson Bay watershed, though the regency government was careful that such measures would not breach the articles of peace and provoke war with Britain.[27] Intelligence gathered from both colonial agents and backcountry specialists proved crucial for navigating the post-Utrecht landscape in North America.

Most intelligence concerning western North America gathered by backcountry specialists made its way into the Delisle *atelier* (workshop) on the Quai de l'Horloge, which was a short distance from the French court at the Palais-Royal in Paris. For the last twenty years, the Delisle family, a veritable map-making dynasty, had hypothesized and propagated the existence of an inland western sea flowing into the Pacific, a view based initially on the travel narratives from navigators, like Sir Francis Drake (1579), Juan de Fuca (1592), and Martín de Aguilar (1602), who had reconnoitred the Pacific Coast. The Delisle map-makers equally relied upon English and Spanish historians and writers, like Francisco López de Gómara (1553), Richard Hakluyt (1589), Antonio de Herrera y Tordesillas (1601–15), Juan de Torquemada (1615), and Samuel Purchas (1626), to promulgate the existence of such a body of water.[28] In 1697, father-son team Claude and Guillaume Delisle presented a manuscript globe to Louis Boucherat, chancellor of France, depicting the Western Sea for the first time. In 1700, Guillaume Delisle presented a mémoire about the Western Sea to Jérôme Phélypeaux, Comte de Pontchartrain, minister of the marine and colonies, who was in the process of amassing charts, maps, and globes within the Ministry of the Marine's newly established Bureau des archives. In February 1717, Guillaume Delisle presented another mémoire titled *Conjectures sur l'existence d'une Mer dans la partie Occidentale de la Nouvelle France* to the French court.[29] In these initial years, Claude and Guillaume did not go public with their hypothesis, but only informed the government in secret, largely out of fear that rival map-makers would profit off their theory or that opposing imperial powers would steal France's glory by making the "discovery" before them. Over the years, bureaucrats from the Ministry of the Marine and Colonies, like Pontchartrain and Raudot, gathered maps, charts, logs, letters, and reports from the Delisle workshop and elsewhere, which they secretly compiled and analyzed at the Parisian offices of the Bureau des Colonies and the Dépôt des cartes et plans, established in 1710 and 1720, respectively.[30]

Taking over the Western Sea project from his father and basing his hypothesis on the available data transmitted through a vast transatlantic intelligence network, Guillaume Delisle surmised that the sea existed in the middle latitudes of North America and opened a passage to the Pacific Ocean through a strait between 43° and 45° latitude, and that from the Continental Divide some kind of "Rivière Longue" or "Rivière de l'Ouest" flowed into the Western Sea. Somewhere on the shores of the sea there was a wealthy and sophisticated Indigenous city named Quivira, which was ready for European trade and might have already been trading with Chinese or Japanese mariners. Delisle concluded that it was improbable that so many different sources could demonstrate such a degree of consistency if no such body of water actually existed.[31] Since Christopher Columbus's 1492 landfall in the Bahamas, European powers had sought the Northwest Passage to circumvent the Americas en route to Asia. The English, French, and Spanish Empires alike sought the elusive passage.[32] The French regent was a former pupil of Claude Guillaume and had a keen interest in cartography and the pursuit of scientific advancement. The discovery of the Western Sea promised a strategic advantage over the Spanish and British Empires and thus became a principal concern for metropolitan officials in the decades following the Treaty of Utrecht.

During the early spring of 1717, Jean Bobé, an abbot and Lazarist priest of the Congregation of the Mission, pondered the question of the Western Sea as he strolled through the nearly empty halls of Louis XIV's magnificent Palace of Versailles. When the Duke of Orléans moved the French court to the Palais-Royal in Paris, Bobé had remained behind, bound by his priestly duty to tend to the local population at Versailles.[33] Despite Bobé's isolation from the government and from the scientific community in the capital, he frequently corresponded with his friend and colleague Guillaume Delisle, who, alongside Cardinal André-Hercule de Fleury, was responsible for Louis XV's education at the Palais des Tuileries. Over the past four years, Bobé had toiled to present a case for the Western Sea to prominent members of the French court, such as Victor-Marie d'Estrées, a marshal of France and Marine Council member, and Antoine Crozat, one of the richest men in France and the first proprietary owner of Louisiana. In the aftermath of the War of the Spanish Succession, the newly founded colony of Louisiana seemed to be a land of infinite (but ultimately unattainable or illusory) possibilities – gold, silver, and cash crops – and with the Trans-Mississippian West largely unexplored by the French, Bobé hypothesized that the Western Sea was indeed near at hand.[34]

Bobé appealed to Delisle to communicate any new tidings regarding the Western Sea. The abbot understood that Delisle was better positioned and much more scientifically minded than he was; indeed, he even asked the cartographer "to tell me sincerely your feelings on my report on the Western Sea in which I do not doubt that there are many things to correct," adding that he did not have "the necessary instruments to measure latitude and the meridians."[35] But rather than basing his information of North America off such precise measurements, Bobé based most of his findings on information provided by a vast transatlantic communication network stretching from the Missouri River to Versailles.

Unlike many other geographers and cartographers, Bobé had already named and designated an immense portion of the Trans-Mississippian West, what he called "Bourbonie." He theorized "that Bourbonie was not separated from New France by any sea or strait, but was the same continent as Tartary [Asia]."[36] Bobé supported his theory that "Bourbonie" was connected to Eurasia by relaying a story of a captive Chinese woman who the Dakota had purportedly acquired from an even more distant western nation.[37] Based on the various colonial reports and travel accounts that Bobé had read, he imagined that many Tatars, Canaanites, and Israelites had immigrated to North America from Eurasia after the Biblical conquest of Canaan. And he was not alone in this position. When Antoine de la Mothe Cadillac was commandant at Michilimackinac, he speculated that all Indigenous peoples in North America were "descended from the Hebrews and were originally Jews, which may also be observed from the terms they use in conversation and in their speeches and customs."[38] Antoine-Denis Raudot wrote that the Dakota "language bears no resemblance to that of the other Natives," but rather "contains some Chinese pronunciations."[39] Bobé agreed with Cadillac and Raudot and insisted that many Dakota resembled Tartars, although he had never actually met any Dakota or East Asians in person.[40]

Backcountry specialists visiting the French court regularly provided first-hand information about western North America that fuelled French imperial fantasies. When former coureur de bois Pierre-Charles Le Sueur visited Paris, he assisted cartographer Jean-Baptiste Louis Franquelin in drawing the first accurate map of the Upper Mississippi watershed.[41] Moreover, Le Sueur, who had lived among the Dakota for several years, also met with Delisle, to whom he transmitted a story the Dakota had once told him. On one occasion, when a Dakota war

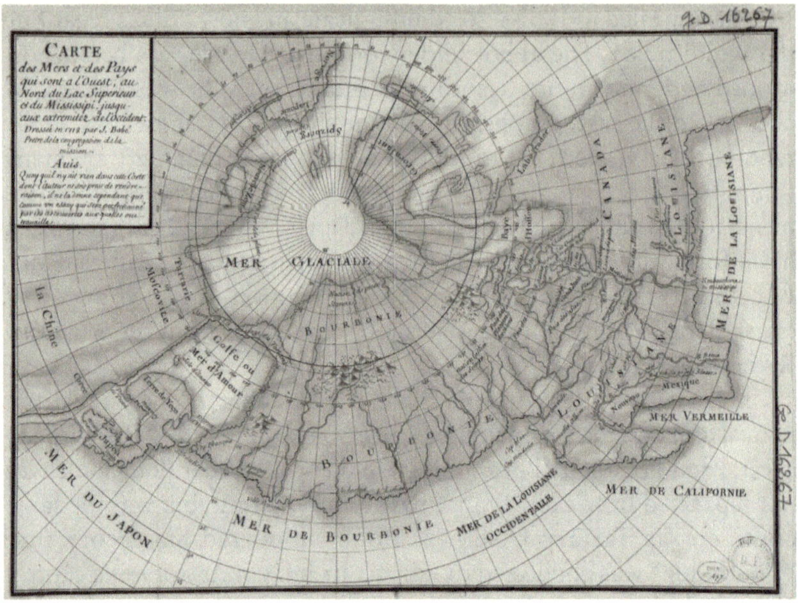

2.1 L'abbé Jean Bobé's imaginative, but not scientifically informed, map of "Bourbonie" included la Mer de l'Ouest in Louisiana's territory.

party travelled fifteen days toward the west, they discovered that they had reached the seashore and were surrounded by massive stone fortresses, inhabited by strange men in silk robes who traded steel knives that differed in both make and design from the more familiar French merchandise.[42] Le Sueur died in 1704, but the valuable information he provided Franquelin and Delisle was later incorporated into Bobé's work as well.

L'abbé Bobé regularly drew upon his vast transatlantic intelligence network to convey information concerning western North America to Delisle. Bobé was "a broker of information" for Delisle, connecting him with both colonial administrators and backcountry specialists.[43] For example, Bobé served as an intermediary between Delisle and Father François Le Marie, a Louisiana missionary, who worked among different Indigenous congregations from 1706 to 1719.[44] Bobé asked Father Le Marie to send reports, maps, and travel narratives from voyageurs who had ascended the Missouri and Platte Rivers, which he then forwarded to Delisle.[45] Based on his experiences, Le Marie shared Bobé's conviction that the route to the Western Sea lay through the more southerly territory of Louisiana. In his 1717 report, Le Marie theorized that searching for the Western Sea too far north would be futile because freezing temperatures and pack ice would make any potential seaway impenetrable.[46] Bobé urged Delisle to send a draft of his map on the next vessel bound for Louisiana so that Father Le Marie could look it over and suggest corrections.[47]

Bobé also wrote to Delisle whenever notable Canadiens visited Paris. On one occasion, Jacques-Charles de Sabrevois, a former officer stationed at Detroit, who Bobé professed "perfectly knew the country," visited France. Bobé redirected Sabrevois to Delisle, writing that his knowledge would be "useful in perfecting your beautiful map of Louisiana as well as the other maps of New France which you have designs to draw."[48] Perhaps Delisle was somewhat annoyed by the abbot's constant queries, suggestions, corrections, and visitors. On 9 July 1718, Bobé wrote to Delisle that he hoped that he was not "mad to have seen Monsieur de Sabrevois," assuring Delisle that he always aimed to please him.[49] Although these types of visits may have been a bit of a nuisance at times for map-makers, they were necessary to ensure geographic accuracy; the quality of the maps depended heavily upon a solid network for transmitting first-hand information to royal cartographers in France. In addition to consultations with North American experts, Bobé and Delisle both voraciously read past and contemporary récits de voyage, mémoires, and epistolary accounts, such as the works of Jacques Marquette, Louis Hennepin, Henri Joutel, Antoine de la Mothe Cadillac, and Pierre Le Moyne d'Iberville, whose writings mostly suggested that the source of the "Rivière de l'Ouest" would be found somewhere up the Missouri River.

Unlike navigators, engineers, and hydrographers – and later British map-makers such as Samuel Hearne, Philip Turnor, and David Thompson – the geographers and cartographers of the ancien régime rarely, if ever, left their offices to make observations and measure the terrain themselves in the field.[50] Rather, Delisle and the other *géographes de cabinet* worked from their Parisian offices, located in the heart of the kingdom's political and scientific capital. At its Île de la Cité location in central Paris, the Delisle workshop was an easy ten-minute walk to most of Paris's engravers, printers, booksellers, and scientific instrument makers. As a member of the Académie des sciences, Delisle was also aware of recent discoveries, especially in astronomy and measurement.[51] Since he never travelled outside of France (and rarely outside of Paris) himself, he collected and voraciously consumed "all the sources available, ancient and modern,

2.2 Guillaume Delisle surmised that a gulf-like interior sea that opened a passage to the Pacific Ocean, otherwise known as la Mer de l'Ouest, existed in the middle latitudes of North America. This map was drawn by his brother, Joseph-Nicolas Delisle, in 1737 in Saint Petersburg and was published in 1752. Joseph-Nicolas carried on and expanded upon his elder brother's hypothesis.

geographical and historical, textual and graphic, printed and manuscript," which enabled him to visualize and illuminate the world on maps.[52] Delisle also worked in conjunction with astronomical observations to fix latitude and longitude, making the maps produced in the Delisle workshop some of the most scientifically accurate and precise drawings to come out of the eighteenth century. The Conseil de Régence and the Marine Council were receptive to Bobé and Delisle's appeals to discover a passageway to the Western Sea. And yet, despite the French state's best intentions and attempts to acquire accurate geographic information, mapping an expanding French overseas empire remained a highly imaginative process. Despite their evident skills and their strong connections to the Académie des sciences, the Delisle family's interpretation of western North America represented one of the most salient imperial fictions of the eighteenth century.[53]

Récits de voyage, mémoires, and epistolary accounts influenced how map-makers like Bobé and Delisle imagined western North

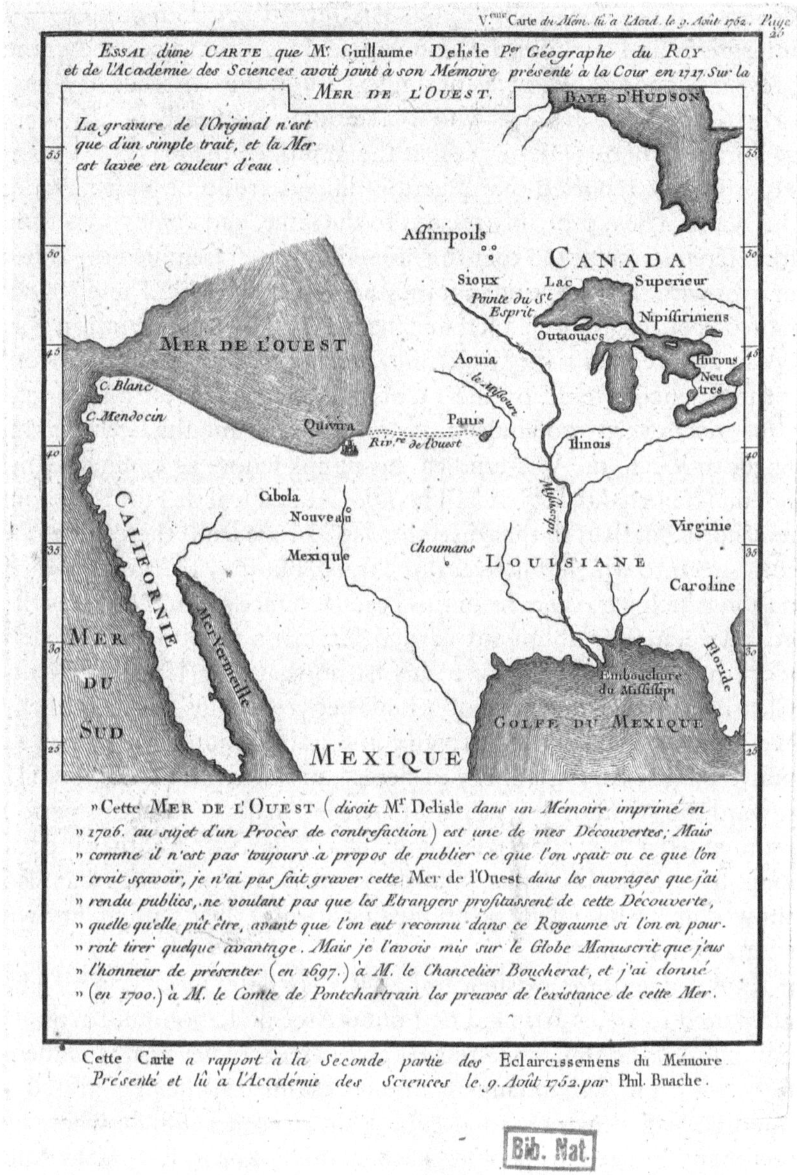

2.3 Guillaume Delisle's conjecture and suppositions about the existence of la Mer de l'Ouest continued well into the eighteenth century, being reprinted, reproduced, and copied by numerous publishers and other map-makers. In 1750, Philippe Buache, who had trained under Guillaume Delisle (his father-in-law) and inherited the Delisle workshop, finally went public with the Western Sea, presenting his treatise entitled *Carte des Nouvelles Découvertes au Nord de la Mer du Sud* to the Académie des sciences in Paris.

America. Take, for example, Nicolas Jérémie *dit* Lamontagne, an interpreter and clerk for the Compagnie du Castor (discussed in the previous chapter), who was optimistic about the existence of a passage to the Pacific. Jérémie, who was stationed for nearly twenty years at Fort Bourbon (1694–1714), at the mouth of the Hayes River on Hudson Bay, reported that a certain inland group of Natives from the Western Sea, probably related to the Cree, had come to visit the fort. Jérémie remarked that this inland group "resembled the other natives with the exception that they have frizzy hair."[54] These "frizzy haired" Natives informed Jérémie that near Lake Winnipegosis it was possible to reach a river "which flows to the west."[55] All other rivers hitherto encountered by the French in the Northwest discharged either northward into Hudson Bay or eastward into the Great Lakes. Eager to locate the Western Sea during his tenure as commandant, Jérémie reported that "I did all I could, while I was at Fort Bourbon, to send the natives in that direction, so as to learn if there were not some sea into which this river discharged, but they are at war with a nation which bars them from this road."[56] Once again, Bobé was the go-between. The abbot forwarded Jérémie's account to Delisle's workshop with a comment to his friend that "he [Jérémie] speaks Clearly and with certainty of a Link between Hudson Bay and the Western sea."[57] Jérémie's account and good reputation convinced many French cartographers to depict an occidental river flowing toward the Western Sea. Many of Delisle's maps around this period represented a "Grande Rivière coulant a l'Ouest."[58] Another French map-maker, Nicolas de Fer, published a map of New France that also showed an ambiguously positioned occidental river with no known source or mouth.[59]

Knowledge of the existence of a "Rivière de l'Ouest" can also be attributed to Louis-Armand de Lom d'Arce de Lahontan, Baron de Lahontan. Lahontan, an unremarkable career soldier turned influential writer and Enlightenment thinker, claimed to have explored a hundred leagues westward along a great river in 1688–89 where he met many Indigenous peoples, such as the Eokoros, Essanapes, and Gnacsitares, who cannot definitively be identified.[60] According to Lahontan's account, the Gnacsitares warned him not to proceed any further westward because their enemies the Mozeemlek "were a turbulent and warlike Nation ... [who] never took the Field without twenty thousand Men at least."[61] With a visit to the Mozeemlek deemed too dangerous and impractical, Lahontan "was forc'd to be instructed at second hand by these Mozeemlek Slaves," who "gave me a Description of their Country … represented by way of a Map upon a Deer's Skin."[62] Based on the slave's description and map, Lahontan believed that the river on which he travelled flowed westward until it discharged into a "salt Lake … three hundred Leagues in Circumference, and thirty in breadth, its Mouth stretching a great way to the Southward."[63] This large "salt lake" fit the description of the sought-after interior seaway to the Pacific. Delisle surmised that Lahontan's "Rivière Longue" could be a potential fluvial route through the heart of North America, but cautioned his readers that it was difficult to tell if the baron "had not invented all these things, which is difficult to figure out, he being the only one that has penetrated into these vast lands."[64] L'abbé Bobé was more critical of Lahontan's narrative, even urging Delisle not to include Lahontan's "Rivière Longue" in his maps: "Would it not be well to efface that great river which Lahontan says he discovered? All the Canadians [Canadiens], and even the Governor-General have told me that this river is unknown; if it existed the French who are in the Illinois and at Ouabache would know of it."[65] For a long time, most scholars dismissed Lahontan's "Rivière Longue" narrative as a pure fabrication, but more recently some historians have reaffirmed the veracity of the baron's voyage by suggesting different plausible hypotheses – for example, that Lahontan might have ascended the Minnesota, Missouri, or even the Platte River.[66] Not all information provided by backcountry specialists was taken at face value, especially when it could not be corroborated by other reliable sources, but it nevertheless still managed to fuel the French imperial imagination.

If Lahontan's narrative temporarily dampened some of the enthusiasm for a riverine passage to the Western Sea, interest was resurrected in 1715 when a new story emerged to whet the appetites of French geographers. Intendant of New France Michel Bégon (1712–26) interviewed coureur de bois Jacques de Noyon, who reported a story similar to Lahontan's "Rivière Longue." In 1688, de Noyon had led a small clandestine trading party from Lake Superior up the Kaministiquia River to Rainy Lake, where he wintered among the Cree and their allies the Nakoda. De Noyon left no written record of his voyage and seems to have kept the details of the sojourn to himself until Bégon interviewed him in 1715. The Bégon–De Noyon interviews resulted in an account of the journey to Rainy Lake replete with details of rivers, lakes, and portages between Kaministiquia and

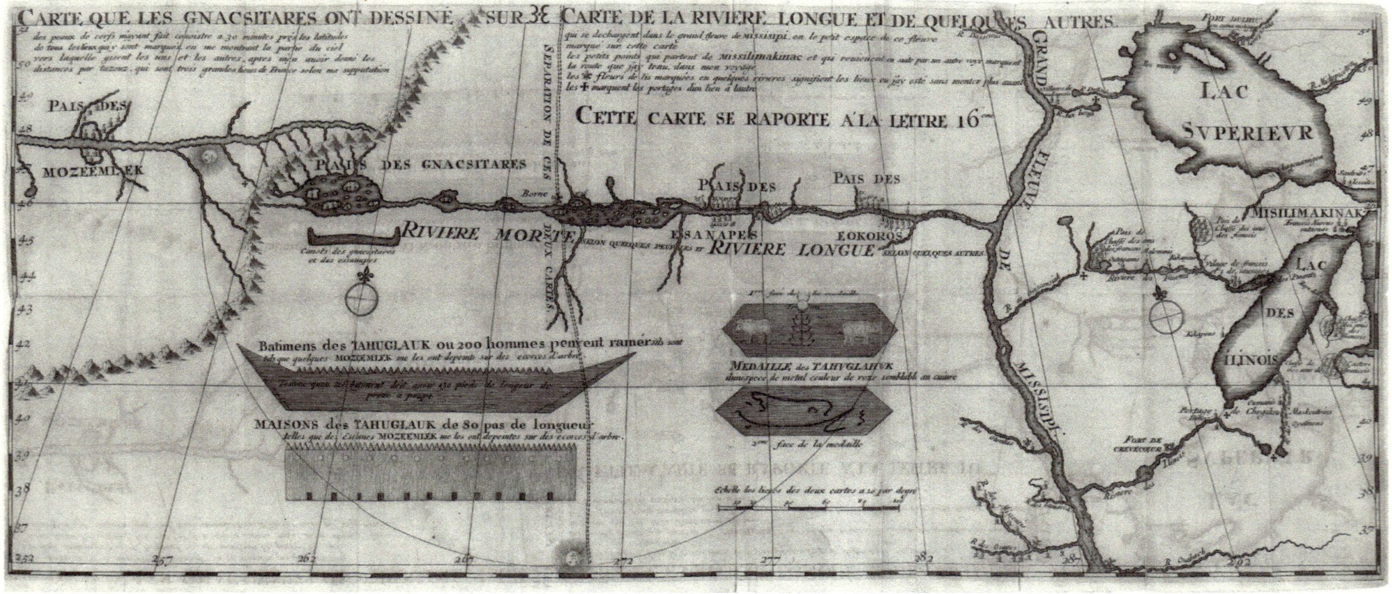

2.4 Not all ministers and geographers found the Baron de Lahontan's voyage down the "Rivière Longue" convincing, but it nevertheless provided knowledge, however ambiguous, that fundamentally drove the imperial appetite for western expansion and discovery.

Lake Winnipeg. Although de Noyon did not voyage as far west as Lake Winnipeg, he nevertheless reported that his Nakoda interlocuters had informed him that they were going to follow a long western river to make war against a race of dwarves, "a nation where the men were three and a half to four feet tall, and very stout."[67] Despite the somewhat fanciful narrative, de Noyon's report helped to substantiate claims of the Western Sea for imperial planners and colonial officials. Delisle and Bobé, who never travelled overseas themselves, had little choice but to trust the often quixotic récits de voyage, accounts, and mémoires transmitted to them from North America. As historian Paul W. Mapp observes, "bewigged cartographers pondered western rivers and inland seas whose existence they suspected and imagined but could not confirm."[68]

Seeking further corroboration of the initial accounts that had been transmitted to Bobé and Delisle, Cardinal Guillaume Dubois (chief minister for the regent) and the Marshal d'Estrées dispatched Father Pierre-François-Xavier de Charlevoix to New France to personally investigate the numerous rumours concerning the existence and whereabouts of the Western Sea.[69] In contrast with Bobé or Delisle, Charlevoix had lived in Canada from 1705 to 1709, where he taught at the Jesuit college in Quebec.[70] Unlike fur traders, adventurers, and explorers, French officials saw Charlevoix as an ecclesiastical agent of empire because the missionary goals of proselytizing to and converting Indigenous peoples aligned more closely with the expansionist imperial agendas of the new Marine Council and New France's colonial government.

Much to Bobé's surprise, Charlevoix's expedition to investigate the Western Sea launched from Canada and not Louisiana.[71] Frequent correspondence with his Louisiana interlocutor Father François Le Marie had convinced Bobé that French explorers were much more likely to reach the Western Sea from France's southwestern colony. Governor Vaudreuil, however, had undermined Bobé by convincing Marshal d'Estrées and the rest of the Marine Council to search for the Western Sea within his jurisdiction of Canada. The governor's suggestion to pursue the discovery of the Western Sea from Canada was likely motivated by a jurisdictional feud following the transfer of the Illinois Country from Canada to Louisiana in 1717. Technically, this never should have been a point of contention because the colony of Louisiana fell under the jurisdictional subordination of the governor general of New France, who outranked his counterpart in

New Orleans and his lesser commission of lieutenant governor.[72] Even though this jurisdictional hierarchy existed in the form of archival paper trails, it was never put into administrative practice in North America because of the vast distances separating Quebec and New Orleans.[73] Louisiana's colonial administrators reported directly to the Ministry of the Marine in France, and, in turn, they received instructions directly from the minister of the marine or the Marine Council (depending on the period).[74] Carefully guarding his own interests, Vaudreuil declared that he "would not allow any habitant from this colony [Canada] to go to Louisiana without his permission," and that any traders who trespassed into Canadian territory from Louisiana would have their goods confiscated.[75] Vaudreuil maintained, moreover, that Louisiana's annexation of the Illinois Country had simply moved the northern frontier to the Illinois River, as he sought to fix the boundaries between the two colonies.[76] Therefore, it was no surprise that Vaudreuil advocated for a more northerly route of discovery that lay within his colonial jurisdiction, despite Bobé's theories regarding the proximity of the Western Sea to Louisiana.[77] Contradictory reports, competing interests, and colonial jurisdictions meant that plans for French westward expansion and discovery were often highly contested.

Throughout Charlevoix's mission, he interviewed voyageurs, coureurs de bois, and other backcountry specialists at Quebec, Michilimackinac, and La Pointe regarding the whereabouts of the Western Sea.[78] At La Pointe, he questioned the elderly Jesuit father Pierre-Gabriel Marest, who had accompanied Nicolas Perrot to the Upper Mississippi valley in the seventeenth century. Although Marest was helpful, Charlevoix claimed that the voyageurs at La Pointe were far more knowledgeable about the West and its Indigenous inhabitants than was the elderly Jesuit. Near Michilimackinac, coureur de bois Jean Viennay-Pachot informed Charlevoix that just beyond the Dakota was another prominent nation. To substantiate his claims, Pachot introduced Charlevoix to a young slave and showed him seashells that supposedly hailed from the shores of the Western Sea.[79] Charlevoix praised Pachot as the one "man in Canada who was the most knowledgeable" about Indigenous peoples and who had the most "astonishing faculty to learn [their] languages."[80] Backcountry specialists like Pachot were crucial for Charlevoix's intelligence-gathering expedition to North America.

In his final report to the Marine Council, Charlevoix concluded that the Western Sea was between 40° and 50° latitude, closer to the pays d'en haut than to the more southerly Louisiana. Charlevoix reported that re-establishment of a post in Sioux Country (the Upper Mississippi valley) would facilitate contact with Indigenous peoples further west, who would serve as guides into unknown regions. This was a victory for Vaudreuil, who had convinced the Marine Council that the Western Sea was seemingly within the jurisdiction of the governor of New France. However, the geographic scope of New France is difficult to define since it was not an empirically demarcated territory in any conventional sense. Instead, as historians Catherine Desbarats and Allan Greer posit, New France "tended to serve as a vaguely delineated expression of limitless imperial ambitions" rather than a precisely bounded territory.[81] Despite New France's somewhat nebulous and ill-defined boundaries, past precedent clearly dictated that Sioux Country fell within Quebec's administrative jurisdiction.[82]

According to Charlevoix's informants, the height of land, or drainage divide, was near the headwaters of the Mississippi and Missouri Rivers, where many smaller rivers flowed toward the Western Sea. Finally, he concluded that an unknown Indigenous people occupied the territories west of the Dakota, probably lived near the seashore, and had occasional contact with the Spanish.[83] Unlike Bobé and Delisle, Charlevoix had travelled throughout the interior of North America and visited the most important French posts in the pays d'en haut, the Illinois Country, and Louisiana; he had interviewed voyageurs, missionaries, coureurs de bois, and Indigenous peoples. As a result, Charlevoix provided the Conseil de Régence, as well as Vaudreuil's colonial administration, with a practicable and pragmatic plan to pursue the establishment of French posts in the Hudson Bay watershed in pursuit of the Western Sea. Within the halls of the Palais-Royal and the Bureau des Colonies, metropolitan ministers and colonial officials consulted Charlevoix's report, which was based on intelligence gathered largely from backcountry specialists and Indigenous peoples, who thereby contributed to the complex and imaginative process of imperial westward expansion. At the end of the day, France's policies regarding the Hudson Bay watershed were ultimately driven by imperial speculation based on the complex flow of information (however ambiguous or imperfect) from backcountry specialists and Indigenous peoples on the ground.

COUREURS DE BOIS AND FRENCH IMPERIALISM IN THE HUDSON BAY WATERSHED

When Vaudreuil returned to Canada in October 1716, he and Intendant Michel Bégon energetically began work on a program to expand the French presence in western North America. Interim governor general of New France Claude de Ramezay informed Vaudreuil that British traders out of Albany, New York, were encroaching into the pays d'en haut and attempting to entice Indigenous peoples away from the French alliance.[84] Just as the French saw options for expansion into the Hudson Bay watershed, the British similarly interpreted the Treaty of Utrecht to their advantage as it related to a number of imperial borderlands – the New England frontier, the Great Lakes, and the Mississippi valley. The threat of British imperial expansion provided further incentive for Vaudreuil to pursue France's new policy of westward expansion. Vaudreuil imagined coureurs de bois as integral agents of empire and cross-cultural mediators in what he saw as French sovereign territories, even if this was in reality still an Indigenous West.

Vaudreuil was acutely aware that the French colonial government lacked the resources to punish errant and illicit French traders beyond the Saint Lawrence valley. Concurrent with metropolitan discussions about the Western Sea, the French colonial government attempted to draw coureurs de bois back into the colonial fold. Officials feared that the illicit fur trade was straining New France's limited labour and capital resources by pulling colonists and funds away from the centralized colony and market of the Saint Lawrence valley. French-Indigenous unions in the western interior of the continent meant that coureurs de bois lived much of their lives beyond both ecclesiastical and colonial control. These "country marriages" placed coureurs de bois outside the bounds of the Catholic Church and frequently kept men away from family farms in the Saint Lawrence valley, which were a cornerstone of the colonial project in Canada.[85] French administrators worried that the fur trade had led to idleness and economic unproductivity, de-Christianization, and the upheaval of the colonial social order.[86]

Despite these persistent anxieties, Vaudreuil was well acquainted with coureurs de bois, having previously employed them to combat the British during the War of the Spanish Succession. Most notably, in 1710, Vaudreuil had charged soldier and coureur de bois Nicolas de Manthet with the task of attacking Fort Albany on James Bay with a force of seventy coureurs de bois and thirty Kahnawake Mohawk warriors.[87] Vaudreuil's close association with illicit fur traders occasionally allowed him to project French imperial power against British territorial pretensions in western North America. These occasions, however, were few and far between, and were only possible through the co-operation of local Indigenous peoples, who maintained true on-the-ground sovereignty over the Hudson Bay watershed. Vaudreuil refrained from officially organizing coureurs de bois for military expeditions against the HBC following the Peace of Utrecht, but instead granted permission to voyageurs to trade within the Hudson Bay watershed at the expense of British trade. Throughout the 1720s, the governor awarded congés to Montreal merchant Paul Guillet to trade at Fort Témiscamingue at Lake Timiskaming, intercepting Natives journeying to Fort Albany and Moose Factory on James Bay.[88] By issuing congés, Vaudreuil hoped to contest the HBC's dominance over the fur trade and to secure New France's pick of prime northern furs without breaching the peace treaty.

While voyageurs were employed in the Hudson Bay watershed fur trade, Vaudreuil also used coureurs de bois as part of his strategy for crushing the Mesquakie, who the French referred to as "Renards" (Foxes). In 1716, Vaudreuil made a declaration of amnesty to illicit traders, hoping to secure coureurs de bois as expert guerilla warriors in the conflict that came to be known as the First Fox War (1712–16).[89] Amnestied coureurs de bois, such as Michel Bisaillon and Jean Viennay-Pachot, distinguished themselves both as combatants and cultural mediators.[90] In addition to subduing the Mesquakie, Vaudreuil wanted to harness the knowledge, expertise, and kinship networks of coureurs de bois as these men had lived and travelled throughout the pays d'en haut and the Hudson Bay watershed for decades and were crucially embedded in Indigenous information and communication networks.

While seeking to recruit coureurs de bois as agents of empire, Vaudreuil also recognized the impracticality of reintegrating these illicit traders into agrarian colonial society. The governor argued that New France "should not hope to have all the coureurs de bois return to the colony ... These people are not accustomed to working the land, nor would they ever adjust."[91] Instead, he suggested that they "must be looked upon as useful for the colony."[92] Vaudreuil argued that "coureurs de bois were very useful in Canada for the fur trade" because they could bring merchandise directly into Indigenous villages, thus preventing Native traders from seeking out trade goods from British posts in New York or Hudson Bay, which would in turn keep them within the political and economic orbit of New France.[93]

In a 1707 report to the French court, Intendant Jacques Raudot, who quarrelled frequently with Vaudreuil, was inclined to agree with the governor's assessment of coureurs de bois as useful agents of empire. Intendant Raudot boasted that "the inhabitants of New England are not brave and do not know how to go in the woods like the French."[94] Going back even further to 1701, Governor Louis-Hector de Callière (1698–1703) opined that "New England ... has twice the population of New France, but the people there are surprisingly cowardly, absolutely unprepared to fight, and lacking any experience of war; the smallest Native war party has always made them run away."[95] While clearly mythologizing their own colonists, Raudot and Callière alike recognized the survival skills and backwoods potential of *some* French colonists and their advantages over British settlers.[96] Vaudreuil, like other colonial officials, understood the salient role that coureurs de bois played in safeguarding French interests and helping to secure French influence in the Hudson Bay watershed. These itinerant and illegal traders opened the geography of western North America to the French colonial government.

In 1716, Vaudreuil and Bégon forwarded to their superiors in Paris a plan for the discovery of the Western Sea via the rivers north of Lake Superior that drained into the Hudson Bay watershed. They estimated that it would take at least fifty voyageurs, six Troupes de la Marine officers, and 28,985 livres to establish a series of forts extending from Kaministiquia at Lake Superior to the Western Sea.[97] The Marine Council approved the ambitious project, and the following summer Zacherie Robutel de La Noue launched an expedition to establish posts at Kaministiquia, Rainy Lake, Lake of the Woods, and Lake Winnipeg, where he would attempt to form alliances with local Anishinaabe-Ojibwe, Cree, and Dakota bands. Vaudreuil also secured the services of Jean Viennay-Pachot, a veteran coureur de bois from the First Fox War who had also aided Father Charlevoix on his travels. The Marine Council hoped that the establishment of French-Indigenous alliances in the territories west of Lake Superior would challenge the HBC's monopoly over the northern fur trade.[98]

La Noue's expedition, however, did not make any concrete foothold further inland than Kaministiquia. La Noue's report to the Marine Council in 1721 suggested the possibility of establishing posts further west at Rainy Lake, but with no mention of a post at either Lake of the Woods or Lake Winnipeg. He advised the Marine Council that a trading post at Rainy Lake would prevent prime furs from slipping into the hands of the HBC. From his interviews with local Native leaders, La Noue optimistically concluded that it would not be difficult to convince Indigenous peoples northwest of Lake Superior to trade with the French instead of the HBC by generously gifting them tobacco, gunpowder, and bullets.[99]

What La Noue failed to realize was that there was an ongoing conflict between an Ojibwe-Cree coalition against the eastern woodland Dakota (Mdewakanton, Sisseton, Wahpeton, and Whapekute) dating back at least two generations to the Sault Sainte-Marie massacre of 1674. More recently, the Dakota had witnessed unmitigated French violence against the Mesquakie during the First Fox War and were not ready to welcome the French into their territory, preferring instead to maintain their alliance with the peoples of the Fox-Wisconsin watershed (Mesquakie, Sauk, Kickapoo, and Mascouten).[100]

The Dakota had another potential motive for refusing an alliance with New France. Increasing numbers of coureurs de bois from New Orleans had reached the Upper Mississippi valley and the Fox-Wisconsin watershed by the 1720s, and they were steadily supplying the Dakota and their allies with firearms, powder, shot, knives, and other European weaponry. This gave the Dakota the economic freedom to deny peace overtures from official representatives of the French colonial government. Vaudreuil suspected that coureurs de bois from Louisiana had a hand in urging the Dakota to break off negotiations with La Noue and the Ojibwe-Cree coalition that he represented.[101]

Trade with the French aside, the Dakota and their allies were repositioning themselves toward the western interior in pursuit of the abundant bison herds that stretched from the confluence of the Mississippi and Minnesota Rivers to the Lower Missouri River.[102] These "buffalo grounds" fuelled Dakota, Yankton, Yanktonai, and Lakota demographic growth, and firearms and iron weapons imbued with *wašíču* (extraordinary qualities) peddled by their coureurs de bois kinsmen gave them a technological advantage in their westward military expansion against the Iowa, Omaha, Pawnee, Ponca, and Otoe along the Lower Missouri.[103] To the west, Dakota, Yankton, Yanktonai, and Lakota war parties assailed Arikaras, Hidatsas, and Mandans of the Upper Missouri.[104] The Očhéthi Šakówiŋ (or Seven

Council Fires, a term the Dakota and their allies used to refer to themselves collectively) were not alone in this transformation; throughout the seventeenth and eighteenth centuries, many other Indigenous peoples, including the Haudenosaunee, Illinois, and Comanche, emerged as formidable confederacies, leagues, and empires in the wake of the Columbian Exchange.[105] Forging a veritable Očhéthi Šakówiŋ empire in the heart of North America, the people of the Upper Mississippi valley had little reason to acquiesce to a French-mediated alliance with the Crees and Ojibwes of Lake Superior.

Ongoing warfare, which pitted Cree and Ojibwe bands against the Dakota of the Upper Mississippi valley, had prevented La Noue from constructing permanent trading posts beyond Kaministiquia. Since the 1680s, the French, using frontier diplomats like Nicolas Perrot and Pierre-Charles Le Sueur, had tried to impose a peace between the peoples of the Upper Mississippi valley and the western Great Lakes. However, by attempting to make peace with the Dakota, the French alarmed and infuriated their long-standing Great Lakes allies – principally the Wendat, the Anishinaabeg Confederacy (Odawa, Ojibwe, and Potawatomi), and the Illinois Confederacy. In 1703, a Wendat chief even reproached the governor of New France for attempting to incorporate the Dakota into the broad French-Indigenous alliance, saying, "You make war on the English, so let us go against the Sioux [Dakota]."[106] As more and more French guns fell into the hands of their Dakota adversaries, Great Lakes peoples became increasingly disgruntled with their French trading partners.[107]

In 1718, La Noue sent voyageur and interpreter Jean Viennay-Pachot to Dakota villages in the Upper Mississippi valley, where he was to pursue an alliance between the Dakota and the Ojibwe-Cree. Despite Pachot's peace overtures, however, the Dakota attacked the Ojibwe-Cree village near Kaministiquia, killing seventeen Natives. Alarmed by the attack against Kaministiquia, neighbouring Ojibwes from La Pointe assembled to retaliate against the Dakota.[108] Upon realizing that Pachot's mission to the Dakota was unsuccessful, Cree and Ojibwe from Kaministiquia resolved to continue the war against the group, despite the harangues of La Noue.[109] It should have come as no surprise to French colonial officials that incorporating the Dakota into the broad French-Indigenous alliance within the pays d'en haut was an arduous task. At the Great Peace of Montreal less than twenty years earlier, the Dakota had been excluded from the peace treaty by New France's Great Lakes allies, who had "refused to extend the roots of the Tree of Peace westward," and thus rejected overtures "to broaden the network of alliances as the French desired."[110] Ongoing warfare between the Ojibwe-Cree and the Dakota, along with competition from the HBC, prevented the French post at Kaministiquia from becoming a major collection point for furs in the 1720s. La Noue returned to Montreal in 1721 after four years at the periphery of the Hudson Bay watershed, having accomplished relatively little. The expedition was by most accounts a failure, even though Vaudreuil had employed veteran voyageur and backcountry specialist Jean Viennay-Pachot. At the same time, independent French traders, despite this setback, continued to challenge their British rivals in the Hudson Bay watershed.

At York Factory in 1716, HBC governor James Knight complained that the Natives "have gone to the lake as they call it wch lyes at the south from their country where there are svll [several] settlements of the French wood runners [coureurs de bois]."[111] Knight concluded that "many of the Indians ha[ve] great friendship for the French here." [112] Eleven years later, the situation was seemingly unchanged, with the chief factor at Albany, Joseph Myatt, believing that "this part of the country was never so pestered with the wood-runners as at this time, for by all report they are daily among the upland Indians."[113] At York Factory in 1728, Thomas McCliesh reported "forty canoes of Indians this summer, most of them clothed in French clothing that they traded with the French last summer."[114] On 3 February 1732, a coureur de bois named Joseph Delestre visited Fort Albany "to look after some Indians that formerly traded with them and still remained in their debt."[115] Joseph Adams, chief factor at Albany, suspected that Delestre "came to spy the market and to draw all the Indians he could to their settlement" and to pry "into the strength or fortification of the factory."[116] Adams managed to send the Frenchman away, but Cree traders at Albany informed him "that the French had finished two settlements up this river, and they see them making a third which is close by this river's side about four days paddle from this factory, in order to intercept all those Indians from coming down this river and compelling them to trade."[117] At Fort Albany, which was a continuous hotspot for French fur trade competition, the value of HBC Made Beaver (MB) decreased from 15,900 in 1725 to 11,000 in 1735.[118] The presence of coureurs de bois and the establishment of temporary posts on both the Moose and Albany Rivers most certainly contributed to the weakening fur returns at Fort Albany and Moose Factory.

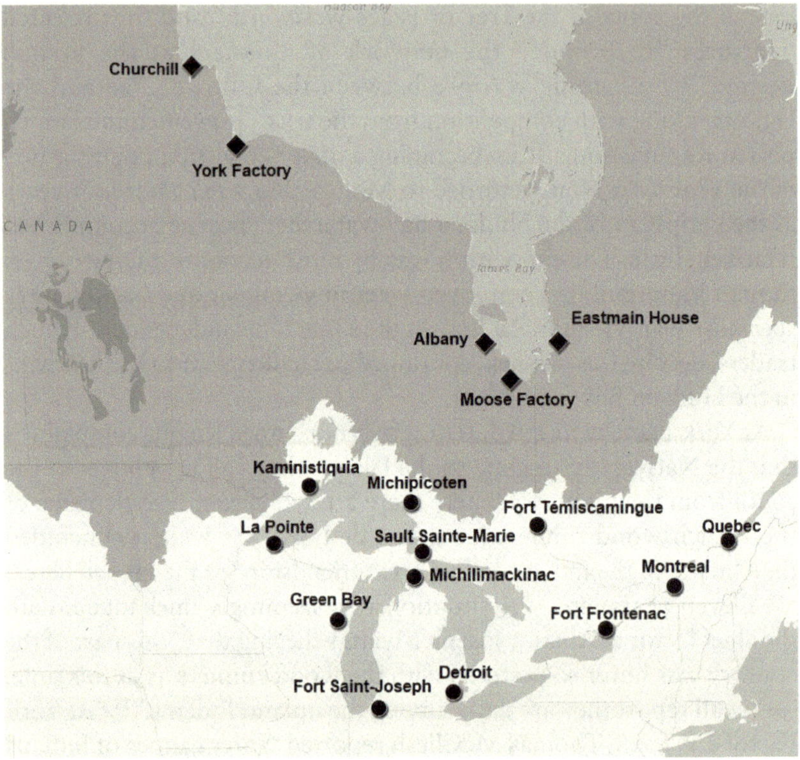

2.5 Hudson's Bay Company posts (diamonds) along the Hudson Bay lowlands and French posts (circles) of the pays d'en haut in the 1720s. The British Crown designated the Hudson Bay drainage basin (shaded) as Rupert's Land, a territory in which a commercial monopoly was operated by the Hudson's Bay Company for two hundred years from 1670 to 1870.

As previously noted, Governor Vaudreuil had officially ceased sending coureurs de bois to assault HBC posts following the Treaty of Utrecht. Meanwhile, the Duke of Orléans, Cardinal Dubois, and the rest of the Conseil de Régence worked to improve relations with Great Britain.[119] Coureurs de bois, however, were illicit traders, and as such were not beholden to French colonial policies or imperial directives. In truth, they had never really been as resolutely in league with Vaudreuil as his detractors had claimed. Because coureurs de bois were outlaws, Vaudreuil and other colonial officials enjoyed a sort of plausible deniability in the face of British accusations that they were breaching the peace, while the actions of these rogue Frenchmen still weakened British imperialism in the Hudson Bay watershed.

In 1729, a sizeable force composed of coureurs de bois and their well-armed Native allies attacked Fort Albany on James Bay. The fort's chief factor, Joseph Myatt, recorded that "the Factory was Alarmed by an Enemy"; he knew "full well that we must not Expect any Quarter from the Woodrunners and Mohawkes, if they Should Overcome Us."[120] Myatt repulsed the French-Indigenous assault on 7 June, noting that two servants posted on watch fired at a "French Spy," though their muskets were loaded only with "Duck Shott," thus leading Myatt to suppose that the spy was only "slightly Wounded."[121] Nevertheless, the chief factor proudly reported that the "men all Appeared to be very forward in the Defence of the factory."[122]

The French-Native war party reappeared a week later, just before midnight on 17 June. The sentries, spotting "at the Least Ten or twelve Men Walking up to the outward Gate," called "out to Alarm the Factory that all Men might repair to their Respective Quarters."[123] Myatt remarked that the men then fired a volley, which "put the Enemy in Such a fright, that they made off wthout Ever Attacking us."[124] The French returned once again the following night and attempted to use an explosive to burn down the fort. Myatt recorded that "we Saw a Great flash of fire fall by the Outward Palisades & Extinguish in a Moment, & Observed a Great Smell of Sulphur arise from it, but Could not Conceive by what Means it Derived from."[125] The fourth and final confrontation between the Albany men and the French occurred at one o'clock in the morning on 20 June, when the sentries "Discovered three Spies" lurking outside Albany's palisades.[126] Rowland Waggoner, an HBC servant, shot and killed one of the coureurs de bois, who "was Crawling a Long in the Grass Endeavouring to Escape after he found he was Discovered."[127] The Fort Albany men did not recover the body because "his Companions Carried him off"; they nonetheless suspected that "he soon after died."[128]

The attack on Fort Albany was ultimately unsuccessful, but the assault indicated the degree to which French backcountry traders were able to conduct their own foreign policy according to the needs of the moment. The confrontation demonstrated that coureurs de bois were following their own agenda because it so evidently clashed with metropolitan designs in post-Utrecht North America, which mandated a peaceful but firmly guarded co-existence with Great Britain. Coureurs de bois and their Native kinsmen continued to cause other hardships for the HBC in the 1720s. At York Factory, Nakoda traders informed HBC governor Henry Kelsey that "the Poets [Dakota] ...

are Encouraged by the French to warr against all country Indians that came here to trade."[129] At Fort Albany, Joseph Myatt recorded the damaging effect that coureurs de bois had on HBC trade: "it is certaine the Kannaday wood runners doe all they can to intercept our trade and set the Inds at variance one wth another that comes to trade wth us."[130] Thomas McCliesh, the chief factor at York Factory, wrote that some Frenchmen "were gone to warrs ... Last Summer with the poets [Dakota] against our Senipoetts [Nakoda] with A Design to Destroy them or force them to trade with them."[131] A few days later, McCliesh noted that the French were constantly encouraging the Dakota to go to war against the Nakoda who traded at Fort Albany. McCliesh also confirmed that several French coureurs de bois had accompanied the raids against the Nakoda: "we have Been In formed by most of the upland Indians this Summer that 8 French wood Runners went to warrs Last Summer with the poets [Dakota]."[132] Corroborating HBC accounts of the Dakota raids against the Nakoda, a Lakota winter count records the killing of six Nakoda as the most important event for 1728–29.[133] In the 1720s, Dakota bands and their French kinsmen began raiding the Nakoda, a pattern that would persist into the early nineteenth century.

The efforts of coureurs de bois in the 1720s to directly antagonize the HBC clashed with Vaudreuil's carefully articulated imperial design. Certainly, the governor had wanted to divert furs away from Hudson Bay and toward New France, but that did not involve French traders like Delestre showing up in person at HBC posts, and it certainly did not involve a full-blown assault on Fort Albany. Coureurs de bois joining the Dakota in raids against the Nakoda also directly challenged the French imperial policy of enforcing a *Pax Gallica* (French-mediated peace) among France's Native allies. Recent scholarship posits that coureurs de bois were ineffectual soldiers and warriors, seeing only brief service in the military campaigns against the Haudenosaunee Confederacy in the 1670s and '80s.[134] However, from the vantage point of the Hudson Bay watershed, the martial prowess of coureurs de bois in service of their own interests (and not imperial goals) was indeed significant. Coureurs de bois participated in at least ten separate military excursions against the British and Nakoda between 1718 and 1729; this was done entirely on their own initiative and largely outside the purview of French colonial administrators. Although the application of violence by coureurs de bois contravened official French policy, it nevertheless laid the groundwork for French influence and eventual westward expansion into the Hudson Bay watershed. In other words, where Troupes de la Marine officers like La Noue had failed, coureurs de bois, acting on their own, were carving out a potential French imperial space, breaking the rules of French-Indigenous and imperial diplomacy along the way.

By the early eighteenth century, coureurs de bois had apparently achieved what French colonial officials could not – an alliance with the Dakota. How did coureurs de bois succeed where the French colonial government seemed wholly incapable? The answer lies largely in the establishment of kinship bonds through marriage. According to Wahpeton Dakota oral tradition, "In their travels, some of the Sioux had come upon a French colony along or at the mouth of the Mississippi River, made peace and stayed a while to work there ... The French colony gave fifty French girls to the Sioux boys to marry, and the Sioux in turn gave fifty Sioux girls to the French to marry."[135] The one-to-one exchange of wives seems unlikely given the dearth of female French settlers in North America, especially along the Upper Mississippi River. However, the oral tradition affirms the importance of marriage in the fostering of kinship ties for the Dakota. Familial bonds and kinship patterns provided the glue that bonded the society together as family members relied heavily on relatives in times of need. Like their Anishinaabeg neighbours, the Očhéthi Šakówiŋ framed society as an essential dichotomy – insiders versus outsiders. Adoption or marriage were the only ways to incorporate outsiders into the *thióšpaye* (extended family group).[136]

Contemporary accounts fail to reveal the number of coureurs de bois that married into Dakota thióšpayes and settled in the Upper Mississippi valley in the early eighteenth century, but French officials made at least one concerted effort to convince these deserters to return to the Saint Lawrence valley colony. Troupes de la Marine officer Paul-Louis Dazenard, sieur de Lusignan, visited Sioux Country with the express purpose of convincing coureurs de bois to return to Canada. They staunchly refused to leave their Dakota wives and their adopted homeland.[137] These coureurs de bois adjusted to Očhéthi Šakówiŋ social practices and adopted those customs, gestures, and rituals that were necessary for full acceptance into the Očhéthi Šakówiŋ thióšpayes.[138]

British, French, and Očhéthi Šakówiŋ records document Canadiens living with and fighting alongside the Očhéthi Šakówiŋ. A Yanktonai winter count confirms that some Frenchmen resided locally in Očhéthi

Šakówiŋ villages scattered throughout the vast territory that stretched from the Upper Mississippi River to the Missouri River. The John K. Bear winter count recorded that 1708 was the year that "a white man joined in a sacred ceremony," probably indicating that a French coureur de bois had at least achieved some degree of cultural integration into Yanktonai society.[139] Even as early as the 1690s, a few coureurs de bois were trading near the vestiges of Fort Saint-Antoine at Lake Pepin, first abandoned by Nicolas Perrot and subsequently reoccupied and then abandoned once again by Pierre-Charles Le Sueur.[140] In 1700, French carpenter André Pénicaut reported the presence of coureurs de bois among eastern Dakota bands at Fort L'Huillier near the confluence of the Le Sueur and Blue Earth Rivers (Mankato, Minnesota).[141] Around this time, Pelée Island on Lake Pepin had become the main rendezvous of illicit French traders after Fort Saint-Antoine was abandoned. Coureurs de bois had built cabins along with large platforms for drying buffalo meat. These Europeans had established kinship relations with the eastern Dakota.[142]

Vaudreuil was unable to take immediate advantage of these relationships and advance the interests of French governance. The Mesquakie had organized the peoples of the Fox-Wisconsin watershed (Sauk, Kickapoo, and Mascouten) as well as the Dakota into a loose coalition to control the western trade and to raid the Illinois Confederacy.[143] The Dakota barred an official French presence in the Upper Mississippi valley, but coureurs de bois with proper kinship relations were still welcomed and permitted to trade.[144] By the 1720s, French colonial policy revolved around neutralizing and eventually destroying the power of the Mesquakie, who opposed French western imperial expansion in a conflict known as the Second Fox War (1728–33).[145] Vaudreuil was reluctant to establish an official post among the Dakota because the Mesquakie "had so predisposed the Sioux [Dakota] against us by leading them to believe that we would betray them that it was impossible to convince them of the contrary."[146] The Dakota abhorred the violence committed by the French against the Mesquakie in the last war, and for that reason they were reluctant to welcome an official French outpost in their territory. However, coureurs de bois who identified as Dakota kinsmen and who traded out of the Illinois Country and Louisiana continued to furnish the Dakota with a generous number of firearms, powder, shot, knives, and hatchets.[147]

The establishment of official French posts in the Hudson Bay watershed and the Upper Mississippi valley was not possible prior to

Vaudreuil's death, but the groundwork had been laid for western imperial expansion when coureurs de bois established kinship relations and commercial connections with the Dakota.[148] In 1727, the French colonial government commissioned René Boucher de La Perrière, a Troupes de la Marine officer, to establish Fort Beauharnois on the Upper Mississippi River. Accompanying him was Father Michel Guignas and Father Nicolas Degonnor, who sought to proselytize to the Dakota.[149] Coureurs de bois had made it possible for the eventual extension of French colonialism into the Hudson Bay watershed, but their own agendas often ensured that western expansion and French imperial designs advanced at an erratic and often oscillating pace.

CONCLUSION

In 1715, ancien régime France underwent a profound political and economic transformation. Amid a host of imperial administrative changes, Governor Vaudreuil emerged as a central figure advising the Marine Council on the pursuit of an expansionist North American policy. The prospect of limiting an imperial rival's access to the fur trade, along with the possibility of discovering the Western Sea, incentivized French imperial expansion into the Hudson Bay watershed. Backcountry specialists such as Jacques de Noyon, Jean Viennay-Pachot, and Nicolas Jérémie, embedded within Indigenous information and communication networks, provided intelligence that was crucial for fulfilling the imperial mandate of western expansion. Pursuant to this period of information acquisition, metropolitan and imperial bureaucrats believed that they would harness Canadiens, particularly coureurs de bois, as agents of empire, thereby giving France extraordinary power and control in post-Utrecht North America.

Colonial officials like Vaudreuil tried to co-opt coureurs de bois and convert them into imperial agents, but these efforts often failed because these men proved highly resistant to governmental control. Initially, it was these coureurs de bois, fur traders, and clerks who fuelled the metropolitan dream of reaching the Western Sea by laying out the feasibility of the project based on their ties to local Indigenous peoples, as well as their linguistic and geographical knowledge of western North America. Despite the information they provided to imperial geographers and metropolitan decision-makers, however, these French cultural brokers often disrupted imperial progress. They attacked the posts of an imperial rival with whom France was trying to maintain peaceful relations and they often allied themselves with Native bands independent of any French governmental authorization or accountability.

Ambitious Canadiens ended up frustrating many imperial goals in the Northwest, but they nevertheless promoted haphazard and ill-defined expressions of French imperialism in the heart of North America during the transitional and transformative period that followed the Treaty of Utrecht. Though not exactly what French metropolitan officials and imperial planners envisioned, the Canadiens' activities slowly began to leave an imperial footprint in the Hudson Bay watershed, especially insofar as they limited the HBC's commercial activities and Britain's imperial expansion. This was a partial French success – it was a far cry from the firm imperial control exercised in urban colonial centres like Quebec and Montreal – but it was a foundation upon which to launch future expeditions and to continue seeking the elusive Northwest Passage.

Further attempts to discover the Western Sea would have to wait until the 1730s, when an enterprising Troupes de la Marine officer named Pierre Gaultier de Varennes, sieur de La Vérendrye, would establish les postes de la Mer de l'Ouest (the posts of the Western Sea). As La Vérendrye struggled to forge alliances with the Indigenous peoples of the Hudson Bay watershed, it would again become apparent that voyageurs and coureurs de bois were more able to determine the form and implementation of colonialism at the edge of empire. Backcountry specialists were proving to be beyond the effective control of the Crown and were establishing themselves as holders of the keys to colonialism in the Hudson Bay watershed.

3

Pierre Gaultier de La Vérendrye and the Western Posts, 1731–1743

On 10 October 1725, Philippe de Rigaud, Marquis de Vaudreuil, died in Quebec at the age of eighty-two. Officers, merchants, habitants, and voyageurs alike mourned the loss of their governor general, whom they held in high esteem. Canada had become Vaudreuil's adopted country, and in 1724 he had even referred to it as his children's *patrie*.[1] The annals of the Ursuline nuns of Quebec record that "We had every reason to mourn him, for under his vigilant administration Canada enjoyed a prosperity unknown until that time."[2] But despite the Ursulines' lofty praise, Vaudreuil was not loved by all; he quarrelled frequently with Claude de Ramezay, governor of Montreal, as well as Louisiana's colonial officials. Still, Vaudreuil had left an indelible mark on the colony, and he had played a crucial part in French westward expansion by advocating for the use of voyageurs and coureurs de bois for imperial projects in the Hudson Bay watershed. Vaudreuil's death marked a shift in French colonial governance. He had contributed significantly to policies of imperial expansion into the Hudson Bay watershed following the deaths of Jean-Baptiste Colbert and Louis XIV, and his own death had very real implications for French imperial ambitions. The subsequent administration of Governor Charles de la Boische, Marquis de Beauharnois (1726–48), represented a radical turn away from the governing style of La Barre, Denonville, and Vaudreuil, each of whom had readily and cleverly used backcountry Canadiens as ambassadors, peacemakers, and diplomats in the pays d'en haut and the Hudson Bay watershed. Vaudreuil, in particular, had tried to utilize voyageurs and coureurs de bois against the HBC in post-Utrecht western North America. Regardless of whether the governor's orders were closely followed, coureurs de bois operating both under and outside of Vaudreuil's purview had demonstrated the potential of French imperial expansion into the Hudson Bay watershed.

In the 1730s and '40s, Beauharnois eschewed Vaudreuil's previous strategy of co-opting the talents of specialized voyageurs, soldiers, and coureurs de bois, and instead adhered to the strict hierarchical protocol of the ancien régime. Beauharnois placed Pierre Gaultier de Varennes, sieur de La Vérendrye, a nobleman, member of the colony's military elite, and lieutenant in the Compagnies Franches de la Marine, in charge of an enterprise that sought to establish a series of forts northwest of Lake Superior that would become known as the Western Posts. French colonial administrators hoped that La Vérendrye's posts would help reinforce claims of sovereignty as well as undermine the British fur trade in the Hudson Bay watershed. However, La Vérendrye lacked inexperience in western Indigenous diplomacy. Ill-prepared for the complex entanglement of Indigenous geopolitics and a protracted conflict involving the Cree, Monsoni, Ojibwe, Nakoda, and Dakota, La Vérendrye was unable to effectuate peace and assert French imperial authority in the region.[3] La Vérendrye's missteps therefore offer a powerful window into the weakness of French imperial control in the Hudson Bay watershed in the 1730s and '40s. Moreover, La Vérendrye's inability to extend the French-Indigenous alliance system of the pays d'en haut into the Hudson Bay watershed speaks to the power and agency of Indigenous peoples in that region during this period.

Unlike his predecessors Radisson, Du Lhut, and Jérémie, La Vérendrye could exert little on-the-ground influence in what remained an Indigenous space. By conceptualizing La Vérendrye's efforts to fulfill imperial projects in the Hudson Bay watershed as an imperial setback, this chapter refutes most of the extant literature on La Vérendrye and the Western Posts.[4] Rather than painting him and his sons as the "tireless explorers of the West," in what follows I seek to more accurately portray the La Vérendrye family as mere pawns in an Indigenous power struggle between two warring coalitions, a conflict that had been simmering for generations.[5] Their lack of power over Indigenous diplomatic and kinship networks ultimately subverted French imperial ambitions in the Hudson Bay watershed.

PEACE PREVAILS: LOUIS XV, CARDINAL FLEURY, AND MAUREPAS

On 25 February 1723, Louis XV, now old enough to assume his position as ruler of France, appointed the Duke of Orléans as his prime minister. With the king in charge, the Regency Council effectively ceased functioning. Four months later, when the Duke of Orléans passed away, Louis XV overhauled the royal court's governing structure. He dissolved the ministerial councils and reinstated the secretaries of state that had operated under Louis XIV. The goal was meant to re-centralize government and restore political power to the high nobility.[6] When Jean-Frédéric Phélypeaux, Comte de Maurepas, assumed the role of the minister of the marine and colonies in 1723, he took over the position vacated by his father, Jérôme Phélypeaux, Comte de Pontchartrain, a decade prior.[7] As a military and naval strategist, Maurepas's chief concern in the 1730s and '40s was to plan for the defence of France's far-flung and inadequately garrisoned overseas empire. Under his guidance, the French navy regained much of the strength and prestige that it had lost at the end of Louis XIV's reign and during the period of the Régence. France built up a small navy of well-designed and solidly built ships supported by improved arsenals and adequate stockpiles of naval stores, thus restoring France's reputation as a maritime power.[8] Realizing the demographic disadvantage in French North America (the populations of French Canada and Louisiana were less than one-tenth of that of British North America), Maurepas thought in terms of a defensive war. If Britain attacked New France, French forces would retreat, prepare interior lines, and regroup around strategic fortresses. They were then to hold those positions until France and its allies emerged victorious on the battlefields of Europe.[9]

During this period, Cardinal André-Hercule de Fleury became Louis XV's chief minister, thereafter ruling France with the king's assent. Cardinal Fleury refused the formal title of prime minister, but his close relationship with the king confirmed his dominance over all others at court.[10] The cardinal, following the precedent set by the Régence, believed that maintenance of the status quo was the best protection of France's interests; he therefore pursued a rapprochement with both Britain and Austria.[11] During the so-called Long Peace between Britain and France (1713–40), Fleury and Maurepas tried to increase the commercial productivity of New France by encouraging an ambitious shipbuilding program at Quebec, the creation of an iron foundry near Trois-Rivières (Forges du Saint-Maurice), and the expansion of the grain trade from Montreal to Île-Royale (Cape Breton) and the French Antilles.[12] Under Fleury and Maurepas, Canada experienced an expansion of commercial activity beyond subsistence farming and the fur trade. Increased trade and communication between Canada and France can largely be attributed to the foundation of the fortress of Louisbourg and its ice-free port on Île-Royale, which functioned as a central hub for French transatlantic trade and correspondence between North America, the Caribbean, and Europe.[13] In order to anticipate the possibility of a British attack, Maurepas improved upon Colbert's vast transatlantic intelligence networks to keep himself apprised of the movements of the British Royal Navy.[14] Adherence to the principles of mercantilism, along with his vision of a centralized empire and expanded imperial intelligence networks, made Maurepas a worthy successor to Colbert.

Two years after taking up his post as minister of the marine, Maurepas was faced with the task of appointing a new governor to replace Vaudreuil. Unlike the inexperienced Marine Council that had preceded him, Maurepas's Ministry of the Marine was largely uninterested in harnessing voyageurs and coureurs de bois to the larger effort to extend imperial claims in the western interior of North America. Instead, he sought a governor firmly tied to the metropole, someone who would adhere to his vision of a centralized and defensive empire. And so, in February 1726, Charles de la Boische, Marquis de Beauharnois, sailed for New France. The newly appointed governor had formerly served at the French port city of Rochefort and was related to Maurepas through marriage into the Pontchartrain family. But perhaps most importantly, in Maurepas's eyes, Beauharnois had no close connections with Canadien families.[15]

GOVERNOR BEAUHARNOIS, LA VÉRENDRYE, AND THE SEARCH FOR THE WESTERN SEA

Governor Beauharnois arrived in Quebec in August 1726 aboard the ship *Eléphant*. The incoming governor was a strict adherent of the patronage networks of the ancien régime. The previous two chapters have described the gradual securing of a French imperial foothold in the Hudson Bay watershed, with colonial officials consistently employing Canadien voyageurs and coureurs de bois as agents of empire. In contrast to Vaudreuil's administration, Beauharnois largely eschewed the usage of Canadiens in favour of French elites and noblemen. When it came to dealing with coureurs de bois and Indigenous peoples in colonial hinterlands, Beauharnois was attempting to move away from the earlier reliance on backcountry specialists; as we have seen, these men were difficult to manage and control. Instead, he would empower those who were more directly answerable and amenable to a firmer imperial hand. This departure from previous practice would have serious consequences for French-Indigenous alliances and western imperial expansion.

Because of his adherence to the patronage networks of the ancien régime, Beauharnois promoted members of elite colonial families over experienced and capable Canadien voyageurs and coureurs de bois. In 1729, the colonial government commissioned the well-connected Troupes de la Marine officer Pierre Gaultier de Varennes, sieur de La Vérendrye, to establish a series of forts northwest of Lake Superior that came to be known as the Western Posts.[16] La Vérendrye was a battle-scarred man in his mid-forties who had served with distinction on North American and European battlefields during the War of the Spanish Succession (1701–14).[17] In 1726, he joined a fur-trading partnership with his brother Jacques-René to operate the poste du Nord, a fur trade district that included Michipicoten, Nipigon, and Kaministiquia on the northern shore of Lake Superior. A Cree trader named Auchagah drew a charcoal map on a piece of birchbark for La Vérendrye representing the waterways leading to the long-sought Western Sea. While serving as commandant of the poste du Nord in 1728 and 1729, La Vérendrye also consulted with Cree leaders Pako, Lefoye, Petit Jour, Tacchigis, and La Marteblanche, who provided oral testimony describing western lands and waters.[18] Based on this new geographic knowledge, La Vérendrye saw an opportunity for his family to achieve great recognition and renown in French society. Discovery of the Western Sea would guarantee not only promotion in New France's military hierarchy and a lucrative fur trade monopoly, but also the intangible prospect of recognition, renown, and glory that drove the ethos of the noblesse d'épée throughout France's Atlantic empire.[19]

When La Vérendrye was at Michilimackinac, he encountered Father Nicolas Degonnor, who was on his way back to Quebec from a newly established Jesuit mission in Sioux Country. La Vérendrye showed Degonnor the birchbark map and shared with him his plan to discover the Western Sea. Auchagah's map, in particular, piqued the interest of the Jesuit father, who agreed to help La Vérendrye prepare a report to Governor Beauharnois. In the report, Degonnor was careful to mention that La Vérendrye's father, René Gaultier de Varennes, had been the governor of Trois-Rivières for twenty-two years, and that La Vérendrye and his eldest brother Louis had both served in the Régiment de Bretagne in Europe during the War of the Spanish Succession.[20] Clearly, La Vérendrye's noble status and military record were relevant to his appointment to undertake and lead an expedition to Lake Winnipeg. By the autumn of 1730, when the last ships prepared to depart for France via the Saint Lawrence before the annual freeze-up, Beauharnois wrote to Maurepas that he had approved La Vérendrye's plan to establish a series of posts northwest of Lake Superior. Beauharnois assured Maurepas that La Vérendrye would undertake the whole enterprise at minimal cost to the Crown, apart from a few customary presents from the royal coffers to solidify French-Indigenous alliances along the way.[21]

In Quebec, a military engineer working for the Ministry of the Marine, Gaspard-Joseph Chaussegros de Léry, drew a parchment copy of Auchagah's birchbark map.[22] Beauharnois attached copies of Degonnor's report and de Léry's copy of Auchagah's map and notified Maurepas that La Vérendrye had founded his whole enterprise "on the reports of natives," whose services as guides would be indispensable to the French.[23] In France, Philippe Buache, who had trained under Guillaume Delisle, enthusiastically received the report and map, which he incorporated into Delisle's earlier map of North America.[24]

With this valuable new geographic knowledge in hand, it was time for French imperial expansion into the Hudson Bay watershed to recommence in earnest. New France had loosely maintained relations with various Cree bands since the mid-seventeenth century, but the colonial government now sought to firmly ally itself with the Cree in order to assert French claims in the Hudson Bay watershed.[25] Beauharnois suggested that a strong alliance with the Cree and the establishment of the Western Posts would secure the northern fur market for New France while simultaneously diverting trade away from the HBC.[26] The Western Posts would also serve as a base for an ongoing French effort to discover a northwest passage to the Pacific Ocean, which, for the past two decades, France's pre-eminent geographers and cartographers had hypothesized was located in western North America between 40° and 50° latitude.

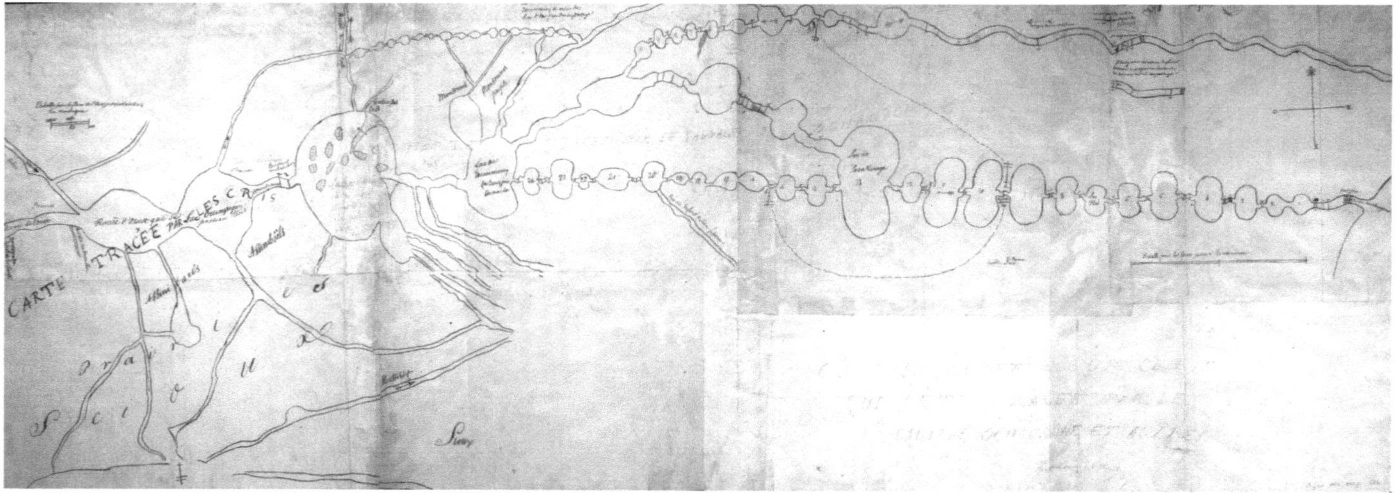

3.1 Military engineer Gaspard-Joseph Chaussegros de Léry drew parchment copies of Auchagah's birchbark map to send to Delisle's workshop in Paris and to the Bureau des Colonies along with La Vérendrye's report outlining the feasibility of the project.

3.2 Philippe Buache superimposed La Vérendrye's new geographic findings on Guillaume Delisle's 1722 map of North America, probably sometime around 1730, when Chaussegros de Léry's copy of Auchagah's made it to Delisle's workshop.

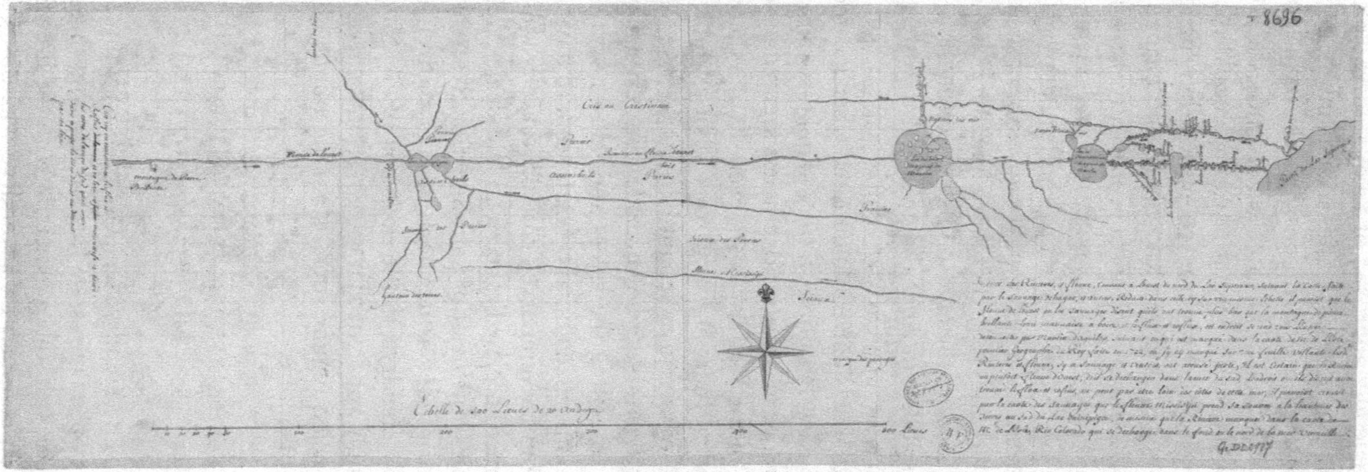

3.3 Auchagah's map re-copied by Philippe Buache.

Beauharnois generally approved of La Vérendrye's plan but questioned his desire to have Abenaki guides accompany the expedition. The motivations behind this bizarre proposal perplexed the governor, who insightfully opined that "it has not seemed necessary to take any Abenakis for the journey ... What advantage could the Sieur de la Vérendrye possibly have derived from people who have no idea whatever of those regions nor the slightest knowledge of the languages spoken there?"[27] The Abenaki were (and are) a people native to eastern Quebec, the Maritimes, and New England, and Beauharnois therefore made the very sensible suggestion that La Vérendrye instead draw his guides from the peoples of western Lake Superior. The governor posited that Ojibwe and Cree guides were not only cheaper to hire, but that they would be much more familiar with the Hudson Bay watershed.[28]

La Vérendrye's choice of Abenaki guides for a western expedition demonstrated that, although he was an aristocrat and an experienced soldier, he was still fairly naive and untested when it came to western Indigenous diplomacy. His noble status and military rank as a lieutenant in the Troupes de la Marine nonetheless secured his commission as commandant of the Western Posts, even though there were other more experienced and capable men around. For example, coureur de bois Jacques de Noyon and merchant Nicolas Jérémie were still alive and well in 1730, aged sixty-two and sixty-one, respectively, and both had experience travelling the rivers and lakes northwest of Lake Superior. Oddly enough, colonial officials seem to have neglected to contact them about La Vérendrye's enterprise, even though they were among the few men in New France who had dealt extensively with Indigenous peoples northwest of Lake Superior. Reservations regarding his choice of guides aside, Beauharnois showed unwavering confidence in La Vérendrye, to the exclusion of all others. Indeed, it became increasingly apparent that the governor's uncompromisingly elitist view of ancien régime social standing blinded him to more qualified agents of empire.

THE ESTABLISHMENT OF THE WESTERN POSTS, 1731–34

On 8 June 1731, La Vérendrye left Montreal with three of his sons, his nephew Christophe Dufrost de La Jemerais, a few licensed traders, about fifty engagés, and some soldiers.[29] With the French court providing only token support, La Vérendrye was obliged to turn to

Montreal merchants to finance his undertaking. Accordingly, between March and June 1731 Montreal merchants formed four distinct partnerships; these later coalesced into a larger partnership that included La Vérendrye and his family.[30] This larger nine-man commercial entity, known as the Associés de la Mer de l'Ouest, was composed of La Vérendrye, his eldest son Jean-Baptiste, his nephew La Jemerais, and Montreal merchants Louis Hamelin, Laurent-Eustache Gamelin *dit* Châteauvieux, Nicolas Sarrazin, Joseph-Marie Lescuyer, Louis Lériger *dit* La Plante, and Gilbert Lériger *dit* Gourville. The partners pooled their investment capital to recruit voyageurs and procure merchandise, and Governor Beauharnois granted them a three-year monopoly over the fur trade in the Lake Winnipeg region.[31]

To La Vérendrye's profound disappointment, the plan to establish the Western Posts in 1731 was dashed when, upon reaching Grand Portage at the end of August, at the western shore of Lake Superior, his engagés mutinied and refused to proceed any further because they were "dismayed at the length of the portage."[32] This was a strenuous route that required traversing fourteen kilometres of steep, slippery, and rocky trails to reach Pigeon River. La Vérendrye had little choice but to acquiesce to his workers' demands and was forced to winter at Kaministiquia, also on the lake's western shore.[33]

When news of the expedition finally reached Beauharnois, La Vérendrye complained that he was progressing more slowly than expected due to "the impossibility of getting men [to follow] on account of their fear of dying of starvation in those parts."[34] In the event, the engagés' caution was justified (though not so much on account of the risk of starvation, as game was more than plentiful) as the expedition entered into a war zone. Throughout the 1730s, eastern Dakota oyátes – Mdewakanton, Sisseton, Wahpeton, and Whapekute – and the Ojibwe who lived at Zhaagawaamikong (La Pointe), or Chequamegon Bay, an inlet of Lake Superior, frequently raided Cree and Monsoni villages around Kaministiquia, Rainy Lake, and Lake of the Woods. Likewise, Crees and Monsonis retaliated by attacking Dakota and Zhaagawaamikong-Ojibwe encampments in the Upper Mississippi valley and southern Lake Superior.

The Dakota and Zhaagawaamikong-Ojibwe had recently entered into a military compact to secure joint access and control of the rich hunting territory west of Lake Superior.[35] The strategic alliance safeguarded Dakota access to the French post at La Pointe and allowed the Zhaagawaamikong-Ojibwe to hunt the abundant bison herds

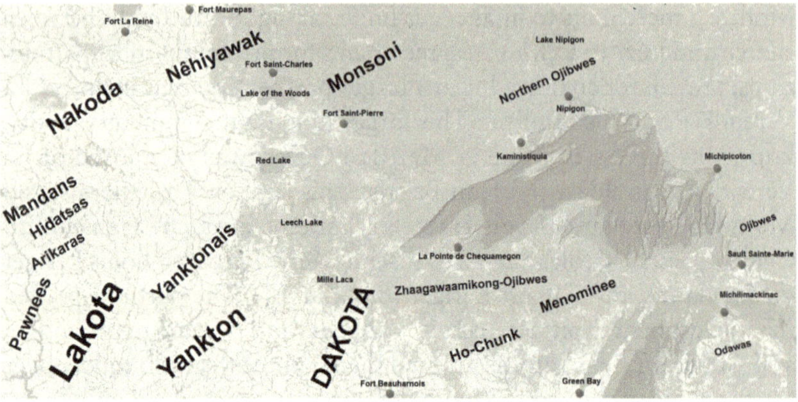

3.4 The five-hundred-mile borderland between Lake Superior and the Upper Missouri valley where the two warring coalitions fought for control of the Upper Mississippi valley and northeastern prairie parklands. To the north, Monsonis, Crees, and Nakoda forged a military coalition, which included some northern Ojibwes. To the south, the Očhéthi Šakówiŋ (Dakota, Yankton, Yanktonai, and Lakota) secured an alliance with the Zhaagawaamikong-Ojibwes, which allowed them access to Lake Superior markets. For the most part, the French were merely passive witnesses to the unfolding conflict between the Cree-Monsoni-Nakoda coalition and the Očhéthi Šakówiŋ.

stretching west from the confluence of the Mississippi and Minnesota Rivers to the Missouri River.[36] The Zhaagawaamikong-Ojibwe and Dakota alliance concerned the Monsoni and Cree, who feared that the new partnership would jeopardize their economic well-being by potentially cutting off their access to French trade and the Lake Superior market. Since the Monsoni were the Moose doodem (clan) of the Anishinaabeg, they were particularly alarmed at the prospect of an intra-Anishinaabe conflict with the Zhaagawaamikong-Ojibwe, who were composed mostly of the Crane, Loon, and Wolf doodemag from La Pointe.[37]

French imperial expansion had unknowingly fuelled this conflict between the Zhaagawaamikong-Ojibwe, Dakota, Monsoni, and Cree by funnelling European firearms, knives, and hatchets into the region. While French posts had the effect of levelling the technological playing field in the East, French firearms and iron weapons gave the Očhéthi Šakówiŋ a decisive technological advantage in their westward and southward military expansions against other groups whose access to European arms were more restricted.[38] For example, westering oyátes of the Očhéthi Šakówiŋ turned their attention toward the peoples of the Missouri valley – Arikaras, Mandans, Hidatsas, Omahas, Pawnees,

Poncas, and Otoes – who lacked firearms and iron weapons. Dispersing their enemies, the Očhéthi Šakówiŋ eventually claimed "an enormous reservoir of water, grass, game, timber, and shelter" for themselves.[39] The rise of an Očhéthi Šakówiŋ empire in the heart of North America represented an unprecedented threat to the Monsoni and Cree because of its enormity, manpower, and capacity for growth. To further complicate matters for the Monsoni and Cree, some Lakota oyátes, like the Sicangus and Oglalas, as well as some Yankton and Yanktonai, were beginning to acquire horses, which they initially christened *šúŋka wakȟáŋ* (sacred dog), from plains-based raiding and trading networks to the southwest.[40] These inter-village patterns of warfare would draw the French into a political conflict in which the two Native coalitions battled for control of hunting and trade territory west of Lake Superior.

Returning to the engagé mutiny at Grand Portage, La Vérendrye, with the help of Jesuit father Charles-Michel Mesaiger, convinced a handful of voyageurs to accompany his eldest son Jean-Baptiste and his nephew La Jemerais in establishing a small fort at Rainy Lake.[41] Coureurs de bois initially made it difficult for the French to establish an alliance with the Nakoda, who were the third member of the Monsoni-Cree northern coalition. In the preceding decades, many coureurs de bois had allied themselves with the Dakota and sought to undermine the British trade at Hudson Bay by attacking the Nakoda, who were steadfast trading partners with the HBC. They pushed the Nakoda farther west in an attempt to limit their access to European trade and weaponry. HBC records confirm that the "Poetts [Dakota] had Destroyed most of our Senipoetts [Nakoda] by the Instigation of the french."[42] The effect of Dakota assaults upon the Nakoda was drastic, driving them to take refuge far to the northwest, beyond the range of enemy war parties.

La Vérendrye complained that none of the Nakoda "have yet come to the fort as they have in some way been made afraid of us."[43] La Jemerais later explained to the governor that the Nakoda refused to come "to the fort of the Lake of the Woods, because they had been scared by being told that the French wanted to eat them."[44] Given that coureurs de bois circulating in the West had essentially armed and purportedly encouraged the Dakota to attack the Nakoda, it was no wonder that they were reluctant to establish contact with La Vérendrye. In other words, the coureurs de bois' interest in trading with the Dakota conflicted with Beauharnois's overarching strategy to build a grand western alliance with the Dakota, Cree, Ojibwe, Monsoni, and Nakoda to secure safe passage for French trade and exploration.[45]

In support of La Vérendrye's enterprise, Governor Beauharnois instigated a synchronized plan to promote a French-mediated peace west of Lake Superior. In the eighteenth century, the main principle of French imperial policy was to enforce such a peace, sometimes referred to as a *Pax Gallica*, among all France's Indigenous allies. La Vérendrye established Fort Saint-Pierre (1731) at Rainy Lake, Fort Saint-Charles (1732) at Lake of the Woods, and Fort Maurepas (1734) at Lake Winnipeg, squarely in the territory of the Crees and Monsonis, which in theory would prevent them from raiding the Dakota and Zhaagawaamikong-Ojibwe. Conversely, Beauharnois directed other Troupes de la Marine officers, who managed the posts in Sioux Country and on the southern shores of Lake Superior, to prevent the eastern Dakota and Zhaagawaamikong-Ojibwe from attacking Cree and Monsoni villages in the proximity of La Vérendrye's newly established Western Posts. Beauharnois failed to realize that these thinly garrisoned outposts would not be able to mitigate violence in the borderlands between these two warring factions. In fact, French posts in the western interior actually provided the commercial infrastructure for a violent confrontation between the Cree-Monsoni-Nakoda and the Dakota-Zhaagawaamikong-Ojibwe coalitions, and the officers who garrisoned them were mostly relegated to the role of passive witnesses to the unfolding events in the Hudson Bay watershed, albeit through a French colonial lens.

The Western Posts allowed Crees and Monsonis to enlist French help in the ongoing war against the Očhéthi Šakówiŋ. Even in the short time it had taken the French to establish themselves at Rainy Lake and Lake of the Woods, several southbound war parties moved against the Dakota and their allies with French-manufactured arms and munitions in hand. In the first weeks of the summer of 1733, three hundred Monsoni warriors struck out southwest from Lake of the Woods via the Warroad River (at present-day Warroad, Minnesota) onto the prairie parkland. Shortly after stowing their birchbark canoes at the forks of the Warroad River, they met and clashed with some Dakota and Ojibwes from Zhaagawaamikong.[46] For the Monsoni, the presence of Anishinaabe doodemag accompanying Dakota thióšpayes (extended family groups) into this region was a troubling new development. To safeguard their interests on the Prairies and in the western Great Lakes, as well as to protect their position within the French-Indigenous alliance system, the Monsoni would have to fight fellow Anishinaabeg. In the same season, a Cree expedition of five hundred warriors made it much further onto the Prairies; they marched for twenty days to the southwest before clashing with an opposing Očhéthi Šakówiŋ expedition, inflicting some casualties, and then effectuating a hasty retreat. Given the distance of the march, this engagement may have taken place as far west as the banks of the James River, in present-day North Dakota.[47]

While La Vérendrye spent much of his time at his main headquarters of Fort Saint-Charles trying to manage the complexities of Indigenous alliances and fruitlessly pursuing a "middle ground," his son Jean-Baptiste and nephew La Jemerais explored and surveyed the land for the best strategic sites for future posts. During Jean-Baptiste and La Jemerais's reconnoiter, the Nakoda came forward, with the help of their Cree allies, to make an alliance with La Vérendrye's family, overcoming their initial fear of the French. Despite a language barrier, the Siouan-speaking Nakoda had been stalwart allies of the Algonquian-speaking Cree since at least the mid-seventeenth century, when they began appearing in Jesuit and HBC records.[48] Dakota raiding parties had vigorously assailed the Nakoda since the early 1720s, as evidenced by HBC records and Lakota winter counts. The Nakoda were eager to acquire direct access to firearms and iron weapons. When Jean-Baptiste and La Jemerais first encountered a group of sixty Nakoda in 1733, they observed that only about half of the male warriors carried muskets, with the rest brandishing bows and arrows.[49] The Nakoda sought to lure the French westward in the hope that they would establish posts in their territories southwest of Lake Winnipeg in the watersheds of the Assiniboine and Souris Rivers, as well as on the aspen parkland of southwestern Manitoba.[50]

Despite some initial difficulties, La Vérendrye had established three posts in the Hudson Bay watershed by 1734, not because Indigenous peoples recognized French sovereignty and protection, but rather because local Indigenous peoples saw the benefits of having French trading partners in their homelands. Buying into a French illusion of empire, La Vérendrye and his fellow Frenchmen welcomed Crees, Monsonis, and Nakoda as children of "Onontio" and as clients of the French king. In the East, Iroquoian-speaking peoples had nicknamed New France's governor "Onontio," or "Great Mountain," which was the literal translation of the name of the first governor, Charles Jacques

Huault de Montmagny (1636–48).[51] In the pays d'en haut, the French believed that they had built a French-Indigenous alliance system binding several Algonquian, Iroquoian, and Siouan peoples through "their common standing as children of Onontio, who was the representative of the French king."[52] However, French, Algonquian, Iroquoian, and Siouan peoples all had radically different conceptions of what it meant to be a good father. In French society, a father was the *pater familias*, the oldest living male in a family, who exercised autocratic authority and demanded unwavering obedience. For the French, all authority was patriarchal, from God the Father, to the king (the father of his people), to the father of an individual household. Fathers commanded, and sons obeyed.[53] In many Indigenous societies, however, a father was kind, generous, and protecting; a child owed a father respect, but a father could not compel unwavering obedience.[54] At the end of the day, Onontio and his so-called children were forced to try and reconcile very different understandings of the role and responsibility of the father. On the "Native ground," as ethnohistorian Kathleen DuVal has observed, "European colonialism met neither accommodation nor resistance but incorporation."[55] While La Vérendrye failed to subjugate Crees, Monsonis, and Nakoda as obedient "children" of Onontio and as subjects or clients of the French king, he himself was incorporated into pre-existing Indigenous social and cultural categories of the "Native ground."

As it turned out, from an Indigenous perspective, La Vérendrye's search for the Western Sea was not the most important thing happening in the Hudson Bay watershed at this time. Rather, Crees, Monsonis, and Nakoda recognized La Vérendrye's arrival and the establishment of the Western Posts as an opportunity to further their own geopolitical agendas in a contested borderland. This Cree-Monsoni-Nakoda coalition was one of the most powerful emerging Indigenous polities west of the Great Lakes, and their exploitation of the French would allow them to shape their foreign policies and wartime strategies according to the shifting realties of eighteenth-century North America.

IMPLICATING THE FRENCH, 1734–35

In 1734, Cree and Monsoni leaders pressured La Vérendrye into allowing his son Jean-Baptiste to accompany a raiding party against the Yankton and Yanktonai. At first, this seemed like a reasonable compromise since the violence would be redirected toward the western prairie parkland and away from the Upper Mississippi, which La Vérendrye believed would prevent a rupture in the French-Indigenous alliance system operating in the western Great Lakes. Such a course of action, however, still threatened to antagonize the Dakota, who were related to the Yankton and Yanktonai.[56] This was the first in a series of critical mistakes and mishaps for the French. La Vérendrye also feared for his son's life; as he put it in his journal from this time, "Who could tell whether my son would ever return?"[57] La Vérendrye worried that the French would lose face with their potential allies if he refused to let his son accompany the Cree and Monsoni, noting that "there was much reason to fear that they would attribute [a refusal] to fear and take the French for cowards, with the result of their shaking off the French yoke."[58] La Vérendrye might have assumed that that Cree and Monsoni leaders were testing his family's military prowess and martial valour so as to evaluate whether the French made suitable allies.[59] La Vérendrye confessed to Beauharnois that he was "cruelly tormented by conflicting thoughts."[60] La Vérendrye therefore turned to his most experienced voyageurs: "In this dilemma, I consulted all the most intelligent Frenchmen of my post and those best able to give advice. They were all of opinion that I should grant the request of the savages, and even pressed me to do so. They said that my son would not be the first Frenchman who had gone with savages to war."[61] La Vérendrye's veteran voyageurs had likely already fought alongside Natives. Indeed, accompanying Indigenous allies on a raid against their enemies was clearly old hat for some Canadiens at Fort Saint-Charles, as some of the men even offered to escort Jean-Baptiste, who for his part greatly desired to go.[62]

Realizing this cultural imperative, La Vérendrye allowed the twenty-year-old Jean-Baptiste to accompany the expedition alone. To express his approval, La Vérendrye fumbled his way through a ceremony in which he "sang the war chant" with axe in hand.[63] With Jean-Baptiste translating for his father, La Vérendrye gave "a brief account of the manner of making war in France, where men did not fight behind trees but in open country, etc. I showed them the wounds I had received in the battle of Malplaquet, which astonished them."[64] Twenty-five years earlier, La Vérendrye had been left for dead on the Flemish battlefield of Malplaquet after suffering a severe gunshot wound and eight sabre cuts. The victorious English had thereafter taken him prisoner for a year. Drawing from his own wartime experiences, La Vérendrye endeavoured to appeal to Cree-Monsoni understandings of warfare and to emulate those attributes in his discourse, though with mixed results. He recounted his own experiences as a soldier in Louis XIV's army to garner Indigenous support for an alliance with the French and to enhance his own reputation as a warrior. La Vérendrye's account of European warfare would have resonated with the Cree and Monsoni, who respected a warrior's combat reputation. His boasting about fighting "not behind trees but in open country," however, would probably not have impressed the Indigenous audience, whose own culture of warfare valued low-casualty encounters.[65]

With the ritual ceremonies completed and the war party ready to depart, a dispute arose between the Crees and Monsonis over Jean-Baptiste. Warriors from both groups seem to have greatly desired to carry him in their canoes. Jean-Baptiste was able to resolve the situation diplomatically by saying, "My brothers, do not be vexed, I beg of you, if I embark with the Cree; we are all marching together; your cabins are mine and we are all one."[66] Jean-Baptiste seemed to have been of paramount importance as a figurehead to both the Cree and Monsoni warriors. Unbeknownst to the French, however, both groups had insisted that Jean-Baptiste accompany the expedition as a stratagem to sever the Očhéthi Šakówiŋ's commercial connection to the French. By implicating Jean-Baptiste in a raid against the Yankton and Yanktonai, the Cree-Monsoni positioned the French as co-belligerents in their war against the Očhéthi Šakówiŋ, thus shaping the contours of the geopolitical landscape of the Hudson Bay watershed.[67]

Jean-Baptiste departed with the Crees and Monsonis from Lake of the Woods via the Warroad River to attack the Yankton and Yanktonai. Unfortunately, only fragmented accounts of the prairie parkland raid survive, but Jean-Baptiste's presence with the Cree-Monsoni expedition was a clear indication that the French supported the war against the Očhéthi Šakówiŋ – a stance that ultimately served to undermine French diplomacy and trade with the Dakota. To further exasperate matters, at some point in the middle of the battle, the beleaguered Yanktons and Yanktonais called out, "Who is killing us?," to which Crees and Monsonis responded, "It is the Frenchman." It was at that moment, Governor Beauharnois later mused, that the Očhéthi Šakówiŋ "resolved on vengeance [against the French], and put into practice all possible means for accomplishing it." [68] With this ruse, Cree and Monsoni leaders had entangled the French as participants in their protracted war with the Očhéthi Šakówiŋ. Jean-Baptiste returned unscathed to his father's headquarters at Fort Saint-Charles after the raid, but his participation would have dire repercussions for the fledgling French presence in the Northwest.

The offensive continued the following year. During the winter of 1735–36, a Jesuit missionary at Fort Saint-Charles, Father Jean-Pierre Aulneau, observed that most of the resident Crees and Monsonis at Lake of the Woods "have been out on a warlike expedition against the Maskoutépoels or Prairie Sioux."[69] As French observers were beginning to learn, when Crees, Monsonis, and Nakoda went to war together, they rendezvoused at a place on the Prairies called "Pointe du Bois." La Vérendrye described Pointe du Bois as "the usual rendezvous for Assiniboine [Nakoda], Cree and Monsoni, distant about fifty leagues from fort St Charles, in order to reach the Sioux [Očhéthi Šakówiŋ]."[70] As the name suggests, the rendezvous was a sheltered wood amid an expansive prairie where warriors could gather covertly, with the treeline providing protection from both the elements and their enemies. According to a contemporary map, Pointe du Bois was located on the western shore of Red Lake, in what is now the state of Minnesota.[71] That winter, Father Aulneau observed that the successful war party returned triumphantly to Fort Saint-Charles having "destroyed a few lodges, and some have returned with a few scalps, which are prized as the most precious trophies of their victories."[72] Yanktonais, Yanktons, and their eastern Dakota kinsmen now resolved to retaliate against the Monsoni, Cree, Nakoda, and French for the series of raids that had occurred in 1733, 1734, and 1735.

THE LAKE OF THE WOODS RAID AND ITS AFTERMATH, 1736–40

In 1736, many Dakota, Yankton, and Yanktonai bands converged on Lake of the Woods and Rainy Lake to retaliate against the Cree, Monsoni, and French for the raids conducted in the previous years. Most significantly, the Očhéthi Šakówiŋ wanted revenge for the attack in which the French were most explicitly involved – the expedition that Jean-Baptiste had accompanied two years earlier, in 1734. The fact that Jean-Baptiste had fought alongside Crees and Monsonis clearly signalled to the Očhéthi Šakówiŋ that the French were now also their enemies. In Cree society, military participation and political leadership were inexorably linked. A male warrior who refused to participate in raids would be socially ostracized and denied a voice in councils.[73] And as we saw, La Vérendrye, recognizing these cultural imperatives, believed that he had had no choice but to allow his son to accompany the 1734 war party against the Očhéthi Šakówiŋ. This had been a critical mistake for the French. The increased presence of Canadien merchants throughout the Rainy Lake and Lake of the Woods districts also alarmed the Dakota, who feared that the French were arming their enemies. La Vérendrye's actions, both political and commercial, had further entangled the French in the Cree-Monsoni conflict with the Dakota.

On 5 June 1736, an Očhéthi Šakówiŋ raiding party composed of thirty canoes carrying between ninety and a hundred warriors captured René Bourassa, a Montreal merchant, at Lake of the Woods and pillaged his wares. The Dakota complained "that they had a grievance against the French for distributing arms to their enemies wherewith to kill them."[74] Bourassa later described his captors as "Prairie Sioux" (Yankton and Yanktonai) and "Lake Sioux" (Dakota).[75] The Očhéthi Šakówiŋ warriors tied Bourassa to a pole and prepared to torture him and then burn him at the stake. However, Bourassa's Dakota slave, a young woman, pleaded for his life, and indicated that there was a much worthier target nearby in the form of Jean-Baptiste de La Vérendrye, who had just departed Fort Saint-Charles bound for Michilimackinac.[76] The Očhéthi Šakówiŋ war party headed to intercept Jean-Baptiste's fur brigade, which was only one day out from Fort Saint-Charles. The French were making their way east through the sheltered waterways between what is now known as the Aulneau Peninsula to the north and Big Island to the south.

The following morning, a hundred Očhéthi Šakówiŋ warriors surrounded Jean-Baptiste, along with Jesuit missionary Father Aulneau and nineteen voyageurs, on a small island on Lake of the Woods. Jean-Baptiste and his voyageurs were outnumbered at least five to one, but they were well-armed with knives, axes, firearms, powder, and shot. They held the heights of the island, a rocky outcropping well above the shoreline that provided a defensible position with a commanding view of the lake. Despite their stout resistance, however, the Dakota ultimately overwhelmed Jean-Baptiste and his men, killing, mutilating, and scalping all twenty-one Frenchmen.[77]

Indigenous warriors, including those from Algonquian and Siouan societies, regularly took war trophies as symbols of status and prestige. Scalps offered a tangible token of a warrior's bravery and prowess on the field of battle. Returning to one's home community with scalps clearly demonstrated that a warrior had killed opponents in battle, while also serving as confirmation of a successful raid into enemy territory.[78]

La Vérendrye, alarmed at rumours of a Dakota war party prowling Lake of the Woods, dispatched a small search party from Fort Saint-Charles, "a canoe with a crew of eight men commanded by a sergeant," to look for his son's fur brigade. A parent's worst fears were realized when the party located the slain Frenchmen on what henceforth came to be known as Île du Massacre (Massacre Island). A colonial report described the grisly aftermath of the battle: "The heads [of the Frenchmen] were placed on beaver robes, most of them scalped; the missionary had one knee on the ground, an arrow in his side, his breast split open, his left hand against the ground, his right hand raised. The Sieur de la Vérendrye [Jean-Baptiste] was lying on his face, his back all scored with knife cuts, a stake thrust into his side, headless."[79] The Dakota had wrapped the decapitated heads in beaver robes to mock the French love for beaver. It was a violent reprisal for their having taken sides and disturbing the balance of power by meddling in regional Indigenous geopolitics. Yet, as ethnohistorian Gary Clayton Anderson has observed, La Vérendrye and the French "seemed oblivious to the impact their growing commercial system was having on intertribal relations."[80] The Lake of the Woods raid had dire ramifications for French colonial policy in the Hudson Bay watershed. Crees, Monsonis, and later Nakoda had drawn La Vérendrye and his surviving sons into a destructive pattern of raiding and warfare to retaliate against the Dakota for the Lake of the Woods raid.

Following the raid, La Vérendrye, fearing an imminent Dakota attack, had "fort Saint-Charles rebuilt and put it in such a condition that four men could defend it against a hundred."[81] It is unclear if La Vérendrye actually believed that the modest Fort Saint-Charles would be able to hold out against a hundred-man Dakota assault, but the comment helps to illustrate his anxiety that the official French presence northwest of Lake Superior was on the verge of collapse. The Dakota threat continued to loom until the onset of winter. Voyageurs and soldiers at Fort Saint-Charles refused to retrieve a package of goods cached at the Savanne portage, near Lake of the Woods, until the lakes and rivers had frozen over.[82] They knew that winter conditions would preclude Dakota raiding parties from travelling efficiently via canoe; the Dakota also traditionally retired to winter hunting camps, far away from Lake of the Woods. Until then, however, fear paralyzed all summertime operations at the Western Posts.

Following the Dakota raid at Lake of the Woods in 1736, defence of Fort Beauharnois, in the Upper Mississippi valley, became untenable. Jacques Legardeur de Saint-Pierre, the fort's commandant from 1734 to 1737, wrote that a Dakota chief with three young warriors, "one of whom had a silver seal hung from his ear," appeared one day.[83] Saint-Pierre demanded to know where the young warrior had acquired the token, but the Dakota responded only with mocking laughter. Enraged, Saint-Pierre ripped the ornament from the Dakota's ear and barred him from entering the fort.[84] The Dakota warrior had acquired the Jesuit seal (with its telltale "IHS" monogram surmounted by a cross) as a war trophy from Father Aulneau, whom the Dakota had slain in the Lake of the Woods raid.[85]

Saint-Pierre soon learned that the Lake of the Woods raid was not an isolated incident; the Dakota had killed and scalped two French traders at the confluence of the Mississippi and Illinois Rivers.[86] Saint-Pierre learned that the Dakota were also raiding Ho-Chunk communities in the Fox-Wisconsin watershed, even burning down entire villages.[87] During the fall hunting season, a party of thirty-six Dakota arrived near the French post and burned down a Ho-Chunk stockade.[88] Perhaps most troubling to Saint-Pierre and his French garrison was the fact that Dakota warriors partook in scalp dance ceremonies outside the fort's palisade, "without saying what Nations they had killed."[89] Peering at the scalps hanging outside the fort, Saint-Pierre and his men would have pondered if the Dakota had slain even more Frenchmen. When Saint-Pierre queried an important Dakota chief, Oüakantapé (Sacred Born), why his people continued to insult the French, he replied coldly that all had been done with the utmost "reflection and design."[90] In 1727, Oüakantapé had welcomed the French and solidified fictive bonds of kinship with Troupes de la Marine officers and Jesuits at Saint Anthony Falls, on the Upper Mississippi (Minneapolis, Minnesota), but now he reproached the French, asserted Dakota sovereignty, and deliberately broke those bonds of kinship.[91]

The Dakota were divided over the merits of having a French post in their country. They certainly valued French goods, but they already had access to coureurs de bois circulating throughout the west. In addition, Fort Beauharnois brought the trespassing children of Onontio – and particularly the Ho-Chunk – to Dakota territory and hunting grounds. When the French had first established Fort Beauharnois on the Upper Mississippi in 1727, they were followed into the region by eighty lodges of Ho-Chunks, who were eager to use the French commercial centre and the adjacent Dakota lands to advance their own economic well-being.[92] Pursuant to the attacks on the Ho-Chunk, the Dakota also terminated their alliance with the Zhaagawaamikong-Ojibwe. The reason for this schism is unclear, but it quite possibly resulted from the refusal of the Zhaagawaamikong-Ojibwe to participate in the Lake of the Woods raid against the French; they may not have been willing to sever their kinship connection with Onontio and their other Ojibwe kinsmen at Kaministiquia and the Monsoni (an Anishinaabe doodem̍) at Rainy Lake. The Zhaagawaamikong-Ojibwe then joined the northern Cree-Monsoni-Nakoda coalition and began to organize raiding parties against the Dakota, their former allies, as part of the coalition's retaliation for the Lake of the Woods raid. The Dakota did not break off their alliances with the Zhaagawaamikong-Ojibwe, Ho-Chunk, and French without serious contemplation and forethought. Beginning in the early eighteenth century, the Očhéthi Šakówiŋ's power base was establishing itself more concretely in the west. Large numbers of Očhéthi Šakówiŋ thióšpayes migrated deep into the West in pursuit of bison herds, whose population had grown impressively during a particularly wet period on the Great Plains.[93] The Dakota had terminated their alliances with the Zhaagawaamikong-Ojibwe, Ho-Chunk, and French knowing full well that their strength lay in that direction.

Troubled by these events, as well as by increasing warfare between Dakota, Ho-Chunks, and Ojibwes, Saint-Pierre held an assembly with René Godefroy, sieur de Linctot (his second-in-command), Jesuit father Michel Guignas, and the other Frenchmen at the post to determine the next course of action. The French merchants, voyageurs, and soldiers all pleaded with Saint-Pierre that they had no other choice but to abandon the post since every day they ran the risk of Dakota attacks.[94] Saint-Pierre patiently listened to his men, and on 30 May 1737, the French abandoned Fort Beauharnois and fled Sioux Country. The French withdrawal from the Upper Mississippi valley represented the end of the French-Dakota alliance and signalled to Crees, Monsonis, and Nakoda that they could retaliate for the Lake of the Woods raid without endangering their alliance with the French.

Beauharnois, however, realized that the French colonial government was in no position to retaliate against the Dakota. The majority of New France's fighting forces (in both Canada and Louisiana) were engaged in a disastrous campaign against the Chickasaw in 1736.[95]

Beauharnois simply did not have the manpower or the munitions for a punitive campaign against the Očhéthi Šakówiŋ, a social formation that, as the French were now beginning to understand, was one of the most populous in North America.[96] In the early eighteenth century, the Očhéthi Šakówiŋ encompassed somewhere between 24,000 and 30,000 people.[97] The most pragmatic course of action was reconciliation. This would not have been unprecedented; on the margins of empire, the French were often humiliated and forced to offer a tentative peace or general pardon to their Indigenous enemies, as had been the case in the concluding years of the Fox Wars.[98] Since the Great Peace of Montreal, colonial policy in North America had largely been to mediate disputes and to maintain peace among France's Indigenous trading partners and military allies in the pays d'en haut.[99]

Although grief-stricken by the death of his eldest son, La Vérendrye followed Beauharnois's directives and harangued Cree, Monsoni, and Nakoda leaders to make peace with the Dakota to prevent further bloodshed and the spread of warfare throughout the region. And yet La Vérendrye's behaviour and refusal to avenge the deaths of his fellow Frenchmen frustrated Cree, Monsoni, and Nakoda chiefs because it went against their own cultural axioms, which mandated the consideration of honour, prestige, and vengeance. Indigenous leaders expected La Vérendrye to avenge his son as well as the other Frenchmen. In addition, La Vérendrye's call for restraint denied the Cree, Monsoni, and Nakoda an excuse to execute their own long-term plans to make war on the Dakota with the help of their French allies, who, as per alliance and kinship obligations, would have naturally provided gifts of tobacco, weapons, firearms, and other goods.[100]

Still reeling from the Lake of the Woods raid, Cree and Monsoni deputies at Fort Saint-Charles told La Vérendrye that they "were weeping incessantly day and night" for the death of his son, "whom they had adopted as chief of the two nations."[101] Similarly, Crees from Lake Winnipeg asked La Vérendrye to let them know when he intended "to go and avenge the blood of the French," and particularly that of Jean-Baptiste, "whom they had adopted as their chief," and "whose death they had all never ceased to bewail."[102] As this rhetoric would indicate, Indigenous peoples were using Jean-Baptiste's death as the necessary catalyst for the escalation of warfare against the Dakota. The Nakoda had also adopted Jean-Baptiste for the role that he had played in the establishment of Fort Maurepas, in the vicinity of Lake Winnipeg.[103] Thus, La Vérendrye was not only refusing to avenge the deaths of Frenchmen – he was refusing to avenge the death of his own son, who had become a figure of paramount importance in Cree, Monsoni, and Nakoda society. Throughout the summer, Crees, Monsonis, and Nakoda arrived weekly at Fort Saint-Charles seeking to assemble war parties to go avenge Jean-Baptiste's death. As La Vérendrye later reported, one group of Crees and Monsonis proposed placing him "at their head and go to avenge the death of my son and the other Frenchmen."[104] In another instance, a prominent leader of the alliance assured La Vérendrye that "they were all ready to move against the enemy, and asked me for vengeance."[105] La Colle, a Monsoni *ogimaa* (leader), was foremost among Indigenous warriors in lamenting Jean-Baptiste's death, insisting to La Vérendrye that "he did not cease to weep for my son and all the Frenchmen, that the lake was still red with their blood, which cried for vengeance."[106] La Vérendrye refused these overtures, however, and fell in line with French colonial policy. What kind of father and leader was La Vérendrye, his Indigenous allies demanded to know, if he did not march to war to avenge the death of his own son? And with hundreds of brave warriors from three different nations at his disposal? La Colle berated La Vérendrye for his lack of action and denied him a place at the war council, saying, "It is no longer you who are taking any part in it [the war]; it is I and the chiefs of the three tribes."[107]

In the aftermath of the Lake of the Woods raid, Crees, Monsonis, and Nakoda took advantage of a moment of crisis to assert their own interests and to further entangle La Vérendrye and the French in their conflict with the Dakota. Although they knew they could not count on the French to provide soldiers, they hoped for material support in the form of presents from Onontio to combat the Dakota. It became clear that La Vérendrye had been strategically outmanoeuvred by those he sought to bring under French dominion. He had struggled to navigate the complex Indigenous geopolitical landscape of the Hudson Bay watershed; he had at the very least failed to foresee the imperial repercussions of his actions. The decision to send Jean-Baptiste to accompany the raid in 1734 prompted a Dakota response in 1736, which ultimately rendered the French presence in Sioux Country untenable. Jacques Legardeur de Saint-Pierre's hasty retreat from the region in 1737 had opened the door for Crees, Monsonis, and Nakoda to retaliate against the Dakota without risking accidental French casualties. These Indigenous peoples used Jean-Baptiste's death as a pretext to justify a fresh round of violence and warfare against the Dakota.

In the years following the Lake of the Woods raid, Troupes de la Marine officers throughout the western Great Lakes and the Hudson Bay watershed sought to smooth relations between warring Indigenous coalitions. Despite these efforts, the Cree, Monsoni, and Nakoda, led by a prominent Monsoni ogimaa named La Colle, waged what they deemed to be a retaliatory war against the Dakota. At La Pointe on Lake Superior, Louis Denys de La Ronde wrote that "War has raged very bitterly, and the Sioux [Dakota] have killed more than thirty persons."[108] When La Ronde admonished the local Ojibwe leaders for attacking the Dakota, they replied that they had wished to avenge the deaths of "the 22 Frenchmen in the North."[109] News of the Lake of the Woods raid spread from the Hudson Bay watershed to the western Great Lakes, reaching a variety of Indigenous peoples who then used it as a pretext to attack the Dakota. At French posts, such as La Pointe and Kaministiquia, Indigenous orators and war chiefs used the Lake of the Woods raid to rally Ojibwe, Cree, Monsoni, and Nakoda warriors, as well as to elicit presents of weaponry from French commandants.

LA COLLE'S RAID AND INDIGENOUS SLAVERY, 1741–43

In 1741, La Colle declared to the French in no uncertain terms that "the Sioux were only good to be eaten," and that he wanted to "kill enough of them to feed his villages."[110] La Colle united Native peoples from western Lake Superior, Lake of the Woods, and Lake Winnipeg and led them on a devastating raid that resulted in the killing of seventy Dakota warriors and the capture of two hundred slaves.[111] Under La Colle's leadership two hundred Crees, Monsonis, and Nakoda warriors invaded Sioux Country, fought the enemy for four days straight, and lost only six warriors in the melee. Victorious, La Colle's expedition marched the captives almost five hundred kilometres through a country of rivers and lakes full of gnawing horseflies and mosquitoes to Fort Saint-Charles, where some of the captives would be sold to the French as slaves. La Colle's arrival at the fort would have been a sight to behold as allegedly the captives "occupied in their [single file] march more than four arpents," or nearly eight hundred feet.[112] That year, Beauharnois, who described La Colle as a decisive man of great influence, remarked that "there will be more slaves than packages [of fur]."[113] In light of La Colle's decisive blow against the Očhéthi Šakówiŋ, a Jesuit missionary sent to replace the slain Father Aulneau described him as "a man of resolution whose intrepidity makes an impression on others."[114] Even La Colle's name (which La Vérendrye might have translated from Anishinaabemowin into French) literally means "The Glue" in English.[115] Clearly, the role that the Monsoni ogimaa played in uniting Monsonis, Crees, and Nakoda into a coalition powerful enough to challenge the Dakota and their allies was not altogether lost on the French. In the aftermath of the Lake of the Woods raid, La Colle had emerged as a principal figure who sought "to go and avenge the French blood that had been spilt."[116]

Historical geographer Paul Hackett posits that La Colle's slave raid may have been a response to a deadly 1737–39 smallpox epidemic in the Rainy Lake district. Similar to the Haudenosaunee cultural practice of the mourning war to cope with population decline, Hackett suggests that Monsonis may have gone on military expeditions to capture enemy women and children to replace those lost in the epidemic.[117] La Colle likely saw Dakota captives as a means to "requicken" the dead and to replenish a population recently depleted by smallpox. La Colle also gifted male Dakota captives to the French in order to solidify the alliance with his European counterparts and to elicit trade goods.

La Vérendrye, while he pleaded with La Colle not to go to war against the Dakota, was not above accepting Dakota war captives as slaves to relieve his considerable debt (a daunting 40,000 livres), which he had amassed in order to fund the enterprise in the first place. Struggling to adhere to Beauharnois's directives, by the 1740s La Vérendrye was voraciously acquiring Indigenous slaves, who were shipped via Michilimackinac and sold at Montreal.[118]

La Vérendrye's sons followed suit and participated in the Indigenous slave trade. Louis-Joseph Gaultier de La Vérendrye, who went by the moniker "the Chevalier," was La Vérendrye's youngest and most well-educated son, having spent a year at Quebec receiving rigorous scientific training in mathematics and cartography. Like his father, Louis-Joseph was a proficient slave trader.[119] The Sainte-Anne's parish registry at Michilimackinac records that in 1750, Father Pierre Du Jaunay "solemnly baptized in the church of this mission, jean françois Regis, a young slave about seven years old, given to this mission last year out of gratitude by Mr. the Chevalier de La Vérendrye on his return from the extreme West."[120] At Michilimackinac in 1754, Father Marin-Louis

Le Franc had baptized another one of Louis-Joseph's slaves, a seventeen-year-old Native boy named Joseph.[121] When Louis-Joseph boarded the *Auguste* in 1761 to go to France after the British conquest of Canada, he brought his Indigenous slave Étienne with him.[122]

The exchange of captives was a symbolically powerful gesture used by many Native peoples to define the parameters of their alliances with each other, and by extension with European newcomers. Brett Rushforth has argued that the French-Native slave trade was derived from Indigenous customs of forging friendships and alliances.[123] Captives were symbolically powerful gifts because they signified the opposite of warfare, "the giving rather than the taking of life."[124] Thus, the slave trade became a useful symbolic exchange in the consolidation of alliances. Starting in the early eighteenth century, however, traders, prominent merchants, and colonial officials began to acquire Native slaves. These slaves, originally exchanged as a symbolic representation of flesh and life, were eventually purchased by various traders and artisans in Montreal and Quebec, both as labourers and as domestic servants.[125]

The Indigenous peoples of the Hudson Bay watershed capitalized on French demand and a growing market for slaves to define their own position within the French alliance system. Crees, Monsonis, and Nakoda were able to employ slavery as a device to prevent the French from achieving any sort of reconciliation with the Dakota of the Upper Mississippi valley. Certainly, the Dakota would have been unwilling or unable to become one of Onontio's children with the knowledge that he held a great number of their own kin as slaves. La Vérendrye benefited economically from the slave trade, but his participation in it also ensured that he would be unable to broker a peace with the Dakota. The Dakota interpreted the La Vérendrye family's acceptance of Dakota captives as an act of French aggression toward them. In this way, the Cree, Monsoni, and Nakoda effectively used slavery to block the French alliance with the Dakota.[126]

Beauharnois was horrified. He recognized that the purchase of Dakota slaves by Frenchmen would further endanger the lives of colonial officials and traders in the Hudson Bay watershed. Beauharnois dispatched orders to Michilimackinac forbidding the purchase of any more Dakota slaves: "You will positively forbid, sir, all the Frenchmen of Your post to buy any Indian slave from the Assiniboines [Nakoda], it being of Infinite consequence for the colony to prevent this trade. Thus, I order you to see it consistently that does not happen, and in case you learn that there might be several at your post, you will make the decision that you Deem the most appropriate for having them sent back to Their home."[127] La Vérendrye disregarded the orders and continued exporting Dakota slaves to Montreal via Michilimackinac. In a later report to the governor, he even went so far as to boast of the slaves he had obtained for the colony.[128] Brett Rushforth nonetheless observes that "La Vérendrye never acknowledged his own culpability" in the slave trade. Moreover, it seems that he never stopped selling Indigenous slaves at Michilimackinac.[129] Another Troupes de la Marine officer, Paul Marin de La Malgue, who was commandant at Green Bay, reported to Beauharnois that La Vérendrye had sold him two Dakota slaves. Beauharnois responded with explicit orders for Marin to return the slaves to their proper villages.[130] At Michilimackinac, Troupes de la Marine officer Jean Jarret de Verchères also followed Beauharnois's orders and returned two Dakota slaves that La Vérendrye had sold to him.[131]

In 1742, Dakota delegates travelled to Montreal with Paul Marin de La Malgue, who was sympathetic to their cause. At Montreal, Mdewakanton Dakota chief Oüakantapé met with Governor Beauharnois and complained of incessant and unrelenting attacks by "Outa8acs, Sauteux, and other Nations," who had killed "more than 160 men, without counting the women and children," the previous spring.[132] While the Očhéthi Šakówiŋ had confidently attacked the French at Lake of the Woods in 1736, the Mdewakanton and other eastern Dakota oyátes – Sisseton, Wahpeton, and Whapekute – now realized that they had few friends left in the Lake Superior watershed and would benefit from French intercession to retain control over the Upper Mississippi valley. If the French wished to maintain any semblance of a relationship with the Dakota, they had to halt these attacks immediately. Of course, Indigenous peoples were sovereign polities, and while New France's governor could give them advice, he could not coercively control their actions.

While visiting Montreal, Oüakantapé and the other Dakota delegates were aggrieved to see many of their Očhéthi Šakówiŋ kinsmen enslaved as domestic labourers, dock loaders, millers, shop workers, and tradesmen in the bustling fur trade settlement. Wishing to placate his grief-stricken guests, the governor reluctantly returned some slaves to the Dakota, which was not an easy task considering that slavery had been legalized in New France in 1709. Even Governor

Beauharnois, who was himself complicit in Indigenous slavery, had difficulty rectifying slaveholders' claims on Natives as property with the efforts to reconstitute an alliance with the Očhéthi Šakówiŋ, which mandated a more flexible exchange of captives and slaves than French property law would allow. In other words, Beauharnois could not force colonists to give up their legally protected slave property without considerable effort – either compensating or coercing them to do so.[133] Beauharnois allowed four Dakota slaves to return with Oüakantapé, "to make them feel the compassion that the French had for them."[134] Beauharnois promised to return the remaining slaves if the Dakota kept their pledge to cease hostilities and returned to Montreal the following year with another peaceful delegation.[135]

Conspicuously absent from the Montreal peace conference were Cree, Monsoni, and Nakoda delegates.[136] Despite the absence of representatives from the Western Posts, Beauharnois assured the Dakota that he had "for a long time now ... been sending an officer [La Vérendrye] with Frenchmen to the Crees, Monsonis, and Assiniboines [Nakoda] to tell them my word ... that they make peace with you."[137] This was at best an extreme exaggeration, at worst an outright lie, because in spite of Beauharnois's orders, La Vérendrye was actively thwarting the peace process by continuing to promote and participate in the trade of Dakota slaves brought to him by his Cree, Monsoni, and Nakoda allies. As the Dakota delegation was departing, Beauharnois gave Marin orders to emancipate and return to Oüakantapé any slaves who had been captured in La Colle's raid and were being shipped by the French to Montreal for sale.[138] Beauharnois's confidence in La Vérendrye had been shattered. La Vérendrye had chosen immediate profit over French imperial interests. In other words, he had acted like a coureur de bois, but without the proper insight and wherewithal that came with experience and well-established kinship relations in the Hudson Bay watershed. La Vérendrye had ignored Beauharnois's orders and embraced the financially lucrative Indigenous slave trade, which ultimately threatened French plans for alliances and imperial expansion throughout the western Great Lakes and the Hudson Bay watershed.

As minister of the marine and colonies, Maurepas had consistently accused La Vérendrye of being more interested in profit than exploration, noting his preoccupation with finding a "sea of beaver" rather than the Western Sea.[139] At first, Beauharnois defended La Vérendrye against these accusations, noting that after "twelve years spent at these posts," La Vérendrye had accumulated considerable debt in order to fund the enterprise in the first place.[140] In response to Maurepas's accusations, La Vérendrye himself opined that, "if debts that I have on my shoulders to the amount of more than forty thousand livres are an advantage, I can flatter myself that I am very rich."[141] However, it was for precisely these reasons that La Vérendrye ignored French colonial policy in the first place and neglected his explorations. The La Vérendrye family's relentless pursuit of the slave trade ultimately prevented French imperial sovereignty from being actualized in the Hudson Bay watershed, which was what the Cree-Monsoni-Nakoda coalition had intended to prevent in the first place.

CONCLUSION

Starting in the 1730s, Governor Beauharnois took an interest in French imperial expansion in the Upper Mississippi valley and the Hudson Bay watershed. Beauharnois attempted to reorient French imperialism away from Canadiens. This shift sought to restore authority to those who wielded the levers of power in New France – governors, Troupes de la Marine officers, and other members of the military elite. This change in policy, however, brought the French no closer to realizing imperial sovereignty in the Hudson Bay watershed.

Beauharnois granted his client La Vérendrye an important commission as the first commandant of the Western Posts. Because of the conflict between the Cree, Monsoni, Nakoda, Ojibwe, and Dakota, La Vérendrye failed to implement the French colonial policy of *Pax Gallica*, preferring instead to participate in the Native slave trade to alleviate his crippling financial debts. La Vérendrye's own lack of understanding of western Indigenous affairs prevented him from navigating an increasingly delicate geopolitical situation. Vaudreuil and later Beauharnois had made efforts to establish good relations with Dakota bands in the early eighteenth century, only to have these relations subsequently destroyed by La Vérendrye's commercial activities and slave trading at the Western Posts.

La Vérendrye pursued commercial policies that horrified his Troupes de la Marine contemporaries, like Paul Marin de La Malgue and Jean Jarret de Verchères, who recognized that the French enslavement of Dakota captives would prevent any rapprochement between the French and Dakota. La Vérendrye's frequent bungling of colonial policy exacerbated regional tensions and undermined French attempts to assert authority at the Western Posts, or any form of sovereignty in the Hudson Bay watershed, for that matter. La Vérendrye's mistakes and miscalculations came at a crucial moment in French-Indigenous diplomacy, thereby resulting in a missed opportunity. French elites would ultimately fail as architects or builders of empire in the Hudson Bay watershed. As the following chapter will explore, however, Canadien voyageurs and coureurs de bois continued to prove crucial to the maintenance of a French presence in the Hudson Bay watershed.

4

Canadiens at the Western Posts, 1731–1743

René Bourassa *dit* La Ronde was tremendously lucky – indeed much luckier than any other Canadien who had been caught in the open at Lake of the Woods by Dakota warriors on 5 and 6 June 1736: he survived to live another day. When Dakota warriors captured Bourassa and were preparing to torture and put him to death, Bourassa's female Dakota slave interceded on his behalf, calling out to the warriors to spare his life and urging them to attack Jean-Baptiste de La Vérendrye instead, who she proclaimed was a much worthier target for their martial prowess.[1] In the spring of 1737 Bourassa went east to Michilimackinac and then on to Montreal. Although the Bourassa family would eventually make Michilimackinac their home in the 1740s, for the time being, they called the parish of La Prairie, on the south shore opposite Ville-Marie, home.[2] René Bourassa was well-known in the Saint Lawrence valley, the pays d'en haut, and the Haudenosaunee borderlands, especially Mohawk territory, which spanned New France to New York via the Richelieu and Hudson Rivers. Bourassa was a notorious coureur de bois who had been caught by French officials smuggling furs between Montreal and Albany, New York, in July 1722, a crime for which he had been fined five hundred livres. In 1729, Bourassa colluded with Montreal's governor, Charles Le Moyne de Longueuil, to smuggle furs to British colonial markets under the guise of an intercolonial letter delivery to New England.[3] It was not uncommon for colonial officials to be involved in the illicit trade. For example, Governor Frontenac had been a known patron of opportunistic coureurs de bois like Daniel Greysolon Du Lhut. In 1725, Longueuil was passed over for promotion to the position of governor general of Canada, so he would have been especially ambivalent about enforcing strict colonial policy under Beauharnois, whom he saw as a metropolitan upstart with no real knowledge of the colonial milieu.[4]

Longueuil passed away in Montreal on 7 June 1729, and thus did not live to see the results of Bourassa's trip.[5] Longueuil, however, had not been the only colonial official to trust Bourassa, and many others – including his rival Governor Beauharnois – trusted and relied upon Bourassa's services and expertise. Placing trust in a mere travelling merchant at first appears out of character for Beauharnois, given his adherence to the precepts of ancien régime social hierarchy (as explored in the previous chapter). But the governor was starting to lose his once unshakable confidence in La Vérendrye, and although still vehemently opposed to the illicit trade, was not above using Canadiens as informants when circumstances warranted. In the spring of 1737, Bourassa reported to Beauharnois on the Lake of the Woods raid. Because the Dakota had taken Bourassa captive, robbed him of his wares, and then released him, he was uniquely positioned to give an account of the composition of the war party. He reported that "Prairie Sioux" (Yankton and Yanktonai), "Lake Sioux" (Mdewakanton, Sisseton, Wahpeton, and Whapekute), as well as some Ojibwes from La Pointe, had participated in the raid. Because of Bourassa's extensive experience trading in the western Great Lakes and the Hudson Bay watershed he was even able to recognize individual members of the raiding party, noting that there were certain Ojibwes present who were "from the post of Monsieur de la Ronde" at La Pointe.[6] Bourassa further explained to Beauharnois "that the Sioux [Dakota, Yankton, and Yanktonai] complained to him that the French furnished arms and munitions to the Cree."[7] In addition to Bourassa, Beauharnois also "inquired from old voyageurs" in Montreal about the identities of the Indigenous peoples who had ostensibly taken part in the attack.[8]

While La Vérendrye seriously considered rallying Cree, Monsoni, and Nakoda warriors to avenge his son's death, Bourassa and other experienced voyageurs perceived colonial policy in the West in more pragmatic terms.[9] Bourassa counselled Beauharnois to allow Crees, Monsonis, and Nakoda to retaliate against the Dakota, but to disengage the French from the conflict. Following this advice, Beauharnois told a Cree chief visiting Montreal that he and his people "were free to pursue the war that they had always been waging with them [the Dakota]," but that the French would postpone their attack on the

Dakota until they should "find a suitable occasion for doing so."[10] Beauharnois did not prevent a retaliatory war against the Dakota – an interdiction that he would not be able to enforce anyway – but rather successfully withdrew French support from the conflict, albeit temporarily. From a French colonial perspective, this was the most practical solution given the circumstances.

Beauharnois had been quick to disregard Canadiens at the beginning of his tenure as governor in favour of the colony's military elite – Troupes de la Marine officers and their families. However, in moments of crises he still turned to voyageurs and coureurs de bois with intimate knowledge of Indigenous politics, customs, and languages. French colonial officials relied heavily upon Canadiens like Bourassa to acquire information in an attempt to consolidate imperial control over the Hudson Bay watershed. In the 1730s and '40s, Canadiens were instrumental to the French presence at the Western Posts, even though they were excluded from the patronage networks of the ancien régime. Under Beauharnois, everyday Canadiens would never achieve ennoblement, seigneurial concessions, and the Croix de Saint-Louis – the ultimate mark of distinction. Yet they still shaped the outcome of imperial projects in the Hudson Bay watershed. Even those most resistant to using Canadien backcountry specialists, like Beauharnois, were left with little choice but to depend on the intelligence and services provided by voyageurs and coureurs de bois.

Whereas the previous chapter emphasized the setbacks experienced by La Vérendrye at the Western Posts, this chapter articulates the aptitude and agency of Canadiens in the Hudson Bay watershed during the same period of the 1730s and '40s. Canadiens played an essential role in maintaining a French presence in the Hudson Bay watershed through their mastery of Indigenous languages and diplomatic protocols, their ability to locate natural resources (which promoted empire-wide economic growth), and their skills as hunters, fisherman, and general provisioners of French posts. Lastly, voyageurs transported goods, furs, and Troupes de la Marine officers between Montreal and the Western Posts. This was a vital part of securing any semblance of a French imperial presence in the Hudson Bay watershed. Several Canadiens at the Western Posts, both named and unnamed in the sources, extended New France's political, territorial, and commercial goals in fundamental ways during this period.

The first section of the chapter examines the careers of Louis Galloudek and Pennesha Gegare, who learned Nų́ų́ʔetaa íroo (the

Mandan language) and helped to secure trade connections between Fort La Reine on the Assiniboine River and the Mandan villages of the Upper Missouri valley. The second section demonstrates how Canadiens in general, but particularly voyageurs (fur trade workers), through their relationships with Indigenous peoples, provided information (or misinformation, as the case may be) that drove the French imperial imagination even further westward and fuelled colonial officials' fervent searches for gold, silver, and other precious metals in western North America. The third section examines the vital role that voyageurs played in provisioning the Western Posts, and how they learned to hunt and fish from their Indigenous allies in the Hudson Bay watershed. The final section examines the labour history of voyageurs in the 1730s and '40s, positing that many of these Canadiens, like Jean-Baptiste Pion, challenged French imperial authority, shaped the contours of their own working environment, and pursued lucrative trading opportunities outside of their indentured contracts at the Western Posts. Overall, this chapter argues that, even when colonial officials largely eschewed voyageurs and coureurs de bois in favour of Troupes de la Marine officers, ordinary Canadiens still proved vital to maintaining a French presence in the Hudson Bay watershed, especially in terms of on-the-ground geopolitics, trade, and kinship.

LANGUAGE AND DIPLOMACY AT THE WESTERN POSTS

On 28 April 1738, the mother of a young boy named Louis Galloudek gave permission for her son to work as a voyageur and domestic servant for La Vérendrye.[11] Galloudek had just turned sixteen when a Montreal notary drew up a three-year indentured contract.[12] That spring, he journeyed with La Vérendrye to the Western Posts. From Fort La Reine, on the banks of the Assiniboine River, La Vérendrye, Galloudek, and about twenty other Frenchmen (voyageurs, merchants, and soldiers) followed Nakoda families on their seasonal expedition over the northern Great Plains to visit and trade with the Mandan villages on the banks of the Upper Missouri.[13] La Vérendrye greatly anticipated meeting the Mandan, a sedentary agricultural people with vast trade connections throughout western North America, not only to open new lucrative markets, but also to explore the Missouri River, which he thought might flow toward the Western Sea.

Shortly after arriving at the principal Mandan village (near present-day Bismarck, North Dakota), La Vérendrye's Native interpreter (who spoke the Cree, Nakoda, and Mandan languages) abandoned the French. La Vérendrye fretted that he and the other Frenchmen were stuck alone with the Mandan "trying to make ourselves understood by signs and gestures."[14] Frustrated that any further communication with their hosts would therefore be impractical and limited to gesturing, La Vérendrye decided to leave Galloudek behind in order to live with the Mandan and learn their language, while he returned to Fort La Reine. La Vérendrye described Galloudek as a boy of "quick intelligence, a good memory, a great faculty for learning languages, and a prudent God-fearing man."[15] Two Nakoda volunteered to remain with Galloudek while he took his crash course in Nų́ų̨ʔetaa íroo, and they also agreed to accompany him back to Fort La Reine the following summer.[16] True to their word, six months later, the Nakoda brought Galloudek back to La Vérendrye at Fort La Reine.[17]

Galloudek reported to La Vérendrye all that he had learned and witnessed during his half-year stint with the Mandan. He had seen visitors on horseback from the West coming to trade with the Mandan. Galloudek even spoke to a trading captain from either the Crows or Kiowas, who showed off a Spanish bridle – almost certainly from New Mexico. The trading captain spoke at length about the Spaniards, who wore cotton clothes, lived in stone buildings, and "prayed to the great Master of Life in books."[18] The captain had either visited New Mexico personally or had at least heard tales about the Spanish and acquired the bridle through the expansive Great Plains trading network that was only growing thanks to the proliferation of the horse trade in the eighteenth century.[19] From an imperial perspective, the information that Galloudek provided La Vérendrye was invaluable. Galloudek connected the Western Posts to new trade opportunities with the Indigenous peoples of the Great Plains. This was a vast new market for the French and a brand-new means to access it – horses. And indeed, in short order, some voyageurs adopted horses as an efficient means of traversing the expansive Great Plains.[20]

Coureur de bois Pennesha Gegare also assisted La Vérendrye in securing trade connections between Fort La Reine on the Assiniboine River and the Mandan villages of the Upper Missouri valley. Unlike Galloudek, who contracted to serve La Vérendrye in Montreal, Pennesha Gegare encountered the French in the Upper Missouri valley and seems to have only informally worked for them starting in the 1740s.[21] According to one contemporary observer, Gegare began his career as a soldier in the Illinois Country and deserted his post at Fort de Chartres: "[He] toock his Boat up the Miseeurea among the Indans and Spant Maney years among them ... He [eventually] Got among the Mondans [Mandans] whare he found Sum french traders who Belonged to the french facterey at fort Lorain [La Reine] on the Read [Red] River this facterey Belong to the french traders of Cannaday."[22] Likely no voyageur contract for Gegare exists because he only worked informally for La Vérendrye after being discovered living among the Mandans during one of the three French visits between 1738 and 1743.[23] Gegare was a huge asset to La Vérendrye and the Montreal merchants at Fort La Reine because he had integrated himself into the vast kinship networks of a variety of Central Siouan and Caddoan peoples who resided between the Illinois Country and the Missouri River, such as the Otoe, Omaha, Pawnee, Hidatsa, and Arikara.[24]

During their sojourns with the Mandan, Galloudek and Gegare might have formed kinship ties with their Mandan hosts through marriage à la façon du pays. In Mandan society it was commonplace to marry and even exchange children with outsiders, which allowed commerce to flow along far-flung kinship lines. It should not be surprising that Mandans would have integrated early Canadien visitors like Galloudek and Gegare through marriage, as they would later do the same with Canadien traders, like René Jusseaume and Old Menard, in the late eighteenth and early nineteenth centuries. These later Canadien traders lived semi-permanently in Mandan villages, married Mandan women, spoke Nų́ų?etaa íroo, and commercially linked the Upper Missouri villages with HBC posts like Brandon House, at the confluence of the Assiniboine and Souris Rivers.[25]

Galloudek and Gegare played an important role in helping La Vérendrye advance imperial projects in the Upper Missouri valley and on the northern Great Plains. In the 1730s and '40s, the Mandan villages were located at the literal crossroads of the bourgeoning horse and firearm trade of the North American continent. The sedentary Mandan cultivated an agricultural surplus of maize, beans, and squash, which they traded to the Comanche, Wichita, and Caddo of the Southwest for Spanish horses.[26] To the northeast, the Mandan also traded their agricultural surplus to the Cree and Nakoda for second-hand European weapons, tools, and trinkets. To the west, Crows,

Cheyennes, Arapahos, Kiowas, and Pawnees all visited the Upper Missouri villages.[27] In addition to learning the rudiments of Nų́ų̨ʔetaa íroo, Galloudek and Gegare may have also familiarized themselves with Plains Indian Sign Language, also known as Plains Sign Talk.[28] Whenever linguistic obstacles arose on the Great Plains between neighbouring Indigenous peoples, they turned to what scholars have deemed "one of the most effective means of nonverbal communication ever devised."[29] One nineteenth-century observer found it "surprising how dexterous all these natives of the plains are in communicating their ideas by signs. They hold conferences for several hours, upon different subjects, during the whole of which time not a single word is pronounced upon either side, and still they appear to comprehend each other perfectly well. This mode of communication is natural to them; their gestures are made with the greatest ease, and they never seem to be at a loss for a sign to express their meaning."[30] Historian Céline Carayon has argued that sign language, pantomime, and other non-verbal means of communication were crucial to establishing French-Indigenous intercultural relations, thereby contributing to the emergence of cultural hybridity in the French Atlantic world.[31] Through their understanding of a variety of forms of verbal and non-verbal communication, Galloudek and Gegare were able to connect New France's fur trade empire to an important exchange market in the heart of North America.

Galloudek's and Gegare's language skills were integral to the larger effort to push colonial frontiers in western North America. In the fur trade, linguistic knowledge was essential, and many Troupes de la Marine officers reluctantly utilized voyageurs and coureurs de bois as interpreters. Louisiana's *commissaire-ordonnateur*, Edmé-Gatien Salmon, noted the importance of having good interpreters to maintain French-Indigenous relations, but lamented that the only men capable of this job were the "coureurs de bois and people of this sort, who live with the natives, purchase their meats and furs, marry them, and often fight alongside them."[32] Another colonial official complained that "very often the interpreters do not say what we command them to say ... sometimes purposefully and sometimes by accident, and are mostly lower class people, who are illiterate."[33] Colonial officials found it difficult to locate polyglot Troupes de la Marine officers and Jesuit missionaries for service in the western fur trade territories, and instead had no other choice but to rely on Canadiens as interpreters and diplomats.

Not only were language skills integral for communication, but they also legitimized the French presence in Indigenous social, diplomatic, and commercial networks. Mastery of idioms, expressions, and cultural symbolism facilitated entrance into and operation within the culturally hybrid networks of the pays d'en haut and the Hudson Bay watershed. The French had learned the importance of Indigenous metaphorical discourse from their first contacts with Native peoples in the Saint Lawrence valley and the Great Lakes region. Intendant Raudot even wrote in 1709 that interpreters had to adopt "a Native style [of speech] to speak to the nations," meaning a discourse "full of hyperboles, allusions, and other figurative Expressions."[34] In other words, French interpreters and diplomats had to learn a variety of metaphors and allusions to converse successfully with Native audiences. For example, many Indigenous peoples employed the metaphor of "boiling the kettle" or "eating their enemies" to express notions of warfare.[35] In 1742, Monsoni chief La Colle told La Vérendrye "that the Sioux [Dakota] were only good to eat."[36] Native peoples also used a myriad of expressions to articulate alliance-making with strangers and reconciliation with former enemies. Diplomatic kin metaphors were central to understanding how Indigenous peoples conceived of their relations with colonizers. Kin metaphors that transformed strangers into family were at the heart of Indigenous diplomacy and alliance.[37] The metaphor of "becoming one and the same people" was particularly prevalent in concluding peace treaties and alliances.[38] When trying to negotiate an alliance with La Vérendrye, for instance, the Cree proclaimed to the French that they were together now one and the same body.[39]

Canadien diplomats and interpreters also learned the necessity of employing wampum cords or belts – composed of short, tubular marine shells strung together – as mnemonic devices in concluding treaties and alliances with Indigenous peoples.[40] Algonquian and Iroquoian peoples used wampum belts in diplomacy from the Atlantic Seaboard to the western interior. When Europeans forgot to employ wampum while engaging in diplomacy with Algonquian and Iroquoian peoples, they were often reprimanded. For example, in 1703, a Wendat chief reproached the French by saying, "We were spoken empty words, that is to say without wampum."[41] The Baron de Lahontan remarked that, without the use of wampum belts, "there's no business to be negotiated with the Savages; for being altogether unacquainted with writing, they make use of them for Contracts and Obligations."[42]

The exchange of wampum cords was also commonplace at the Western Posts. The Cree, Monsoni, and French frequently exchanged wampum during diplomatic ceremonies and negotiations.[43] For example, a Monsoni chief offered La Vérendrye a wampum cord representing their alliance, which he used to urge the French commandant to bring more trade goods and merchandise to the Western Posts.[44] Canadiens helped La Vérendrye navigate the cultural and linguistic landscapes of the Hudson Bay watershed, interpreting not only words but also signs, allusions, diplomatic conventions, and the symbolic meaning of material objects.

GOLD, SILVER, AND OTHER PRECIOUS METALS: LOCATING MINERAL WEALTH IN WESTERN NORTH AMERICA

On 14 February 1734, Cree visitors from the Lake Winnipeg region (Cris du Oüinipigon) presented La Vérendrye with a slave and a wampum cord at Fort Saint-Charles and asked that the French come establish a post on the shores of Lake Winnipeg.[45] La Vérendrye agreed and dispatched "two well-disposed" voyageurs as ambassadors to the Crees from Lake Winnipeg, where they would inspect the place and determine where it would be most convenient to build a fort.[46] La Vérendrye gave the two voyageurs "rules for their guidance on the journey, both as to talking to the savages and as to visiting the different spots and choosing a convenient one for the fort, recommending them also to take notes of any mines which there might be in those localities or any kinds of wood different than ours."[47] In doing so, the top French official in the West entrusted voyageurs with establishing good relations with Indigenous peoples and laying the foundation for further French expansion into the Hudson Bay watershed.

A couple months later, the two French envoys returned with a Cree chief and eighteen men and reported that they had found a considerable Cree population and had been well-received by their hosts.[48] The French emissaries described the area's resource potential, noting that the Lake Winnipeg region had high timber forests, including a great deal of white oak, and even a salt spring, from which they brought a small sample. Most importantly, the Frenchmen brought descriptions of the mines of the Lake Winnipeg region and a small specimen of the ore, which HBC traders had earlier thought to be silver.[49] Manitoban geologist George Reynolds speculated that the Crees gave La

Vérendrye's voyageurs hematite or red iron from a large deposit located on the southeastern shore of Black Island on Lake Winnipeg.[50] Iron ore was a valuable metallurgical resource, but it was commonplace in the Saint Lawrence valley, especially in the vicinity of the Forges du Saint-Maurice, the first successful ironworks in New France.[51] A mineral as common as red iron ore would not have been worth the trouble to mine and transport from the Lake Winnipeg region back to the Saint Lawrence valley.

The discovery of mineral deposits had always been a French imperial priority in the Americas. In the sixteenth century, Jacques Cartier had considerably exaggerated the mineral wealth of the Saint Lawrence valley; he collected what he believed to be diamonds and gold, but upon his return to France, these were discovered to be merely quartz crystals and iron pyrites – which gave rise to a French expression: "Faux comme les diamants du Canada" (As false as Canadian diamonds).[52] In the early eighteenth century, John Law's Compagnie d'Occident fruitlessly pursued tales of gold and other precious metals in Louisiana, eventually leading to economic collapse – the so-called Mississippi Bubble – the revocation of the company's charter, and the incorporation of Louisiana as a royal colony.[53] Concurrent with Law's daydreaming about mineral wealth in Louisiana, Pierre-Charles Le Sueur searched in vain in the Upper Mississippi valley for precious metals, only to turn up "four thousand pounds of greenish dirt."[54] Beginning with the Spanish conquests of Mexico and Peru, the search for gold, silver, and other precious metals had consistently been one of the driving forces behind the European exploration, conquest, and colonization of the Americas.

Based on the reports of La Vérendrye's voyageurs and Indigenous informants, French geographers improved and redrew the maps of western North America in the 1750s to include the location of certain natural resources – timbers, salt springs, and mines. For example, Jacques-Nicolas Bellin's 1755 map of western North America portrays a massive mineral deposit along the fabled "Rivière de l'Ouest," described as a "Mountain of sparkling stone following the report of the Natives."[55] The blacksmith posted at Fort Saint-Charles, Michel Baillargeon *dit* Durivage, never commented on the small specimen of ore, but based on descriptions that made it into Bellin's map, French colonial officials were led to believe that La Vérendrye had discovered a great silver mine in North America, perhaps one to rival even the great Spanish mine of Potosí in Peru.

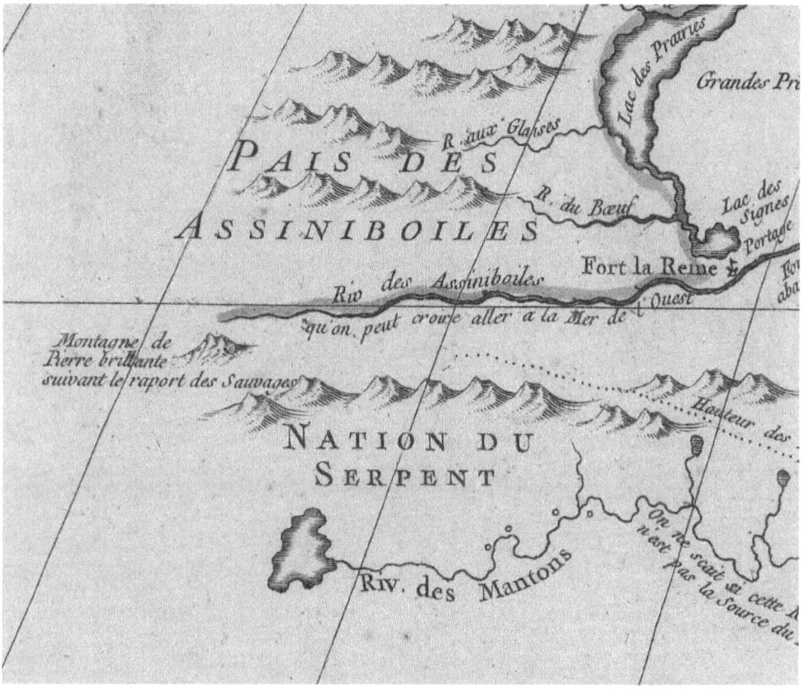

4.1 Detail of "Mountain of sparkling stone following the report of the Natives," in map by Jacques Nicolas Bellin, French hydrographer and geographer for the Ministry of the Marine

With La Vérendrye mired in Indigenous geopolitics at Fort Saint-Charles, Canadiens fanned out across the rivers and lakes of the Hudson Bay watershed contacting future allies and surveying potential resources. Encountering hitherto unknown Indigenous groups, French interlocutors reported back to Troupes de la Marine officers with tales, reports, and rumours provided by their Native hosts. Historian Gregory Evans Dowd shows how groundless news, rumours, and hoaxes shaped the history of the original American colonies and drove European exploration of the North American interior. Dowd contends, moreover, that when it came to gold, silver, and other precious metals, rumours spread like wildfire and contributed to the spread of imperialism in western North America.[56] Similarly, historian Paul W. Mapp posits that rumours, particularly the rumour of the Northwest Passage, helped ignite western imperial expansion and even a global war between France and Britain.[57] In other words, even false information had the power to influence colonial policy and imperial projects.

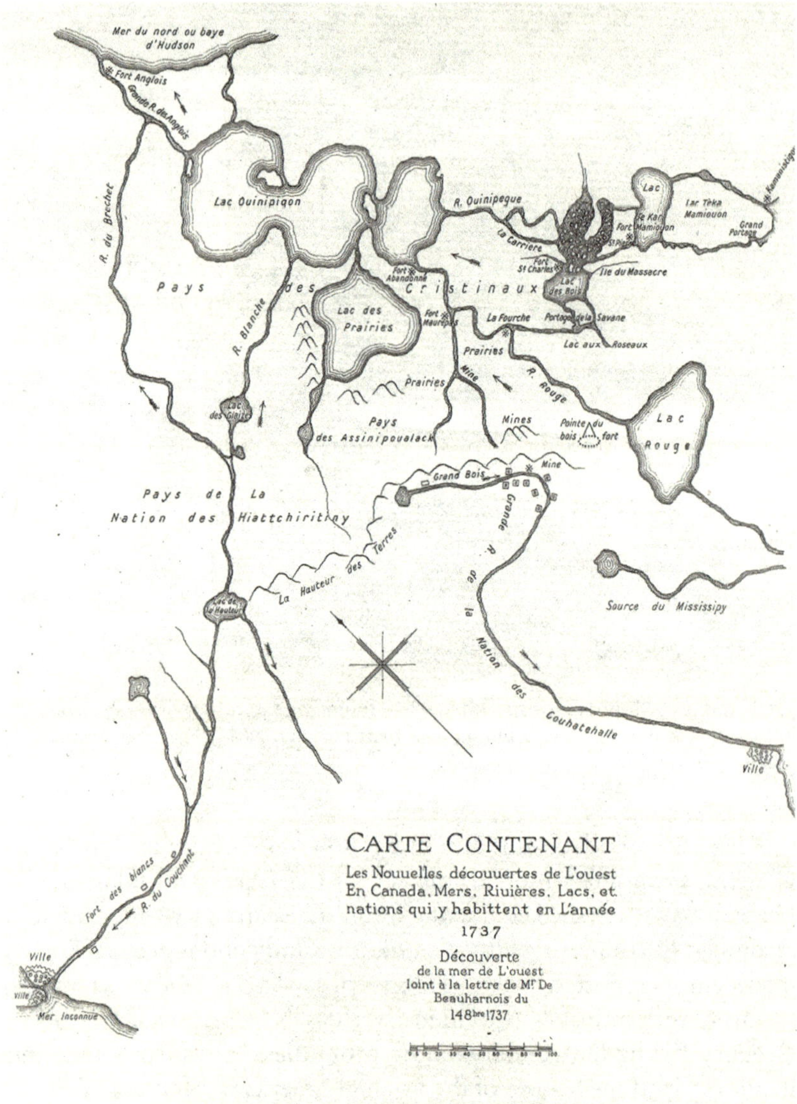

4.2 A 1737 map drawn from La Vérendrye's journals, possibly with the assistance of Quebec military engineer Gaspard-Joseph Chaussegros de Léry. This map indicates several mines in one of the rivers above the headwaters of the Mississippi River. This is a paper copy reprinted and published by the Champlain Society to accompany the 1927 transcription and translation of La Vérendrye's journals and letters describing the search for the Western Sea. According to Library and Archives Canada, the original is housed in the archives of the Service historique de la Défense in Vincennes, France.

The resource potential of the Lake Winnipeg region was greatly exaggerated and misunderstood by French imperial agents, who for over two centuries had seen mineral wealth as one of the top priorities of French empire building.[58] The abstract and often intangible possibility of gold, silver, and other precious metals continued to drive and justify French exploration, conquest, and colonization. Canadiens were central figures in the proliferation of these rumours and hearsay.[59] What made Canadiens such salient holders of power in these peripheral imperial spaces were their relationship with and access to Indigenous peoples. Through their connection to Natives, Canadiens played a crucial role in securing new trade connections and identifying potentially valuable resources. At the end of the day, Canadiens provided both information and misinformation that proved pivotal in shaping expansionist imperial ambitions in the Hudson Bay watershed.

PROVISIONING THE WESTERN POSTS

At first, Troupes de la Marine officers and voyageurs alike feared that they would starve to death in the region northwest of Lake Superior. These fears were largely unfounded, however, as the Europeans for the most part possessed adequate hunting and fishing skills and game and fish were more than plentiful in the area.[60] On 29 August 1733, La Vérendrye and his voyageurs feasted on "meats, moose and beef fat, bear oil and wild oats" at Fort Saint-Charles.[61] Throughout much of the winter of 1736–37, Canadiens ate bison meat and fat daily from the opulent herds inhabiting the prairie parkland southwest of Lake of the Woods.[62] At the Western Posts, Canadiens also consumed a variety of fish (northern pike, walleye, lake trout), bear, deer, moose, and other smaller game animals (beaver, fox, and hare). Many Canadiens were proficient hunters and secured vital stores of food for La Vérendrye's posts.

In the winter of 1733, La Vérendrye sent ten men to the opposite shore of Lake of the Woods from Fort Saint-Charles "with tools for building themselves a shelter ... and with nets for fishing."[63] He later recorded that they caught "more than 4,000 big whitefish, not to speak of trout, sturgeon, and other fish ... [and] thus lived by hunting and fishing at no expense."[64] Voyageurs also fished with Crees at La Barrière aux Esturgeons (literally "sturgeon barrier") in the spring of 1733 while they awaited the late thaw so they could precede up the Winnipeg River.[65] Local Crees had established this "barrier," or dam, at a narrow chokepoint on the Winnipeg River in order to catching fish with wicker baskets, nets, and spears.[66] Such important teachings had long been a staple of French-Indigenous encounters from the Saint Lawrence valley to the pays d'en haut, and finally in the Hudson Bay watershed. For example, a Jesuit missionary remarked in 1663 that "the Frenchmen, having observed how the Savages carried on their fishing, resolved to imitate them, – deeming hunger still harder to bear than the arduous labour and risks attending such fishing."[67] Voyageurs, soldiers, and coureurs de bois learned to fish in North America's lakes and rivers using hook and line, nets, and spears. Indigenous peoples also taught Canadiens how to cure their catches without relying on salt, showing them how to use smoke or sunlight as alternate methods of food preservation.[68]

Voyageurs and soldiers hunted an abundance of game as they trekked overland across the Prairies along the banks of the Assiniboine River in the autumn of 1738.[69] Following their Nakoda guides, Canadiens hunted grouse, deer, and perhaps even bison, which were plentiful in the aspen parkland of the Assiniboine Valley, an ecoregion rich in flora and fauna that straddles the boreal forest and Canadian Shield to the northeast and the northern Great Plains to the southwest.[70] When HBC servants Joseph Smith and Joseph Waggoner visited Fort Bourbon at Cedar Lake, they found that resident voyageurs were wintering and hunting with a Nakoda band in the Porcupine Hills of the Manitoba Escarpment.[71] At French posts in the Hudson Bay watershed, meat comprised the major part of the diet of voyageurs, officers, and soldiers. Large game animals such as deer, moose, bear, and bison seemed to be the favourites, but Frenchmen also consumed beaver, hare, and wildfowl.[72]

French colonial officials came to expect that voyageurs would be able to provision both themselves and the interior posts throughout the trading season. Fur brigades leaving Montreal for the pays d'en haut had their canoes full of merchandise for trading and could not be too encumbered with food and other daily supplies. One colonial official noted that "all their provisions consist of but a little biscuit, peas, corn, and some small barrels of brandy, as they carry the least they can to avoid losing room for merchandise, they are soon reduced to live only from hunting and fishing that they find along their way."[73] That they would be expected to hunt and fish for the entire fur brigade or trading post was in fact included as a clause in many voyageurs' contracts. For example, Augustin Beauvais's 1734 contract indicated that he had to "Hunt ... [and] fish, if there is need."[74] This was an important precursor to regulations later enacted in the British Montreal fur trade (1763–1821), where stark distinctions were made between voyageurs who provisioned themselves and those who did not. In the hierarchical "voyageur world" that emerged following the British conquest of Canada, fur trade workers who journeyed beyond Grand Portage, nicknamed *hommes du nord* (northmen), were expected to provision themselves, whereas the voyageurs restricted to the Great Lakes region relied solely on provisions brought from Montreal or purchased at Michilimackinac, hence their nickname *mangeurs de lard* (pork eaters). The ability to sustain oneself through hunting and fishing, to winter away from the more consistently supplied posts in the pays d'en haut, and to navigate the more treacherous portages and rapids of the Hudson Bay watershed (compared to the flat, open waters of the Great Lakes) was an important indicator of masculinity in North America's fur trade world.[75] In the pays d'en haut, traders at French posts merely supplemented their supplies by hunting and fishing, since they received colonial foodstuffs from Montreal. In the Hudson Bay watershed, by contrast, Canadiens were the primary provisioners of the Western Posts.

French posts benefited from the goodwill of local Native hunters and fishermen, but this support carried with it the assumption of reciprocity.[76] At the Western Posts, the French observed that "without the help of the pot you cannot have friendship."[77] This meant that Indigenous custom dictated that hosts were required to feast their guests (Native visitors to their posts) in order to establish proper kinship relations and alliances. When the French were able to provision their own posts, they were able to fulfill the social obligations of reciprocity with their Indigenous neighbours, as well as feed themselves. In the end, it seems unlikely that the French fur trade could have extended as far west from Montreal as the Assiniboine and Saskatchewan Rivers without the diligent support of Canadiens supplying posts.[78]

PADDLING, PORTAGING, AND TRANSPORTING CARGOES IN WESTERN NORTH AMERICA

Voyageurs were vital for the transportation of human and commercial cargoes in the Hudson Bay watershed. This was perhaps the most obvious requirement of the job. Take, for example, the voyageur contract of Jean Le Vallois, signed in 1731, which reads "[he is] to bring the Canoes, goods, and furs of the aforementioned Sieurs associates, to take care of those And other things necessary for such journeys, to obey the aforementioned Sieurs associates and to serve them faithfully – And Generally to do everything That is Commanded."[79] Under that umbrella of human-powered riverine transportation were subsumed several different roles and skill levels for which voyageurs earned varying degrees of prestige and payment. The least prestigious position in the canoe was the *milieu*, or middleman, which was the most monotonous and required the least skill. These voyageurs were responsible for paddling from dawn to dusk and carrying merchandise or bales of fur over portages. A more skilled position was the *devant*, or foreman, who helped to guide the canoe through treacherous waterways and acted as a lookout. The *gouvernail*, or steersman, was at the back of the canoe. Together, devants and gouvernails directed the paddling, called out commands to commence or cease paddling, set the rhythm, and were also responsible for carrying the canoe over portages.[80]

One voyageur, usually a senior man with experience and knowledge garnered from many previous trips, was the designated guide of the entire fur brigade. Guides had to make difficult and potentially life-threatening or monetarily ruinous choices as to whether canoes should attempt to shoot rapids, be tracked from shore, or be portaged.[81] Navigating birchbark canoes through rivers and streams was a difficult job that required experience and knowledge of waterways and canoe travel. For example, Alexandre Bissonet's three-year voyageur contract indicated that he was to "depart from This city [Montreal] the following spring in the capacity as guide in a Canoe laden with goods, and to lead and Conduct them to the [posts of] the Western Sea, and wherever Will be necessary at the aforementioned posts of the Western Sea."[82] Alexandre Bissonet was an experienced voyageur familiar with the riverine routes of the Hudson Bay watershed; he had signed a previous contract with La Vérendrye and the Associés de la Mer de l'Ouest in 1739 and another contract at Michilimackinac in the 1740s.[83]

In addition to goods and furs, voyageurs also transported their fur trade masters, usually Troupes de la Marine officers, to and from the Western Posts. There is no indication that these elite officers paddled or portaged during the three-thousand-kilometre journey from Montreal to the Western Posts. La Vérendrye even cautioned the Cree and Monsoni that his son Jean-Baptiste was "not as accustomed to fatigue as you," which suggests that Jean-Baptiste de La Vérendrye did not exert himself beyond the normal duties of an aristocratic officer in the Compagnies Franches de la Marine.[84] Fur trade and labour historian Carolyn Podruchny argues that these masters enacted a "theatre of authority" by performing less physical labour than the voyageurs under their command. Accordingly, they were usually the only passengers aboard fur trade canoes and they only assisted in paddling and portaging in cases of extreme necessity.[85] Although Podruchny's analysis of the "voyageur world" pertains to the post-1760 context, her argument holds true for the 1730s and '40s. In this earlier period as well, masters did not participate in the vigorous round of activities that kept the forts and trading posts functioning smoothly, such as constructing and maintaining buildings, fabricating and repairing canoes, and hunting, fishing, and preparing meals. Rather, fur trade elites kept account books, managed the merchandise and provisions, and initiated authorized trade and diplomacy with Indigenous peoples.[86]

The annual salaries of voyageurs in the first half of the eighteenth century was usually somewhere between 150 and 350 livres, but it could reach up to 500 livres, or even 1,000 livres for the more specialized positions of devants, gouvernails, and guides. For most Canadiens, a voyageur contract was a means to earn two to three times more than was possible in the Saint Lawrence valley.[87] Many voyageurs re-engaged several times for service in the pays d'en haut, the Illinois Country, or the Hudson Bay watershed, whereas others took their earnings and settled down to an agrarian life in the Saint Lawrence valley. Scholars have shattered the historiographical myth that there was an inherent divide between participation in the fur trade and agriculture.[88] In the pays d'en haut, argues Gilles Havard, the system of engagement in the fur trade, based on trips back and forth between the colony and Indigenous communities in the interior, was part of a seasonal labour regime that speaks to "the pendular nature of French colonization."[89] However, the Hudson Bay watershed was distant enough that it was impossible for voyageurs to return home in the same year as their outbound voyage. Once voyageurs passed the threshold of Grand Portage and entered into the waters of the Hudson Bay drainage basin, they were committing at minimum to a one-year stay. As we will explore in the next chapter, because of the enormous distances involved in the fur trade, many voyageurs began to live in the Hudson Bay watershed with Indigenous communities on a semi-permanent and even permanent basis.

On the surface, the arduous labour performed by voyageurs suggested that this was a young man's profession. One French colonial official even remarked that voyageurs were "always young people, or in the prime of life, old age not being capable of enduring the fatigues of the trade."[90] In reality, however, many voyageurs continued to work past the prime of life (into their thirties, forties, and fifties, with a few notable examples of voyageurs working into their sixties and even seventies). Wisdom and experience became significant factors in the hiring of devants and gouvernails, and especially guides, who constantly had to weigh the advantages and risks associated with choosing routes of travel, when to portage, and the overall speed of the brigade.[91] Some exceptional voyageurs maintained their vitality and strength into old age. For example, Father Nicolas Degonnor, a Jesuit missionary, described "an old voyageur named Giguière, seventy-seven-years-old, but still alert for his age, who I have several times seen climb the highest and steepest mountains of the Mississippi, who, this winter, we saw that he knew how to use snowshoes and pursue deer."[92] In many instances, fur trade bourgeois preferred to hire "old hands" over novices, and were willing to pay a premium salary for experienced voyageurs.[93]

Many voyageurs, young and old, frequently increased their wages by engaging in valuable side-trading. Initially, in the seventeenth century, this was a tolerated, albeit heavily regulated, activity. For example, Governor Frontenac granted permission to some voyageurs bound for Michilimackinac to "carry 100 livres worth of merchandise each, which they could trade for their own profit."[94] By the eighteenth century, however, the French colonial government outlawed side-trading by issuing strict trade regulations. Voyageurs were henceforth forbidden from "leav[ing] the posts, whether to return to Montreal, or to go to some other place, even hunting, without the express permission of the Commandant."[95] Another regulation forbade voyageurs from trading away their personal firearms to Natives, with a penalty of three months' imprisonment. Not only was holding on to personal guns a safety precaution, but it also helped to deter voyageur side-trading from eating into the profits of the commandant and the officially licensed merchants.[96] Despite heavy regulations, side-trading continued unabated into the period of the British Montreal fur trade. In the early nineteenth century, notes historian Nicole St-Onge, many voyageurs purposefully and strategically "spent heavily at the company store on goods mainly destined for bargaining with the native population," and companies' tolerance of low-level side-trading would have been enticement for experienced voyageurs to accompany certain fur trade expeditions.[97] Many voyageurs saw side-trading as a valuable supplement to their existing wages, and carefully cultivated kinship relationships with Indigenous peoples in the interior to facilitate these illicit (albeit occasionally tolerated) commercial activities.

Voyageurs blatantly disregarded regulations and frequently engaged in side-trading at the Western Posts and throughout the Hudson Bay watershed. In 1739, Montreal merchant Charles Nolan Lamarque complained that a side-trading voyageur named Lorimier was violating his congé to trade in the Lake Winnipeg region, and that his trade profits suffered severely as result of Lorimier's actions.[98] Unable to remove the voyageur, Lamarque decided to build a new post twenty-five leagues away with five engagés, and yet he was still dismayed with the paltry returns at his new establishment. Lamarque penned an angry letter to La Vérendrye decrying the lack of trade at his new location: "Here we are at the 16th of April and we have not yet seen anybody. God knows what is in store for us!"[99] La Vérendrye wrote back saying that he was very sorry to hear that Lamarque and his brother Jean-Marie Nolan "should go away empty-handed."[100] Financial difficulties at the Western Posts continued for Lamarque, Nolan, and their associates in the ensuing years. In 1741, voyageur Jean-Baptiste Pion submitted a petition to the Montreal court against La Vérendrye and Montreal merchant Pierre Gamelin Maugras for unpaid wages of 500 livres. La Vérendrye and Maugras had withheld Pion's wages because he had gone off to trade independently on the Winnipeg River rather than assist at the Western Posts.[101] The merchant company belonging to Maugras and his partners – Charles Nolan Lamarque, Jean-Marie Nolan, Jean-Baptiste Legras, and Ignace Gamelin – dissolved the same year.[102] Rampant side-trading siphoned off furs and made it increasingly difficult for legitimate Montreal merchants, who had paid exorbitant fees for congés to trade at the Western Posts, to turn a profit. For example, in 1735 the Associés de la Mer de l'Ouest paid Governor Beauharnois 3,000 livres to trade at the Western Posts, as well as an additional 3,000 livres to La Vérendrye, who was supposed to ignore the fur trade and devote himself entirely to exploration and discovery.[103] However, these traders were constantly undercut by voyageurs who clandestinely brought their own merchandise into the Hudson Bay watershed and carried on a profitable side trade with local Indigenous peoples.

When working conditions became unsuitable, unfair, or even dangerous, voyageurs challenged La Vérendrye's authority as commandant. In 1731, as we saw in the previous chapter, La Vérendrye's voyageurs mutinied at Grand Portage, refusing to proceed inland because they were "dismayed at the length of the portage."[104] When La Vérendrye wanted to trek overland to visit the Mandan villages of the Missouri valley in 1737, he noted that "the Frenchmen were afraid to accompany me, which defeated all my plans ... Such are our difficulties."[105] Many scholars have examined fur trade labour relations in the Northwest. With regards to the British fur trade, Edith Burley and Scott Stephen argue that HBC labourers were not passive members of some "company family"; rather, they played an active role in determining the structure of their working conditions by showing indifference to authority, protesting bad treatment, and insisting on higher wages and shorter contracts.[106] Canadien voyageurs, too, selectively resisted authority to shape their own working environments in the Northwest. Carolyn Podruchny posits that "voyageurs created a space to continually challenge the expectations of their masters." When masters made unreasonable demands or failed to provide adequate provisions, "voyageurs responded by working more slowly, becoming insolent, and occasionally free-trading and stealing provisions." Voyageurs shaped the contours of their working environments by complaining and mocking their superiors, refusing to share the food they obtained through hunting and fishing, collectively withholding their labour, and even deserting the service altogether.[107] Indeed, throughout the long history of the fur trade, the most "powerful bargaining tool in labour relations was the option of desertion."[108] At the Western Posts, there were opportunities for voyageurs to desert and go live with Indigenous families, or even to operate independently as coureurs de bois.

Voyageurs were the backbone of the fur trade, literally paddling and portaging goods, furs, and Troupes de la Marine officers back and forth between Montreal and the Western Posts. Without this Canadien labour, the fur trade, and French western imperial expansion more broadly, would not have been possible. Voyageur agency, however, also exposes the very limits of French imperial authority. Paradoxically, then, while Canadiens made it possible for the French to establish themselves in the Hudson Bay watershed, they simultaneously limited the scope of French imperial projects by pursuing illicit side-trading, challenging the authority of their superior officers, and shaping the contours of their own working environment.

CONCLUSION

La Vérendrye and his imperial ambitions initially achieved mixed success in the Hudson Bay watershed, but French colonial officials tenaciously clung to the Western Posts until the Seven Years' War (1754–63). In large part, the efforts of Canadiens accounted for the continued French presence in the Hudson Bay watershed. Some of these Canadiens acted as important cultural brokers through their understanding of Indigenous customs and languages. Likewise, voyageurs who married into Indigenous families à la façon du pays were able to acquire a familiarity with the cultural, commercial, and diplomatic landscapes of the Hudson Bay watershed. As a result, Canadiens were often some of the first Europeans to arrive at new territories, preceding Troupes de la Marine officers bogged down with the work of enforcing imperial agendas and haranguing their new Native allies into conforming to the expectations of the French-Indigenous alliance that had previously been established in the pays d'en haut.

From an Indigenous perspective, voyageurs and coureurs de bois were much more relaxed and tolerant than the seemingly uptight Troupes de la Marine officers. Unburdened by French colonial policies or mandates, Canadiens acquiesced to their Native hosts and easily adhered to local societal norms. While La Vérendrye and his successors were mired in Indigenous geopolitics at Fort Saint-Charles and Fort La Reine, Canadiens spent progressively more time among their Indigenous hosts, hunting, fishing, travelling, learning languages, and forging relationships with them. As a result, voyageurs who had initially accompanied La Vérendrye's expedition became instrumental to the success of the establishment of new posts and the formation of new alliances in these remote western territories.

At the same time, Canadiens also exposed the fractures of French empire in the Hudson Bay watershed. The presence of side-trading voyageurs strained New France's already overextended and overtaxed fur trade system. Quite simply, Montreal merchants and Troupes de la Marine officers could not afford to compete with both the HBC and their own voyageurs. The latter, who sidestepped the purchase of exorbitantly costly congés from the colonial government, gravely undercut Montreal merchants and called into question the viability of the western fur trade. While La Vérendrye and his sons searched in vain for the Western Sea and struggled to prevent Native peoples from trading with the HBC, Canadiens laid the foundation for a culturally hybrid French-Indigenous social world in the Hudson Bay watershed. That hybrid world will be explored at length in the following chapter.

5

Métissage and Kinship

Voyageurs and Coureurs de Bois in the Hudson Bay Watershed, 1743–1759

On 17 May 1757, a small flotilla of birchbark canoes entered the upper reaches of Lake Winnipegosis. HBC servants Joseph Smith and Joseph Waggoner had accompanied a Cree band to their hunting grounds in the Swan River area the previous summer. After a plentiful season of hunting bison on the Prairies with their Cree hosts, Smith and Waggoner were returning to York Factory. The HBC servants had convinced several Cree and Nakoda families to accompany them back to York Factory to trade. Around midday, Smith, Waggoner, and their Native companions rested on the shores of Lake Winnipegosis and fished for sturgeon, but not smoking, as Smith complained in his journal, because their tobacco stores were depleted.[1] Later that afternoon, they heard gunfire echo from across the lake; "we thought it was Inds," he would write in his journal, "but it was the french going down with their goods."[2] The HBC servants and their Cree companions paddled across the lake and came upon a group of voyageurs who were resting at the start of a portage located at the narrow isthmus separating Lake Winnipegosis from Cedar Lake.[3] As a gesture of goodwill, the French leader gave the HBC servants some fresh game and tobacco, much to their delight.[4] Smith and Waggoner were elated to smoke tobacco again, which was a favourite pastime at the HBC's bayside posts.[5]

The following day, the French, British, and Natives hauled their merchandise and canoes across the 4.8-kilometre portage. Once they reloaded and re-embarked their birchbark canoes at Cedar Lake, the flotilla paddled along the southwestern shore to Fort Bourbon, a French post strategically located near where the Saskatchewan River enters Cedar Lake.[6] That evening, the leader of the voyageurs, a man named François Jérôme *dit* Latour, generously feasted and entertained

Smith and Waggoner. Together, they all ate meat, imbibed brandy, smoked, and conversed amicably.[7] Smith recorded the revelries at Fort Bourbon in his journal: "att night the Master Invited us both into his house, there was meat and fatt but for bread he had none, then we smoakt and drank brandy all together."[8] James Isham, chief factor at York Factory, remarked that the French traders treated Smith and Waggoner "very Civily."[9] Joseph Smith himself remarked that most of the voyageurs and coureurs de bois they encountered on their journey inland were "very Civill to us" and "behaved Extreamly well to us."[10] François Jérôme even allegedly said to the two HBC servants, "What if the King of England and the King of France are att warrs together, that is no reason why we should, so Lett us be friends."[11] Perhaps, quite like their Indigenous kinsmen, Canadiens had come to recognize that in "Indian Country" interdependence was a form of power rather than weakness.[12] Jérôme was the de facto commandant of Fort Bourbon in the absence of a superior officer in that region. During intervening absences of Troupes de la Marine officers at the Western Posts, voyageurs and coureurs de bois also established new posts and trading houses. In the 1740s and '50s, Canadiens in the Northwest established themselves at locations independent from the Western Posts, including settling directly in Indigenous villages, sites of seasonal aggregation, such as fishing and hunting camps, and gathering places of ceremonial and commercial importance.

The War of the Austrian Succession (1740–48) brought New France's "Golden Age" and "Long Peace" with Britain to an end. This conflict was a watershed moment that caused a shortage of trade goods in North America, and it threw the western fur trade and the French-Indigenous alliance system into disarray.[13] In so doing, the war had a marked effect on French aspirations in the Hudson Bay watershed, which from an imperial standpoint had largely ceased to be a priority. During this period, hundreds of coureurs de bois ranged beyond the network of official trading posts then under the nominal control of the French colonial government. While Troupes de la Marine officers were preoccupied with squabbling over command, promotion, and trade at the Western Posts, voyageurs and coureurs de bois made themselves at home in an increasingly familiar landscape. While New France was dealing with escalating imperial tensions and war between 1744 and 1760, Canadiens flourished in the Hudson Bay watershed.[14] They shaped the geopolitical and cultural character of the region, as their unbroken presence gave rise to a

French-Indigenous social world in the outermost sphere of French North America that was increasingly defined by political, economic, and cultural hybridity. The Hudson Bay watershed epitomized a borderland contact zone where disparate peoples utilized métissage (cultural hybridity) to navigate a fluid and shifting geopolitical, social, and cultural landscape.

The first half of this chapter examines the Hudson Bay watershed during the War of the Austrian Succession, shedding light on a region hitherto neglected in the historiography of the war's North American theatre – a branch of the conflict otherwise referred to as King George's War. During this period, the influence of Troupes de la Marine officers in Indigenous geopolitics reached its nadir, with the war spelling disaster for French imperial designs in the Hudson Bay watershed. The second half of the chapter analyzes the activities of Canadiens during the same period. The French imperial setbacks of the 1740s and '50s signified even more latitude for Canadiens hoping to build a world of kinship and métissage with the Indigenous residents of the Hudson Bay watershed. The War of the Austrian Succession was the beginning of a period of Canadien ascendency and the formation of a culturally hybrid French-Indigenous social world, a process that occurred largely outside the purview of the French colonial government.

TROUPES DE LA MARINE OFFICERS AT THE WESTERN POSTS AFTER LA VÉRENDRYE

On New Year's Day 1743, a breaking dawn revealed the shapes of lofty mountains in the distance. Louis-Joseph Gaultier de La Vérendrye and his brother François stared in dismay at the snow-capped peaks of the Bighorn Mountains.[15] Born at Île aux Vaches on Lac Saint-Pierre, near Trois-Rivières, Louis-Joseph was familiar with the sprawling, forest-covered Laurentian Mountains that rise above the north shore of the Saint Lawrence River, but the Bighorn Mountains were probably the highest peaks the young Troupes de la Marine officer had ever seen. As Louis-Joseph would write in his journal, "On the 1st of January 1743 we found ourselves in sight of the mountains … I had a strong desire to behold the Sea from the top of the mountains."[16] The La Vérendrye brothers had been exploring the northern Great Plains for six months in the company of various Indigenous peoples – Mandans, Arikaras, Cheyennes, Crows, and Kiowas.[17] After more than a decade in the Hudson Bay watershed, this was the La

Vérendrye family's last chance to discover the Western Sea before Governor Beauharnois would revoke their commission and recall them to Canada.

The La Vérendrye brothers had spent their adult lives following their father's dream. They believed that once they reached the height of land – the Great Continental Divide – they would look back east to see New France's fur trade empire, and to the west, a great interior sea, la Mer de l'Ouest. In the middle latitudes of North America, the French had sought a vast inland sea that in theory was supposed to provide a passageway to the Pacific Ocean. The discovery of the Western Sea would have given France a distinct advantage in global imperial trade by providing a more direct route to the Pacific Ocean. Yet North America was far more immense than French explorers and geographers had ever imagined. As historian Paul W. Mapp has observed, the French "continued to understate, and probably underestimate, the magnitude of the Rockies, to imagine inland seas where sagebrush grew."[18] The existence and immensity of the Rocky Mountains belied the maps of French cartographers, such as Guillaume Delisle and Philippe Buache, who had portrayed the Western Sea's existence to the southwest of Hudson Bay. Confronted with reality, the La Vérendrye brothers were disappointed and disillusioned, and returned to Fort La Reine to report the news to their father, who anxiously awaited them. When La Vérendrye learned that his sons had not in fact reached the Western Sea, he claimed to be in ill-health and resigned his position as commandant of the Western Posts, perhaps wanting to avoid the humiliation of being replaced by another officer.[19] La Vérendrye returned to Canada and enjoyed a socially active retirement before Beauharnois reappointed him as commandant of the Western Posts in 1749. Before he could resume his position, however, La Vérendrye died in Montreal on 5 December 1749, where he was entombed in the Notre-Dame Basilica.[20]

Geopolitical and geographical considerations made further French imperial exploration of the Missouri and Mississippi Rivers untenable. By the time La Vérendrye's sons had reached the Rocky Mountains in 1743, French attempts to find the Northwest Passage using the Missouri River and the northern Great Plains had proven futile.[21] Additionally, an exploratory expedition led by Joseph Marin de la Malgue in 1750 suggested that the Sioux Country and the headwaters of the Mississippi River did not drain into the Western Sea. Warfare between the Dakota and the Illinois Confederacy, squabbling between

Troupes de la Marine officers over trade territories, and severe winter weather also prevented Marin from making significant westward progress.[22] Prior to his death in 1749, La Vérendrye had advocated following the Saskatchewan River to discover the Western Sea. The failure of La Vérendrye and his sons to "discover" such a seaway, however, did not deter enterprising Troupes de la Marine officers from continuing to pursue the western fur trade, particularly up the now seemingly promising Saskatchewan River.

The Ministry of the Marine had a difficult time finding Troupes de la Marine officers who were serious about exploring new routes rather than seeking riches in the fur or liquor trades. Jacques Legardeur de Saint-Pierre, commandant of the Western Posts from 1750 to 1753, engaged in a prolific trade in liquor in the Hudson Bay watershed; in the process, he not only met growing Indigenous consumer demands, but also lined his own pockets. Introduced into the Hudson Bay watershed in the early eighteenth century, liquor rapidly became a coveted trade good among Cree, Nakoda, Ojibwe, and Dakota peoples, who sought alcohol for its social, spiritual, and medicinal functions.[23] Élisabeth Bégon, a noblewoman in New France, pronounced that "it is said that brandy has been very much in fashion at [the posts of] the Western Sea, thanks to Saint-Pierre."[24] Saint-Pierre had amassed a prodigious amount of liquor to sell at fur trade posts before his life was cut short in the opening salvos of the Seven Years' War, during which he perished at the Battle of Lake George on 8 September 1755.[25] Upon his death, his cellar was found to contain forty quarts of brandy, worth about 3,000 livres.[26]

Saint-Pierre also engaged in the Indigenous slave trade at the Western Posts, as evidenced in a letter from a Montreal merchant who claimed to have received six Indigenous slaves from the commandant in Montreal during the spring of 1752.[27] The Indigenous slave trade continued unabated in the Hudson Bay watershed throughout the 1740s and '50s. A metropolitan overview of all of New France's fur trade and military posts stated that at the Western Posts the French traded "more than fifty to sixty Indian slaves, or Jatihilinine panis, a nation situated on the Missouri, and who play in America the same role of the negroes in Europe. Only in this post are we engaged in this [slave] trade."[28] Commandants of the Western Posts ignored the imperial mandate to explore and instead sought self-enrichment. The last such commandant, Charles-René Dejordy de Villebon, was overwhelmingly preoccupied with the fur and liquor trades; the French court accused him of unlawfully dealing in brandy as part of the so-called *l'Affaire du Canada*, the trial for treason brought against many Troupes de la Marine officers following the Seven Years' War.[29]

Despite the wealth a Troupes de la Marine officer could derive through the liquor, fur, and slave trades, metropolitan and colonial officials still emphasized exploration and the search for the Western Sea. In 1739, Louis-Joseph de La Vérendrye had explored the northern peripheries of Lake Winnipeg, Lake Manitoba, Lake Winnipegosis, and Cedar Lake. Louis-Joseph had even entered the lower stretches of the Saskatchewan River, travelling upriver as far as the Saskatchewan River Forks, which was an important rendezvous point for various Cree bands. Louis-Joseph thought he might have discovered a waterway to the Western Sea when the Crees told him that the Saskatchewan River "came from very far, from a height of land where there were very lofty mountains; that they knew of a great lake on the other side of the mountains, the water of which was undrinkable."[30] Following Louis-Joseph's visit to the Forks, the Ministry of the Marine and the French colonial government ordered all future commandants of the Western Posts to follow the Saskatchewan River in pursuit of the Western Sea.

Nicolas-Joseph de Noyelles de Fleurimont succeeded La Vérendrye – his uncle by marriage – as commandant of the Western Posts in 1744. De Noyelles was unable to follow the proposed Saskatchewan River route and likely journeyed no further than the southwestern forts of the Red and Assiniboine Rivers. De Noyelles explained that his lack of success was due to his inability to acquire a reliable Native guide. Beauharnois was disappointed that de Noyelles had not made any significant discovery, which he mostly blamed on "the lack of tranquility that prevails among the nations of this continent, which the Sieur de Noyelles found very alarmed upon his arrival."[31] Indeed, arriving at Fort La Reine, his uncle's former headquarters, de Noyelles was dismayed to find a panicked atmosphere, with Crees and Nakoda still reeling from a Dakota attack that had destroyed five Cree cabins and resulted in the deaths or capture of all their inhabitants. Crees and Nakoda did not go trade with the HBC that season, but instead rallied their warriors to retaliate against the Dakota for the destruction of an entire Cree band.[32] De Noyelles was relieved that the Natives at his post would not go to trade with the HBC, but he was still concerned that warfare between the Indigenous peoples of the Hudson Bay watershed would hinder further exploration. Similar to his uncle, de Noyelles was unable to enforce a *Pax Gallica* west of the Great Lakes.

Because of a renewed Anglo-French conflict in 1744, de Noyelles failed to secure enough merchandise and trade goods to make his appointment as commandant of the Western Posts profitable. For example, merchant records indicate that de Noyelles brought only six canoes full of merchandise to the Western Posts, considerably less than La Vérendrye, who in 1735 arranged to have twelve canoes worth of merchandise brought to the posts.[33] Indigenous peoples were not pleased that de Noyelles lacked the necessary trade goods to renew ties of kinship and alliance in the Hudson Bay watershed. Formal relationships between Europeans and Indigenous peoples were not premised on a one-time payment – they had to be regularly renewed through negotiations and gift giving.[34] Because of the lack of trade goods from Montreal, de Noyelles reported that on 24 August 1746 "the Sauteux [Ojibwe] had accepted the hatchet from the English and were to prepare ambuscades in Lake Superior to prevent any Frenchmen leaving the next spring."[35] Fearing for his life, de Noyelles tendered his resignation and returned to Canada.[36]

De Noyelles's lack of success can be blamed in part on the political and commercial crises precipitated by the War of the Austrian Succession, which not only strained supply lines but threw the entire French-Indigenous Great Lakes alliance system into disarray. The disagreement over who would succeed Holy Roman emperor Charles VI (1711–40) triggered a succession crisis that ultimately led to a war between France and Great Britain as well as other European nations in 1740. The War of the Austrian Succession spread to North America in 1744, where the conflict was known as King George's War (1744–48), and led to renewed hostilities between New France and the Thirteen Colonies.[37] In 1745, New Englanders aided by a British fleet captured the French maritime fortress of Louisbourg.[38] The British followed up on their seizure of Canada's only ice-free deepwater port with a naval blockade of the Gulf of Saint Lawrence, which effectively cut off French transatlantic supplies.[39] Anglo-American traders increased their efforts to get British goods into the interior, most notably at Fort Oswego, on the south shore of Lake Ontario, which undermined French influence in the pays d'en haut.[40] The War of the Austrian Succession made the far-flung French posts of the Hudson Bay watershed immensely difficult to supply and provision because of the scarcity and high cost of trade goods. This all resulted in a great shortage of French merchandise and a dramatic increase in prices, which exacerbated existing tensions between New France and its Indigenous allies.[41]

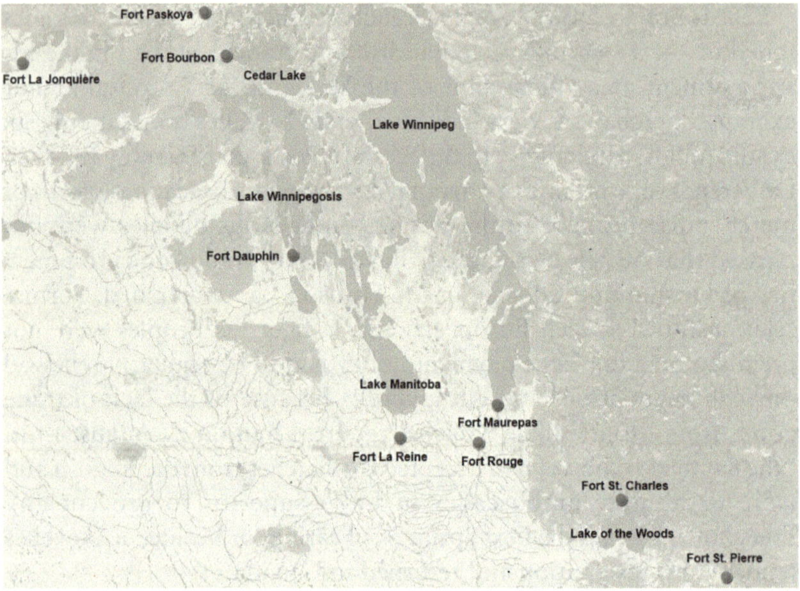

5.1 For part of the War of the Austrian Succession and its aftermath, there were years during which the Western Posts lacked an official commandant (1746–50). In this period, prolonged interactions between Indigenous peoples and Canadiens saw salient patterns of métissage take root in the Hudson Bay watershed.

French colonial historiography has traditionally centred the political and commercial crises of the 1740s around Michilimackinac, Detroit, Oswego, and the Ohio Valley.[42] By reorienting our gaze away from the pays d'en haut toward the Hudson Bay watershed, it becomes clear that the War of the Austrian Succession also had an immeasurable impact on this more peripheral French imperial region. Fur trade returns at the Western Posts declined considerably, just as they did at the Great Lakes posts. In light of the decreased French trade in the Hudson Bay watershed, HBC records indicate that the company's fur trade revenues rose in the late 1740s. The total number of pounds of beaver received by the HBC rose considerably during this period, from 39,505 in 1746–47 to 52,716 in 1747–48.[43] At Fort Albany, which was a continuous hotspot for French fur trade competition, there was an increase in animal furs received from 10,432 skins in 1735 to 23,689 in 1748.[44] The value of MB (Made Beaver) generated at Albany rose from 8,900 in the early 1740s to 12,100 by 1749.[45] The European fur trade – both French and British – would never return to seventeenth-century levels for the simple reason that beaver populations had been depleted from decades of intense competition between traders from both countries in the more easterly portions of the Hudson Bay watershed.[46] Depletion of fur-bearing animals around Hudson and James Bays meant that the French and the British were left to fight for smaller returns, and eventually, seek out new peltries further west.

French colonial officials had considered various schemes for attacking the British in the Hudson Bay watershed following the outbreak of King George's War in 1744. Beauharnois had even sent orders to Paul Guillet, a Montreal merchant who had traded at Témiscamingue since 1724 and who had strong connections to local Anishinaabeg, Crees, and Innu, to invite these Natives to join the French in an attack upon the James Bay posts tentatively planned for the spring of 1745.[47] In addition, Beauharnois expedited orders to Michilimackinac, Nipigon, Michipicoton, and other northern posts to invite local Natives to prepare their warriors, so that "all can collaborate together in the destruction of English settlements on the north shore."[48] Yet the winter of 1744–45 passed without the dispatch of a French-Indigenous force to Témiscamingue, and in 1745 the northern offensive was quietly and indefinitely suspended.[49] Beauharnois instructed Paul Guillet at Témiscamingue to keep the Natives in readiness to join in an attack "if the circumstances become more favourable," but the HBC was left in peace for the remainder of the war.[50] New France's failure to launch even an overland French-Native raid against the HBC demonstrated once again the limits of French imperial power during this period.[51]

The War of the Austrian Succession exacerbated a variety of factors relating directly to the viability of the French fur trade in the Hudson Bay watershed, such as the higher costs of transportation due to longer travel distances, heavier interest rates for merchants, restrictions on canoe cargo space, and higher manufacturing costs in France compared to Britain.[52] Whereas the HBC could ship their goods directly from London via large seafaring cargo ships, the French had to offload seafaring cargoes at Montreal, which they then transferred to birchbark cargo canoes to be paddled and portaged approximately three thousand kilometres to the Western Posts.[53] An overall decline in French voyageur contracts and congés (see figure 5.2) in the late 1740s, as well as the precipitous rise of HBC fur trade revenue, suggests that the crisis triggered by the Atlantic blockade during the War of the Austrian Succession also significantly affected commercial returns at the Western Posts.

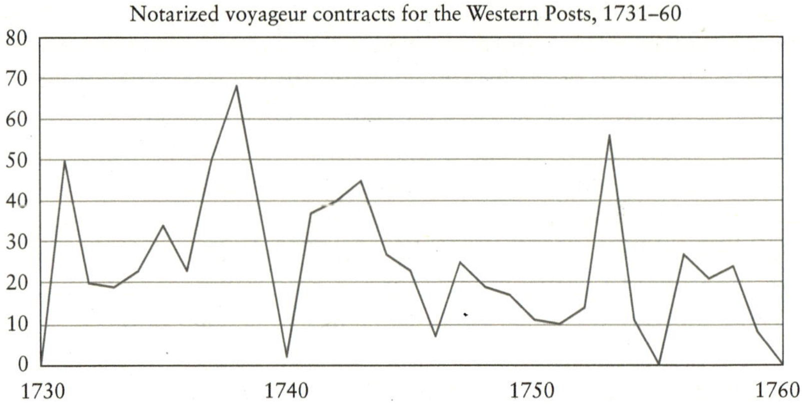

5.2 This graph indicates a clear downward trend in voyageurs signing contracts for indentured labour in the Hudson Bay watershed during the War of the Austrian Succession in North America (1744–48). A similar can trend can be observed for the Seven Years' War in North America (1754–63).

While the War of the Austrian Succession occupied the French in the Great Lakes region and the Ohio Valley, many Cree, Nakoda, Monsoni, and Ojibwe bands who had previously frequented the Western Posts returned to trade with the HBC. When Jacques Legardeur de Saint-Pierre arrived to take up his position as commandant of the Western Posts in 1750, he observed that the British had wrested Cree and Nakoda trade away from the French. Saint-Pierre mistakenly believed that the HBC had gained complete mastery over the Cree and Nakoda, assuming that they feared the British and were "foolish enough to give credence to every dire thing they predict for them."[54] Saint-Pierre attempted to divert trade away from the HBC posts and back into French hands, but Indigenous leaders saw no practical reason to limit themselves to a single European market. Even while Saint-Pierre restored an official French presence at the Western Posts, Crees, Nakoda, Monsonis, and Ojibwes continued to frequent both French and HBC posts. Indigenous peoples of the Hudson Bay watershed liked the convenience of trading at closer French posts but preferred the HBC's reliability, as the company's posts always had merchandise in stock. Once again, the French were powerless to demand that Indigenous peoples trade with them exclusively. Saint-Pierre also had little success when it came to imposing a *Pax Gallica* in the area, noting that Crees and Nakoda were "constantly waging [war] against the Sioux [Dakota]."[55] In the years following the War of the Austrian Succession, Troupes de la Marine officers were unable to renew kinship bonds due to lack of trade goods, and thus lacked the necessary influence in Indigenous societies to pursue French imperial projects in the Hudson Bay watershed.

Saint-Pierre and his lieutenant, Joseph-Claude Boucher, Chevalier de Niverville, barely survived at the Western Posts. Indigenous ambivalence and food scarcity brought Saint-Pierre and Niverville to the brink of starvation and commercial destitution in the early 1750s. At Fort La Reine, Saint-Pierre grumbled that "a very strict fast upset my health so badly that I was rendered incapable of undertaking anything to fulfill my mission."[56] At Fort Paskoya, Niverville suffered such serious malnutrition that an illness left him bedridden; he was unable to even write to Saint-Pierre.[57] The Cree and Nakoda felt no obligation to provision Troupes de la Marine officers, such as de Noyelles, Saint-Pierre, and Niverville, since these men had failed to provide them with adequate trade goods. For that matter, experienced Canadiens who had resided in the Hudson Bay watershed during the War of the Austrian Succession as coureurs de bois would also have refused to supply Saint-Pierre, who was under orders to apprehend illicit fur traders. Therefore, knowledgeable Canadiens would likely have avoided the Western Posts during Saint-Pierre's tenure as commandant.

Saint-Pierre's inability to wrangle coureurs de bois at the Western Posts is not surprising. In fact, Saint-Pierre had disastrously failed to apprehend coureurs de bois earlier in his career when he was stationed at Fort Ouiatenon, on the Wabash River. At the time, Saint-Pierre complained to his superiors, "despite all my attention for the implementation of your orders I could not prevent the passage of the ones named Marié and La Framboise who did it [evaded me] with the help of the Natives who transported them through the woods ... It is not surprising that the Natives help them since they are married to *Sauvagesses* [Native women] who are their allies."[58] Although this example is from the Wabash River valley, and probably involved the Wea (a Miami-Illinois-speaking people), it still helps to explain how Canadiens used family ties and kin connections forged through marriage to evade the French state in colonial hinterlands.

In addition to his failure to acquire a trade monopoly or to impose a French-mediated alliance at the Western Posts, Saint-Pierre also made several diplomatic missteps that offended his Cree and Nakoda hosts. Driven by a desire for profits, he became frustrated over the lack of beaver and other pelts that Cree and Nakoda traders brought to his posts. Although Europeans often essentialized Indigenous peoples as ardent hunters and traders, Natives often defied European preconceptions by engaging in other productive economic activities such as agriculture, bison hunting (rather than beaver trapping), harvesting wild berries or rice, and fishing.[59] In response to the low yields of furs being brought to Fort La Reine, Saint-Pierre even wrote to his merchant partners back in Montreal to say that he planned to personally lead a Cree hunting expedition to a nearby beaver-rich region near the confluence of the Assiniboine and Souris Rivers. Saint-Pierre was certain that his enthusiastic presence on the mission would produce "a considerable profit to the Partnership."[60] However, a European newcomer leading a hunting expedition without proper integration into Cree and Nakoda society would have been extremely unlikely. Cree and Nakoda chiefs followed a prescribed code of acceptable and customary behaviour. A leader's reputation, charisma, consensus-driven decision-making, and redistribution of wealth to their followers were the most important factors governing social and political status.[61] The avaricious Saint-Pierre, who had failed to earn a reputation as either a warrior or a diplomat among the Cree and Nakoda, would have lacked the privileged position needed to lead a hunting party.

Saint-Pierre's un-kin-like behaviour must not have won him many supporters among the Indigenous inhabitants of the Hudson Bay watershed. On 22 February 1752, Nakoda warriors attacked Saint-Pierre's headquarters at Fort La Reine. Around nine o'clock in the morning, two hundred Nakoda stormed the fort and overwhelmed the small garrison of five Frenchmen. Saint-Pierre recorded that the Nakoda warriors raided the armoury with the desire "to kill and pillage me."[62] According to Saint-Pierre's own account, he acted quickly and seized a flaming firebrand, broke open the door of the powder magazine, and knocked in a keg of powder.[63] Saint-Pierre then held the torch over the gunpowder and shouted to the intruders that he would "not perish at their hands, and that in dying I would have the honour of making all of them suffer my very fate."[64] The Nakoda interlopers purportedly took Saint-Pierre's posturing seriously, and "all flew to the fort's gate," fearing that the French commandant may very well blow up the entire fort.[65] As reported by Saint-Pierre, this whole series of events seems very unlikely; not one Frenchman or Native was harmed in the commotion, nor do the Nakoda appear to have seized any of the French trade goods, weapons, or provisions. In the pays d'en haut, as historian Richard White has previously demonstrated, the maintenance of the French-Indigenous alliance sometimes required good acting, clever staging, and the occasional elaborately scripted cultural fiction.[66] Whether Saint-Pierre was aware of it or not, the Nakoda interlopers may have been trying to impose proper kin-like behaviour on the French at Fort La Reine without wanting to actually kill anyone. This staged attack in which no Frenchmen were even injured would have ensured that Saint-Pierre was punished and humiliated for his un-kin-like behaviour, but was not so severe that it made reconciliation with Onontio impossible once a new officer arrived to replace Saint-Pierre – after all, no French blood had been spilled. Fearing for his men's lives, Saint-Pierre remained for the rest of the winter at Fort La Reine, where he survived on meagre rations. He decided to return to Kaministiquia in the spring to gather fresh provisions for the Western Posts.[67]

Given what he perceived as the perilous conditions in the area, Saint-Pierre surmised that no Frenchman could reasonably be asked to garrison Fort La Reine in his absence. However, some Crees and Nakoda had arrived near the end of the winter, ostensibly to beg for forgiveness. Saint-Pierre recorded that "they made great and long harangues, which aimed at obtaining a pardon for their brothers. I answered them that I was not the one who was able to grant it to them, that they had the General as a father, who had sent me to them, that I would report everything to him, and that he would see what he would have to do ... I would persuade their father to forgive them, being convinced of the sincerity of their repentance."[68] To compensate for the supposedly hostile actions of their kinsmen, Saint-Pierre asked the Nakoda band to watch over the post in his absence. Returning the following season, Saint-Pierre was "pained to learn from the Crees that four days after my departure from Fort la Reyne, the same Indians to whom I had entrusted it had set fire to it."[69] Once again, the Nakoda expressed their dissatisfaction with Saint-Pierre's behaviour, as well as his troubling lack of tradable goods. On 31 October 1753, Governor Duquesne reported to Antoine-Louis Rouillé, the new minister of the marine and colonies who had replaced Maurepas in 1749, that Saint-Pierre had failed not only in his mission to discover the Western Sea, but also in his efforts to reconcile the Cree, Nakoda, and Dakota to a French-mediated alliance.[70] De Noyelles's and Saint-Pierre's experiences at the Western Posts clearly illustrated the limits of French imperial power in the 1740s and '50s. The Indigenous peoples of the Hudson Bay watershed retained their own political sovereignty and economic autonomy. During the period immediately following the War of the Austrian Succession, naive elites like Saint-Pierre tried to impose their will on an unfamiliar region. Saint-Pierre's reluctance to utilize Canadiens, who had always been the keys to French diplomacy and influence in the Hudson Bay watershed, was particularly problematic. In short order, local Crees and Nakoda demonstrated to Saint-Pierre and other Troupes de la Marine officers that they would much rather deal with their kinsmen among the coureurs de bois.

VOYAGEURS AND COUREURS DE BOIS IN THE HUDSON BAY WATERSHED, 1743–59

Many voyageurs took control of the Hudson Bay watershed fur trade during the intervening absences of Troupes de la Marine officers from the Western Posts, particularly the four-year period between de Noyelles's departure and Saint-Pierre's arrival (1746–50). Voyageurs and coureurs de bois exercised extraordinary autonomy and enjoyed relatively amicable kin relations with Indigenous peoples in the Hudson Bay watershed in the 1740s and '50s. This period marked an important transition for Canadiens, who moved away from contractual employment and toward greater autonomy and mastery of the region's geographic, political, and cultural landscapes. In many ways, they were important precursors to the *gens libres* (freemen) of the northern Great Plains whose contracts had expired or who had fled company service during the era of fur trade competition between the HBC and the North West Company (NWC).[71] In following a similarly independent trajectory, Canadiens (especially coureurs de bois) in the Hudson Bay watershed took advantage of the War of the Austrian Succession. First, they asserted their political and economic prowess to challenge the HBC's fur trade monopoly. Second, Canadiens began to display markers of a coalescing cultural identity, particularly through expressions of sartorial, spiritual, and gastronomical hybridity. Lastly, many Indigenous women and Canadiens formed "tender ties" by marrying à la façon du pays (in the custom of the country), which helped to entrench voyageurs and coureurs de bois in Indigenous communities in the Hudson Bay watershed. While elements of cultural hybridity and marriage à la façon du pays were present from the beginnings of French-Indigenous relations in the region, the absence of imperial power in the form of Troupes de la Marine officers in the 1740s and '50s – even if their power was by this point largely illusory – helps to explain the increase in scale and pervasiveness of these processes of métissage.

Illicit Traders: Coureurs de Bois Challenge the HBC

It is impossible to determine the exact number of coureurs de bois who traded in the Hudson Bay watershed during the French regime. Even general estimates of the number of illicit fur traders varied widely from one official to the next and were largely a matter of speculation since coureurs de bois tended to evaded the French state. For example, in 1714, Governor Vaudreuil and Intendant Michel Bégon estimated that at least two hundred coureurs de bois had absconded from their obligations as colonists in the Saint Lawrence valley.[72] Around the same time, Governor Claude de Ramezay of Montreal lamented the fact that more than two hundred and fifty coureurs de bois traded liquor with Indigenous peoples in the pays d'en haut.[73] Just a few years later, a missionary report claimed that a thousand habitants had become coureurs de bois.[74] During his tenure as governor, Beauharnois never provided an overall estimate of coureurs de bois, but he did remark that there was a community of about thirty coureurs de bois at the Straits of Mackinac.[75] In the late 1740s and '50s, Beauharnois's successors as governor, Roland-Michel Barrin de La Galissonière (1747–49) and Jacques-Pierre de Taffanel de La Jonquière (1749–52), believed that the activities of coureurs de bois had increased drastically due to the economic pressures of the War of the Austrian Succession, but they did not provide any substantive numbers.[76]

Estimates of coureurs de bois specifically in the Hudson Bay watershed have been even more difficult to determine, but a few sporadic appraisals exist. In 1700–01, French carpenter André Pénicaut reported seven coureurs de bois west of Lake Superior trading with the Dakota.[77] In the summer of 1728, the HBC factor at York Factory indicated that there were at least eight coureurs de bois trading with the Dakota and warring against the Nakoda in the area.[78] In 1731, HBC officials at York Factory and Governor Beauharnois each remarked on how a small group of coureurs de bois in three canoes (between six and nine men, based on the size of their *canot du nord*) traded at the south end of Lake Winnipeg.[79] Judiciously guarding the illusion that he was in control of French imperial projects in the West,

La Vérendrye was careful to never disclose the number of coureurs de bois operating in the Hudson Bay watershed in contravention of the dictates of the colonial authorities at the Western Posts. Nevertheless, French colonial officials believed that the number of coureurs de bois west of Lake Superior had increased over time, especially during the War of the Austrian Succession. In particular, Governor La Jonquière believed that coureurs de bois were an endemic problem in the Hudson Bay watershed, and it was for this reason that he ordered La Vérendrye's successor, Jacques Legardeur de Saint-Pierre, to stop and arrest all coureurs de bois he came across during his attempt to re-garrison the Western Posts.[80] Even the upper administration of the Ministry of the Marine, like Maurepas, opined that in western North America the number of coureurs de bois "increases yearly."[81] By the end of the 1750s, HBC officials at York Factory gave an astonishingly large estimate of two hundred coureurs de bois in the Hudson Bay watershed alone.[82]

Based on the observations of French colonial officials and HBC factors, it is clear that an increasing number of coureurs de bois were taking advantage of the absence of French officials at the Western Posts during the War of the Austrian Succession. These men began to establish small independent trading posts at Cedar Lake, Moose Lake, the northern shore of Lake Winnipeg, and the lower stretches of the Saskatchewan River. HBC post journals and letters attest to the increased activity of the Canadiens in these more northerly waterways. In 1743 at Fort Albany, Joseph Isbister fretted that "we have got a new neighbour of 3 french pedlars come and placed themselves on ye maine branch of this river [the Albany] ... All Indians that have come in here is all clothed with french cloth."[83] In 1747, at York Factory, HBC governor James Isham wrote that "our Enemys ye french" were "Incroaching near our frontiers and building of huts for trade."[84] The same year, John Potts at Moose Factory, was distressed that coureurs de bois were establishing little trading houses along Moose River to intercept Native traders on their way to the HBC factory.[85] In 1748, Isham reported to the company's London Committee that coureurs de bois were trading in such close proximity to York Factory that they were siphoning off the main portion of the fur trade.[86] Henry Ellis, a scientific observer aboard a vessel engaged in the search for the Northwest Passage, observed that coureurs de bois were "making daily Encroachments upon" and "intercepting the choicest Kind of Furs, such as Otters, Martins, or Sables; which they purchase, because they are lightest, and, consequently, fittest for Carriage, as the Places where they buy them are at a great Distance from the French Settlements."[87] In 1752, George Spence at Fort Albany noted that local Crees had traded with coureurs de bois the previous winter, and that the Canadiens intended to build a trading house at the source of the Severn River (Deer Lake, Ontario).[88]

To counteract the activities of coureurs de bois, the chief factor at York Factory, James Isham, began a policy of sending adventurous company men inland to encourage Indigenous peoples to come trade at bayside posts. This led to the increased presence of HBC explorers and traders along the interior waterways of the Hudson Bay watershed. These men's travels and writings help to shed light on the activities of Canadiens during this period. In 1754, Isham conceived of a plan to send Anthony Henday, a labourer, net maker, and former smuggler, on a journey inland with a Cree leader named Attickasish (Little Deer). Henday had "gone in Land ... [to] Encourage the Indians to come to Trade," and he was especially meant to "bring the Earchethe to Trade, who are very Numerous."[89] The HBC was only vaguely aware of these Natives, whom they knew as the "Archithinues" or "Earchethe" but who called themselves "Niitsítapi," otherwise known as the Blackfoot Confederacy, which comprised three Indigenous nations: the Kainai (Blood), Piikani (Peigan) and Siksika (Blackfoot).[90] Because coureurs de bois were pulling away the HBC's traditional Cree customers located in the Lake Winnipeg, Cedar Lake, and lower Saskatchewan River regions, James Isham and other company officials wanted to open new, untapped markets. Aware of the lingering presence of coureurs de bois in the regions that Henday would have to pass through, Isham warned him:

> It's not unlikely of the french or wood Runners, in hearing of your being amongst the Indians, may way Lay you, to prevent which, take perticular Care to make the Indians your friends, that in case They shou'd attempt Such a thing, you may be able to head the Indians against the said wood Runners, for your own preservation, but otherwise do not offer, or Let the Indians molest the Said wood runners, unless they are the first transgressors, as already observ'd.[91]

HBC officials like Isham were acutely aware of the influence that Canadiens wielded in the Hudson Bay watershed.

Rather than challenging the HBC, some coureurs de bois opted to engage in "private trade" with company servants. For example, voyageur François Jérôme *dit* Latour took advantage of the situation to assert control of the French fur trade in the region of Fort Bourbon, at Cedar Lake. In the absence of trade goods from Montreal, though, Jérôme tried to strike a contraband deal with the HBC, sending a letter with a Native courier to John Newton, interim chief factor at York Factory. Along with the letter, Jérôme sent his broken oboe and asked if they could repair it; incidentally, this was the first mention of a musical instrument of this kind in the Hudson Bay watershed.[92] Jérôme offered them some of his own contraband items in return, urging the British to come visit him at Fort Bourbon and "settle a little private trade," telling them that they had nothing to fear from the Canadien traders as long as they "Leave the Indians quiet as we do."[93] John Newton replied haughtily that the HBC paid its employees too well for them to be tempted to trade illegally and to associate with coureurs de bois.[94]

This does not appear to be the first time that coureurs de bois tried to open contraband trade with the HBC during the absence of a commandant at the Western Posts. When HBC surveyor and engineer Joseph Robson was visiting York Factory in 1746, he recorded that he had caught a glimpse of a letter addressed to the HBC from Canadien fur traders north of Lake Winnipeg. Robson claimed that the intent of the letter was to establish a trade between the Canadiens and the British at York Factory involving those heavy goods of which the French stood in great need but could not easily transport from the Saint Lawrence valley, such as guns, kettles, knives, and hatchets. The letter beseeched the British to indicate how much beaver they wanted in exchange for some of these bulkier items.[95] Robson was also surprised and suspicious when he heard the post's surgeon, one "Mr. Brady," conversing in French with some Native traders who had come to the post.[96] When Anthony Henday, following Isham's instructions, descended the Saskatchewan River in 1755, voyageurs and coureurs de bois asked him if he could bring or send "a piece of Brazile tobacco, & a quart, or pint, japanned drinking mug."[97] In the absence of Troupes de la Marine officers, voyageurs and coureurs de bois not only piggybacked on French trade networks, but also occasionally crossed imperial lines to attempt to trade directly with the British.

In 1759, Humphrey Marten, another interim chief factor at York Factory, learned from a visiting voyageur that a group of coureurs de bois had established a post nearby at Moose Lake.[98] Coureurs de bois also traded on Lake Winnipeg, particularly at the mouth of the Winnipeg River, at Big Bullhead Point, and at Fort Saut-au-Pas, where the Saskatchewan River discharges into Lake Winnipeg (present-day Grand Rapids, Manitoba).[99] These illicit traders radiated out from the Western Posts in search of more advantageous places to engage in the fur trade. For example, rather than trading out of Fort La Reine, many coureurs de bois operated at the more strategically located Fort à Blondeau and Pointe-aux-Trembles, near the confluence of the Assiniboine and Souris Rivers, in order to trade with the Nakoda.[100] Similarly, independent traders at Portage du Île and Fort Bourguignonin, in the Winnipeg River and English River watersheds, strategically positioned themselves to intercept more Cree and Ojibwe traders travelling to Hudson Bay than their counterparts at Fort Saint-Charles and Fort Saint-Pierre.[101] Taking into account these unofficial or illegal trading locations, the French presence in the Hudson Bay watershed nearly doubles during this period.[102] By 1759, the same year that Quebec City fell to the British at the Battle of the Plains of Abraham, there were still an estimated two hundred coureurs de bois in the Hudson Bay watershed.[103] From that first lonely winter of 1659–60, when Radisson and Des Groseilliers were the only coureurs de bois wintering in the area northwest of Lake Superior, the number of Canadiens in the Hudson Bay watershed would increase exponentially over the next century.

During the 1740s and '50s, Canadiens regularly operated outside of the confines of imperial trade regulations, much to the chagrin of both French and HBC officials. These voyageurs and coureurs de bois not only requisitioned pre-existing French trade networks, they also attempted to transcend imperial borders to trade with the British, a grave threat to both French mercantilism and imperialism in the Hudson Bay watershed. In addition to the fact that these illicit French traders were beyond imperial control, there was now the possibility that they might defect and thus change the balance of power at the edge of empire. As HBC officials were soon to learn, Canadiens used métissage and kinship relations to maintain their positions of prominence in Indigenous trade and diplomatic networks in the Hudson Bay watershed.

Cultural Hybridity at the Western Posts

When Anthony Henday, HBC explorer and trade promoter, visited the French posts in the Saskatchewan River valley, he described a world of cultural hybridity in which Canadiens were adapting to the ways of their Cree trading partners and kinsmen. On 30 May 1755, Henday expressed his surprise at how one French trader was "dressed very genteel yesterday, but to day he is dressed like the natives excepting his white ruffled shirt, silk handkerchief tied round his head and laced hat."[104] As historians Timothy J. Shannon and Sophie White have demonstrated, sartorial expressions of "cultural cross-dressing" fundamentally mediated encounters between Europeans and Natives. In other words, dress and clothing could serve as symbolic cross-cultural expressions that helped Natives and newcomers find common cultural meanings.[105] French colonial officials usually clothed Native chiefs visiting Montreal by giving them linen shirts, capotes, and leggings, which served as symbolic representations of their alliance with the French as well as their fictive kin relationship with Onontio.[106] Similarly, Frenchmen donned Indigenous garb and wielded certain aspects of material culture, such as the calumet, in an attempt to engender accommodation and find common meaning with their military allies and partners in the fur trade. In both cases, "cultural cross-dressing" was not a form of sartorial acculturation so much as a continuation of traditions of cultural borrowing and flexible identity for both French and Indigenous participants.[107] For example, during the negotiations leading up to the Great Peace of Montreal in 1701, Mesquakie orator Miskouensa emulated French dress and mannerisms by donning an old wig that was "heavily powdered and very badly combed" and saluting Governor Callière in the French aristocratic manner. Historian Gilles Havard argues that Miskouensa's performance illustrated "the creative aspect of the encounter and highlights the intensity of the cultural exchange. Each side was attempting to adapt to the other by mirroring its culture."[108] In other words, if one wanted to exert cultural influence in the host society, whether Indigenous or European, one had to be ready to dress the part.

In many instances, Native and Canadien cultural cross-dressers were not always necessarily seeking mutual understanding; sometimes, they were simply looking for expedient adaptations to the local environment of the Northwest. Canadien voyageurs and coureurs de bois, for example, dressed primarily for the constraints of long-distance canoe voyages, adapting their clothing to the requirements of strenuous paddling and portaging. During the summer, most Canadiens went about wearing only an oversized linen shirt that fell to the knees and a *brayet* (breechcloth) in order to alleviate the intense heat. One observer wrote that Canadiens, when paddling and portaging canoes, "are generally barefooted and barelegged, wearing only their shirts."[109] Another remarked that, "when the French are travelling about in this country, they are generally dressed like the natives; they wear then no trousers."[110] Voyageurs and coureurs de bois also carried a powder horn around their necks, a fire bag, a tobacco pouch, a cooking pot, a hatchet, and a gun. In winter, voyageurs traded their summertime outfits for beaver mittens, capotes, pairs of *mitasses* (gaiters), wool toques, and moccasins. One Jesuit described moccasins as "socks made of elk-skin, and lined inside with hair or with wool, [which] take the place of shoes"; these were "absolutely necessary for the purpose of adjusting their snowshoes."[111] Inversely, Native peoples often traded their animal skins for woollen or linen garments and fabrics, which not only dried much faster than furs but could also be dyed with a variety of coloured pigments. One eighteenth-century observer noted that "a great number of the natives ... had already begun to dress like the French: the same kind of jacket and vest, while on journeys they wore the same red cap or hat."[112] According to historian Susan Sleeper-Smith, ready-made clothing, bolt cloth, blankets, and the items to transform cloth into clothing – scissors, thread, pins, and needles – became the most desirable trade items, constituting 60 per cent of merchandise exchanged in the fur trade.[113]

Religious and spiritual syncretism matched the superficially visible métissage of sartorial expression. At first glance, the often disparaging way that Catholic missionaries and clergymen wrote about voyageurs and coureurs de bois gives the impression that Catholicism was not an important factor in these men's lives. For example, when Daniel Greysolon Du Lhut rescued Father Louis Hennepin somewhere on the Upper Mississippi River, the Récollet priest fretted that Du Lhut and his men "had not receiv'd the Sacraments in the whole two Years and a half that they had been out upon their Voyage."[114] Similarly, Intendant Jean Bochart de Champigny exclaimed that voyageurs and coureurs de bois "live in the woods like Natives and go for two or three years without receiving any sacraments."[115] A Jesuit missionary criticized the itinerant nature of the fur trade and worried that "This Sending of the french among the savages must appear

Infinitely harmful to them. It Takes them away from all the holy places; it separates them from all Ecclesiastical and religious persons; It abandons them to a total deprivation of all Instruction, both public and private, of all devotional Exercises, and, finally, of all the spiritual aids to Christianity."[116] Despite the reservations of some colonial officials and missionaries as to the piety of Canadien fur traders, many voyageurs and coureurs de bois stationed in the Hudson Bay watershed were devoted to their Catholic beliefs, some journeying quite far to the distant mission of Michilimackinac to seek out clergymen who could administer sacraments.

Michilimackinac's parish register indicates that Canadiens from the Hudson Bay watershed often travelled there to visit resident priests Father Pierre Du Jaunay or Father Jean-Baptiste de Lamorinie, who baptized their children (and sometimes slaves), admitted them to Holy Communion, and consecrated their "country marriages." For example, in 1747, Father Lamorinie "baptized a young child about 3 years old, natural son of Charles Chevalier tallier and of a Sioux [Dakota] slave. The said child was born at lac de la pluye [Rainy Lake]."[117] In 1752, Father Lamorinie baptized a teenager, "about thirteen or fourteen years old," who took the name of Louis and who was the "natural son of Mr. la plante and of a woman Savage of Cammanettigouia [Kaministiquia]."[118] In 1762, Father Du Jaunay baptized the child of Sieur Hyppolite de Rivières and his wife Marie, who was "born at Alimipigon [Nipigon] on the 19th of December of last year."[119] Prominent families of Michilimackinac, like the Bourassas and the Langlades, often acted as godparents to children or slaves from the Western Posts, which served to solidify kinship ties between the pays d'en haut and the Hudson Bay watershed.[120] As historian Susan Sleeper-Smith argues, Catholicism acquired increased centrality in the fur trade because of its social ramifications. Indigenous peoples and Canadiens used "frontier" Catholicism to construct networks mostly through kinship ties (godparentage) with distant and dispersed communities throughout western North America that shaped the emergence of a fur trade society.[121]

While Michilimackinac served as a conduit for Catholic kinship networks in the pays d'en haut, Catholic beliefs and rites were very important for voyageurs and coureurs de bois even before missionaries formally implanted the institutions of the Catholic Church in the Hudson Bay watershed. Historian Émilie Pigeon has examined the ways that Canadien and later Métis people practised "lived

Catholicism" outside of the institutional control of the church. As Pigeon explains, "when priests were unavailable, laypeople became evangelists and disseminated Catholic teachings to their families."[122] In the Hudson Bay watershed, Canadien voyageurs and coureurs de bois relied upon their own understanding of the faith and engaged in Catholic rituals and practices on their own terms. In the absence of clergy in the region, Canadiens practised syncretic religious customs – for example, by substituting pemmican for the traditional host in the celebration of the Eucharist, Indigenous medicines like sage and oak for the blessed palms distributed on Palm Sunday, and by repurposing the Canadien folkloric tale of the *loup-garou* (werewolf) to reinforce Lenten practices.[123]

Many French officers marvelled at the strangely syncretic spiritual customs of Canadien voyageurs, such as mock baptisms. For example, during a 1686 expedition, Pierre de Troyes, a nobleman and high-ranking military officer, commented on how Canadiens reacted to a spiritually charged Indigenous site called Oiseau Rock, which is located along the Ottawa River at the upper end of Lac aux Allumettes. De Troyes described the sacred site as

> a high mountain which drops straight and sheer into the water. The middle of this rock wall appears black, caused perhaps by the natives' offerings of tobacco which they shoot at the rock by attaching them to the ends of their arrows. The natives call this rock "The Bird." According to the custom of our people, a man must be baptized here the first time he passes this rock. Several of our men, not wishing to abandon this time-honoured custom, dived into the water so we camped at the foot of the portage.[124]

Sacrificing arrows and tobacco was a common practice among many Indigenous peoples, and voyageur ritual baptisms occurred at these thresholds of spatial and cultural significance. Fur trade historian Carolyn Podruchny has posited that voyageur ritual baptism was a religiously syncretic practice that combined Roman Catholic rites with Indigenous spiritual customs. Podruchny suggests that it was not an accident that the spiritually transformative "Pointe aux Baptêmes" was situated at Oiseau Rock, a pre-existing site of Indigenous spiritual meaning.[125] Canadiens respected another Indigenous spiritual site at Mackinac Island, which was said to house a great manidoo who lived under the island and controlled the currents and winds of the Straits of Mackinac. The Canadiens were somewhat reserved in their reverence for the manidoo because they had previously mocked the Indigenous superstition, but when feasting in sight of Mackinac Island they always "mutter[ed] something between their teeth which resembles the prayer that they offer to these spirits [*manidoog*] of the island."[126] Clearly, Canadien voyageurs had over time come to appreciate the spiritually charged landscape of Native North America.

In the absence of priests and missionaries, lay practitioners – whether Canadiens, Europeans, or Natives – participated in rites usually reserved for the clergy, such as the performance of baptisms, nuptials, administering last rites, and catechizing neophytes.[127] While lay baptisms and marriages might be consecrated by clergymen at a later date, unforeseen or accidental deaths in the Northwest necessitated ad hoc Christian burial and funerary rituals. Following the Lake of the Woods raid, the French mostly sequestered themselves inside Fort Saint-Charles throughout the summer, but finally, on 17 September 1736, La Vérendrye "dispatched the sergeant with six men to go and raise the bodies of the Reverend Father Aulneau and my son, and on the eighteenth I had them buried in the chapel, together with the heads of all the Frenchmen killed, which they also brought in accordance with my orders."[128] Although these are La Vérendrye's only written comments on the burial, the later excavation of Fort Saint-Charles by an expedition from St Boniface College in the summer of 1908 suggests that Jean-Baptiste de La Vérendrye, Father Aulneau, and the voyageurs were interred according to the rites of the Roman Catholic Church. The St Boniface College expedition unearthed nineteen skulls and five bodies, "two of which were in a box side by side." Within the makeshift coffin, the St Boniface College team excavated "beads of a rosary and a bunch of keys."[129] This conformed to Catholic burial practices, according to which rosaries are often placed in the hands of the deceased prior to burial. The reason for interring the keys is less evident, but it might symbolize the keys of heaven Jesus entrusted to Saint Peter, which were also the heraldic symbols of the Holy See.[130] Although the Lake of the Woods raid constituted the single largest loss of life for voyageurs in the Northwest – larger even than the Pemmican War (1812–21) – many voyageurs also perished from starvation, injury, and illness. Canoeing and portaging accidents resulting in hernias, broken and fractured bones, and drowning were commonplace.[131] When voyageurs died while on the job, their comrades performed funerary rites in an ad hoc, syncretic blending of Catholic ritual and spiritual customs that had developed à la façon du pays, perhaps offering some tobacco or uttering a small prayer to riverine and whitewater manidoog.

Miracles also played a role in the "lived Catholicism" of the Northwest in the period prior to the arrival of Red River missionaries Father Joseph-Norbert Provencher and Father Sévère Dumoulin in 1818. The Roman Catholic Church never officially recognized these miracles, but they survived in the voyageur folkloric tradition of the Northwest. Father Aulneau's death produced several miraculous occurrences that circulated in voyageur folklore. After interviewing several voyageurs, Father Pierre Du Jaunay of the mission at Michilimackinac wrote that as soon as the Dakota warriors had killed Aulneau, "a deafening peal of thunder struck terror into the whole band. They fled the spot, believing that Heaven was incensed at what they had done."[132] Du Jaunay seems to have learned about the miraculous crash of thunder from visitors to Michilimackinac, and he cautiously endorsed the account, asserting, "here is what I have learned from hearsay, and some of my sources of information seem trustworthy."[133] The voyageur folkloric tradition recorded by David Thompson in 1797 attests to the pervasiveness of the Father Aulneau miracle in subsequent decades. Canadiens informed Thompson that the moment the Dakota slew Aulneau with a well-placed arrow, "the rocky isle trembled and shook," which frightened the Dakota warriors, who retired to the south shore of Lake of the Woods, sparing Fort Saint-Charles.[134] Despite the tradition surrounding Aulneau's miraculous death at Lake of the Woods, it appears that he never became a staple in the Canadiens' spiritual repertoire in the Northwest as there are no recorded instances of voyageurs praying to him to intercede with God on their behalf.

However, one of Aulneau's *confrères* from the seventeenth century, Father Jacques Marquette, who died on the eastern shore of Lake Michigan in 1675, seems to have enjoyed much more prominence in the fur trade country. Father Charlevoix (whom we met in chapter 2) observed during his journey through the pays d'en haut that Canadien voyageurs often prayed to Father Marquette "when they are in any danger on lake Michigan. Several of them have affirmed that they believed themselves indebted to his intercession for having escaped very great dangers."[135] Aside from Marquette, Canadiens also prayed for intercession from saints officially recognized by the Roman

Catholic Church, with Saint Anne and the Virgin Mary being the most venerated.[136] For example, when crossing the threshold from the Saint Lawrence valley into the pays d'en haut, voyageurs always stopped at Saint Anne's church at the western extremity of the Island of Montreal to pay homage to the patron saint of voyages and ask for her protection during their expedition. Sailors and fishermen from Brittany had brought Saint Anne to New France in the seventeenth century by building a chapel in her honour at Beaupré.[137] During a seaborne naval expedition to Hudson Bay, Jesuit army chaplain Father Pierre-Gabriel Marest explained how strong headwinds and an advancing winter season compelled Canadien sailors and soldiers to turn to Saint Anne for succour. Marest observed that Saint Anne was "especially reverenced by the Canadians as their advocate with God."[138] During the Iroquois Wars, Canadien habitants recruited as soldiers often wore devotional scapulars of the Immaculate Conception. These objects of popular piety devoted to the Virgin Mary ensured that soldiers who fell in battle would be guaranteed a "good death" and prompt deliverance from purgatory.[139] In 1690, the Virgin Mary thwarted an English seaborne invasion of the Saint Lawrence valley meant to conquer Quebec. A Jesuit chronicler wrote that when thirty-four English warships appeared before Cap Diamant, "the banner of Our Lady was continually displayed from the top of the steeple of the great Church; it was under this sacred flag that our poor habitants fought and Conquered."[140] David Thompson observed in the late eighteenth century that Canadiens who had taken root in the Hudson Bay watershed, while they seemingly knew very little about the more formal aspects of religious practice, nonetheless worshiped the Virgin Mary.[141] Devotion to Saint Anne and to the Virgin Mary travelled easily with canoe brigades via rivers and lakes into the heart of North America.[142] When fur trader and diarist Daniel Williams Harmon travelled through the watershed of the Assiniboine and lower Souris Rivers, he claimed to have encountered Indigenous peoples who recited "some short prayers in the French language" purportedly taught to them by a French missionary fifty years prior.[143] In all likeliness, Harmon had encountered the offspring of fur trade marriages, who remembered some of the prayers that their French fathers had taught them. Belief in the Virgin Mary and Saint Anne, alongside manidoog that dotted the riverine and lacustrine landscapes, were important to the syncretic spiritual tapestry of the Northwest.

During his stay at the French posts along the Saskatchewan River in 1754–55, HBC explorer Anthony Henday dined several times with Canadien traders and described how the food and beverage consumption at the Western Posts was remarkably hybrid.[144] Henday described how they feasted on pemmican and liberally drank French brandy, but he complained that "we had no bread until we were done [supper]; then He presented me with [only] half a biscuit."[145] The French diet in the Saint Lawrence valley consisted of European and tropical staples such as bread, beef, poultry, cheese, milk, peas, beans, cabbage, cucumbers, eggs, milk, coffee, brandy, wine, and even chocolate, but such luxuries were rarely available for consumption at distant fur trade outposts.[146] For the most part, fur traders' diets generally consisted of fresh game, wild rice, berries, fish, bear fat, and maple sugar, as well as mostly preserved foods such as pemmican when on the move.[147] As one Sulpician writer observed, "one manages in the woods of Canada to fare well without bread, wine, salt, pepper, or any condiments."[148] In the pays d'en haut, *sagamité*, a corn-based stew seasoned with bear grease, beans, wild rice, pumpkin, and chunks of meat or fish, was a daily dish for Indigenous peoples and Canadiens at places like Michilimackinac and Detroit.[149] A Récollet observer described it as a "Meal of Indian Corn boil'd with Water, and season'd with Grease."[150] *Sagamité* was far less common in the Hudson Bay watershed because Crees, Monsonis, and Nakoda did not cultivate corn. However, the dish was not completely unknown in the Northwest because Crees and Nakoda of the Red and Assiniboine River valleys frequently traded second-hand European merchandise – axes, knives, firesteels, and kettles – with their agriculturist neighbours to the south, like the Mandans, Hidatsas, and Arikaras, for bushels of corn and beans.[151] During their sojourn with the Mandan, La Vérendrye and Canadiens feasted daily on "corn, beechnuts, pumpkin ... always cooked."[152] Likewise, Canadiens shared provisions brought with them from Montreal with Indigenous peoples. At Fort Saint-Charles, Crees and Monsonis might have tasted biscuits, peas, salted pork, smoked beef, and brandy for the first time.[153] Similar to hybrid sartorial expressions and religious syncretism, the diets of coureurs de bois reflected salient processes of métissage. At the Western Posts, the diets of Indigenous peoples and French traders basically constituted a "fusion cuisine," a term later coined by modern-day restaurateurs and foodies to describe the multicultural fusing or blending of flavours and culinary traditions.

This was nothing new for Crees, who had been forging a "fusion cuisine" with European newcomers since the early eighteenth century, when Cree leaders compelled HBC traders to share company provisions with them as part of a reciprocal relationship that ensured survival in the harsh subarctic climate of the Canadian Northwest. At HBC posts, factors held preparatory feasts for Cree goose hunters and their families, generously supplying oatmeal, peas, salted fish, tobacco, and brandy as encouragement to the hunters prior to the arrival of the geese.[154] In return, Cree hunters provisioned HBC factories with three to four thousand geese annually.[155]

HBC servants and Canadiens alike enjoyed bison meat and pemmican when travelling alongside Crees and Nakoda on the northern Great Plains. When HBC servants Joseph Smith and Joseph Waggoner spent the winter on the Prairies, in what is now southwestern Manitoba and southeastern Saskatchewan, they encountered groups of French traders who were also wintering with Indigenous peoples and consuming prodigious amounts of bison flesh. Later Catholic tradition from North Dakota reveals that Canadiens on the Prairies substituted sacramental bread for pemmican as Eucharistic hosts.[156] Although Smith and Waggoner record no such observations, it was not inconceivable that Canadiens were adapting rituals around the Holy Eucharist to life in the Northwest as early as the 1750s. In addition to the consumption of sacramental pemmican during the Catholic rite of the Eucharist, Canadiens adhering to "lived Catholicism" also had to circumvent other restrictions that forbade the consumption of red meat on certain days, which would have been difficult on the limited diet of the Prairies and the Canadian Shield. Swedish botanist Pehr Kalm observed upon his visit to the Saint Lawrence valley that "beaver meat is eaten not only by the Indians but likewise by the Europeans, and especially by the French, on their fasting days; for his Holiness the Pope has ... classified the beaver among the fishes."[157] The Roman Curia had indeed classified the beaver, with its aquatic adaptations, as a fish; this meant Canadiens were permitted to consume the animal during the forty days of Lent, as well as on Fridays and Saturdays. Ultimately, the Eucharistic pemmican and the piscine beaver constituted a blend of religious syncretism and gastronomical hybridity in the Northwest.

Despite the shortages of French trade goods and merchandise, métissage seems to have kept Canadiens in a preferential position for diplomacy and trade in Indigenous political and commercial networks in the Hudson Bay watershed. When Anthony Henday later attempted to persuade the Crees to trade exclusively at York Factory, Cree chief Monkonsko was adamant that they were "more conveniently supplyed from the french houses," but he agreed to visit and trade at HBC posts on occasion. Henday bemoaned the fact that the Crees were "strongly attached to the french Interest."[158] James Isham opined that the HBC's debilitating trade situation was due to logistical problems, and especially the fact that the company's posts were stretched out over vast distances. Simply put, the French brought merchandise directly to Indigenous peoples, whereas the HBC's posts were several months of hard travel away from most Native communities, which made it difficult for Cree hunters to provision their families in the difficult subarctic environment.[159] Still, Henday had achieved some success in his inland mission. On 6 September 1754, he met a group of "Eagle Indians," a Nakoda band who had supposedly never traded with Europeans before. Henday's diplomacy was apparently effective, for Eagle Nakoda trading parties subsequently went down to York Factory annually. Several other band leaders also agreed to trade at York Factory exclusively, but it is difficult to track whether they kept their promise or continued to trade with the French posts on the Saskatchewan River as well.[160]

Following the moderate success of Henday's expedition, Isham sent more young men inland to coax various Native bands to come trade at Hudson Bay. Between 1756 and 1763, Joseph Smith and Joseph Waggoner, whom James Isham often referred to as "the two Josephs," made five inland journeys. Smith kept journals on his 1756, 1757, and 1763 trips, but it is difficult to pinpoint his routes because his entries are often crude and laconic. The two explorers were certainly the first Englishmen to journey as far as the Assiniboine River region. On 4 July 1758, Isham sent Issac Batt and an "Esquimay Boy," George Potts, inland with Sturgeon River Crees, who were "the same Inds the 2 Josephs were with."[161] Not since the days of Henry Kelsey in the 1690s had the HBC so earnestly pursued the exploration of the interior of North America.[162] If the HBC had "for eighty years slept at the edge of a frozen sea," as surveyor and engineer Joseph Robson had once criticized, they had indeed now awoken.[163]

Anthony Henday described the voyageurs and coureurs de bois along the lower stretches of the Saskatchewan River as traders whose "Master and men were gone down to Montreal with the Furs."[164] Regarding the motley assortment of Canadiens that remained along the Saskatchewan River, Henday found it "suprizing to observe what great influence the French hath over the natives ... [They] got above 1,000 of the richest Skins."[165] Henday attributed their success to métissage and the language skills they possessed, noting that "the French talk several Languages to perfection: They have the advantage of us in every shape."[166] The clothing of Canadiens reflected this métissage, and Anthony Henday further observed that Canadiens in the Hudson Bay watershed "wore nothing but thin drawers, and striped cotton shirts ruffled at hand and breast, they all talk the Language as well as the Natives themselves, and has a command over the Natives."[167] Joseph Robson also admired the success of French traders in the Hudson Bay watershed, noting that Natives "behave well to the English, but better to the French, because the French have taken more pains to civilize their manners, and engage their esteem."[168] Robson recognized that voyageurs and coureurs de bois retained good relations with the Cree, but mistakenly believed that it was because Canadiens were "civilizing" or "Frenchifying" their Native trade partners. In reality, trade relations were amicable because voyageurs and coureurs de bois were adhering to and even practising Indigenous customs, languages, and material culture.

Marriages à la façon du pays

Indigenous peoples and Canadiens maintained kinship relations through enduring and salient processes of métissage centred around calumet ceremonies, exchanges of gifts, and the bestowing of kin names, each of which helped to transform "outsiders" into "insiders," or to make European newcomers into relatives in Indigenous society.[169] In particular, though, French-Native marriages, or marriages à la façon du pays (in the custom of the country), created kinship ties that solidified political and commercial relations between Canadiens and Indigenous peoples in the Hudson Bay watershed. Native wives served as cultural and often political liaisons between their male kin and Canadien husbands, providing the latter access to Indigenous trading networks through kinship ties.[170] In the fur trade, argue scholars like Jennifer Brown, Sylvia Van Kirk, and Susan Sleeper-Smith, Indigenous women were not merely casual bedmates, but rather essential "negotiators of change" and contributors to the spread and conduct of the trade itself, often embracing métissage and the hybrid set of cultural values that comprised fur trade society in the Northwest.[171]

Even though marriages à la façon du pays occurred in the fur trade country outside the purview of the church, they were true marital unions in every sense of the word. As Sylvia Van Kirk concludes, "in spite of its many complexities and complications, 'the custom of the country' should be regarded as a bona fide marital union."[172]

Initially, some Troupes de la Marine officers had recognized the strategic advantages of French unions with Indigenous women. These marriages allowed officers to acquire insider perspectives on local Indigenous communities, which was especially valuable during tenuous periods marked by shifting alliances and warfare.[173] Notwithstanding these obvious strategic, diplomatic, and economic advantages, the French colonial government had officially condemned French-Indigenous marriages by the beginning of the eighteenth century due to a solidifying racial ideology based in the stigmatization of "mixed-raced" descendants. Colonial officials feared French-Native marriages and emphasized the importance of "never mixing a bad blood with a good one," and they argued that "mixed-blood" children were as lazy as Indigenous peoples were purported to be.[174] An official from New Orleans stressed that children of mixed-marriages were "naturally idlers, libertines and … rascals."[175] Another colonial official complained that children of mixed unions "are more mischievous than the natives themselves."[176] The racialization of Indigenous peoples eventually made its way into French colonial discourse because of Jean-Baptiste Colbert's failed cultural-assimilationist policy (francisation) in the seventeenth century. Disillusioned by New France's "cultural defeat," French officials drew upon the metropolitan discourse of mésalliance (inferior blood or blood corruption), and further employed a biological discourse to stigmatize the idea of French-Indigenous intermarriage.[177]

And yet Canadiens still frequently married into Indigenous families and extended kinship networks irrespective of the official government condemnation. Voyageurs and coureurs de bois who married into Indigenous families benefited from relationships that helped improve their quality of life considerably. While a husband was away engaging in the fur trade or military duties, Indigenous women managed hearth and home, preparing food, chopping wood, mending clothing, and even making valuable survival items such as moccasins or snowshoes.[178] As an Algonquin neophyte told Jesuit father Paul Le Jeune in 1639, "To live among us without a wife is to live without help, without home, and to be always wandering."[179] The Algonquian-speaking Crees and Monsonis of the Hudson Bay watershed shared many similarities with the Algonquins encountered by Father Le Jeune almost a century prior. On the other side of the cultural and linguistic divide, Siouan peoples of the Upper Mississippi valley (Očhéthi Šakówiŋ) and northern Great Plains (Nakoda) also engaged in strategic fur trade marriages with European newcomers.[180]

It is important to note, however, that not all French-Indigenous relations resulted in the same cross-cultural sexual and marital relationships described by Brown, Van Kirk, and Sleeper-Smith. Marriage à la façon du pays was not a forgone conclusion in all French-Indigenous relations because the gender norms that regulated various Indigenous societies differed greatly across place and time. Certain Indigenous peoples, like the Quapaws of the lower Arkansas valley or the Apalachee refugees at Mobile, consistently rejected exogamous trade or political marriages with the French.[181] On the "Native ground," or in "Indian Country," the French alone did not determine the sexual and marital landscape; rather, it was local Indigenous peoples who largely set the guidelines for gender relations, marital practices, and sexual interactions between Indigenous women and French men. As Kathleen DuVal argues, "Indian women and men alike worried about how best to maintain their societies in the face of disease, war, and other agents of change, and they weighed the advantages and disadvantages of marriage with foreigners."[182] In other words, if marriages between Indigenous women and French men occurred at the Western Posts, it was because Cree, Monsoni, and Nakoda women and men desired such unions with the French newcomers in order to forge commercial, political, and military alliances. Thus, Indigenous peoples dictated the gendered terms of kinship that defined French-Indigenous relations in the Hudson Bay watershed.

The degree of influence that Canadiens attained among Cree, Nakoda, Dakota, and Ojibwe bands was based on the seriousness with which they took their marriage and kinship obligations. Those who became community fixtures by returning seasonally to bring trade goods and to raise families generally found that their influence grew.[183] Indigenous peoples themselves played an important role in ensuring that the usual patterns for sexual relations between Indigenous women and European traders took the form of sanctioned marital unions. Voyageurs and coureurs de bois who wished to marry a woman had to first obtain the consent of her parents. Once permission was obtained, the fur trader had to pay a bride price in the form of blankets, woollen cloth, kettles, or alcohol.[184] Traders who sought to sidestep the formalities of marriage à la façon du pays, or who offended Native customs, ran the risk of serious reprisal. As one old NWC voyageur would later explain, custom had to be observed: "Almost all nations are the same, as far as customs are concerned ... There is a danger to have your head broken if one takes a girl in this country without her parents' consent."[185]

Many of the Canadiens at the Western Posts seem to have had strong kinship connections to local Indigenous peoples, particularly the Ojibwe, through marriage. According to Anishinaabe oral tradition recorded by William W. Warren in the nineteenth century, marriages between Ojibwe women and French men were ubiquitous in the western Lake Superior region, the gateway to the Northwest, in the decades prior to the British conquest of New France: "The main body of the French traders and common voyageurs who had so long remained amongst them [the Ojibwe], had many of them become united to the Indian race by the ties of marriage; they possessed large families of half-blood children whom the Indians cherished as their own."[186] At Grand Portage, which had become an important entrepôt for the transshipment of cargoes of merchandise and peltries between the West and the East, Ojibwes insisted on marriage alliances to cement reciprocal social obligations with French newcomers. Because the Ojibwe world view recognized essentially two categories of people – *inawemaagen* (relative) and *meyaagizid* (foreigner) – they had to reimagine kinship networks and social formations before a socially reciprocal relationship with European newcomers could be established. Through marriage, Ojibwes transformed French foreigners into relatives.[187]

The Ojibwes, and more broadly the Anishinaabeg, identified themselves as members of kinship groupings, or doodemag (totemic clan designations), such as Amikwa (Beaver), Kiskakon (Cut-Tail or Catfish), and Monsoni (Moose). Doodem identity was, and still is, important for Anishinaabe social organization and kinship. Doodemag provided lineage identification, shaped kin obligations, granted access to territory and resources, facilitated long-distance travel, and determined marriage and alliance patterns. The Anishinaabeg communicated their doodem identity through sartorial expressions, material culture, body modification (the Amikwa, or Beaver people, always pierced their noses, for example), and pictographic communications on sacred scrolls, birchbark missives, treaty documents, and rock paintings. Doodem identity connected Anishinaabe peoples to other-than-human progenitor beings, such as the First Beaver or First Bear, from creation stories in the earth-diver genre. These origin narratives connected specific clans to the land where the ancestral members of their doodem first came into being. These individual Anishinaabe clans were responsible for taking care of their lands and local resources and were required to maintain and nurture a reciprocal relationship with the "non-human world." The clan-based descent system organized the socio-political world of the Anishinaabe by dictating marriage patterns and relatedness between doodemag. Since members of the same doodem regarded each other as siblings, there was a strong taboo against intra-clan marriage. Therefore, Anishinaabe women married in from other doodemag, a practice that shaped regional politics by fostering lateral marital alliances with exogamous villages, which in turn created a geographically diverse and widespread kinship network throughout the pays d'en haut and beyond.[188]

Understandably, then, the Anishinaabeg sought to make alliances with French newcomers in the same way that they did with other doodemag. However, because Anishinaabeg inherited their doodem identities through their fathers, marriage between Ojibwe women and Frenchmen complicated the traditional Anishinaabe kinship system. French fathers did not have a doodem to pass down patrilineally to their half-Anishinaabe children. Doodem identity, however, was flexible and adaptable enough to accommodate marrying into a non-clan-based society.[189] For example, as Heidi Bohaker has persuasively argued, it was possible for maternal grandfathers to claim and adopt their Anishinaabe-European grandchildren as members of their own doodem.[190] This meant that mixed-descent sons and daughters of Anishinaabe-French marriages probably would have joined their maternal doodem. On the other hand, as Nicole St-Onge has recently argued, some Anishinaabeg may have regarded French newcomers as belonging to a "new" doodem. While not linked to a powerful other-than-human progenitor being, French fathers all shared a common geographic origin (the Saint Lawrence valley), spiritual belief system (Catholicism), language, and access to spiritual power or a manidoo (trade goods).[191] Whether or not Anishinaabeg conceived of the French as belonging to an emerging doodem, they still recognized the socio-economic importance of incorporating these French newcomers into their broader kinship network.

When French traders initially tried to enter the Northwest, the Ojibwe community at Grand Portage acted as gatekeepers of the important fourteen-kilometre portage, which bypassed the difficult terrain along the eastern portion of the Pigeon River. The Ojibwes ensured that they would benefit from any trade that travelled through their territory. To access the portage, many Canadien voyageurs fulfilled the diplomatic and even practical aspects of the fur trade through cultural adaptations and by marrying Ojibwe women à la façon du pays. Subsequently, Native wives and Canadien husbands negotiated their respective gender roles. Canadien fur traders and voyageurs provided generous gifts and issued ample trade goods on credit in the winter for repayment in the summer. In return, Ojibwe women fulfilled traditional gender roles such as food production (primarily through berries, maple sugar, and small game), netting snowshoes, making and mending clothing, and constructing birchbark canoes.[192] Within the context of fur trade marriages, Anishinaabe women continued to enjoy close relations with their paternal doodem. Thus, Canadiens who married into Anishinaabe bands drew on their wives' clan identities to access areas available for hunting, wild rice harvesting, maple syrup sugaring, and fishing. Kin and alliance affiliations granted them access to territory and resources, which reinforced the connection between the doodem and a specific territory.[193] In the end, for Canadien newcomers, marriage to Anishinaabe women transformed the local environment from a harsh and foreboding wilderness to a legible and comprehensible landscape with clearly articulated relationships, resources, territorial boundaries, and reciprocal obligations to both the human and non-human worlds.

Another example of a French-Indigenous relation concerns Montreal merchant René Bourassa, whom we encountered at the beginning of chapter 4. Bourassa's connections to the Dakota through his female slave literally saved his life during the Lake of the Woods raid in 1736. As Dakota warriors were about to torture and burn Bourassa at the stake, his female Dakota slave interceded on his behalf, calling out to the warriors, "My friends, what are you going to do? I owe my life to this Frenchman: he has done me nothing but good: if you want to be avenged for the attack made on you, you have only to go further on and you will find twenty-four Frenchmen, amongst whom is the son of their chief [Jean-Baptiste de La Vérendrye], the one who slaughtered us."[194] Why did the Dakota slave plead for Bourassa's life, rather than partake in the torture and murder of her master and then abscond with her kinsmen?

Historian Brett Rushforth, the leading expert on Indigenous slavery in New France, cautions that sexual relations that occurred in the context of such unequal power relations should be considered a form of sexual violence. The large numbers of Mesquakie and Dakota women that made their way into French hands as slaves in the early eighteenth century were subjugated to the unbalanced power relations of colonialism and patriarchy, and they were unquestionably vulnerable to physical and sexual abuse from their masters.[195] Yet, as Rushforth argues, some Indigenous women were able to navigate a complex colonial slave system that allowed them or their children to potentially emerge as free people. As Kathleen DuVal states, "In an irony that enslaved women have endured throughout history, sex with masters sometimes offered freedom, security, and community."[196] However asymmetrical the power dynamics of these master-slave relationships were, some mutual affection between male masters and enslaved women may have also developed.[197] This appears to have been the case for Bourassa and his Dakota slave. Bourassa lived to see another day because of her intercession with her Dakota kinsmen, while other voyageurs on the lake were killed in the attack.[198]

Relations between Canadiens and Indigenous women, whether through the structured practices of marriage à la façon du pays or even through slavery and captivity, sometimes led to serious long-term relationships characterized by lasting loyalty and mutual affection. Some of these examples evoke HBC chief factor James Douglas's phrase of 1842 to describe some fur trade marriages between HBC servants and Cree and Ojibwe women: "the many tender ties, which find a way to the heart."[199] There was, however, a less savoury side to marriage à la façon du pays. Not to be romanticized, abuses, abductions, rape, and abandonments were commonplace in these unions. European and Indigenous men alike forced Native women into opportunistic marriages to secure trade partnerships and kinship ties. These marital alliances were not always long-lasting or loving and many fur traders, like Patrick Small, John McDonald of Garth, George Nelson, and William Connolly, shirked marital and paternal responsibilities, eventually abandoning their Native wives and in some cases their fur trade families altogether. As the rivalry between the NWC and the HBC intensified in the Athabasca Country in the late eighteenth century, Dene women in particular suffered abuses at the hands of extortionist traders who sometimes forcibly seized Native women as commodities for unpaid wages or debts.[200] As ethnohistorian Jennifer Brown points out, scholars examining the more negative aspects of the fur trade "have found ample grounds to argue that abuse of women, neglect, prostitution, family breakup, and other social problems were also part of fur trade life."[201] At the end of the day, there was considerable variability to the relationships between Indigenous women and European men in the Hudson Bay watershed.

CONCLUSION

By the 1740s, the period of official French political and commercial expansion in western North America had come to end. Rather than focusing on expanding the frontiers of their North American empire, French colonial officials instead redirected their efforts toward consolidating imagined borders, frontier posts, and Indigenous alliances against their Anglo-American neighbours to the south and their HBC commercial rivals to the north. A succession crisis in 1740 threatened to upset the balance of power in Europe and eventually led to imperial war in North America in 1744. The British navy's disruption of French transatlantic shipping and its seizure of Louisbourg disrupted the flow of goods that the French required to effectively carry out gift diplomacy and maintain New France's Indigenous alliances. Though certainly not the only factor, this episode demonstrates how events in the Atlantic could, and did, have serious consequences for French-Indigenous alliances in the interior of North America, thereby exposing a potential weakness for New France's defence against its imperial rivals.

Governor La Jonquière's decision to dispatch Joseph Marin de La Malgue and Jacques Legardeur de Saint-Pierre in the early 1750s was the last attempt by colonial officials to discover the Western Sea and to wrest control of the Hudson Bay watershed away from both coureurs de bois and the HBC. Subsequent Troupes de la Marine commandants of the Western Posts were principally preoccupied with furs, slaves, and the liquor trade, rather than exploration in the Hudson Bay watershed. While French officers like Nicolas-Joseph de Noyelles and Jacques Legardeur de Saint-Pierre struggled to make inroads in Indigenous diplomacy and western exploration, coureurs de bois expanded their influence through métissage, kinship, and commerce, thus tightening their grip on the Northwestern fur trade.

In large part, voyageurs and coureurs de bois were successful at ensconcing themselves in the fur trade because they maintained strong kinship relations with the Indigenous peoples of the Northwest through intermarriage and métissage. The War of the Austrian Succession was an opportunity for Canadiens to assert political, economic, and cultural agency in the Hudson Bay watershed. Voyageurs and coureurs de bois displayed separate markers of cultural identity, particularly through expressions of sartorial, spiritual, and gastronomical hybridity, often predicated upon a strong foundation of marriage à la façon du pays. These were all part of the recurring patterns of métissage that helped Canadiens entrench themselves within Indigenous communities in the Hudson Bay watershed during the final years of French imperialism in North America. In addition to entering Indigenous fur trade and kinship networks, voyageurs and coureurs de bois also took the initiative to found new posts throughout the Hudson Bay watershed. While Troupes de la Marine officers began to withdraw from the Western Posts, Canadiens and Indigenous peoples actually expanded their economic, social, and cultural networks in an effort that defied the shifting boundaries and overlapping trade interests of New France and the HBC. Canadiens and Indigenous peoples shaped not only empires, but also an increasingly hybrid world that thrived despite waning French imperial interest and power in the Hudson Bay watershed.

6

From Métissage to Métis

Canadiens and Natives in the Hudson Bay Watershed after the Conquest of Canada, 1760–1782

The French ministers, bureaucrats, and imperial planners who had sought to fulfill imperial projects in the Hudson watershed could hardly have foreseen that the French presence in the West would, despite the vicissitudes faced by France's North American empire, have a much more enduring and salient legacy. Failed imperial aspirations – whether in the fur trade, Indigenous alliances, or the "discovery" of the Western Sea – ultimately resulted in the creation of a new Indigenous culture, language, people, and nation: the Métis. While French colonial thinkers and dreamers like Guillaume Delisle, Jean Bobé, Governor Vaudreuil, and La Vérendrye had spent decades chasing a *rêve fou* in the form of the non-existent Western Sea, they had unknowingly engendered crucial processes that contributed to the beginnings of political self-determination and collective identity that eventually led to the emergence of the Métis people. Indeed, under the very noses of Troupes de la Marine officers, Jesuit missionaries, and colonial officials, a dynamic cultural exchange had taken place at the Western Posts, which saw the entrenchment of métissage alongside the emergence of group identity, ultimately leading to the ethnogenesis of the Métis people. French imperial expansion into the Hudson Bay watershed had contributed to a complex environment characterized by Native-newcomer exchange and in which the Canadiens tended to thrive. By the 1750s and '60s, a dynamic French-Indigenous social world born of cultural hybridity was no longer dependent on the foil of French Empire for its existence. The French colonial structures of the ancien régime had collapsed in the Hudson Bay watershed following the British conquest of Canada, but a new world was beginning to rise from the ashes.

In the 1750s, Troupes de la Marine officers, unable to wrest control of the fur trade away from the HBC or to locate the fabled Western Sea, withdrew ignominiously to defend Canada in the Seven Years' War (1754–63).[1] Rejecting the call to arms, many former voyageurs, soldiers, and coureurs de bois remained in the Hudson Bay watershed among their Indigenous fur trade families. Consequently, when British pedlars from Montreal, such as Alexander Henry the elder, James Finlay, Peter Pond, and Thomas and Joseph Frobisher, arrived in the Northwest in 1767, they encountered well-established, cohesive, and dynamic French-Indigenous communities. Between 1754 and 1775, the HBC made fifty-six wintering trips inland with the goal of attracting Native customers to come and trade at their bayside posts, only to be confronted by long-time resident Canadien traders. The journals kept by many of these inland travellers, among them William Tomison, William Pink, Matthew Cocking, Samuel Hearne, Philip Turnor, Peter Fidler, and David Thompson, recorded a culturally hybrid French-Indigenous world in the Hudson Bay watershed.

The first half of this chapter examines HBC and NWC sources to challenge the previous scholarly interpretation that the French presence in the Hudson Bay watershed vanished during the Seven Years' War. By taking an in-depth look at the cases of two individuals – François Jérôme *dit* Latour and Louis Primeau – alongside numerous other examples, I posit that the Hudson Bay watershed remained a French-Indigenous space even after Troupes de la Marine officers withdrew to the East and the battlefields of the Seven Years' War. Through Indigenous kinship networks, many Canadiens had gained detailed knowledge of the geographic, political, and cultural landscapes of western North America, and this allowed them to carve out a salient socio-cultural space even once the hierarchy of the ancien régime had collapsed at the Western Posts. Unfortunately, most scholars have dismissed the notion of a Canadien presence in the Hudson Bay watershed following the outbreak of the Seven Years' War.[2] Despite this oversight in the early Canadian and fur trade historiography, Canadiens remained in the interior after the withdrawal of the last French commandant of the Western Posts and were key players in the era of fur trade competition between the HBC and the NWC during the late eighteenth and early nineteenth centuries.

This chapter also examines the transition from métissage to Métis peoplehood in the Hudson Bay watershed. A massive demographic upheaval brought about by a smallpox epidemic in 1780–82 combined with the western expansion of the fur trade to form a crucible of French-Indigenous métissage. This ultimately created favourable conditions for the formation of Métis political self-consciousness and collective identity. The rise in culturally hybrid, or *métisé*, Canadien voyageurs due to an expanding fur trade, as well as the cataclysmic plummeting of the Cree population due to devastating disease epidemics, resulted in the striking of an important demographic balance in the Hudson Bay watershed. This demographic equilibrium allowed significant Métis population growth, particularly in the Saskatchewan River valley. This interpretation challenges traditional Métis historiography, which has hitherto tethered the birth of the Métis people, as well as their political and cultural awakening, to the Battle of Seven Oaks in 1816, to the Sayer Trial in 1849, or even to their battle against the Yanktonai at Grand Coteau in 1851.[3] Prominent scholars who have focused predominately on Métis kinship and family have located Métis ethnogenesis in the early nineteenth century – a framing that tends to dismiss the eighteenth century as a superfluous prelude.[4] Perhaps most notably, these scholars have largely deemed patterns of métissage established prior to the conquest of New France as inconsequential, preferring instead to focus on the influence of the English and Scottish pedlars from Montreal, who subsequently formed the NWC, as a key catalyst in the rise of the Métis people.

This chapter challenges not only the chronology of Métis ethnogenesis, but also the spatial limitations of traditional Métis historiography, which has previously positioned the Red River Valley as the sole Métis homeland. Historians Trudy Nicks and Kenneth Morgan coined the phrase "Red River myopia" to articulate the unbalanced academic focus on Métis communities in the Red River region.[5] In a similar manner, Frits Pannekoek used the expression "the bog of Red River" to emphasize the limited number of studies of the Métis outside of the Red River Valley.[6] J.R. Miller has also stated that most early Métis studies were negatively effected by an exclusionary focus on the Red River Settlement.[7] In this respect, I follow the more recent works of Nicole St-Onge, Heather Devine, Brenda Macdougall, and Michel Hogue, who have moved beyond the Red-River-as-homeland paradigm and instead position Métis history in a more expansive transregional or transnational framework.[8] In an important article examining buffalo-hunting brigades, Brenda Macdougall and Nicole St-Onge argue that the excessive concentration on the Red River as the cradle of Métis society can be explained by the richness of archival sources from that region. They write that "the Red River settlement was an important node in the fur-trade system and the HBC's administration after 1821, but it was not the centre of the Plains Metis world. In many respects, it was its eastern periphery."[9] In other words, and as this chapter will show, the Métis did not arise in the Red River Valley alone; they were also a salient presence along the North and South Saskatchewan Rivers, along the Hayes and Nelson Rivers north of Lake Winnipeg, on vast stretches of grasslands and the Prairies of western North America, and even as far northwest as the Athabasca basin.

Such an analysis offers an opportunity to rethink the chronology of Métis people- and nationhood, connecting it more squarely to the long history of French-Indigenous métissage in the Hudson Bay watershed. Throughout the latter half of the eighteenth century, Canadiens continued to navigate complex Indigenous geopolitical and cultural landscapes, entrenching the saliency of métissage in the Hudson Bay watershed. Pursuant to the processes of métissage, a competitive fur trade environment and a devastating smallpox epidemic (1780–82) provided the necessary groundwork for nascent French-Indigenous communities to begin asserting political self-determination and self-consciousness. Culturally hybrid, or métisé, Canadiens were able to leverage cultural and political capital to secure a continued place and status for themselves and their children in a newly emerging French-Indigenous social world. These developments would ultimately result in the rise of the Métis Nation in western North America.

FRENCH-INDIGENOUS CONTINUITY IN WESTERN NORTH AMERICA

In the summer of 1759, all was quiet on the shores of Hudson Bay, where HBC governor James Isham was enjoying a good trading season at York Factory. Unbeknownst to Isham, though, on 13 September 1759, while he was supervising HBC servants at York Factory as they busily loaded provisions and trade goods into a sloop (one-masted sailboat) destined for Severn House, the armies of James Wolfe and Louis-Joseph de Montcalm were clashing on the Plains of Abraham in a battle that would help decide the fate of the French and British Empires in North America.[10] A year later, Pierre de Rigaud, Marquis de Vaudreuil-Cavagnial, New France's last governor general (1755–60), surrendered the embattled colony to British general Jeffery

Amherst. Three years later, in European council chambers, the British conquest and occupation of Canada was ratified with the 1763 Treaty of Paris, which confirmed a British takeover of most French possessions in North America, except for Louisiana west of the Mississippi River, which France had secretly ceded to its ally Spain the previous year in the 1762 Treaty of Fontainebleau.[11]

With the Saint Lawrence valley, the pays d'en haut, and even the Hudson Bay watershed ostensibly open to British commercial markets following the Seven Years' War, some merchants and traders from Great Britain and the Thirteen Colonies, like Alexander Henry the elder and Peter Pond, flocked to the British Empire's most recent colonial acquisition hoping to make a profit. English and Scottish traders did not lose much time before they attempted to tap into French fur trade networks. The British first entered the pays d'en haut to begin trading in 1760, but the sluggish mobilization of financial capital and military setbacks suffered in Pontiac's War (1763–66) slowed the advancement of British traders and merchants and ensured that Canadiens would once again take the lead within Indigenous fur trade networks.[12] In the 1760s, even as the British fought for their lives in Pontiac's War and struggled to untangle the intricacies of Euro-Indigenous alliances in the pays d'en haut, Canadien traders continued with "business as usual" along a vast and expansive fur trade network that connected Sault Sainte-Marie, Michilimackinac, Detroit, and Montreal to the Hudson Bay watershed.[13] Historians have demonstrated the continuity of French commercial and kinship networks in the pays d'en in the aftermath of the British conquest.[14]

Perhaps the most successful fur trading family at Michilimackinac were the Langlades, who had married into the Nassauaketon doodem, an influential Odawa clan at Waganawkezee (L'Arbre Croche) near the Straits of Mackinac.[15] Following the British conquest, the French-Odawa Charles Langlade and his father, Augustin Langlade, made plans to leave Michilimackinac and live instead with some Odawa relatives at Green Bay, attracting trade from all around the Fox-Wisconsin watershed and the Upper Mississippi valley. As Michael McDonnell has argued, "the Langlades could capitalize on this trade [at Green Bay] only because their Anishinaabe kin networks allowed them access – and ensured they could trade in relative safety."[16] Unlike British newcomers to the pays d'en haut, the Langlades were perfect intermediaries who could not only access goods from newly established British merchants at Montreal but could also supply themselves from French traders at Prairie du Chien, Fort de Chartres, and St Louis. The Langlades provide a telling, and oft-referenced example, of how métissage allowed families to successfully navigate a fluid Euro-Indigenous world in the wake of the 1763 Treaty of Paris.[17]

Considering the relative success and prosperity of families such as the Langlades in the pays d'en haut, the British colonial government soon recognized the importance of Canadiens as guides and interpreters in "Indian Country." The British governor of Quebec, Guy Carleton (1768–78), believed that British success in western North America would depend on the help of Canadiens, "who are well acquainted with the country [and] the language and manners of the natives."[18] Similarly, General Thomas Gage, commander-in-chief of the British forces in North America, admitted in late 1766 that the British traders in the pays d'en haut were hard-pressed to keep up with their Canadien competitors, with their "long connections with those Indians and their better knowledge of their languages and customs."[19] Canadiens and their bicultural offspring dominated the northwestern fur trade's political and commercial networks as voyageurs, guides, interpreters, and traders well into the nineteenth century.[20]

Noting the success of the fur trade in the pays d'en haut, entrepreneurial Montreal pedlars and Canadien traders soon turned their attention toward the Hudson Bay watershed. There, they found a number of métisé Canadiens prepared to act as guides, interpreters, cultural brokers, and on-the-ground traders willing to gather furs directly (*en dérouine*) from Indigenous peoples. Certainly, many French posts had been abandoned due to lack of trade goods from Montreal during the Seven Years' War, but many Canadiens nevertheless remained in the Hudson Bay watershed with various Indigenous bands. For example, when William Tomison journeyed inland in 1769, he encountered a former voyageur who had been living with a Cree band for so long that he had apparently forgotten the French language. In his journal, Tomison marvelled that "in the afternoon one man came to our tent, he told me in Indian that ... [he] is now entirely forgot his owne Langueg and talks [only] the Indian [language]."[21] Similarly, on 3 September 1772, Matthew Cocking, an HBC fur trader, encountered what he described as "a poor forlorn French-man" travelling with a Nakoda band near Eagle Hills in Saskatchewan. The Frenchman recounted that he had been living with his Nakoda kinsmen for the past decade, travelling between the North and South Saskatchewan Rivers and occasionally onto the grasslands to hunt bison.[22] These Canadiens who remained in the West used the cultural knowledge and capital derived from processes of métissage to navigate fluid ethnic and cultural boundaries as they renewed and forged commercial and kinship networks in the wake of the French imperial defeat in North America.

The names of specific métisé Canadiens also emerge from the sources. For example, Henri Janot *dit* Bourguignon, who signed a voyageur contract for Fort Dauphin in 1758, never returned to Montreal following the British conquest.[23] According to testimony by an old Cree woman reporting to James Sutherland, an HBC trader at Escabitchewan Post in 1793, a Canadien named "Burdino" or "Burdigno" had operated a post at Ball Lake in the English River watershed, a tributary of the Winnipeg River, during her youth, which would have been in the 1750s and '60s.[24] Sutherland discovered the ruins of Bourguignon's long-forgotten trading post but lamented the fact that all traces of the structure would soon be lost: "The corners of the House by which its dimensions may be known is still standing, but on the slightest touch moulders into dust. I carried a piece of one log home and tied it to the ledge of my House as a rare piece of antiquity in this wild Country where history is unpreserved."[25] According to the Cree woman, the old trader died at Grand Portage in 1780 at an advanced age, although according to Bourguignon's baptismal record, he would have only been in his early sixties.[26] HBC observers also reported that other "French inland masters," such as Jean-Baptiste Proulx and Maurice-Régis Blondeau, were also actively engaged in the Hudson Bay watershed fur trade, where they were firmly entrenched in Indigenous kinship networks. Proulx had traded along the lower Saskatchewan River since as early as 1754 and he had solicited HBC servants at York Factory to engage in the illicit trade, demanding items such as a few fathoms of tobacco, a pair of double-soled shoes, and a fiddle with some strings for it.[27] In 1767, Maurice-Régis Blondeau, alongside his younger cousin Barthélemi Blondeau, received permission to go with two canoes manned by at least two contracted voyageurs – Albert Lebeau and Louis Lasonde – to trade in the Assiniboine River valley.[28] During this voyage, Blondeau established his own independent trading house called Fort à Blondeau, or "Blondishe's Fort," near the confluence of the Assiniboine and Souris Rivers.[29] Another notable presence in the post-conquest landscape of the Hudson Bay watershed was Charles Boyer, a Canadien merchant based out of Michilimackinac who had been trading in the Rainy Lake district since at least as far back as 1744.[30] Because of Boyer's familiarity with the region he had an enduring (albeit pendular) presence in the Northwest, which continued after the conquest. From 1766 to 1769, Boyer, whom the Crees called "Paquatick," and his newfound English partner, Forrest Oakes, traded along the Red and Assiniboine Rivers, most notably at Fort des Épinettes, along the Assiniboine. During this period, Boyer also distinguished himself by his talent for building birchbark *canots du nord* at Rainy Lake and Lake of the Woods.[31] The examples of Henri Janot *dit* Bourguignon, Jean-Baptiste Proulx, Maurice-Régis Blondeau, and Charles Boyer demonstrate the continuity of the Canadien presence in the Hudson Bay watershed from the era of the Western Posts to the arrival of Montreal pedlars following the conquest.

HBC inland travellers' accounts reveal a dynamic Canadien presence in the Hudson Bay watershed. Rather than withdrawing to the Saint Lawrence valley, many voyageurs and coureurs de bois and their fur trade families remained embedded within Indigenous kinship networks in the Northwest. The close connections and familial affection that existed between Natives and Canadiens consistently astonished Matthew Cocking, who in the early 1770s was surprised "to perceive what a warm side the Natives hath to the French Canadians ... I observe plenty of french goods amongst them."[32] In 1767–68, William Pink, another HBC inland traveller, also acknowledged that Canadien traders must have been well-established in Indigenous communities because he recognized that many Cree bands possessed hats, shirts, kettles, woollen cloth, blankets, and tobacco from Montreal, distributed by Canadien traders.[33] Canadiens had maintained amicable relations with the Indigenous peoples of the Hudson Bay watershed since before the beginning of the Seven Years' War, and the ratification of the 1763 Treaty of Paris seemingly opened the possibility for British merchant capital to flow into the Hudson Bay watershed. Métisé Canadiens would be the vanguard of this commercial revolution in the Northwest.

MÉTISSAGE IN THE HUDSON BAY WATERSHED: THE CAREER OF FRANÇOIS JÉRÔME *DIT* LATOUR

As early as the summer of 1761, Cree traders reported to HBC officials at Moose Factory that Canadiens employed by Montreal pedlars were "as thick as Muskettos" on the Nottaway River and other rivers flowing into James Bay.[34] Many newly arrived English and Scottish merchants from Montreal were fortunate that their newfound Canadien trading partners had long and enduring connections in the rich fur-bearing territories of the Hudson Bay watershed. Throughout this period, Canadiens, some of whom had retained ties to the Northwest even during the tumultuous events of the Seven Years' War, were able to leverage their backcountry skills and Indigenous networks to advantageously position themselves within the region's shifting political and commercial landscapes. The English and Scottish pedlars of Montreal adopted the same view as the former French regime – namely, that the HBC's chartered territory and fur trade monopoly was confined to the Hudson Bay shoreline and strait. They believed, therefore, that the entirety of western North America was open to commercial expansion, except for a few bayside posts, such as York Factory, Churchill, Albany, and Moose Factory.[35] In less than a decade, Canadien traders working with (but mostly for) English and Scottish merchants came to dominate the fur trade of the Hudson Bay watershed.

Canadien voyageurs and coureurs de bois were vital assets to the new Montreal pedlars, as evidenced by William Pink's first encounter with a group of Montreal-backed traders on the lower Saskatchewan River. Just four years after the ink had dried on the Treaty of Paris, Pink wrote: "This Day as we Ware paddleing Down the River I see all on a Sodon on the North Side of it some of the people of Canada and Likewise a Little up from the Rivers side I see thare house ... they are consisting of Twelve Persons in Nomber, the chiefest persons name is Shash they are all French men that are heare upon the account that the English Did not [k]now the way."[36] Unlike Canadiens, English and Scottish newcomers had no knowledge of the interior waterways of the Hudson Bay watershed. The leader whom Pink called "Shash" was in fact Canadien trader François Jérôme *dit* Latour, the same coureur de bois that Joseph Smith and Joseph Waggoner had encountered at Cedar Lake in 1757. In addition to "Shash," Jérôme also went by the nicknames "Saswee," "Sas'wow," and "Franceway."[37] Indigenous names did not necessarily represent familial lineage or patrimony; rather, they expressed an individual's personal traits, dispositions, and exploits. Indigenous hosts frequently bestowed such names to help integrate adopted members into their community.[38] Ethnohistorian James Carson suggests, for example, that Indigenous peoples incorporated certain French newcomers into their kin groups by conferring inherited names or titles passed from one person to the next and representing particular traits like leadership, healing, and peacemaking.[39] Jérôme's name of "Saswee" might be derived from the Cree verb *Saswekittew*, which in Father Albert Lacombe's French-Cree dictionary is translated as "to disperse," "to scatter," or "to sow grain."[40] This nickname could have reflected Jérôme's particularly itinerant nature (even by Cree standards). Linguist Carol Jean Léonard suggests another plausible explanation for Jérôme's sobriquet, positing that "Saswee" (pronounced "sassooway") is a phonetic English adaptation, itself derived from a Cree reworking of Jérôme's given name of François. According to Léonard, the linguistic leap to Saswee from François can be explained by the following two observations. First, in the eighteenth century, the name François was pronounced "Françoué" ("fransooway"). Second, the absence of the letters *f* and *r* from the phonological systems specific to some Algonquian languages made "Françoué" sound like "sassooway" to native Cree speakers.[41] Whatever the origin of Jérôme's moniker, the well-travelled Saswee was married à la façon du pays to a Cree woman, with whom he had children.[42] HBC traders William Tomison and Matthew Cocking both marvelled at Jérôme's expansive kinship network and strong trade connections with the Saskatchewan River Crees.[43]

Jérôme was continuously active in the fur trade before, during, and after the Seven Years' War. He briefly departed the Hudson Bay watershed in 1756 after he signed a contract to go to Fort Ouiatenon on the Wabash River southwest of Lake Michigan.[44] The following year, Jérôme had saved enough money to hire his own voyageurs and thus became a *négociant* (merchant) himself. He established trade operations northwest of Lake Winnipeg at Cedar Lake and hired Gabriel Saint-Michel and Joseph Beaunoyer to meet him at Michilimackinac to bring merchandise up from Montreal and return with his peltries.[45] Jérôme's hiring of these voyageurs to go to Michilimackinac and back is an indication that he may have stopped returning to Montreal on a regular basis. Following the British conquest, there was a general reorientation of the fur trade away from Montreal and toward secondary hubs, such as Michilimackinac, Detroit, Green Bay, St Louis, and Portage-des-Sioux.[46] After the conquest, François Jérôme partnered with several different British merchants based out of Montreal and trading via Michilimackinac. For example, in 1767, British merchant Alexander Baxter financed Jérôme to take six canoes to Fort Dauphin and Fort La Reine (at the former Western Posts), valued at 2,400 livres. This was the most significant consignment of trade goods that year.[47]

While still maintaining Indigenous kinship relations in the Hudson Bay watershed, Jérôme also forged politically advantageous relationships with British colonial officials, who garrisoned the pays d'en haut following Pontiac's War. For example, when Robert Rogers was appointed commandant at Michilimackinac in 1766, Jérôme seems to have made a good impression on the British army officer. Rogers had dispatched two expeditions under Jonathan Carver and James Tute to the Northwest and later entrusted Jérôme to carry some letters to Carver and Tute in the Lake Superior region.[48] Rogers praised Jérôme in his letter to Carver and Tute informing his subordinates that the Canadien trader was advancing toward Lake Winnipeg with ten canoes full of merchandise, while also assuring them that "by François you shall have all the news of every kind."[49] Robert Rogers and François Jérôme seem to have enjoyed a mutually beneficial relationship. Jérôme would not only supply Rogers's Northwest expedition but would also presumably introduce them to the Indigenous peoples of the Hudson Bay watershed, who were unfamiliar to the British outside of the HBC.[50] Through Rogers's patronage, Jérôme enjoyed access to British merchandise to trade as well as the security and protection of an official fur trade licence in the Northwest.

In the ensuing years, Jérôme partnered with several of Montreal's leading British merchants. One of Jérôme's more lucrative partnerships appears to have been with British merchant James Finlay, who backed the venture with the financial capital necessary for ensuring that trade goods flowed from Montreal into the Hudson Bay watershed, thus successfully cutting off HBC trade on the lower Saskatchewan River.[51] Jérôme's role was to provide the on-the-ground expertise, which allowed the collaboration with Finlay to succeed in the Northwest fur trade. When HBC officer William Pink tried to stop them, Jérôme and Finlay bluntly told him that they had the "Liberty to come & gou as far … [as they] chuses in to the in Land Contry."[52] Cree traders informed Moses Norton at Churchill about Jérôme's occupancy of the Saskatchewan River valley, which Norton subsequently reported to his superior Ferdinand Jacobs at York Factory: "the Master of the Pedlers that has done your Traders much damage his name is Sa'swew and has about 20 Men with Him, this is the Natives Account to me."[53] Together, Jérôme and Finlay established a post below the Saskatchewan River Forks that operated between 1768 and 1773. Archaeologists Alice B. Kehoe and David Meyer have placed the so-called François-Finlay Fort near the town of Nipawin, Saskatchewan. Excavations in the 1960s revealed a hybrid material culture at the fort. Arrowheads, Indigenous pottery shards, and bone tools were found alongside remnants of European trade goods, such as clay pipes, glass beads, steel knives, awls,

6.1 *A Metis Family (A Halfcast with his Wife and Child)*, by Peter Rindisbacher, 1825.

and gun parts.[54] In addition to the François-Finlay Fort, Jérôme and Finlay also occupied trading posts at Cedar Lake, Opāskweyāw (Fort Paskoya or Basquia), and Fort à la Corne, all along the Saskatchewan River trade corridor.[55] As had been the case when he was in command of Fort Bourbon at Cedar Lake in the 1750s, Jérôme continued to occupy a salient liminal space between European and Indigenous societies and cultures, which allowed him to play an important role as an intermediary in the expanding northwestern fur trade.

Not all Canadiens in the Hudson Bay watershed after the British conquest were rooted in the emerging French-Indigenous social world. In fact, many Canadiens arrived in the Hudson Bay watershed for the first time in the 1760s and '70s in the employ of Montreal pedlars. Many métisé Canadiens, like Jérôme, who had remained in the Hudson Bay watershed, welcomed these newly arrived Canadiens as kin because they still shared common markers of linguistic, religious, and cultural identity. Being welcomed into the French-Indigenous social world not only instigated further processes of métissage, but also bolstered the number of métisé Canadiens, who in turn contributed to the entrenchment of group identity and political consciousness that led to the eventual rise of the Métis people. In other words, culturally hybrid Canadiens saw the political advantages of welcoming newly arrived Canadien voyageurs in the employ of Montreal pedlars into their ethnic fold.

Jérôme provides a quintessential example of métissage in the Hudson Bay watershed with wider connections throughout a French river world. From his home parish of La Prairie, near Montreal, Jérôme drew on his local community and kinship relations to recruit more Canadiens for his growing network in the Hudson Bay watershed. In 1769, Jérôme's twenty-nine-year-old nephew Pierre, also from La Prairie, signed a voyageur contract and made his way to Michilimackinac, where he met up with his uncle, who had been seasoned in the fur trade for the last twenty-odd years.[56] Born around 1740, Pierre Jérôme would have been coming of age around the time of the British conquest of New France when his uncle's commercial exploits were expanding in the Hudson Bay watershed. Subsequently, Pierre Jérôme may have joined his uncle's fur trade operations along the Saskatchewan River.[57] At any rate, Pierre would soon come to forge his own path as a Cree interpreter in the Saskatchewan River valley fur trade. It made good sense that Pierre Jérôme worked as a Cree interpreter; after all, his aunt was a Cree woman, his uncle François spoke fluent Cree, and his many first cousins were half-Cree.[58] The Saskatchewan River Crees considered parallel cousins (the children of same-sex siblings) as siblings. Since Pierre Jérôme (born 1740) was the son of Pierre Jérôme (born 1718), who was François's younger brother, the half-Cree cousins in the Saskatchewan Country would have recognized the newly arrived Pierre Jérôme from Canada as their brother.[59]

Allan Greer, Nicole St-Onge, Robert Englebert, and others have demonstrated how engagement in the fur trade was typically a kinship or parish-based enterprise, which regularly saw brothers, brothers-in-law, cousins, sons, nephews, and other distant relatives enter the trade at the behest of an established family member.[60] Although Jérôme was fully integrated into the French-Indigenous social world of the Hudson Bay watershed, he still maintained strong and persistent connections with Canadien kinsmen in his home parish of La Prairie in the Saint Lawrence valley, as well as with the new British ruling class of colonial officials, military officers, and merchants.

By 1774, François Jérôme seems to have entered a new partnership with Charles Paterson and William Holmes that involved them operating a post at Fort à la Corne. HBC officer Samuel Hearne, who had just established Cumberland House on the banks of the Saskatchewan River, was under the impression that Jérôme, Paterson, and Holmes were all equal partners in the trade.[61] The trio also seems to have formed a wider partnership with Thomas and Joseph Frobisher, Isaac Todd, and James McGill to minimize financial risk. To ensure success, the conglomerate of Canadien and British traders set off in different directions and traded widely in a vast area stretching throughout the northern Great Plains, the Saskatchewan River valley, and even northwards to the Athabasca Country.[62]

Samuel Hearne was surprised that Jérôme "gave me an invitation to sup with them," which Hearne "did not think any harm in accepting."[63] Once again, Jérôme extended his warm hospitality to HBC men, as he had previously done with Joseph Smith and Joseph Waggoner at Cedar Lake in 1757, and then again with Matthew Cocking in 1773 at the Forks of the Saskatchewan River.[64] This was an opportunity for Jérôme not to only learn vital new information about the HBC interlopers in the Saskatchewan Country, but also to build a reciprocal relationship with these newcomers to the region. Perhaps Jérôme and other Canadiens, much like his Native kinsmen, saw systems of reciprocity as an avenue to political power in diplomatic relationships in which the respective parties were bound by mutual obligations.[65] Another way Jérôme placed HBC men in a position to reciprocate was his rescuing of HBC servant Robert Flatt, who had purportedly been robbed and "treated very crewilly" by some Crees and then left for dead on the north shore of Lake Winnipeg. Hearne was delighted that Jérôme had saved Flatt's life and returned him safely to Cumberland House even though they were rival traders. Hearne described Jérôme's intervention and subsequent generosity as follows: "Franceway [Jérôme] took care of Robert Flatt and cloath him very well for the Indians had striped him almost Naked. Those Masters were all very kind to him but those above mentioned Particularly so, I thanked them for the care they had taken of my man and offered to satisfy them for the Expense they were at in Cleaning him & which they declined accepting, saying we were very welcome."[66] Other company officers – like Matthew Cocking, for instance – also commented upon the genteel nature of Canadiens engaged in the Saskatchewan River fur trade, who often tried to forge amicable relationships with HBC newcomers.[67] Adopting Cree and Nakoda systems of reciprocity, which differed significantly from a market-based economy, métisé Canadiens like Jérôme sought to entangle HBC newcomers in a political structure that was decentralized, non-hierarchical, and dependent upon mutual obligations.

In the Hudson Bay watershed, many Canadiens besides Jérôme were skilled guides, talented linguists, and competitive traders. This much is evident from surviving HBC sources; company officials frequently bemoaned their disadvantage in comparison to the Montreal pedlars, who more often were able to employ Canadiens. Thomas Hutchins at Fort Albany argued that it was the Canadiens' ability to live like "Indianized Frenchmen" that made them successful traders in the interior.[68] Outside observers like Hutchins clearly perceived that métissage was a significant factor in the success of Canadiens in the Hudson Bay watershed. Hutchins remarked, moreover, that "the Canadians have great influence over the natives by adopting all their customs and making them companions. They drink, sing, conjure, scold with them like one of themselves and the Indians are never kept out of their houses whether drunk or sober, night or day."[69] Many HBC traders found the egalitarianism practised by Canadiens disconcerting to the notions of class they had absorbed in their home societies.[70]

By embracing newly arrived Canadiens from the parishes of the Saint Lawrence valley as kinsmen, Jérôme did his part to cultivate a nascent French-Indigenous social world whose inhabitants were beginning to dominate the Hudson Bay watershed fur trade. Although Jérôme had already built an expansive Indigenous kinship network through his Cree wife's extended family, he now created more kinsmen as Canadiens arrived in the employ of his various Montreal partners, including Alexander Baxter, James Finaly, and William Holmes and Charles Paterson. Compared to La Vérendrye's tenure as commandant of the Western Posts, where on average thirty voyageurs might come to work per year, with no more than fifty to one hundred Canadiens living in the Northwest at any given time due to the multi-year length of most contracts, the number of voyageurs arriving and living in the region had significantly increased under the Montreal pedlars.[71] For example, a 1780 petition to British governor of Quebec Frederick Haldimand (1778–86) by Montreal merchants Simon McTavish, James McGill, Isaac Todd, Benjamin Frobisher, and many others, stated that up to three hundred voyageurs per year now traded in the Hudson Bay watershed.[72] In 1786, William Tomison estimated the total strength of voyageurs from Montreal inhabiting the Northwest at over four hundred men.[73] As a result, the Canadien demographic advantage was beginning to be felt by the HBC, which for the first time suffered a serious commercial reversal as fur trade returns dropped to lows not even experienced during the height of La Vérendrye's operations at the Western Posts. In the 1760s and '70s, HBC officials watched in horror as Montreal pedlars and their Canadien collaborators almost completely siphoned off their trade.

When William Tomison journeyed inland in 1767, he found many Crees at the place where the Winnipeg River empties into Lake Winnipeg, waiting for the arrival of Montreal pedlars.[74] Throughout the summer of 1768, Indigenous peoples at York Factory testified to the presence of Canadien traders in the Hudson Bay watershed. On 21 June 1768, Ferdinand Jacobs's post journal entry stated: "6 Cannoes of Trading Indians ... Inform me of 8 Cannoes of Peddlers from Quebeck being in their Country."[75] Five days later, thirteen canoes of Nakoda traders "also say there is a canoe of peddlers from Quebeck amongst the Indians that Usually came to this Factory to trade."[76] The following day, Cree traders visiting York Factory warned Jacobs that Canadien traders with nine canoes of merchandise and trade goods from Montreal were in the Lake Winnipeg region.[77] From Cumberland House, HBC trader Joseph Hanson remarked that the "Natives in general are not agreeable to go down [to York Factory] as they can be supplied with their Necessaries at home by the Canadian Traders."[78] Samuel Hearne recognized that Canadiens "are distributed through the Country" in great numbers and with a large quantity of trade goods, remarking that more than sixty canoes had entered the Hudson Bay watershed from Grand Portage in 1774.[79] Grand Portage had become the de facto launching point and organizational base for fur trade operations in the Hudson Bay watershed. After the signing of the Jay Treaty in 1796, the Montreal pedlars moved their base of operations to Fort William, near the mouth of the Kaministiquia River (Thunder Bay, Ontario).[80] The organizing of various Montreal pedlars into the NWC in 1779 under the leadership of Simon McTavish and Joseph Frobisher played a significant factor in the east–west movement of even more Canadien voyageurs, as superior financial capital and labour coordination allowed for an accelerated westward expansion of the fur trade into the Hudson Bay watershed.[81]

Old Canadien residents and new arrivals with the Montreal fur brigades joined together and were seemingly everywhere throughout the Hudson Bay watershed in the latter half of the eighteenth century. Mobility was key, and the renewed ties with the East bolstered the political capital of those who could operate freely in the French-Indigenous social world of the Hudson Bay watershed. The competitive fur trade environment shaped by rival HBC and Montreal pedlars also helped Canadiens – both long-term residents and new arrivals – assert political self-determination and pursue a myriad of socio-economic opportunities in the Hudson Bay watershed. Nicole St-Onge and Carolyn Podruchny have argued that mobility and kinship were central, definitional concepts of Métis peoplehood and identity, and as such they liken them to a "spider's web" spun throughout the Hudson Bay watershed connecting kin or tribal structures, shared world views, reciprocal obligations, and economic opportunities.[82] These "webs of connectedness" and patterns of mobility dated back to some of the progenitors of the Métis people – French voyageurs from the Saint Lawrence valley and the Great Lakes region and the Indigenous peoples with whom they formed kinship ties. Robert Englebert has articulated the concept of a "French river world" to describe the mobility and interconnectedness of disparate French populations and communities in North America.[83] A bourgeoning French-Indigenous society in the Hudson Bay watershed employed mobility and far-flung kinship connections to maintain riverine ties with Great Lakes fur trade communities of similar demographic makeup, such as Michilimackinac, Sault Sainte-Marie, Green Bay, Lac La Pluie, Prairie du Chien, and Vincennes.[84] Indeed, in the historiographies of the Great Lakes, the Illinois Country, and Louisiana, many scholars now accept that there was widespread continuity and mobility in French commercial, community, and kinship networks following the 1763 Treaty of Paris.[85] In the Hudson Bay watershed, these far-flung connections prefigured the eventual rise of the Métis in the Red River Valley, with nascent French-Indigenous communities forging initial networks in the Saskatchewan River valley and eventually moving to the northern Great Plains to exploit the socio-economic niche of the buffalo hunt and associated pemmican trade.

Montreal pedlars and Canadiens dominated the Northwest fur trade by utilizing these expansive networks. At Cumberland House, HBC trader William Walker concluded that "the Pedlers are so very Numerous all over the Country ... They have got such great quantities of Goods remaining and now they are gone down to the great Carrying Place They have Canoes and Men at every Place where Indians resort, so that an Indian cannot come from any part of the Country but they see of them."[86] Humphrey Martin, chief factor at York Factory, echoed Cocking's remarks when he told the London Committee that he and his colleagues were "greatly alarmed at the Information We have received from You and Other Persons of the greatly encreased numbers of Canadian Traders that now overspread almost [all] this Country and have absolutely blocked up every Passage to their Honors Inland Settlement." [87] Alexander Henry the elder also reported on the sheer amount of Montreal pedlars and Canadien voyageurs in the Northwest, saying that he had accompanied "a fleet" of 30 canoes and 130 men across Lake Winnipeg.[88] In 1770, Humphrey Marten at York Factory broke down the breadth of Canadien trade patterns throughout the Hudson Bay watershed and noted that the Montreal pedlars had 2 large canoes at Opāskweyāw, 33 Canadiens up past the Saskatchewan River Forks, and 4 traders in the waterways north of Cumberland House.[89] In 1778, a massive trade blockade of 120 Canadien voyageurs on the frozen North Saskatchewan River completely ruined the trade at the HBC's newly established Hudson House.[90] Throughout the 1760s and '70s, Montreal pedlars and Canadien voyageurs continued to intercept Indigenous traders who were making the long and arduous journey to the HBC's bayside posts. The pedlars were also gathering furs directly (en dérouine) from Indigenous peoples, like the Niitsítapi, who typically did not engage in long canoe voyages.[91] It soon became apparent that Montreal pedlars were making serious inroads into the HBC's trade. As had been the case during the French regime, Montreal traders ignored the HBC's supposed monopoly in Rupert's Land. The growing impact on the trade was evident in the steady decline of beaver pelts acquired at York Factory. In 1760, York Factory received 33,000 MB worth of furs, but by 1768 the post's annual total had dropped to only 18,000 MB.[92]

Since the early eighteenth century, Canadien voyageurs and coureurs de bois had actively engaged with Indigenous peoples at a community level. Not only had they developed kinship ties through marriages à la façon du pays, but they also travelled far more extensively along the aquatic pathways of the Hudson Bay watershed, which shaped and enhanced their intimate knowledge of the landscape. Although exact figures for marriages à la façon du pays between Indigenous women and métisé Canadiens after the conquest are difficult to determine because of the paucity of sources, an examination of later Red River census data from 1827 to 1835 indicates that large amounts of

Number of Métis births by decade based on Red River Settlement census data, 1827–35

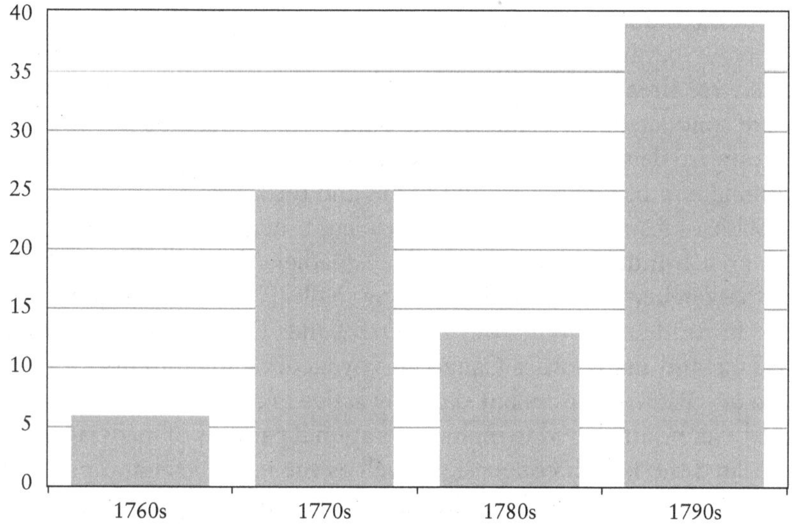

6.2 Métis births in Rupert's Land (Hudson Bay watershed) from the 1760s to the 1790s according to Red River Settlement and Grantown census data between 1827 and 1835.

Métis children were born to these mixed unions in the pivotal decades of the 1760s and '70s. Although many English and Scottish Métis, who referred to themselves by the terms "half-breed" or "country-born," lived in the Protestant parishes (St Andrews and St Clements) of the Red River Settlement by the 1820s and '30s, I have counted only the Métis population derived from French-Indigenous marriages. Beginning in the eighteenth century, French-Indigenous marriages gave rise to what some historians have dubbed the "Plains Métis," who practised Catholicism, spoke Michif, called themselves "Bois-Brûlés," and were committed to the lifestyle of the buffalo hunt.[93]

The Red River census data is incomplete, however, and might only represent a small fraction of the Bois-Brûlés Métis born in the Northwest between the 1760s and the 1790s. The data does not consider Métis individuals born in these earlier decades who might not have been alive at the time of the Red River Settlement censuses of the 1820s and '30s. Moreover, the census data does not consider Métis families who did not move to the Red River Valley. For example, many Métis families remained at Pembina, the Qu'Appelle Valley,

Île-à-la-Crosse, Fort Carlton, and Fort-des-Prairies. We also know that François Jérôme's children, described by William Tomison in 1767, were never mentioned in the Red River Settlement or Grantown censuses, probably because they, their descendants, and the rest of the Jérôme clan were already living in the Pembina region by the time the censuses were conducted. Nevertheless, the data, even if incomplete, indicates an upward demographic trend and suggests that the Métis people were coming into being between the 1760s and the 1790s.

With a substantive number of Canadiens brought into Jérôme's growing French-Indigenous social world, Canadiens flexed their muscles in the Saskatchewan River valley, thereby challenging the HBC's presumptive fur trade monopoly over Rupert's Land. The success of François Jérôme and many other Canadien voyageurs and coureurs de bois, unnamed in the sources but similarly active in the Hudson Bay watershed, can be attributed to multi-generational patterns of métissage that predated the British conquest, as well as the new social and political capital that they accrued as cultural brokers in the competitive fur trade milieu. When the Montreal pedlars and Canadien voyageurs arrived in the Hudson Bay watershed in the 1760s and '70s, they encountered and linked up with their ethnic kinsmen, who had formed a new home in the West – a cohesive and dynamic French-Indigenous world. Without the influx of more Canadiens in the employ of Montreal pedlars, it seems unlikely that this nascent French-Indigenous social world would have survived long enough to produce an independent Métis people within only a few generations; rather, the few Frenchmen who remained in the Hudson Bay watershed, métisé as they were, would likely have been fully absorbed into Indigenous communities. In the end, though, the career of François Jérôme *dit* Latour demonstrates how a combination of well-entrenched métissage and expansive kinship connections (spanning both Indigenous and French worlds) gave the bourgeoning French-Indigenous community enough social and political capital to emerge as an independent people in the Hudson Bay watershed by the close of the eighteenth century.

"A MOST SERVICEABLE MAN FOR YOUR INTEREST INLAND": THE CAREER OF LOUIS PRIMEAU

Following the French government's abandonment of the Western Posts during the Seven Years' War, a few voyageurs and coureurs de bois who remained in the Hudson Bay watershed sought career opportunities with the HBC. There was the seemingly isolated incident of a Canadien, Jean-Baptiste Desjarlais, working for the HBC during the Seven Years' War, but a few others followed suit after the 1763 Treaty of Paris.[94] Similar to Desjarlais, a trader named Louis Primeau showed up at York Factory in 1766 seeking employment after living with his Cree family for six years.[95] Primeau seems to have first entered the Northwest in 1749 at the age of twenty-two after signing a voyageur contract to go to the Lake Nipigon post.[96] Ferdinand Jacobs, chief factor at York Factory, recorded that when twenty-six canoes of "trading Indians" arrived, there "also Came with the Indians a French Man whos Name is Luis Primo, but Commonly Known by the Indians by the Name of Nick'a'thu'tin."[97] The fact that Primeau had an Indigenous name indicated that his adoption into Cree society was complete: his Cree relatives had conferred upon him a new name and identity.[98] Jacobs carefully interviewed Primeau to ascertain the former voyageur's potential contribution to the company. He believed that Primeau could serve the company in the capacity of an inland trader because of his background and experience among the Natives. Jacobs stated that he was going to send Primeau "back with the Natives Fitted Out in a Proper manner to Promote the Companys Trade and bring Down yearly what Natives he Can to Trade."[99] To this end, he gifted Primeau some laced shirts and other items from his "own apparel."[100] Examining the cultural significance of dress, historian Sophie White posits that sartorial expressions permitted individuals to navigate different cultural spaces.[101] By donning clean European clothing – coat, waistcoat, cotton ruffled shirt, breeches, shoes, and stockings – for the first time in six years, Primeau was able to cross a cultural threshold and re-enter a European space. Jacobs said that he also permitted Primeau to "Lye in the Factory," in other words to sleep within the fort's walls, a privilege not usually permitted to visiting Indigenous peoples, who were required to set up their tents outside the factory.[102] In the context of colonial Louisiana, Sophie White argues that European notions of cleanliness (freshly laundered linens, for example) allowed mixed-heritage voyageurs to clearly mark their bodies as European in order to enter urban spaces that were considered off limits to Indigenous visitors.[103] Similarly, by donning new clean garments, Primeau demonstrated his Europeanness to fellow HBC servants, while simultaneously signalling his position as a cultural broker to his Indigenous kinsmen and trade partners.

To enter company service as a wage-earning employee and not simply a Cree trading captain, Primeau had to reassert his European identity. With one foot still in the Cree world, however, Primeau was a salient asset to the HBC. As Jacobs observed, "he is very Talkative man Says he Can Neither read nor write" but he was a "Master of the Indian Language."[104] Most HBC servants, with the exception of only a few adventurous inland winterers, were not given opportunities to learn Indigenous languages thanks largely to the London Committee's anxieties over private trade. The HBC's method of hindering such trade was to put all dealings with Indigenous peoples, at least nominally, in the hands of its governors or chief factors and a select few interpreters.[105] His close kinship ties with the Cree made Primeau a valuable asset to the HBC, but the risk that he could engage in side-trading without the company's consent meant that he was also a potential liability.

Primeau was taken into the company fold and became central to the HBC's plans to leave the bayside posts and expand into the interior of the continent. At York Factory, Andrew Graham assured the London Committee that "Lewis Primo ... [was] an able & serviceable Man for your Interest Inland."[106] A few days later, Graham sent Primeau with a Cree band travelling to the Beaver River, an eastward-flowing river into which drains Lac La Biche before turning sharply north to flow into Lac Île-à-la-Crosse on the Churchill River. Graham hoped that by sending Primeau up the Beaver River he would bring about an exponential increase in trade returns at York Factory that season. Graham praised Primeau as a "very good Servant to his Employers ... He talks the Language as well as the Natives themselves."[107] Language skills were crucial to growing the HBC's inland fur trade network, and Primeau used them to great effect. From 1766 to 1772, he wintered nearly every season with the Cree or Nakoda and promoted HBC trade interests – all of this at a time when HBC trade was being increasingly threatened by the activities of English and Scottish pedlars from Montreal. Primeau emphasized to Andrew Graham the absolute necessity of building inland posts. The HBC subsequently established Cumberland House on the Saskatchewan River in 1774, the company's first permanent post in the interior.

Primeau regularly returned to York Factory from the interior with Indigenous trading partners and canoe loads of prime beaver pelts. For example, on 7 July 1771, Ferdinand Jacobs recorded that "Lewis Primo Came here with 20 Canoes of Trading Indians, Saluted them & Clothed their Leaders, gave them also the Other Customary

Presents."[108] Primeau also continued to warn company officials of the growing commercial threat of the Montreal pedlars. Jacobs wrote that "Leuis Primo ... Confirms the Acctt of the French Pedlers being in the Heart of the Country, & that they Invited him to come to them but he Declined it."[109] Indeed, the influence of the Montreal pedlars had grown to the point that they even threatened to recruit Primeau himself, by now one of the HBC's most valuable inland agents.

Not all company traders trusted Primeau. Matthew Cocking, for example, disliked him and thought he was beginning to show signs of divided loyalty. He gave a scathing account of Primeau, writing, "I am certain he hath a secret kindness for his old Masters, & is not to be depended on."[110] Cocking also heard from Cree traders that Primeau had been wearing clothing he received from Montreal pedlars, and that he was alleged to have received over a hundred beaver pelts from trading goods he had brought inland.[111] Cocking was well-aware of company rules and regulations, which strictly forbade any engagement in private trade.[112] Cocking's suspicions were proven correct when Primeau abandoned company service in 1773, shortly after boasting that he was going down to Grand Portage to visit friends. Cocking admonished Primeau, reminding him that he had signed a written contract and was legally bound to serve the HBC for its duration.[113] In 1773, Andrew Graham learned of Primeau's betrayal from visiting Cree traders before Cocking even had a chance to inform him.[114] Graham rushed orders down to Samuel Hearne at Cumberland House that "If you should see Lewis Primo [*sic*] acquaint him he has forfeited all the Money ... by his breach of contract in deserting the Company service," adding that he intended to sell the new cloths that he had brought from London for Primeau in order to recoup the money he had cost the company.[115] The HBC had been wary of Canadiens, who for most of the past century had sought to undermine the company's operations in the Hudson Bay watershed. And yet, the HBC was intrigued, at least for a while, by the possibility of hiring experienced Canadiens like Primeau. Ultimately, though, the experience with Primeau soured the HBC on its plans to harness Canadien employees until at least the period of the Pemmican War (1812–21).[116]

Soured by Primeau's desertion, Ferdinand Jacobs informed the London Committee that he was "determined not to employ any more of these renegades who turns out to be the worst enemies of your interests."[117] Matthew Cocking offered a similar caution: "as to employing Canadians, who are certainly well versed in this kind of business, I am of the opinion they are very improper persons, for they would be constantly roaming off to the pedlars and laying open all they knew. Indeed, when they are engaged on the peddling business, they often elope from their employ and go with the natives."[118] Primeau's desertion simply reinforced the company's belief that Canadien traders were too independent and unpredictable to be trusted.

Canadiens largely maintained their own agency in an increasingly competitive fur trade environment. Switching allegiances between the HBC and Montreal pedlars was commonplace, especially when a more lucrative contract presented itself, but also when an employer or partner infringed on Canadiens' independence. The competitive environment of the 1770s provided opportunities for expressions of French-Indigenous collective identity and political self-determination, as more and more culturally hybrid Canadiens realized their unique advantage in the fur trade milieu. Canadien traders soon came to understand their own inherent value and technical ability and were not to be shortchanged in dealing with company officials. Philip Turnor, the HBC's first inland surveyor and map-maker, commented upon the problem of not paying Canadien inland servants enough to keep them in the company's service. Writing to the London Committee, he offered his "opinion [that] your Honors need never be surprised should you find great difficulty in keeping your Inland Officers" because the HBC simply did not place enough monetary value on actual experience.[119]

In 1773–74, Primeau returned to the West in the employ of Thomas and Joseph Frobisher as their chief guide and trader. He appears to have been a significant factor in the Frobisher brothers' success in cutting off the HBC's trade along the Churchill River and limiting peltries arriving at both York Factory and Churchill (Prince of Wales Fort).[120] Moses Norton, chief factor at Churchill, remarked that Denes who came down the Churchill River to trade barely brought any furs that year and were clothed in mantles and blankets provided to them by Montreal pedlars as they passed through the northerly route to Hudson Bay.[121] The following year, Andrew Graham accused Joseph Frobisher and Louis Primeau of robbing York Factory and Churchill of all its incoming trade.[122] Similar to the influential roles played by Pierre-Esprit Radisson and Médard Chouart des Groseilliers a century prior, commercial success in the Hudson Bay watershed seemed to wax and wane in accordance with whichever company Louis Primeau aligned himself with.[123]

Primeau became such a prominent trader in the waterways north of Cumberland House linking the Saskatchewan River to the Athabasca basin that his name was even used to designate geographic features on maps. Philip Turnor's large composite map of North America depicts "Primo's [*sic*] Lake" as an oxbow lake of the Churchill River system near the larger Frobisher trading post at Île-à-la-Crosse.[124] Turnor described "Primo's Lake" in his 1790 journal: "[we] came to a lake called Nick-ey-thu-tins-Sack-a-ha-gan or Lewis Primoes Lake ... At this place Lewis Primo formerly had a house from which the Lake takes its name, this was then the farthest house in this Country."[125] From this advantageously positioned post, Primeau intercepted Cree and Dene traders using the northern route of the Churchill River to reach Hudson Bay.[126]

By 1776, Primeau was wintering and trading at Île-à-la-Crosse. The site was strategically located at a place where fur brigades could reach the Athabasca Country to the northwest via the Methye Portage, the Saskatchewan River valley to the southwest via the Sturgeon-Weir River, and the Churchill River to the northeast flowing toward Hudson Bay through a series of labyrinthian lakes. Île-à-la-Crosse was founded as a modest trading post manned by Montreal pedlars and Canadien voyageurs but would eventually become a vibrant French-Indigenous community and a flashpoint for Métis ethnogenesis following a devastating smallpox epidemic that ravaged the Hudson Bay watershed from 1780 to 1782.

Between 1779 and 1782, a smallpox epidemic originating in Mexico City devastated the entire continent of North America.[127] The virulent epidemic reached the northern Great Plains in 1780, and its impact was disastrous. Farther north at York Factory, Matthew Cocking wrote that "Much the greatest part of the Indians whose furs have been formerly and hitherto brought to this Place, are now no more having been carried off by that cruel disorder the Small Pox."[128] Smallpox is a serious and often deadly infectious disease that causes headache, backache, fever, vomiting, fatigue, malaise, and, eventually, telltale skin rashes, lesions, pustules, and scabs. At Gloucester House, John Kipling received a group of Ojibwes from Rainy Lake, who reported that "there is a great mortality among the Indians and that most of the Indians in and near the raney [Rainy] Lake is dead, and

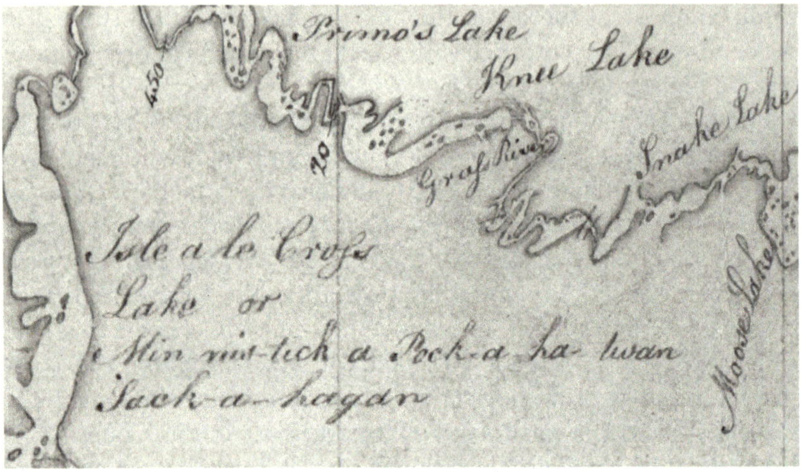

6.3 In 1790, Philip Turnor, inland surveyor and cartographer for the HBC, left Cumberland House with Malchom Ross and Peter Fidler. The men wintered at Île-à-la-Crosse, where they were hosted by Patrick Small, one of the original members of the 1779 North West Company partnership. From Île-à-la-Crosse, Turnor surveyed the Churchill River system looking for a direct connection to the Athabasca basin that would bypass the Methye Portage.

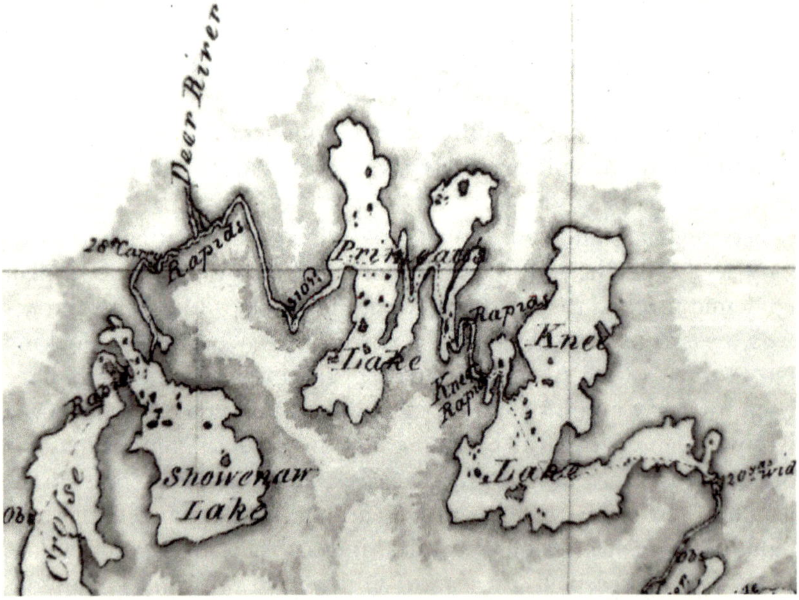

6.4 In his 1826 map of northwestern North America, Thompson accurately portrayed the labyrinth of lakes that form the Churchill River system.

that the assineybols [Nakoda] country is depopulated."[129] At Severn House, two families of Ojibwes reported that they had "seen but one Indian during the winter, that they are all dead inland."[130] William Tomison at Cumberland House also described the devastation that the smallpox epidemic had wrought along the Saskatchewan River: "the Small Pox had destroyed most of the Indians Inland ... The whole tribe of U'Basquiou Indians ... are extinct except one child, and that of the several Tribes of assinnee Poet [Nakoda] Pegogomew [Cree] and others bordering on Saskachiwan River ... not one in fifty have survived."[131] William Falconer, also at Severn House, likewise confirmed that "the Small Pox having been communicated to the Natives about Cumberland House and the Upper Settlement have almost entirely rooted [routed] them, and the Bungees [Ojibwe] having also caught the infection ... are either dying or dead."[132] Between 1779 and 1782, this smallpox epidemic claimed tens of thousands of lives in North America, and marked an important ethnic and demographic transition on the northern Great Plains and the Hudson Bay watershed in particular.[133]

As devastating as the smallpox epidemic was to the peoples of the Hudson Bay watershed, it also opened a space for Canadiens and their bourgeoning intercultural families to establish themselves in advantageous positions and exploit new avenues of political power in the Northwest. As HBC sources indicate, the epidemic wiped out almost the entire band of "Basquia Indians," a Cree group who maintained an important trade rendezvous at Opāskweyāw (where the French had built Fort Paskoya along the Saskatchewan River).[134] David Thompson, travelling through the Hudson Bay watershed in the 1790s, observed the significant population decline due to the smallpox epidemic: "When Hudson's Bay was [first] discovered, and the first trading settlements made, the Natives were far more numerous than at present. In the year 1782, the small Pox from Canada extended to them, and more than one half of them died."[135] During his 1819–22 Coppermine expedition, Sir John Franklin also described how the Saskatchewan River Crees had never fully recovered from the 1780–82 smallpox epidemic: "The tribe of Indians who reside in the vicinity, and frequent these establishments, is that of the Crees, or Knisteneaux. They were formerly a powerful and numerous nation, which ranged over a very extensive country ... but they have long ceased to be held in any fear, and are now, perhaps, the most harmless and inoffensive of the whole Indian race."[136] Scholars David Meyer and Dale Russell argue that, following the 1782 epidemic, the Basquia "ceased to exist," and that the few "survivors formed new social groups."[137] The smallpox epidemic also decimated the Pegogamaw, another dominant Cree group further upstream from the Basquia along the North Saskatchewan River.[138]

This left a power vacuum in the Saskatchewan River trade corridor from Cedar Lake in the east to the divergent branches of the North and South Saskatchewan rivers in the west. The smallpox epidemic also left vast swathes of territory abandoned and unoccupied in the Hudson Bay watershed. In its wake, Cree and Nakoda leaders encamped along the Pembina Escarpment invited Ojibwes from western Lake Superior to move west into their heavily depopulated lands: "the children of the forest [Ojibwes] were formally invited to dwell on the plains – to eat out of the same dish, to warm themselves at the same fire, and to make common cause with them against their enemies the Sioux [Očhéthi Šakówiŋ]."[139] The Cree and Nakoda invitation for the Ojibwe to relocate into depopulated lands probably paralleled the general movement of Canadiens and their Indigenous wives, who would prefigure the rise of the Métis people. Whereas some historians, like Laura Peers, have emphasized the general Ojibwe movement into the Hudson Bay watershed following the 1780–82 smallpox epidemic, others have emphasized the implications of the pestilence for the emergence of the Métis.[140] Gerhard Ens and Joe Sawchuk, for example, posit that "the Métis of the plains and Upper Missouri emerged in the shadow of smallpox epidemics, shifting patterns of indigenous occupation, and inter-ethnic warfare."[141] Bill Waiser writes that the 1780–82 smallpox epidemic "literally remade the map of the region by wiping out one-half to two-thirds of some band populations."[142] In many cases, it seems that Ojibwe relocation patterns correlated with that of former Canadien voyageurs and traders. In fact, many Métis families can trace their ancestry to unions between Ojibwe women (sometimes widowed by the epidemic) and Canadiens.[143] In other words, the 1780–82 epidemic helped create the necessary conditions for the eventual rise of the Métis as a distinct socio-political group.

Unsurprisingly, then, the nascent Métis community of Île-à-la-Crosse grew into existence shortly after these major demographic changes. Culturally hybrid Canadiens became important figures in the post-epidemic world of the Hudson Bay watershed. In time, as more and more resident Canadien traders married local Indigenous women,

Île-à-la-Crosse would grow into an important and vibrant Métis community.[144] The ability of these mixed-descent children to straddle both worlds made them respected leaders and dominant players in the local trade.[145] Following the smallpox epidemic, the French-Indigenous social world that had been built up over multiple generations in the Hudson Bay watershed had room to grow and to become something else entirely – the Métis Nation. For his part, Primeau remained in the region for the rest of his life and oversaw the NWC's Cumberland House post, a position he held when David Thompson visited the region in 1798.[146]

By remaining in the Northwest during and after the Seven Years' War, Louis Primeau deftly navigated liminal cultural spaces between Cree and British worlds. Already moving fluidly between European and Indigenous political and cultural spaces, Primeau also crossed commercial lines to work for rival Montreal pedlars, much to the chagrin of his former HBC employers. Working with Thomas and Joseph Frobisher, Primeau used his Indigenous connections to help dominate the Churchill River waterways north of Cumberland House, not only effectively cutting off trade to Hudson Bay, but also securing access to the fur-rich Athabasca Country, what historian Gerald Friesen has designated the "El Dorado" of the Canadian fur trade.[147] As a founding member of Île-à-la-Crosse, Primeau played a role in asserting an early Métis political identity in the aftermath of the 1780–82 smallpox epidemic.

The epidemic had brought about a major demographic shift in the Saskatchewan Country that gave métisé Canadiens, their Indigenous wives, and their offspring a demographic advantage in the Northwest fur trade. The proven success of the Athabasca Country guaranteed that Île-à-la-Crosse would develop into an important entrepôt on the Churchill River system, which was already connected to the well-known Saskatchewan Country to the south via the Sturgeon-Weir River and was now linked to the rich northern furs of the Arctic watershed via the Methye Portage. Starting in the 1780s, Montreal-based traders began to inhabit Île-à-la-Crosse year-round, marrying local Cree and Dene women. The Métis community at Île-à-la-Crosse quickly grew.[148] By 1819, Sir John Franklin's travel narrative indicates that sizeable Métis populations had taken root along the Saskatchewan and Churchill Rivers and their environs.[149] Over time, many of the Métis communities that had emerged in the Saskatchewan Country in the 1780s moved to the Red River Settlement to take advantage of the buffalo hunt and provisioning trade. Of course, many Métis stayed at Île-à-la-Crosse and other Saskatchewan and Churchill watershed fur trade communities in the Northwest, like Cumberland House, Lac La Loche, Lac La Ronge, and Fort Carlton. The developments of the period – the 1780–82 smallpox epidemic, the influx of more Canadien voyageurs, and a permanent settlement at Île-à-la-Crosse and adjacent sites in the Saskatchewan district – struck an important demographic balance in the Hudson Bay watershed that allowed Métis collective consciousness and political self-determination to develop.

Louis Primeau's son, Joseph Primeau, was born in 1785 to a Cree mother from the lower Saskatchewan River region.[150] This marital union occurred around the time that Primeau had switched his services from the HBC to the NWC in the 1780s. Primeau likely went through the formalities of Cree marriage customs, which would entail applying for the consent of the woman's father, brother, or other male relative and making him a present (bride price) of furs or European trade articles like blankets, woollen cloth, kettles, or alcohol. If the proposal was accepted, the marriage would be formalized, with no particular ceremony marking the occasion. The newly married couple would then move into a dwelling furnished by the bride's family. The husband was expected to provide an initial period of bride service before the wife took up residence in her husband's tent on a more permanent basis. For Canadien, English, and Scottish fur traders, this may have resembled a season or two of trading, hunting, and generally living en dérouine among his wife's community, before she eventually returned with her husband to the fur trading post or factory to live permanently.[151] Therefore, following long-term patrilocal residency patterns, young Joseph Primeau grew up around the NWC's Cumberland House, where his father was in charge. Joseph would have observed how his father conducted day-to-day trade with Cree and Nakoda visitors. By the early nineteenth century, Joseph Primeau was himself an interpreter, albeit at Fort Edmonton, which Canadiens called Fort-des-Prairies.[152] Interpreters and those with facility in Indigenous languages and customs were often dispatched from Fort Edmonton to winter with Native bands and return with furs for the trade and meat to provision the fort.[153] After working and trading for a number of years along the North Saskatchewan River, Primeau eventually moved to the Red River Settlement, ostensibly still in the employ of the NWC.

CONCLUSION

According to conventional Métis historiography, the Métis people emerged as a salient political force in the early nineteenth century following the Pemmican Proclamation (1814) and the Battle of Seven Oaks (1816).[154] A century-long investigation of French-Indigenous interaction in the Hudson Bay watershed demonstrates, however, that the earliest emergence of significant patterns of métissage in the Hudson Bay watershed can be traced back to the late seventeenth century. A global imperial war between Britain and France (1754–63) compelled colonial elites – Troupes de la Marine officers and wealthy merchants – to withdraw from the Western Posts to defend their professional and familial interests in the Saint Lawrence valley. Many voyageurs and coureurs de bois did not heed the call to defend *la Patrie*, but instead remained in the Hudson Bay watershed, attached as they were to their fur trade families and Indigenous kinship networks.

Following the British conquest of Canada in 1760 and the Treaty of Paris in 1763, Canadien traders, such as François Jérôme *dit* Latour and Louis Primeau, who would never have thought of themselves as Métis, nevertheless played important roles as progenitors of the Métis people. A dynamic Métis world was emerging from the vestiges of New France's Western Posts. They were the heirs of an ambivalent empire in the Northwest. Although they were few in number, métisé Canadiens and their Indigenous wives of the 1760s and '70s were the spark that would ultimately kindle the sacred fire of the Métis Nation. Female-centred Indigenous kin networks constituted the centripetal force that incorporated outsider males (métisé Canadiens) into a distinct regional and cultural world view rooted in family obligations, responsibility, and relatedness. The union of these Indigenous women and métisé Canadiens gave rise to what historian Brenda Macdougall has dubbed the "proto-generation," children who took their fathers' last names but resided in the homelands of their mothers' families, eventually intermarrying with each other and developing a sense of peoplehood and claiming a homeland.[155] Their children, grand-children, and great-grandchildren married each other to form new and distinct communities and kin networks, slowly moved onto the northern Great Plains, and gradually developed a unique sense of themselves as totally separate from other European or Indigenous communities in the Hudson Bay watershed. They were multilingual, great horsemen, expert buffalo hunters, acted as important cultural brokers between European and Indigenous societies, and dominated the trade in buffalo hides and pemmican.

Following this general pattern, Jérôme's descendants moved away from the fur trade corridor along the Saskatchewan River and embraced the buffalo hunt, eventually moving into modern-day North Dakota, in the vicinity of the Pembina posts, close to buffalo migration routes.[156] Likewise, Primeau's descendants made their way to the Red River Valley and northern Great Plains. In 1869, a descendant of Primeau, Jean-Baptiste Primot (Primeau), who was living in the parish of St Norbert, likely joined a group of young Métis agitators (mostly boatmen and farmers of the colony under the leadership of Louis Riel) to build "La Barrière" across the Pembina Trail, thereby preventing incoming land-survey parties from Ontario from entering the colony.[157] This was the start of the Red River Resistance (1869–70), which resulted in the Manitoba Act and the territory's official entry as a province into the new Canadian nation-state. Historian Jacqueline Peterson once described the Great Lakes as one of the "many roads" leading to Métis ethnogenesis in the Red River Valley. Peterson has since revised her position, arguing instead that the term "Métis" should only be applied when historical self-ascription and political consciousness can be identified. I would, note, however, that within the Hudson Bay watershed itself there were many roads to Red River, and that the Saskatchewan River was one such road; it was the crucible in which the Jérôme, Primeau, and many other families' Métis identities were forged before their eventual relocation to the Red River Valley.[158] Eventually, Métis families that emerged in the fur trade communities of Île-à-la-Crosse, Fort Carlton, and Fort-des-Prairies made the move to the Red River Valley to take advantage of new economic opportunities presented by the buffalo hunt and the pemmican trade. By the beginning of the nineteenth century, the Hudson Bay watershed (and the Saskatchewan River valley in particular) had truly emerged as a Métis homeland.

EPILOGUE

A Métis Homeland

It was a chilly fall morning in 1821; frost had covered the grass around the wooden palisade of Fort Carlton (Duck Lake, Saskatchewan), though the freeze-up had not yet set in on the North Saskatchewan River. The extended kin group of the Jérôme family had gathered within the fort's walls to mourn the death of their family's patriarch, Pierre Jérôme. The HBC officer in charge of Fort Carlton, John Peter Pruden, recorded the notable loss to the fur trade community, and said that Jérôme had been "[for] many years in the service of the NWC [North West Company] as Interpreter for the Crees and I should suppose he must be upwards of 80 years of age."[1] Pierre Jérôme had been an interpreter at Fort Edmonton (Fort-des-Prairies), on the North Saskatchewan River, from 1799 to 1804.[2] Born around 1740, Pierre Jérôme was the nephew of François Jérôme *dit* Latour, whom we followed in the preceding chapters. When he arrived in the Hudson Bay watershed in 1769 at the age of twenty-nine, Pierre Jérôme likely joined his uncle's fur trade operations in the Saskatchewan River valley. Unsurprisingly, Pierre Jérôme probably developed his language skills through kinship connections to his aunt (a Cree woman) and his many half-Cree first cousins.[3] According to Jérôme family history, Pierre Jérôme married à la façon du pays an Oji-Cree woman named Virginia with whom he had four children – two boys and two girls.[4]

Pierre Jérôme's son Martin (*père*) and grandson Martin (*fils*), both of whom were in the employ of the NWC (and later the HBC after the two companies merged in 1821), were present at Fort Carlton on that chilly fall morning in 1821. Alexander Henry the Younger had hired Martin Jérôme (*père*) as his interpreter at Fort Vermilion (located at the mouth of the Vermilion River, Alberta) in the winter of 1809–10.

In addition to interpreting, Jérôme worked as an itinerant trader collecting furs en dérouine from Cree camps.[5] Martin Jérôme (*fils*) was born and worked at Fort Edmonton, on the banks of the North Saskatchewan River. Alexander Henry the Younger referred to Martin (*fils*) as a "half Breed young man" and a "Native of Fort des Prairie."[6] When Norway House chief factor Colin Robertson prepared for a trip to Fort Edmonton in 1822, he noted that "Jérôme and the White Eagle's son are supposed to be the best guides."[7]

Employment in the fur trade, including work as guides, interpreters, and diplomats, was an intergenerational vocation. Three generations after François Jérôme *dit* Latour's exploits around Lake Winnipeg, the Red River Valley, and the lower Saskatchewan River in the 1760s and '70s, the extended Jérôme family was still energetically participating in a socially and culturally hybrid fur trade world. In the early 1820s, Martin (*fils*) quit company service and moved to the Red River Settlement. The Jérôme family's relocation to the Red River Valley paralleled the general movement of early Métis families who sought seasonal access to the bison herds of the northern Great Plains. Eventually, the Jérômes became what is often described in the abundant historical literature as a typical Métis family: residing in the Red River Valley, multilingual (French, Cree, and Anishinaabemowin), and skilled bison hunters and Prairie traders with no remaining ties to the Saint Lawrence valley.[8]

From the very beginning of a French presence in the Hudson Bay watershed in the 1660s until the British conquest of New France in 1760, Canadiens had navigated complex Indigenous geopolitical and cultural landscapes. Canadiens were salient intermediaries between Indigenous peoples and French imperial agents at the edge of empire. The French Crown was initially receptive to employing Canadiens as informants, explorers, linguists, diplomats, fur traders, and military leaders in the Hudson Bay watershed. In time, however, the French metropolitan and colonial governments became more reluctant to acknowledge and reward ennoblements, commissions, and seigneuries to Canadiens for their services, preferring instead to adhere to the protocol and hierarchy of the ancien régime, in which rank, status, and nobility outweighed ability and experience. The governorship of Charles de la Boische, Marquis de Beauharnois, attempted to regulate mobility in the fur trade and imposed strict guidelines on who could head imperial projects in western North America. In the 1730s, Beauharnois tasked Pierre Gaultier de Varennes, sieur de La Vérendrye, a member of New France's military elite and an officer in the Compagnies Franches de la Marine, to establish the Western Posts. However, as La Vérendrye and other French colonial officials struggled to forge alliances with the Indigenous peoples of the Hudson Bay watershed, it became increasingly apparent that voyageurs and coureurs de bois were still better equipped to determine the form and implementation of colonialism in western North America.

Whether or not French metropolitan and colonial governments always attempted to utilize Canadiens as agents of imperial power, voyageurs and coureurs de bois pursued their own agendas and exercised agency in the Hudson Bay watershed. Canadiens initially made it possible for French imperialism to extend into the region, but their own ambivalent relationships with the colonial government and its representatives led to a fragmentation of French imperial authority in western North America. Within these contact zones, Canadiens were indeed ambivalent and roguish agents of empire, sometimes promoting imperial projects and at other times resisting and fragmenting official French influence. These rogue Canadiens, operating largely in their own self-interest, ended up frustrating many imperial goals in the West, but they nevertheless promoted haphazard and ill-defined expressions of French imperialism in the heart of North America, which facilitated overseas expressions of empire, even if they were negotiated at times.

The French imperial presence in the Hudson Bay watershed constituted an ambivalent empire, one that emerged between the dichotomies of idealized imperial projects envisioned by the metropole and personal interests, ambitions, and initiatives pursued by local Indigenous, Canadien, and Métis actors. While Canadiens, along with their Indigenous wives and kinsmen, ultimately thwarted imperial designs, the accompanying effects of empire – trade goods, technologies, global markets, disease epidemics, military alliances, new cultural and religious practices, and an influx of marriageable Frenchmen – still profoundly affected the social, cultural, political, and demographic landscapes of the Northwest. While the effects of French imperialism were often devastating and destabilizing, local actors siphoned and channelled these forces in productive ways – sometimes to amass considerable prestige and personal fortune, like Radisson, Des Groseilliers, and Du Lhut; other times to conduct trade and expand power and influence across Indigenous, imperial, and commercial borders, like Louis Primeau; or, finally, to build families, form new and distinct communities and kin networks, and forge new identities from the ashes of New France's Western Posts, like the extended Jérôme family.

The Hudson Bay watershed had never been a "middle ground," at least not in the sense that Richard White has utilized that term to refer to both a process (between Algonquian-speaking peoples and the French colonial government) and a space (the pays d'en haut). In the Hudson Bay watershed, the necessary ingredients for a "middle ground" – an equal balance of power and a desire for cross-cultural accommodation and common meaning – never came together. State-sponsored European newcomers were always at the mercy of their Anishinaabe, Cree, Nakoda, and Dakota partners. Despite a lack of actualized sovereignty, or even "middle ground" accommodation in the Hudson Bay watershed, French imperial officials gazed covetously upon a region that was much more valuable, from an imperial standpoint, than French colonial historians have hitherto acknowledged. The Hudson Bay watershed was a salient asset of French empire because its geography, at least according to the expert geographers and map-makers of the day, promised to reveal a northwest passage. Although the Western Sea ultimately proved to be an imperial fiction, the enduring belief in its existence made the Hudson Bay watershed a potential bridge connecting the French Atlantic world with France's aspirations in the Pacific Basin. In other words, the Western Sea and the Hudson Bay watershed fuelled a French dream of an "extra-Atlantic" global empire that spanned from western North America to the Pacific.[9]

In the end, however, France's bid for hegemony and imperial sovereignty in the Hudson Bay watershed was unsuccessful, at least as it was conceived at Paris and Versailles. French imperial representatives in North America were unable to take control of the fur trade away from the HBC (a company that endures to this day, albeit strictly as a retail department store). The French were also unable to "discover" the fabled Western Sea, and the Northwest Passage would remain an imperial pipe dream. Even a century after the British conquest of New France, Sir John Franklin, Captain Francis Crozier, and the entire crews of the HMS *Erebus* and the HMS *Terror* perished in the Canadian Arctic near King William Island in a fruitless and hubristic search for the Northwest Passage. Throughout the history of French North America, the "West" – whether sought via Louisiana or the Hudson Bay watershed – remained the stuff of dreams, representing endless possibilities for metropolitan ministers and imperial planners who envisioned mineral wealth, valuable trade, and the Northwest Passage. Those same metropolitan ministers and imperial planners could hardly have foreseen that the French presence in the Hudson Bay watershed would have a much more permanent and significant legacy – the creation of a new Indigenous people and nation.

In 1754, a violent imperial skirmish in the Ohio Valley sparked what is referred to in French-speaking Canada as *la guerre de la Conquête*, and the fighting spread like wildfire to Lake Champlain and the upper reaches of the Hudson River valley corridor, Lake Ontario, and Acadia, particularly the Isthmus of Chignecto and Cape Breton. In a final denouement, British forces breached the Saint Lawrence valley, besieging and capturing the citadel of Quebec, and a year later laid siege to an inadequately fortified Montreal, where the remnants of the French fighting forces in North America had gathered to make a final stand against the British. Dismissing the protestations of the Chevalier de Lévis and Louis Antoine de Bougainville, New France's last governor general, Pierre de Rigaud, Marquis de Vaudreuil-Cavagnial (1755–60), surrendered to the British on 8 September 1760, with the understanding that further resistance would only serve as a meaningless sacrifice of lives and property to an already lost cause.[10] While Troupes de la Marine officers had initially withdrawn from the Northwest to defend Canada, as well as to protect their families and business interests in the Saint Lawrence valley, the majority, realizing that their positions in society had been fatally compromised, later opted to return to France. Even though the first British governor of Quebec, James Murray, guaranteed Canadiens their religious freedom and property rights, most of this French military elite simply refused to be subordinated to British rule.[11]

Both during and after the Seven Years' War, many Canadiens opted to remain with their fur trade families in the Hudson Bay watershed. These Canadiens had gained detailed knowledge of the geographical, political, and cultural landscapes of the Hudson Bay watershed through years of travel, work, intermarriage, and ceremonial inclusion within Indigenous kinship networks. This intimate knowledge allowed them to carve out a salient socio-cultural space even after the hierarchy of the ancien régime had collapsed at the Western Posts. The continuous presence of Canadiens in the Hudson Bay watershed meant that multi-generational métissage went on uninterrupted during a period of imperial transformation, turmoil, and upheaval.

Ojibwe, Cree, and Nakoda women incorporated these Canadiens, initially greeted as outsiders, into female-centred family networks, which allowed these newcomers to situate themselves within an extensive alliance of Indigenous peoples in the Northwest. Through their kin and alliance affiliations, Canadiens gained access to territory and vital resources.

When Canadien voyageurs working for British and Scottish pedlars arrived in the Hudson Bay watershed after the conquest, they encountered and joined their ethnic kinsmen in their new home in the West. It was a cohesive and dynamic French-Indigenous world. The everyday activities and interactions of Indigenous peoples and French voyageurs, soldiers, traders, and coureurs de bois left their mark in the region, with a century-long pattern of seasonal visitation and commercial activity eventually leading to permanent habitation and, by the close of the eighteenth century, the rise of the Métis people in the Hudson Bay watershed. If the tension between localized Indigenous sovereignty and French imperial projects during this era constituted the crucible in which Indigenous and French identities, cultures, and bloodlines were heat blasted into a nascent Métis peoplehood, then later external threats to the Métis way of life – the Selkirk Settlement, the Hudson's Bay Company, and the Dominion of Canada – represented the hammer and anvil by which a Métis national consciousness was forged in the coming generations.

In the spring of 1825, the Letendre extended family and young Martin Jérôme (*fils*) (François Jérôme *dit* Latour was his great-great-uncle) arrived within sight of the Red River Colony. Jérôme had followed his lifelong friend and mentor, Jean-Baptiste Letendre *dit* Batoche, to take advantage of economic opportunities presented by the bourgeoning pemmican trade of the Red River Valley and northern Great Plains.[12] With all their worldly belongings packed into a Red River cart pulled by oxen, the Letendre clan and young Martin Jérôme followed the Carlton Trail, the most prominent of the Red River Trails, a heavily rutted 1,450-kilometre track that ran across the Prairies. Having arrived at the small Red River Colony (comprised of only a few hundred people, mostly retired fur traders and their Indigenous families), Jérôme might have gazed upon the white steeple rising up from the small log chapel of the newly founded Roman Catholic mission, as well as the tall wooden palisade of Fort Garry, the HBC's headquarters, built high on the banks of the confluence of the Red and Assiniboine Rivers. With an estimated fifty million bison still on the Prairies in 1800, he may have even spotted some herds within a few kilometres of the settlement.[13] A couple of months after their arrival, on 5 June 1825, Jérôme married Jean-Baptiste Letendre's sister Angelique, and together they had four children: Angelique, Martin, Jean-Baptiste, and André. This joining of the Letendre and Jérôme clans and their relocation to the Red River followed a similar pattern of mobility that brought other Métis families to the region, where they established buffalo hunting brigades, developed a Métis culture on the northern Great Plains, and carved out their own economic niche in the provisioning trade of the Red River Valley. They were home.

APPENDIX

The Hudson's Bay Company and the Anglo-Métis

The principal subjects of this study are Canadien voyageurs and coureurs de bois, originating mostly from the parishes between Trois-Rivières and Montreal, and their subsequent relations with the Indigenous peoples of the Hudson Bay watershed, which eventually resulted in the rise of the Métis people of the northern Great Plains. While my focus has been on the antecedents of what some historians have dubbed the "Plains Métis," who practised Catholicism, spoke Michif, called themselves "Bois-Brûlés," and were committed to the lifestyle of the buffalo hunt, I also recognize that there is a distinctive Anglo-Métis element to the story of the Métis Nation.[1] By the nineteenth century, mixed-descent populations, derived from marriages "in the custom of the country" between Indigenous women and English and Scottish fur traders, settled the Protestant parishes of the Red River Settlement. Unlike their Bois-Brûlés brethren, the Anglo-Métis called themselves "half-breed" or "country-born," professed an Protestant religion, spoke English or Bungi, and while still participating in the buffalo hunts, increasingly became farmers and merchants.[2] This appendix is an acknowledgment and brief overview of the Anglo-Métis's origins and contribution to the history of the Métis Nation.

The origins of the English and Scottish Métis lay in the history of the HBC. From its 1670 charter onwards, the London Committee demanded celibacy from their servants and officers; they forbade them from fraternizing with Native women at the bay and punished those who permitted such relationships around company factories. As a result, only fifteen instances of company men (typically officers) taking Indigenous wives "in the custom of the country" are documented in HBC records prior to 1770.[3] Nevertheless, Cree interests and social values challenged the company's sternly monastic stance. Cree bands consistently encouraged the formation of marriage alliances between their women and company men to cement social ties and to create reciprocal connections between their bands and the HBC. Because the heads of posts had greater control over commerce and access to merchandise, trading captains placed greater pressure on governors and chief factors to cement trade alliances by accepting these offers of marriage. Unsurprisingly, men such as Robert Pilgrim, Richard Norton, Moses Norton, James Isham, and Humphrey Marten fathered the first "mixed-blood" children born at the company's bayside factories. Many HBC factors did marry "in the custom of the country," but in all cases their Indigenous wives resided with them in the factory; none had joined their wives' communities. "Mixed-blood" sons like Charles Price Isham (born in the 1750s at York Factory) and John America Marten (born in the 1760s at Fort Albany) lived and operated within a predominately British milieu, even travelling to England for schooling before becoming full-fledged members of HBC trading posts, whereas the daughters of such Euro-Indigenous unions usually resided among, and were assimilated into, their Cree extended families. In other words, prior to 1770, the heads of posts skirted the London Committee's strict policy and claimed female companionship at the factories for themselves. The resultant children were not classed as a separate ethnic group in any meaningful sense.[4]

Large-scale intermarriage between Indigenous women and HBC servants began to occur in the late-1770s when the HBC workforce moved inland, reorienting the site of Euro-Indigenous relations away from coastal factories and toward Saskatchewan River posts like Cumberland House, Nipawin, Upper Hudson House, and Manchester House. From these inland posts, HBC fur traders formed itinerant trading parties and ventured directly into far-flung Indigenous camps with a supply of trade goods. By trading *en dérouine* (a fur trade idiom that refers to the practice of travelling with a small complement of goods to Indigenous communities to trade for furs), HBC servants, and not just officers, entered Native worlds and developed positive social connections and kin relations among Indigenous communities.[5] Unlike officers' "half-breed" sons, who were educated in England and later joined the company ranks, the mixed-descent population that emerged from marriages between lower-ranking servants and Native mothers resided predominately among Indigenous bands and worked only informally for the HBC as provisioners and itinerant traders, operating within the fur trade in a manner comparable to that of Cree trading captains in the region.[6]

By 1800, the company had entirely abandoned its official policy of non-fraternization between Indigenous women and British-born officers and servants in response to the exponential growth of the HBC's labour needs. To challenge the NWC, the HBC had established interior posts throughout the Saskatchewan, Churchill, and Athabasca watersheds. Needing to staff these posts, the London Committee turned to Native-born youths who could fulfill apprentice roles locally and immediately, rather than brining young apprentices from England, as had been the policy during the company's long first century (1670–1786). The company even began providing some training and schooling, with the intention of educating the children to play useful roles at the factories, a move encouraged by interested fathers who were already beginning to train their sons in practical skills.[7] Around the same time, HBC fur traders began to view Native-born daughters – who were more likely to stay in "Indian Country" than their mixed-descent brothers – as desirable marriage partners. Because these Native-born daughters grew up in a predominately Indigenous milieu, their mothers had transmitted to them necessary skills, such as preparing furs, netting snowshoes, and securing small game, to fulfill a salient socio-economic role in the fur trade. Moreover, unlike Indigenous women, marriage between HBC apprentices and the Native-born daughters of seasoned HBC fur traders established patronage bonds by linking incoming and established company traders by mutual ties of sentiment.[8]

The merging of the HBC and the NWC in 1821 moved many "mixed-bloods" to embrace a Métis identity. Under the firm hand of Governor George Simpson, who reorganized the post-merger company, unnecessary and superfluous posts were shuttered, and hundreds of redundant employees (over half of the fur trade labourers in Rupert's Land) were laid off. The remaining employees found that the restructured hierarchy became more stratified, especially for "half-breed" or "country-born" labourers.[9] Losing employment opportunities because of a diminished and less competitive labour market, mixed-descent labourers formerly employed by the HBC moved to the Red River Settlement, where they and their families could acquire land, housing, and educational and religious facilities beyond anything provided at the posts.[10] The English Métis lived in the Protestant parishes of St Andrews and St Clements, north of the Forks of the Red and Assiniboine Rivers.

While historian Frits Pannekoek relied on parish records to argue that there was segregation and even hostility between the Catholic Bois-Brûlés and the Protestant Anglo-Métis, Métis community tradition, as well as further archival research into non-clerical sources, suggests that this division among the Red River Métis population has been grossly overstated, and that there was a feeling of co-operation and unity between the two mixed-descent populations. Protestant anglophones and Catholic francophones joined together in the annual buffalo hunt, freighting expeditions (both overland Red River cart trains and York boat brigades on Lake Winnipeg and up the Saskatchewan River), and even marriages, which spanned the alleged cultural gulf between the Anglo-Métis and Bois-Brûlés groups. At important junctures in the history of the Métis Nation, Anglo-Métis joined their Bois-Brûlés compatriots to assert their sovereignty and defend their national interests; this included free trade, an issue that played a major part in the Sayer Trial of 1849, and land rights, which came to a head with the Red River Resistance of 1869–70.[11] Ultimately, the Anglo-Métis of the Protestant parishes of St Andrews and St Clements, on the banks of the lower Red River, were (and still are) an integral part of the Métis Nation and its national narrative.

Notes

ABBREVIATIONS

ANF	Archives nationales de France
ANOM	Archives nationales d'outre-mer
BAnQ	Bibliothèque et Archives nationales du Québec
BnF	Bibliothèque nationale de France
DCB	*Dictionary of Canadian Biography*
DRCNY	*Documents Relative to the Colonial History of the State of New York*
HBCA	Hudson's Bay Company Archives
JCBL	John Carter Brown Library
JR	*Jesuit Relations*
LAC	Library and Archives Canada
PRDH	Programme de recherche en démographie historique
SHSB	Société historique de Saint-Boniface
VCD	Voyageur Contracts Database

PREFACE

1 St-Onge, "The Dissolution of a Métis Community."

2 For the quote, see Combet, *In Search of the Western Sea*, 165.

3 Trémaudan, *Histoire de la nation métisse*, 37–40.

4 In a recent biography on Louis Riel, M. Max Hamon argues that, despite their Quebecois origins, the Lagimodières were for all intents and purposes Métis. Despite their "whiteness" compared to neighbouring Métis families, Hamon posits that "race did *not* determine Métis identity; community, kinship, and religion were far more important." Hamon, *The Audacity of His Enterprise*, 28–9.

INTRODUCTION

1 HBCA, B.198/a/10, Severn post journal, William Tomison, "Observations of a Journey Inland to the Great Lake Performed by William Tomison Steward at Severn House Mr. Andrew Graham Master From June 16th, 1767 to June 30th, 1768."

2 The term *Canadien* typically refers to French colonists born in the colony of Canada (i.e., the Saint Lawrence valley). During this period, reports of Canadiens among the Upland Cree who traded with the HBC steadily increased. The Canadiens were building posts amid the Cree and giving their leaders large presents to discourage them from going to Albany and other HBC factories. Humphrey Marten wrote that "Poor Albany how are thou fallen, the trade at Present, not 5,000 [Made Beaver] the Pedlars ruin us, may the Devil confound them." HBCA, B.3/b/9, Humphrey Marten, Fort Albany correspondence books.

3 HBCA, B.198/a/10, Tomison, "Observations of a Journey Inland."

4 The lower Saskatchewan River is the part of the river in Manitoba and eastern Saskatchewan, and downstream from the Saskatchewan River Forks, where the separate North Saskatchewan and South Saskatchewan Rivers merge to create the singular Saskatchewan River. The "lower" designation refers to it being downstream from the two main branches and to its proximity to the river's discharge at Lake Winnipeg (Grand Rapids).

5 HBCA, B.198/a/10, Tomison, "Observations of a Journey Inland."

6 Cocking, *Journal of Matthew Cocking*, 118.

7 Ibid.

8 Wallace, *Pedlars from Quebec*, 4–7; Swan and Jerome, "Indigenous Knowledge," 41–4.

9 Havard, *Histoire des coureurs de bois*, 319.

10 Little has been written on French-Indigenous relations in the Hudson Bay watershed. The few works that deal with the topic are primarily biographies of French explorers like Pierre-Esprit Radisson and Pierre Gaultier de Varennes, sieur de La Vérendrye. See, for example, Champagne, *Les La Vérendrye et Le Poste de l'Ouest*; Champagne, *Nouvelles Études*; Fournier, *Pierre-Esprit Radisson*; Combet, *In Search of the Western Sea*; Bourrie, *Bush Runner*.

11 For some recent works on Euro-Indigenous relations and Native histories in the Hudson Bay watershed, see Lytwyn, *Muskekowuck Athinuwick*; Bird, *Telling Our Stories*; Bohr, *Gifts from the Thunder*

Beings; Brown, *An Ethnohistorian in Rupert's Land*. The literature on the Métis people is covered extensively in the introduction.

12 During the period of New France (1608–1760), the Canadien settler population would peak at seventy thousand in 1760.

13 Eccles, "Military Establishment in New France," 6.

14 Ibid., 9–11, 18–19.

15 Notable exceptions include Allaire, "Fur Trade Engagés," 15–26; Wien, "Le Pérou éphémère," 160–88; Wien, "Familles paysannes," 167–80; Vézina, "Le Lexique des voyageurs francophones."

16 Podruchny, *Making the Voyageur World*; Englebert, "Diverging Identities and Converging Interests"; Englebert and St-Onge, "Paddling into History"; St-Onge, "'He Was Neither a Soldier nor a Slave"; Barman, *French Canadians, Furs, and Indigenous Women*; Barman, *Iroquois in the West*.

17 Havard, *Histoire des coureurs de bois*.

18 For French (and later British) imperial weakness in Acadia, see Lennox, *Homelands and Empires*, 15–18, 46. For imperial failure in French Guiana, see Regourd, "Kourou 1763." For the French Caribbean in general, see Boucher, *France and the American Tropics*, 62–3, 85–6. For Louisiana, see Dawdy, *Building the Devil's Empire*, 3–4, 19–20, 134–5. For French imperial failure in Canada (the Saint Lawrence valley), particularly during the Seven Years' War, see Frégault, *The War of the Conquest*, 200, 257, 267, 342.

19 Pritchard, *In Search of Empire*, 234–7; Boucher, *France and the American Tropics*, 62–3, 85–6; Dawdy, *Building the Devil's Empire*, 3–4, 19–20, 134–5.

20 Banks is of course paraphrasing and paying homage to David Parker's earlier contention that "absolutism was always in the making, but never made." Banks, *Chasing Empire Across the Sea*, 7; Parker, *The Making of French Absolutism*, xvi.

21 Soll, *The Reckoning*, 61–2.

22 Banks, *Chasing Empire Across the Sea*; Soll, *The Information Master*.

23 James C. Scott sees legibility as the central problem in governance. The state's attempt to make a society legible ignores or dismisses functional, on-the-ground realities and complexities, and thus undermines effective governance. Scott, *Seeing Like a State*, 4–5.

24 Edelson, *The New Map of Empire*, 10–11, 334–5.

25 Banks, "Communications and 'Imperial Overstretch,'" 24–6.

26 Rushforth, "Insinuating Empire," 51.

27 White, *The Middle Ground*, xxvii.

28 Dawdy, *Building the Devil's Empire*, 19.

29 As French Atlantic historian Paul Cohen has demonstrated, the Indigenous peoples of North America inhabited their own "cultural cores" or "world-systems," which, from their perspective, would relegate "Parisian haberdashers and dapper French buyers of beaver felt hats on the outer margins of the Algonquin, Huron [Wendat] and Iroquois [Haudenosaunee] world." The French Atlantic world was both shaped by and peripheral to the Great Lakes and Mississippi watersheds. Cohen, "Was There an Amerindian Atlantic?," 409.

30 Witgen, *An Infinity of Nations*, 118, 149, 165; Morrissey, *Empire by Collaboration*, 11–38, 52–9; Hämäläinen, *Comanche Empire*, 1–17, 345–61; Lee, *Masters of the Middle Waters*.

31 Witgen, *An Infinity of Nations*, 149, 165; Anderson, *Kinsmen of Another Kind*, 45–6; Hämäläinen, *Lakota America*, 11–84.

32 Dawdy, *Building the Devil's Empire*, 11, 19.

33 Scott, *The Art of Not Being Governed*, 24–5, 129, 152–3.

34 Ibid., ix–x, 10, 24.

35 Ibid., ix–x, 3–4.

36 Havard, *Histoire des coureurs de bois*, 45; Greer, *The People of New France*, 58–9; Dechêne, *Habitants and Merchants*, xiv.

37 Coates, *Metamorphoses of Landscape and Community*, 75–99; Moogk, *La Nouvelle France*, 170–3; Trigger, *Natives and Newcomers*, 194–7.

38 Charles Le Moyne and Pierre Boucher were both soldiers, interpreters, diplomats, seigneurs, and governors. Both accompanied Alexandre de Prouville de Tracy's 1666 Carignan-Salières Regiment expedition into the heart of Iroquoia. Pierre Boucher was ennobled in 1661 and eventually became governor of Trois-Rivières in 1662. In 1668, Le Moyne received letters patent of nobility and Governor Antoine Lefèbvre de La Barre recommended him in 1683 for the post of governor of Montreal. When Le Moyne died in 1685, he was the richest man in Montreal. The two men's descendants became some of the key figures in the history of New France, among them Pierre Le Moyne d'Iberville and Jean-Baptiste Le Moyne de Bienville (Le Moyne's sons), as well as Joseph Boucher de Niverville and Pierre Gaultier de Varennes, sieur de La Vérendrye (Boucher's grandsons). DCB, 1:463–5, 2:82–7.

39 Grenier, *Brève histoire du régime seigneurial*, 33–49; Dépatie, Dessureault, and Lalancette, *Contributions à l'étude du régime seigneurial canadien*, 1–3, 62–3, 84, 229; Courville, *Quebec: A Historical Geography*, 6; Miquelon, *New France, 1701–1744*, 194–8. On the other hand, some historians, like Cole Harris, have argued that

the seigneurial system was irrelevant to the colonization, settlement patterns, economic activity, and the society of early Canada. Harris paints seigneurs as largely absent and habitants as fiercely independent people who, forming the largest class in the colony, were largely the ones to fashion the seigneurial system into what they wanted it to be. Harris, *The Seigneurial System*, 8, 139.

40 Participation in military services initially stemmed from necessity in the seventeenth century to safeguard the nascent colony from Haudenosaunee raids (particularly around the Island of Montreal and Trois-Rivières) and from English maritime attacks around Quebec and Acadia. Additionally, Louise Dechêne points out that the "martial character of French society" in the seventeenth century "had been recently refuelled by the wars of religion and the Fronde." Dechêne, *Habitants and Merchants*, 19–20; Havard and Vidal, *Histoire de l'Amérique Française*, 88, 113–14, 93–9, 110–12; Lozier, *Flesh Reborn*, 48–52, 217–18, 220.

41 For more on officers in the Troupes de la Marine and Canadian-born military elites, see Lalancette, "Les capitaines des troupes de la Marine de 1683 à 1739."

42 Eccles, "Military Establishment in New France," 1–22; Crouch, *Nobility Lost*, 27–31, 110; Lesueur, *Les troupes coloniales d'Ancien Régime*, 178–92, 213–14. See also, Moogk, *La Nouvelle France*, 181–91; Dechêne, *Habitants and Merchants*, 210; Dechêne, *Le peuple, l'État et la guerre au Canada*, 93–152; Gagné, *Inconquis*, 15–16; Fournier, *Les officiers des Troupes de la Marine au Canada*, 23–32.

43 Dechêne, *Habitants and Merchants*, 43–5, 91, 94–100, 113–17; Miquelon, *Dugard of Rouen*, 69–73, 140–7; Bosher, *The Canada Merchants*, 9–10, 20, 57–62.

44 Dechêne, *Habitants and Merchants*, 41–3; Crouch, *Nobility Lost*, 28; Greer, *People of New France*, 50.

45 Frégault, "Politique et politiciens au début du XVIIIe siècle"; Zoltvany, *The Government of New France*, 92–7; Coates, "La mise en scène du pouvoir"; Delâge, "Modèles coloniaux, métaphores familiales et logiques d'empire"; Banks, *Chasing Empire Across the Sea*, 194–7; Miquelon, *New France, 1701–1744*, 246–58.

46 Havard, *Histoire des coureurs de bois*, 130–5, 250–8, 295–6, 308–9.

47 For works in the 1990s and early 2000s influenced by *The Middle Ground*, see Thorne, *The Many Hands of My Relations*; Murphy, *A Gathering of Rivers*; Sleeper-Smith, *Indian Women and French Men*; Hinderaker, *Elusive Empires*; Merrell, *Into the American Woods*.

48 Lipman, "No More Middle Grounds?," 24; Sleeper-Smith, "Introduction: The Middle Ground Revisited," 4–5; Sleeper-Smith, *Indian Women and French Men*, 2–3.

49 White, *The Middle Ground*, xxv–xxvi, 50–93.

50 Ibid., 1–49; White, "Creative Misunderstandings and New Understandings," 10.

51 Havard, *Empire et métissages*; DuVal, *The Native Ground*; Bohaker, "Nindoodemag"; Rushforth, "Slavery, the Fox Wars, and the Limits of Alliance"; Hämäläinen, *Comanche Empire*; Rushforth, *Bonds of Alliance*; Witgen, *An Infinity of Nations*; Sturtevant, "'Inseparable Companions' and Irreconcilable Enemies"; Englebert and Teasdale, *French and Indians in the Heart of North America*; Labelle, *Dispersed but Not Destroyed*; McDonnell, *Masters of Empire*.

52 Desbarats, "Following the 'Middle Ground,'" 90–1; Bohaker, "Nindoodemag," 29, 46; Sturtevant, "'Inseparable Companions' and Irreconcilable Enemies," 235

53 DuVal, *The Native Ground*, 5.

54 McDonnell, "Maintaining a Balance of Power," 43. Several Canadian and American scholars have produced narratives from an Indigenous, or "facing east," perspective. See, for example, Richter, *Facing East from Indian Country*; Calloway, *One Vast Winter Count*; Richter, *Before the Revolution*; Warren, *The Worlds the Shawnees Made*; Fenn, *Encounters at the Heart of the World*; Parmenter, *Edge of the Woods*.

55 Grandin, *The Blood of Guatemala*; Metcalf, *Go-betweens and the Colonization of Brazil*; Townsend, *Malintzin's Choices*; Yannakakis, *The Art of Being In-between*.

56 Brooks, *Captives & Cousins*; Barr, *Peace Came in the Form of a Woman*.

57 Berlin, *Many Thousands Gone*, 92.

58 Fausz, "Middlemen in Peace and War"; Merrell, *Into the American Woods*; Steele, *Setting All the Captives Free*, 230.

59 Havard, *Empire et métissages*, 44.

60 For material culture and sartorial expressions, see Shannon, "Dressing for Success on the Mohawk Frontier"; White, *Wild Frenchmen and Frenchified Indians*, 1–20, 98–101, 146, 232. For Indigenous ceremonial tattooing, see Balvay, "Tattooing and Its Role in French-Native American Relations"; Havard, *Empire et métissages*, 603. For spiritual *métissage* or Catholic syncretism, see Morrison, "Baptism and Alliance"; Podruchny, "Baptizing Novices"; Havard, *Empire et métissages*, 681–735; Pigeon, "Au nom du Bon Dieu et du Buffalo."

61 Thorne, *Many Hands of My Relations*; Murphy, *Gathering of Rivers*; Sleeper-Smith, *Indian Women and French Men*; Greer, *Mohawk Saint*; Balvay, *L'épée et la plume*; Leavelle, *Catholic Calumet*; White, "To Ensure that He Not Give Himself Over to the Indians"; Morrissey, *Empire by Collaboration*; Englebert, "Colonial Encounters and the Changing Contours of Ethnicity"; Lozier, *Flesh Reborn*.
62 Sleeper-Smith, "Women, Kin, and Catholicism."
63 Englebert, "Colonial Encounters," 47.
64 For a good discussion of the rise of the eastern "Métis," the evocation of métissage, and the appropriation of Indigenous identity, see Gaudry, "Communing with the Dead"; Gaudry and Leroux, "White Settler Revisionism and Making Métis Everywhere." For a discussion of Mi'kmaq-Acadian relations and the absence of a new and distinct people and nation, see Wicken, "Encounters with Tall Sails and Tall Tales," 206, 236–40; Griffiths, *From Migrant to Acadian*, 34–7; Kennedy, *Something of a Peasant Paradise?*, 66–70.
65 Jacqueline Peterson has distanced herself from her previous research in which she argued that Métis genesis occurred in the Great Lakes region and from there extended westward to the Red River Valley. Recanting her previous "Métis-as-mixed" framework, Peterson has cautioned scholars not to insert Métis consciousness into areas and eras where they did not previously exist. Peterson, "Many Roads to Red River," 39, 64; Peterson, "Red River Redux," 26–7, 30.
66 Andersen, "Moya Tipimsook," 38–9.
67 Andersen, *"Métis,"* 198–9.
68 Andersen, "From Nation to Population," 350.
69 Gaudry and Leroux, "White Settler Revisionism," 120.
70 Colpitts, *Pemmican Empire*, 214; Binnema, "A Fur Trade Historian's View of Seasonal Bison Movements," 166–7.
71 Hickerson, *Chippewa and Their Neighbors*; Bishop, *Northern Ojibwa*; Bellfy, *Three Fires Unity*.
72 McDonnell, "Maintaining a Balance of Power," 39.
73 Witgen, *An Infinity of Nations*, 177; Lytwyn, *Muskekowuck Athinuwick*, xi, 206, Bird, *Telling Our Stories*, 24; Smith, "The Western Woods Cree," 434–48; Russell, *Eighteenth-Century Western Cree*, 3–4; Brown and Long, *Together We Survive*, 283–4; Bishop, "Northern Algonquians," 276–8.
74 Witgen, *An Infinity of Nations*, 178; Denig, *The Assiniboine*, xxviii.
75 Anderson, "French-Indian Relations in the Far West," 104–12; Gibbon, *The Sioux*, 2–5; Witgen, *An Infinity of Nations*, 163–6.

CHAPTER ONE

1 For different interpretations of the Iroquois Wars, see Hunt, *Wars of the Iroquois*; Richter, "War and Culture"; Richter, *The Ordeal of the Longhouse*, 51, 54–5, 58–61; Brandão, *Your Fyre Shall Burn No More*; Starna and Brandão, "From the Mohawk-Mahican War to the Beaver Wars," 725–50; Labelle, *Dispersed but Not Destroyed*, 32–3; Parmenter, *Edge of the Woods*, 45–6, 57, 75, 80–2, 124.

2 Although the Haudenosaunee displaced many Indigenous peoples, they did not destroy their pre-existing cultural identities and kinship networks. Many scholars have argued that membership in a cross-cultural French-Indigenous alliances was not the primordial ingredient of collective identity among Native groups living in the Great Lakes region in the seventeenth and eighteenth centuries. Rather, Indigenous peoples maintained distinct political and cultural identities even under the pressures of French, British, and Haudenosaunee western imperial expansion. Desbarats, "Following the 'Middle Ground,'" 90–1; Bohaker, "Nindoodemag," 29, 46; Sturtevant, "'Inseparable Companions' and Irreconcilable Enemies," 235; Witgen, *An Infinity of Nations*, 49–50, 91.

3 For a discussion of Samuel de Champlain as the visionary founding father of New France, as well as the role of the other founding figures of French Canada, including the Innu leader Anadabijou, see D'Avignon, *Champlain et les fondateurs oubliés*.

4 Richter, *The Ordeal of the Longhouse*, 51, 54–5; Beaulieu, "The Birth of the Franco-American Alliance," 153–62; Fischer, *Champlain's Dream*, 249–50, 254–80, 460–2.

5 Moogk, "Reluctant Exiles," 463–505; Dewar, "Y establir nostre auctorité," 276–77; Havard and Vidal, *Histoire de l'Amérique Française*, 44–129.

6 The Sovereign Council was renamed the Superior Council in 1703.

7 Eccles, *The French in North America*, 66–99; Verney, *The Good Regiment*; Lesueur, *Les troupes coloniales d'Ancien Régime*, 178–92, 272–7.

8 Anishinaabe tribal histories record that in the 1670s, the Odawa, Ojibwe, Nipissing, Mississauga, and Wendat warriors organized successful military campaigns against the Haudenosaunee around Lake Erie, Lake St Clair, Georgian Bay, the north shore of Lake Ontario, and Lake Simcoe. MacLeod, "The Anishinabeg Point of View," 202–4; McDonnell, *Masters of Empire*, 65–6.

9 For a description of the noblesse d'épée and noblesse de robe in the ancien régime, see Ford, *Robe and Sword*, 16–21, 51–8, 68–73.

10 Bruce G. Trigger has argued that some of these youths, such as Marsolet and Lintot, became merchants and landholders (seigneurs) of some importance in the colony, noting that "in the early days [of New France], there was considerable opportunity for enhancing one's status in the colony." Trigger, *Natives and Newcomers*, 194–7.

11 Sayre, *Les Sauvages Américans*, 7; Havard, *Histoire des coureurs de bois*, 25–34.

12 Wien, "Le Pérou éphémère," 160–88; Havard and Vidal, *Histoire de l'Amérique Française*, 273–317; Allaire, "Fur Trade Engagés," 15–26 ; Dechêne, *Habitants and Merchants*, 117–25; Pritchard, *In Search of Empire*, 103–4; Havard, *Histoire des coureurs de bois*, 39–77, 234–7.

13 ANOM, COL C11A 5/fol.331–2v, "Édit du roi défendant à tous les habitants de la Nouvelle-France d'aller à la traite des pelleteries dans les habitations des Indiens et dans la profondeur des bois sans permission expresse des autorités, Versailles, 02 mai 1681."

14 Kellogg, *Early Narratives of the Northwest*, 325–34.

15 ANOM, COL C11A 3/fol.159–71v, "Mémoire de Talon au roi sur le Canada, Québec, 2 novembre 1671." For more on the exploits of Nicolas Perrot, see Havard, *The Great Peace of Montreal*, 119, 206–7; Weyhing, "Le Sueur in the Sioux Country," 35–6.

16 Norall, *Bourgmont*, 31, 87–8.

17 Sale, *The Conquest of Paradise*, 7–183; Taylor, *American Colonies*, 24–49; Burkholder and Johnson, *Colonial Latin America*, 40–7.

18 Sale, *The Conquest of Paradise*, 184–240; Taylor, *American Colonies*, 51–66; Elliott, *Empires of the Atlantic World*, 3–28; Burkholder, *Colonial Latin America*, 52–92.

19 Latimer, *Buccaneers of the Caribbean*, 7.

20 Lacoursière, *Canada-Québec synthèse historique*, 28.

21 Lesueur, *Les troupes coloniales d'Ancien Régime*, 17; Boucher, *France and the American Tropics*, 41.

22 Dewar, "Y establir nostre auctorité," 26, 35; Fischer, *Champlain's Dream*, 42–61; Barbiche, "Henri IV and the World Overseas," 25–6, 28–9; Thierry, *La France de Henri IV en Amérique du nord*, 460.

23 From a Canadian perspective, the failure of Jacques Cartier and Jean-François de La Rocque de Roberval to establish a permanent settlement at Charlesbourg-Royal (Cap-Rouge, Quebec), in the Saint Lawrence valley, in 1542–43 is perhaps the most recognizable example of a false start to the permanent French colonization of the Americas.

For Cartier and Roberval, see Cook, *Voyages of Jacques Cartier*; Litalien, *Explorateurs de l'Amérique du Nord*, 15–88; Allaire, *La rumeur dorée*. For the French Huguenots' attempts to colonize Florida, see Augeron, de Bry, and Notter, *Floride, un rêve français*. For the sixteenth-century French colonization of Brazil, see Eccles, *The French in North America*, 1–31; Seed, *Ceremonies of Possession*, 41–68.

24 For the raids of Acadia's coastal settlements, particularly Virginian adventurer Samuel Argall's raid against Île Sainte-Croix and Port-Royal in 1613 and William Alexander's efforts to oust Charles La Tour from Fort Lomeron (Cape Sable Island, Nova Scotia), see Griffiths, *From Migrant to Acadian*, 23–5, 31–4, 41–5. For the French surrender of Quebec in 1629 to English privateers led by David Kirke, see Nicholls, *Fleeting Empire*, 122–31; Allaire, "The Occupation of Quebec by the Kirke Brothers," 245–57.

25 For the Treaty of Saint-Germain-en-Laye (1632), see Thierry, *La France de Henri IV en Amérique du nord*, 204–6, 221–3; Allaire, "The Occupation of Quebec," 255–7; Fischer, *Champlain's Dream*, 431–41.

26 Dewar, "Y establir nostre auctorité," 4, 158–60, 197–201, 205–6; Carpin, "Migrations to New France," 165, 177–8; Fischer, *Champlain's Dream*, 404–5, 466–70.

27 Leslie Choquette has argued that chartered companies were more successful than they are often credited in the historiography. Choquette posits that during the Compagnie des Cent-Associés's ten-year proprietorship, "immigration had been fairly dynamic," whereas the early years of direct royal rule "was disastrous ... [and] quickly degenerated into complete chaos." Choquette, "Proprietorships in French North America," 124–5.

28 Banks, *Chasing Empire Across the Sea*, 218–19.

29 Ford, *Robe and Sword*, 93; Moote, *The Revolt of the Judges*, 364; Soll, *The Information Master*, 33. See also, Hurt, *Louis XIV and the Parlements*.

30 Beik, "The Absolutism of Louis XIV as Social Collaboration," 195.

31 Beik, *Absolutism and Society in Seventeenth-Century France*, 3–4; Collins, *Classes, Estates, and Order in Early Modern Brittany*, 271–88; Parker, *Class and State in Ancien Régime France*, 6; Beik, "The Absolutism of Louis XIV as Social Collaboration," 195–9. For the historiography of French absolutism, see Cosandey and Descimon, *L'Absolutisme en France*.

32 Hodson and Rushforth, "Absolutely Atlantic," 103.

33 Rule and Trotter, *A World of Paper*, 14–15, 20–1, 36–7; Soll, *The Information Master*, 6–7, 12–14, 50.
34 Soll, *The Information Master*, 13.
35 Ibid., 13–14, 51–2.
36 Ibid., 35–9.
37 Soll, *The Reckoning*, 98.
38 Soll, *The Information Master*, 99–133.
39 Ibid., 52.
40 Ibid., 73–6.
41 Nish, *Canadian Historical Documents Series, Vol. 1*, 46–7.
42 Greer, *Peasant, Lord, and Merchant*, 3–19. For more on the early settlement of the Saint Lawrence valley, its agrarian development, and the seigneurial system of New France, see Trudel, *Les Débuts du régime seigneurial au Canada*; Harris, *Seigneurial System in Early Canada*; Dépatie, Dessureault, and Lalancette, *Contributions à l'étude du régime seigneurial canadien*; Mathieu, Therrien-Fortier, and Lessard, "Mobilité et sédentarité," 211–27; Choquette, *Frenchmen into Peasants*; Coates, *Metamorphoses of Landscape and Community*; Courville, *Quebec: A Historical Geography*, 49–68; Grenier, *Brève histoire du régime seigneurial.*
43 For more on trade, commerce, and mercantilism in the French Atlantic world, see Mathieu, *Le commerce entre la Nouvelle-France et les Antilles*; Røge, "La Clef de Commerce," 431–43; Røge, *Economistes and the Reinvention of Empire*; Pritchard, *In Search of Empire*, 95–7, 228, 236; Banks, *Chasing Empire Across the Sea*, 14–42.
44 Lesueur, *Les troupes coloniales d'Ancien Régime*, 20.
45 Latimer, *Buccaneers of the Caribbean*, 144–5; Soll, *The Reckoning*, 91–2.
46 Pritchard, *In Search of Empire*, 234–7; Soll, *The Reckoning*, 91–2.
47 Boucher, *France and the American Tropics*, 177–9; Klooster, *The Dutch Moment*, 107, 188.
48 Usner, *Indians, Settlers, and Slaves*, 244–56; Klooster, *Illicit Riches*; Pritchard, *In Search of Empire*, 201–8.
49 Miquelon, *Dugard of Rouen*, 28–30; Pritchard, *In Search of Empire*, 197–204, 209–14; Boucher, *France and the American Tropics*, 177–8.
50 Greer, *Peasant, Lord, and Merchant*, 3–19.
51 For some essential works on French commerce and colonialism in the Caribbean, see Mathieu, *Le commerce entre la Nouvelle-France et les Antilles*; Elisabeth, *La Société Martiniquaise*; Garrigus, *Before Haiti*; Boucher, *France and the American Tropics.*

52 Pritchard, *In Search of Empire*, 162.

53 Ibid., 161; Eccles, *The French in North America*, 139, 175.

54 Eccles, *The French in North America*, 73, 104; Eccles, *Frontenac*, 1–4.

55 ANOM, COL B 6/fol.28–35, "Colbert to Frontenac, Versailles, 17 mai 1674." Quoted in Pritchard, *In Search of Empire*, 81.

56 Eccles, *The French in North America*, 93–5; Eccles, *Frontenac*, 77–9, 97; Havard and Vidal, *Histoire de l'Amérique Française*, 66–7, 271.

57 Moogk, *La Nouvelle France*, 96–7; Pritchard, *In Search of Empire*, 16–19.

58 ANOM, COL C11A 2/fol.199–206v, "Lettre du Ministre Colbert à Talon, Versailles, 5 avril 1666."

59 Hennepin, *A New Discovery*, 305–6.

60 Havard and Vidal, *Histoire de l'Amérique Française*, 66–7, 271.

61 Louis XIV's great minister and imperial architect Jean-Baptiste Colbert distrusted Canadian expansionism, considering it drain on Canada's human and material resources from the Saint Lawrence valley. Colbert had attempted to curb this expansion, a policy that Canadian historian W.J. Eccles has labelled "the compact colony policy." Eccles, *Canada under Louis XIV*, 59–76.

62 White, *The Middle Ground*, 24–5.

63 Pritchard, *In Search of Empire*, 234–7.

64 Boucher, *Les Nouvelles Frances*; Hall, *Africans in Colonial Louisiana*; Banks, *Chasing Empire Across the Sea*; Boucher, *France and the American Tropics*; Dawdy, *Building the Devil's Empire*; Greer, *Mohawk Saint*, 24–31; Gray, *The Congrégation de Notre-Dame*; Clark, *Masterless Mistresses*; Leavelle, *Catholic Calumet*; Noel, *Along a River*, 10.

65 Pritchard, *In Search of Empire*, 262–3.

66 Soll, *The Information Master*, 115.

67 McShea, *Apostles of Empire*, xvi.

68 This was especially true with the Wendat in the seventeenth century. Wendat headman Aenon supported and advocated for a Jesuit presence in Wendake to foster a military and trade alliance between the Wendat and the French newcomers. Labelle, *Dispersed but Not Destroyed*, 20–5.

69 Cook, "Onontio Gives Birth," 181–2. See also, Morrison, "Baptism and Alliance," 416–37; Delâge, "La religion dans l'alliance franco-amérindienne," 55–87; Deslandres, "Et loing de France," 93–117.

70 Trigger, *The Children of Aataentsic*, 753–4, 762; Delâge, *Bitter Feast*, 136, 167; Labelle, *Dispersed but Not Destroyed*, 101–4.

71 Salisbury, *Manitou and Providence*, 73.
72 Labelle, *Dispersed but Not Destroyed*, 3.
73 McShea, *Apostles of Empire*, xvii, 68–70, 73–8, 91–2, 130–2, 152–3, 256.
74 Louis XIV championed the divinity of his royal person and coerced the French clergy into supporting the Four Gallican Articles (1682), which diminished the papacy's control over the French regular clergy and lay orders. Louis XIV and Colbert also campaigned against the Jansenists, a movement of theologians and priests who opposed the state control over religion. Banks, *Chasing Empire Across the Sea*, 23; Wolf, *Louis XIV*, 388–92.
75 Greer, *Mohawk Saint*, 80; McShea, *Apostles of Empire*, xvi, 25–33, 196–8.
76 For more on the Society of Jesus in North America, see Jones, *Gentlemen and Jesuits*; Campeau, *La mission des jésuites chez les Hurons*; Anderson, *Chain Her by One Foot*; Beaulieu, *Convertir les fils de Caïn*; Codignola "Competing Networks," 539–84; Blackburn, *Harvest of Souls*; Greer, *Mohawk Saint*; True, *Masters and Students*.
77 ANOM, COL C11A 3/fol.233–51, "Lettre de Frontenac au ministre, Québec, 2 novembre 1672"; ANOM, COL C11A 5/fol.209–17v, "Lettre du roi à Duchesneau, Versailles, 2 juin 1680"; ANOM, COL C11A 17/fol.331–8, "Lettre de Duplessis, Québec, 7 octobre 1698."
78 Blackburn, *Harvest of Souls*, 132.
79 *JR*, 58:81–2.
80 Ibid., 67:21.
81 ANOM, COL C11A 12/fol.125–6v, "Placet des Jésuites du Canada adressé au ministre Pontchartrain, février 1692."
82 For more on the Jesuit Christian missions of the Saint Lawrence valley, see Greer, *The Jesuit Relations*, 10–14; Labelle, *Dispersed but Not Destroyed*, 108–19; Lozier, "Les origines huronnes-wendates de Kanesatake"; Lozier, *Flesh Reborn*.
83 Greer, *The Jesuit Relations*, 12.
84 The first and most famous reference to Frenchification was when Samuel de Champlain promised his Wendat, Innu, and Algonquin allies that "our young men will marry your daughters, and we shall be one people." *JR*, 5:210. Following up on Champlain's promise, Louis XIV's chief minister, Jean-Baptiste Colbert, also declared that the French and Natives would "become one people and one blood." ANOM, COL C11A 2/fol.290–7v, "Lettre de Colbert à Talon, Saint-Germain-en-Laye, 5 avril 1667."

85 In ancien régime France, mésalliance was a marriage with a person thought to be unsuitable or of a lower social position. The marriage of a non-noble or recently ennobled individual into an old aristocratic family belonging to families of noblesse d'épée or noblesse de robe was the quintessential example of mésalliance in ancien régime France. However, in the North American context, mésalliance and blood corruption took on a racial discourse by the end of the seventeenth century, when colonial officials feared that the intermixing of Frenchmen and Indigenous women would lead to the eventual corruption of French blood. Aubert, "The Blood of France," 445–6, 451–3. See also Belmessous, "Assimilation and Racialism," 322–49; Belmessous, *Assimilation and Empire*; White, *Wild Frenchmen and Frenchified Indians*, 117–18.

86 Havard, "Nous ne ferons plus qu'un peuple," 98. See also Havard, *Histoire des coureurs de bois*, 331–6.

87 Gaudry and Leroux, "White Settler Revisionism," 117.

88 Soll, *The Information Master*, 86–7.

89 Banks, *Chasing Empire Across the Sea*, 4–5.

90 Soll, *The Information Master*, 23–4.

91 Ibid., 70–1, 86–7.

92 Bellfy, *Three Fires Unity*.

93 *JR*, 23:225.

94 Witgen, *An Infinity of Nations*, 81–107.

95 Greer, *The Jesuit Relations*, 14–15.

96 Trigger, *Children of Aataentsic*; 789–840; Labelle, *Dispersed but Not Destroyed*, 49–67.

97 Blair, *Indian Tribes of the Upper Mississippi Valley*, 164–5. For more on the establishment of villages of ethnically diverse peoples in the aftermath of the Iroquois Wars, see White, *The Middle Ground*, 1–49; Labelle, *Dispersed but Not Destroyed*, 68–98; McDonnell, *Masters of Empire*, 34–58.

98 Warren, *History of the Ojibway People*, 126–7.

99 Anderson, "French-Indian Relations," 104–12; Gibbon, *The Sioux*, 2–5; Witgen, *An Infinity of Nations*, 163–6.

100 White, *The Middle Ground*, 11.

101 Thwaites, *Father Marquette*, 87.

102 *JR*, 54:190–1.

103 In this sense, the Jesuits can largely be blamed for painting the Haudenosaunee as the "boogeyman" of early Canadian history. For a discussion of the distortion of the Haudenosaunee in New France

and early Canadian historiography, see Brandão, *Your Fyre Shall Burn No More*, xi. For a discussion of the circulation of the *Jesuit Relations* and its readership, especially their reaction to the discourse of "Amerindian cruelty," see True, *Masters and Students*, 83–112.

104 *JR*, 54:190–1.

105 Joan B. Townsend argued that European firearms held no inherent advantage over Indigenous technology and traditional weapons until at least the mid-nineteenth century. Townsend, "Firearms against Native Arms," 1–33. Other scholars posit that, while firearms were not technologically superior to traditional arms, they did constitute a significant psychological advantage in warfare. Trigger, *Children of Aataentsic*, 629; Bishop and Lytwyn, "Barbarism and Ardour of War," 42–3. Other historians, like Armstrong Starkey and Patrick M. Malone, argue that Indigenous peoples valued firearms in warfare because they were much more deadly than traditional bows and arrows. Starkey, *European and Native American Warfare*, 20–5; Malone, *The Skulking Way of War*, 13, 62–6. For recent and more nuanced interpretations, postulating the deadly new potential of firearms but also the practicality of traditional Indigenous technologies, see Bohr, *Gifts from the Thunder Beings*, 109–15, 127–35, 154–5; Silverman, *Thundersticks*, 8, 16, 28–9.

106 Starkey, "Frontier Warfare in North America," 63–4; Skinner, *The Upper Country*, 21–2.

107 For example, many Algonquian and Iroquoian warriors in northeastern North America discarded cumbersome wooden armour that could not protect against firearms, and they also opted to utilize skirmishing and ambush tactics over larger direct assaults. Silverman, *Thundersticks*, 23–4.

108 *JR*, 54:191–2.

109 Thistle, *Indian-European Trade Relations*, 8.

110 *JR*, 54:192.

111 *JR*, 58:257–9.

112 Ibid.

113 Witgen, *An Infinity of Nations*, 140–2, 150.

114 Perrot, "Memoir on the Manners," 170.

115 *JR*, 54:132–4. See also, Mandelbaum, *Plains Cree*, 16–17.

116 Blair, *Indian Tribes of the Upper Mississippi Valley*, 307.

117 Fournier, *Pierre-Esprit Radisson*, 97–125; Havard, *Histoire des coureurs de bois*, 48–9.

118 See, for example, Skinner, *The Upper Country*, 17; for the original quote, see Warkentin, *Pierre-Esprit Radisson*, 1:265.

119 Although the Dakota and other Indigenous peoples practised the Feast of the Dead, most ethnohistorical research has focused on the Wendat Feast of the Dead, the mortuary custom of the Wendat Confederacy. Seeman, *The Huron-Wendat Feast of the Dead*; Labelle "Faire La Chaudière," 1–20.

120 Witgen, *An Infinity of Nations*, 60–2.

121 In Anishinaabemowin (the Anishinaabe language), "Zhaagawaamikong" is a place name that means "sand bar place." For Anishinaabemowin ethnonyms and toponyms in this book, I have relied primarily on the interpretation and helpful advice of Alan Corbiere, a professor at York University and Anishinaabe language historian from M'Chigeeng First Nation. Alan Corbiere, personal communication with the author, 14 May 2020.

122 Warren, *History of the Ojibway People*, 121–2.

123 Ibid., 122; Warkentin, *Pierre-Esprit Radisson*, 1:292–7.

124 Havard, *Histoire des coureurs de bois*, 49–50.

125 The London Committee was a tight-knit group of wealthy metropolitan investors and shareholders who ran the HBC from London. Rich, *Hudson's Bay Company*, 64, 103.

126 Fournier, *Pierre-Esprit Radisson*, 222–40; Warkentin, *Pierre-Esprit Radisson*, 2:7–97. There are few extant studies on the Compagnie du Nord; see, for example, Borins, "La Compagnie du Nord."

127 Borins, "La Compagnie du Nord," 88.

128 Thomson, *Mercenaries, Pirates, and Sovereigns*, 21.

129 Roper and Van Ruymbeke, *Constructing Early Modern Empires*, 1–19. For more on how early modern states used chartered companies to project sovereignty overseas, see Mancke, "Negotiating an Empire," 235–82; Stern, *The Company-State*; Dewar, "Souveraineté dans les colonies," 63–92.

130 Thomson, *Mercenaries, Pirates, and Sovereigns*, 43–4.

131 Fournier, *Pierre-Esprit Radisson*, 253–7; Witgen, *An Infinity of Nations*, 174–6, 179–85.

132 James Daschuk has recently examined how during the era of the Numbered Treaties (or Post-Confederation Treaties), the Canadian nation-state took advantage of Old World diseases and the decline of bison herds and purposefully withheld rations with the aim of annexing western Canada as a national space for white settlement, thereby contributing to the deaths and subjugation of thousands of

Indigenous people. I would argue, however that, until that time, the region that would later become the Canadian provinces of Manitoba, Saskatchewan, and Alberta remained unquestionably a "Native ground." See Daschuk, *Clearing the Plains*.

133 Warkentin, *Pierre-Esprit Radisson*, 2:25.

134 Ibid., 27.

135 Ibid.

136 Fournier, *Pierre-Esprit Radisson*, 251–7.

137 Witgen, *An Infinity of Nations*, 193.

138 Warkentin, *Pierre-Esprit Radisson*, 2:99–107.

139 Ibid., 115–17, 147.

140 Rich, *History of the Hudson's Bay Company*, 1:158–68.

141 Because it was possible to purchase titles, state offices, and military ranks, Mathé Allain argues that the ethos of ancien régime France was the antithesis of capitalism and colonial development. Most members of the French middle class preferred to invest in state offices, which enabled them to enter the first rungs of nobility, rather than invest in chartered companies. In seventeenth-century Canada, suggests W.J. Eccles, a select few enjoyed a speedier entry into the privileged classes after Louis XIV decreed in 1685 that noble residents in Canada could engage in commerce and industry without sacrificing their noble status. Eccles, *The French in North America*, 126; Allain, *"Not Worth a Straw,"* 90.

142 ANOM, COL B 7/fol.39v, "Ordonnance royale portant défense aux habitants du Canada d'aller à la traite des pelleteries avec interdiction au gouverneur et à l'intendant de donner des derogations, 15 avril 1676."

143 Kellogg, *Early Narratives of the Northwest*, 330.

144 Ibid.

145 Ibid., 330–1. For a succinct outline of the career of the Marquis de Seignelay as secretary of state and minister of the marine, see Pritchard, *In Search of Empire*, 237–8.

146 Hennepin, *A New Discovery*, 227–31. See also, Rushforth, *Bonds of Alliance*, 15–18.

147 Kellogg, *Early Narratives of the Northwest*, 332.

148 Hennepin, *A New Discovery*, 293–313.

149 ANOM, COL C11A 5/fol.320–3v, "Mémoire de Duchesneau adressé au ministre sur les désordres causés par les coureurs de bois et sur le commerce frauduleux avec les Anglais, Québec, 13 novembre 1681."

150 ANOM, COL C11A 5/fol.320–3v, "Mémoire de Duchesneau, Québec, 13 novembre 1681."
151 Soll, *The Information Master*, 153–6.
152 ANOM, COL C11A 6/fol.287–8, "Lettre de La Barre au ministre, Québec, 9 juillet 1684"; ANOM, COL C11A 6/fol.284–6v, "Lettre de La Barre au roi, Québec, 9 juillet 1684."
153 Lahontan, *New Voyages*, 72–3.
154 ANOM, COL C11A 9/fol.32–8, "Lettre de Champigny au ministre, 16 juillet 1687"; ANOM, COL C11A 9/fol.61–77v, "Lettre de Denonville au ministre, Montreal, 25 août 1687."
155 For an analysis of the political interplay and strategic considerations regarding coordinated French-Indigenous raids against the Haudenosaunee Confederacy in the lead-up to the Great Peace of Montreal in 1701, see Havard, *The Great Peace of Montreal*, 46–57.
156 ANOM, COL C11A 6/fol.134–44v, "Lettre de La Barre au ministre, Québec, 4 novembre 1683"; ANOM, COL C11A 6/fol.146, "Extrait d'une lettre de La Barre à Seignelay, Québec, 14 novembre 1683."
157 ANOM, COL C11A 6/fol.177–80v, "Lettre de M. de Meulles au ministre dénonçant la conduite de La Barre, Québec, 4 novembre 1683."
158 ANOM, COL C11A 7/fol.138v, "M. de la Barre au Ministre, Québec, 3 novembre 1683."
159 ANOM, COL C11A 6/fol.301–301v, "Extrait d'une lettre de Dulhut à La Barre, 10 septembre 1684."
160 JCBL Map Collection, Nicolas de Fer, "Carte de la Nouvelle France," 1718.
161 BnF, département Cartes et plans, CPL GE DD-2987 (8560), "Partie de la Nouvelle France par Hubert Jaillot, 1700."
162 Ray and Freeman, *"Gives Us Good Measure,"* 26–7.
163 Witgen, *An Infinity of Nations*, 179.
164 ANOM, COL C11A 09/fol.74v, "Lettre de Denonville au ministre, Québec, 25 août 1687."
165 *DCB*, 2:263.
166 Skinner, *The Upper Country*, 6–7; Pritchard, *In Search of Empire*, 155.
167 ANOM, COL C11A 6/fol.340–54v, "Mémoire de La Barre au roi, Québec, 13 novembre 1684."
168 Dawdy, *Building the Devil's Empire*, 11, 19
169 Ibid., 19.
170 Wingerd, *North Country*, 19.

171 For a similar example of a roguish agent working patronage networks within the French state in pursuit of his own personal interests, see Richard Weyhing's work on Antoine de la Mothe Cadillac, "Gascon Exaggerations," 78–87, 97–101.

172 Hennepin, *A New Discovery*, 299–300.

173 Lahontan, *New Voyages*, 133.

174 Le Clercq, *First Establishment of the Faith in New France*, 2:106.

175 In 1700, the French Crown revoked the Compagnie du Nord's monopoly and transferred it to the Compagnie de la Colonie. The Compagnie de la Colonie operated until 1705, when Louis-François Aubert, an Amsterdam merchant and cousin of the late of Charles Aubert de La Chesnaye of Quebec (financier and director of the Compagnie du Nord), joined with Jean-Baptiste Néret and Jean-Baptiste Gayot, Parisian financiers, to buy them out. They took over export duties on beaver and other furs throughout North America (including the Hudson Bay watershed) as the Compagnie du Castor until 1718. ANOM, COL C11A 18/fol.352–5v, "Arrêt du Conseil d'État qui révoque le monopole de la Compagnie du Nord à la baie d'Hudson, 10 janvier 1700."

176 Jérémie, "Description du Détroit & de la Baye d'Hudson," 58.

177 Ibid., 59–60.

178 Ibid., 61.

179 Jérémie, *Twenty years of York Factory*, 42.

180 Ibid., 18.

181 Ibid., 19.

182 Ibid.

183 Ibid.

184 Ibid., 36.

185 Pagden, *European Encounters with the New World*, 10.

186 ANOM, COL C11A 22/fol.134–134v, "Mémoire pour la baie d'Hudson, ca 1704."

187 A metropolitan report concluded that Jérémie, "who had served as an Interpreter at fort Bourbon for the last 10 or 12 years, and who in this capacity had the most contact than anyone else with the Natives … was the person the most admired by the Natives." ANOM, COL C11A 22/fol.134–134v, "Mémoire pour la baie d'Hudson, ca 1704."

188 ANOM, COL C11A 22/fol.134–134v, "Mémoire pour la baie d'Hudson, ca 1704."

189 Jérémie, "Description du Détroit & de la Baye d'Hudson," 63.

190 Larouche, *Le second registre de Tadoussac*, 100.

191 BAnQ Québec, Fonds Conseil souverain, TP1, S28, P5607, "Communication au procureur général du procès de Noël Jérémie dit Lamontagne ... demandant la nullité du mariage de son fils, Nicolas Jérémie dit Lamontagne, avec Marie-Madeleine Tetaouiskoué, sauvagesse de la nation des Montagnais, 8 mars 1694."

192 BAnQ Québec, Fonds Conseil souverain, TP1, S28, P6887, "Nomination de Jacques Gourdeau comme curateur pour Marie-Madeleine Tetaouiskoué, montagnaise, 11 janvier 1694."

193 Jérémie, *Twenty years of York Factory*, 38–40.

194 Ibid.

195 Ibid.

196 Thistle, *Indian-European Trade Relations*, 18, 47.

197 Isham, *Observations on Hudson Bay*, 94–5.

198 Van Kirk, *Many Tender Ties*, 40–1.

199 ANOM, COL C11A 22/fol.134–134v, "Mémoire pour la baie d'Hudson, c.1704."

200 Mandelbaum, *The Plains Cree*, 123–4.

201 Jérémie, *Twenty years of York Factory*, 32.

202 Stephen, *Masters and Servants*, 263, 257.

203 Brown, *Strangers in Blood*, 21, 61–3.

204 ANOM, COL C11B 1/fol.21-21v, "Pontchartrain au sieur Jérémie sur la remise à l'Angleterre de la baie et du détroit d'Hudson, selon les conditions du traité d'Utrecht du 11 avril dernier, 9 août 1713."

205 ANOM, COL C11A 123/fol.121, "Résumé d'une lettre des sieurs Néret et Gayot avec commentaires du ministre, Paris, 19 novembre 1714."

CHAPTER TWO

1 Pevitt, *Philippe, Duc D'Orleans*, 163–85, 231.

2 As regent, the Duke of Orléans dismissed the secretaries of state – marine and colonies, foreign affairs, war, Maison du Roi, etc. – and replaced them with six councils, a system of governance labelled the *polysynodie*. Dupilet and Sarmant, "Polysynodie et gouvernement."

3 Pritchard, *In Search of Empire*, 197–204, 209–14, 234–7; Havard and Vidal, *Histoire de l'Amérique Française*, 66–7, 271; Soll, *The Information Master*, 13–14, 35–9, 51–2, 115.

4 Miquelon, *New France, 1701–1744*, 159; Miquelon, "Envisioning the French Empire"; Miquelon, "Ambiguous Concession."

5 During the preceding two decades, the official Canadian fur trade had come to a standstill because of market oversaturation. In a desperate attempt to cope with the glut of furs, the Ministry of Marine gave orders in 1696 to suspend the beaver trade, to stop issuing congés (fur trade licences), and to abandon all the French posts in the interior. In 1697, in response to pressure from colonial officials fearing loss of control of New France's hinterlands, the court permitted the re-garrisoning of Fort Frontenac (Cataraqui), Michilimackinac, and Fort Saint-Joseph. Following the War of the Spanish Succession, Governor Vaudreuil sought to reverse the 1696 decision and re-establish the western fur trade, thus providing a bulwark against future potential British or Haudenosaunee imperial expansion into the Great Lakes. The Marine Council granted permission to the governor to reorganize New France's fur-trading empire, a step made necessary by the long-awaited recovery of the fur market in 1716. Havard, *Empire et métissages*, 783; Havard, *Histoire des coureurs de bois*, 104–5, 118–20, 234–5.

6 For Vaudreuil in France, see Zoltvany, *Philippe de Rigaud de Vaudreuil*, 143–55. For the Western Sea, see Petto, "From L'état, c'est moi to c'est l'état," 60; Delanglez, "A Mirage: The Sea of the West (part II)," 541–68; Lewis, "Misinterpretation of Amerindian Information," 542–3; Lagarde, "Le Passage du Nord-Ouest," 19–43.

7 Litalien, Palomino, and Vaugeois, *Mapping a Continent*, 136–9. For more on French imperial cartography, see Pedley, *The Commerce of Cartography*; Palomino, "Pratiques cartographiques en Nouvelle-France," 21–39; Branch, *The Cartographic State*, 142–64.

8 MacMillan, *Sovereignty and Possession*, 121, 147–8; Lennox, *Homelands and Empires*, 4, 211; Edelson, *New Map of Empire*, 10–11, 334–5.

9 Banks, *Chasing Empire Across the Sea*, 188.

10 Collins, *The State in Early Modern France*, 66.

11 Hodson and Rushforth, "Absolutely Atlantic," 101–3, 112; Dubois, "The French Atlantic," 137–61; Dubois, *A Colony of Citizens*, 2; Dubois, *Avengers of the New World*, 285–6; Garrigus, *Before Haiti*, 311–14.

12 Dawdy, *Building the Devil's Empire*, 18.

13 Morrissey, *Empire by Collaboration*, 5.

14 Collins, *The State in Early Modern France*, 146, 150–1.

15 Brewer, *The Sinews of Power*, 26–63.

16 Collins, *The State in Early Modern France*, 161–2, 183–5. For more on the wars of Louis XIV, see Lynn, *Giant of the Grand Siècle*, 519; Lynn, *Wars of Louis XIV*, 334.

17 Groulx, *Histoire du Canada français*, 150–1; Lanctôt, *A History of Canada*, 190–1; Groulx, *Notre grande aventure*, 212, 241.

18 Collins, *The State in Early Modern* France, 162–3.

19 The case for the Treaty of Utrecht's colonial clauses being primarily concerned with maritime affairs is made in Miquelon, "Envisioning the French Empire."

20 The French eventually constructed the Fortress of Louisbourg on Île Royale and Fort Beauséjour on the Isthmus of Chignecto to protect the eastern entrance to the Saint Lawrence River. Griffiths, *From Migrant to Acadian*, 253.

21 Chalmers, *A Collection of Treaties*, 378–80.

22 Collins, *The State in Early Modern France*, 151.

23 Dangeau, *Mémoire Du Marquis de Dangeau*, 24.

24 Miquelon, *New France, 1701–1744*, 4, 226.

25 Banks, *Chasing Empire Across the Sea*, 32–3.

26 Collins, *The State in Early Modern* France, 267–9.

27 The Duke of Orléans worried that the sickly Louis XV, his nephew, would die in childhood and that the Bourbon king of Spain, Felipe V (the grandson of King Louis XIV), would rise against France and challenge the House of Orléans's claim to the French throne. Fearing a potential war with Spain, the Duke of Orléans courted England as a potential military ally and backer to his family's claim to the throne. Cardinal Dubois, the Duke of Orléans's secretary and councillor of state, undertook many trips to Whitehall seeking rapprochement with England. Shennan, *Philippe, Duke of Orleans*, 74–5.

28 Buache, *Considerations geographiques*, 26–33.

29 Ibid., 25–6.

30 For the records and information management of the Ministry of the Marine and Colonies, see Houllemare, "Seeing the Empire through Lists and Charts," 374–7.

31 Mapp, *Elusive West*, 161.

32 By the time of Delisle's investigation in the early eighteenth century, French colonizers and explorers like Jacques Cartier, Samuel de Champlain, and Jean Nicollet had been looking for a northwest passage for more than two centuries. For early French efforts to discover a northwest passage, see Biggar, *Works of Samuel de Champlain*, 1:229–32; Cook, *Voyages of Jacques Cartier*, 65; Fischer, *Champlain's Dream*, 503–5.

33 In France, members of the Congregation of the Mission (La congrégation de la Mission) were popularly known as Lazaristes. Rather than

travelling overseas to proselytize to Indigenous peoples in territories claimed by the French, Lazaristes participated in an internal missionization of France as part of the Catholic Counter Reformation that occurred in the wake of the French Wars of Religion (1562–98). Deslandres, *Croire et faire croire*, 130–1.

34 For more on Antoine Crozat and the first joint-stock companies of early Louisiana, see Vidal, "French Louisiana in the Age of the Companies," 133–62.

35 "Jean Bobé, Versailles, 16 août 1718" (ANF, Marine, 2JJ/56, no. X, 26, N), in Dawson and Vincent, *L'atelier Delisle*, 241–2.

36 LAC, MG18-G6 2/fol.428–535, "Mémoire pour la découverte de la mer de l'Ouest présenté par l'abbé Jean Bobé, Versailles, avril 1718."

37 "Jean Bobé, Versailles, avril 1717" (ANF, Marine, 2JJ/56, no. X, 26, A), in Dawson and Vincent, *L'atelier Delisle*, 234–5.

38 Quaife, *The Western Country*, 53–4.

39 ANOM, COL C11G 6/fol.39v–58v, "*Mémoires sur le Canada*, 1706–10."

40 LAC, MG18-G6 2/fol.428–535, "Mémoire pour la découverte de la mer de l'Ouest présenté par l'abbé Jean Bobé, Versailles, avril 1718."

41 Anderson, *Kinsmen of Another Kind*, 23.

42 Buache, *Considerations geographiques*, 30.

43 Petto, "From L'état, c'est moi to c'est l'état," 65.

44 Lagarde, "Le Passage du Nord-Ouest," 27–9.

45 BAnQ Québec, ZF18 Fonds Archives de la marine (France), Série 3JJ, Service hydrographique, papiers Delisle, 388/fol.07–10, "Mémoires et lettres de Mr. le Maire Missionnaire, 17 mai 1719."

46 Delanglez, "A Mirage: The Sea of the West (part II)," 561.

47 Lagarde, "Le Passage du Nord-Ouest," 27.

48 "Jean Bobé, Versailles, 1 juillet 1718" (ANF, Marine, 2JJ/56, no. X, 26, L), in *L'atelier Delisle*, 240.

49 "Jean Bobé, Versailles, 9 juillet 1718" (ANF, Marine, 2JJ/56, no. X, 26, M), in *L'atelier Delisle*, 241.

50 For a good discussion of British innovations in the field surveying and map-making techniques within the context of the HBC, see Mitchell, *Mapmaker*, 38–40.

51 Litalien, *Mapping a Continent*, 136–8; Pedley, *The Commerce of Cartography*, 97–9.

52 Petto, *When France Was King of Cartography*, 59.

53 For the Delisle family's expertise in scientific cartography and connection to the Académie des sciences, see Petto, "From L'état, c'est moi to c'est l'état," 54–5, 60–2, 67–8.

54 ANOM, C11E 16/fol.13–16, "Mémoire intitulé 'Chemin du lac Supérieur au lac des Asiniboiles, d'où on va par une rivière à la mer de l'Ouest,' 12 novembre 1716."
55 Jérémie, *Twenty Years of York Factory*, 33.
56 Ibid.
57 Bobé to Delisle, 2 July 1717, Archives du Service Hydrographique, 115–10: no. 26, D. Quoted in Delanglez, "A Mirage: The Sea of the West (part II)," 556. See also Lagarde, "Le Passage du Nord-Ouest," 27.
58 BnF, Département Cartes et plans, Guillaume Delisle, "Carte d'Amérique dressée pour l'usage du Roy," 1722.
59 JCBL Map Collection, Nicolas de Fer, "Carte de la Nouvelle France," 1718.
60 Lahontan, *New Voyages*, 184–97.
61 Ibid., 187.
62 Ibid., 193.
63 Ibid., 194–5.
64 BnF, Département Cartes et plans, Guillaume Delisle, "Carte du Canada ou de la Nouvelle France et des Decouvertes qui y ont été faites," 1703.
65 Bobé to Delisle, 15 March 1716, in *Historical Magazine*, no. 3 (1859): 232. Quoted in Delanglez, "A Mirage: The Sea of the West (part II)," 554.
66 For scholars who have dismissed Lahontan's voyage as pure fabrication, see Kellogg, *French Régime in Wisconsin*, 240; DeVoto, *The Course of Empire*, 64. For different plausible theories about Lahontan's voyage, see Ouellet and Beaulieu, *Lahontan: Œuvres complètes*, 199, 383; Fenn, *Encounters at the Heart of the World*, 41–7.
67 ANOM, COL C11E 16/fol.13–16, "Mémoire intitulé 'Chemin du lac Supérieur au lac des Asiniboiles, d'où on va par une rivière à la mer de l'Ouest,' 12 novembre 1716."
68 Mapp, *Elusive West*, 194, 262.
69 Jean Bobé, Versailles, 21 juin 1720 (ANF, Marine, 2JJ/60, no. XVI, 123), in *L'atelier Delisle*, 243.
70 *DCB*, 3:104; *JR*, 54:192–3.
71 Jean Bobé, Versailles, 21 juin 1720 (ANF, Marine, 2JJ/60, no. XVI, 123), in *L'atelier Delisle*, 243.
72 Desbarats and Greer, "Où est la Nouvelle-France," 51; Conrad, "Administration of the Illinois Country," 33–4.
73 For an example of this vestigial hierarchy in the archives, Catherine Desbarats and Allan Greer point out that instructions from the Crown

addressed to the governor general of New France in 1755 began with the following words: "New France, which his Majesty has kindly entrusted to the government of Sieur De Vaudreuil de Cavagnal includes Canada, Île Royale and Louisiana with their dependencies." Yet the instructions that followed concerned only Canada. Desbarats and Greer, "Où est la Nouvelle-France," 52.

74 Desbarats and Greer, "Où est la Nouvelle-France," 52; Conrad, "Administration of the Illinois Country," 33–4.

75 ANOM, COL C11A 41/fol. 399–413v, "Résumé d'une lettre de Vaudreuil et Bégon datée du 26 octobre 1720 et délibération du Conseil de Marine, 24 décembre 1720."

76 ANOM, COL C11A 43/fol.99–107, "Résumé d'une lettre de Vaudreuil datée du 4 novembre 1720 et délibération du Conseil de Marine au sujet de nouvelles reçues de Robutel de La Noue, 14 janvier 1721."

77 For more on the rivalry between Canada and Louisiana, and especially the debate over the jurisdiction of the Illinois Country starting in 1722, when a royal ordinance transferred the Illinois Country's governance from Canada to Louisiana, see Conrad, "Administration of the Illinois Country," 31–53.

78 ANOM, COL C11E 16/fol.106–7v, "Lettre du père de Charlevoix au secrétaire d'État, 1 avril 1723."

79 ANOM, COL C11E 16/fol.102–4v, "Lettre du père de Charlevoix au ministre de la Marine, 20 janvier 1723."

80 ANOM, COL C11E 16/fol.96–7v, "Lettre du père de Charlevoix au Ministre, Michilimackinac, 27 août 1721."

81 Desbarats and Greer, "Où est la Nouvelle-France," 31.

82 When the governor of Louisiana, Pierre de Rigaud de Vaudreuil de Cavagnial (son of the Vaudreuil discussed in this chapter), proposed a trade boundary between Louisiana and Canada in 1743–44, he pragmatically observed that the dividing line could never be located any further north than the Wisconsin River because of New France's long diplomatic relationship with the Dakota, a people with which Louisiana's government officials had virtually no diplomatic precedent. Conrad, "Administration of the Illinois Country," 44, 47.

83 ANOM, COL C11E 16/fol.96–7v, "Lettre du père de Charlevoix au Ministre, Michilimackinac, 27 août 1721."

84 ANOM, COL C11A 30/fol.44–84v, "Lettre de Vaudreuil au ministre, 14 novembre 1709."

85 Havard, *Histoire des coureurs de bois*, 142.

86 Ibid., 141, 144–6.

87 Manthet's expedition descended the Moose River and assaulted Fort Albany, at that time commanded by John Fullartine. The HBC repulsed the French and Native attackers, leaving sixteen of them dead (two HBC servants died in the effort). Manthet himself perished in the attack. Vaudreuil blamed the expedition's failure on Manthet's excessive recklessness. Manthet had been a coureur de bois in the governor's inner circle. In 1706, Vaudreuil had even defended Manthet to the Ministry of the Marine, downplaying accusations of Manthet's involvement in the illicit trade. ANOM, COL C11A 30/fol.23–8, "Lettre de Vaudreuil au ministre, 27 avril 1709"; ANOM, COL C11A 31/fol.7–16, "Lettre de Vaudreuil au ministre pour se justifier des accusations portées contre lui, 25 octobre 1710." See also Francis and Morantz, *Partners in Furs*, 36.

88 ANOM, COL C11A 45/fol.124–6, "Permission accordée par Vaudreuil à Paul Guillet, 16 août 1723"; ANOM, COL C11A 45/fol.162–162v, "Permission accordée par Vaudreuil à Paul Guillet, 1 juillet 1724."

89 ANOM, COL C11A 21/fol.103v, "Lettres patentes en forme d'édit qui amnistient les coureurs des bois de la Nouvelle-France, 2 mars 1716."

90 "Le Ministre à M. De Vaudreuil, Versailles, 19 mars 1714," in *Rapport de l'Archiviste de la province de Québec, 1947–1948*, 248; "Mémoire du Roi à MM. De Vaudreuil et Bégon, Versailles, 19 mars 1714," in *Rapport de l'Archiviste de la province de Québec, 1947–1948*, 240–1; ANOM, COL C11A 35/fol.99–100v, "Justification de Michel Bisaillon, ca 1715"; ANOM, COL C11A 35/fol.56–60v, "Copie de la lettre Ecrite par Mr. Dadanour a Mr. de Longueuil, Le Rocher, 22 août 1715"; ANOM, COL C11A 124/fol.32–5, "Délibération du Conseil de Marine concernant principalement la mission de Louis de La Porte de Louvigny à Michillimakinac, 5 janvier 1718"; Zoltvany, *Philippe de Rigaud de Vaudreuil*, 141–2; Edmunds and Peyser, *Fox Wars*, 78–83; Skinner, *The Upper Country*, 103–5.

91 ANOM, COL C11A 33/fol.3–8v, "Lettre de Vaudreuil et Bégon au ministre, Québec, 12 novembre 1712."

92 ANOM, COL C11A 34/fol.228–61v, "Lettre de Vaudreuil et Bégon au ministre, Québec, 20 septembre 1714."

93 ANOM, COL C11A 33/fol.3–8v, "Lettre de Vaudreuil et Bégon au ministre, Québec, 12 novembre 1712"; ANOM, COL C11A 34/fol.228–61v, "Lettre de Vaudreuil et Bégon au ministre, Québec, 20 septembre 1714."

94 ANOM, COL C11G 6/fol.39v–58v, "Autre mémoire de M. Raudot au ministre sur le même sujet, Québec, 20 août 1707."

95 ANOM, COL C11A 19/fol.232, "Callière, 1701." Quoted in Havard, *The Great Peace of Montreal*, 180–1.

96 Although backwoodsmen from New England, Virginia, and the Carolinas certainly existed in early eighteenth-century North America, they were fewer in number than their French counterparts, and thus played a more negligible role as a potential imperial resource. Nevertheless, Anglo-American traders just as readily married à la façon du pays and underwent processes of cultural acculturation like their French counterparts. For example, starting in the 1680s, South Carolina "Indian traders" intermarried among their Creek and Cherokee allies. Havard, *Histoire des coureurs de bois*, 193–230.

97 ANOM, COL C11E 16/fol.28–31v, "Mémoire de MM. de Vaudreuil et Bégon intitulé 'Projet pour la découverte de la mer de l'Ouest,' 15 octobre 1717."

98 ANOM, COL C11A 43/fol.99–107, "Résumé d'une lettre de Vaudreuil datée du 4 novembre 1720, 14 janvier 1721."

99 ANOM, COL C11E 16/fol.94–94v, "Lettre de Zacharie Robutel de La Noue, 15 octobre 1721."

100 Anderson, *Kinsmen of Another Kind*, 40.

101 ANOM, COL C11A 43/fol.99–107, "Résumé d'une lettre de Vaudreuil, 14 janvier 1721."

102 Witgen, *An Infinity of Nations*, 149, 165.

103 Anderson, "Early Dakota Migration and Intertribal War," 26.

104 Hämäläinen, *Lakota America*, 72–3.

105 Jennings, *Ambiguous Iroquois Empire*, xvii–xviii, 8, 19–20, 43, 93–6, 98–105, 111–12; Parmenter, *Edge of the Woods*, 77–118, 124–5; Morrissey, *Empire by Collaboration*, 11–38, 52–9; Hämäläinen, *Comanche Empire*, 1–17, 345–61.

106 ANOM, COL C11A 21/fol.75v, Parolles des sauvages hurons à mr de Vaudreuil, 14 juillet 1703.

107 Anderson, "French-Indian Relations in the Far West," 107–8; Havard, *Empire et métissage*, 472–8.

108 ANOM, COL C11A 43/fol.99–107, "Résumé d'une lettre de Vaudreuil datée du 4 novembre 1720, 14 janvier 1721."

109 Ibid.

110 Havard, *The Great Peace of Montreal*, 123, 158.

111 HBCA, B.239/a/2, James Knight, York Factory post journal, 22 August 1716.

112 Ibid.

113 Davies and Johnson, *Letters from Hudson Bay*, 122.
114 Ibid., 136.
115 Ibid., 166–7.
116 Ibid.
117 Ibid.
118 The HBC used "Made Beaver" as its standard unit of economic evaluation. One MB was equivalent to the value of a prime beaver skin, and the prices of all trade goods, other furs, and "country produce" were expressed in terms of MB. Ray, *Indians in the Fur Trade*, 61–2; Ray and Freeman, *"Give Us Good Measure,"* 166.
119 For French efforts to improve relations with Great Britain following the Peace of Utrecht, see Petitfils, *Le régent*, 391–6.
120 HBCA, B.3/a/17, Joseph Myatt, Fort Albany post journal, 7 June 1729.
121 Ibid.
122 Ibid.
123 HBCA, B.3/a/17, Joseph Myatt, Fort Albany post journal, 18 June 1729.
124 Ibid.
125 HBCA, B.3/a/17, Joseph Myatt, Fort Albany post journal, 19 June 1729.
126 HBCA, B.3/a/17, Joseph Myatt, Fort Albany post journal, 20 June 1729.
127 HBCA, B.3/a/18, Richard White, Fort Albany post journal, 25 July 1730.
128 Ibid.
129 HBCA, B.239/a/7, Henry Kelsey, York Factory post journal, 3 June 1722.
130 HBCA, B.3/a/12, Joseph Myatt, Fort Albany post journal, 1 September 1723.
131 HBCA, B.239/a/11, Thomas McCliesh, York Factory post journal, 9 June 1729.
132 HBCA, B.239/a/11, Thomas McCliesh, York Factory post journal, 12 June 1729.
133 Winter counts were pictographic calendars in which each image represented a remarkable or unusual event from a single year. Pictographs were arranged sequentially in spirals or rows, originally on hide. Greene and Thornton, *The Year the Stars Fell*, 1–2, 79.
134 Dechêne, *Le peuple, l'État et la guerre au Canada*, 58–9, 191–2, 208–9; Havard, *Histoire des coureurs de bois*, 177–82.

135 Mniyo and Goodvoice, *The Red Road*, 109.
136 Anderson, "French-Indian Relations in the Far West," 105, 108.
137 ANOM, COL C11A 85/fol.227–227v, "Lettre de Beauharnois au ministre, Québec, 28 octobre 1746."
138 Gibbon, *The Sioux*, 55–6; Hämäläinen, *Lakota America*, 77–8.
139 Howard, "Yanktonai Ethnohistory," 25.
140 After the suppression of fur-trading licences and the evacuation of the pays d'en haut in 1696, coureur de bois Pierre-Charles Le Sueur maintained contact with the Dakota people by using Du Lhut's old route to their lands via Lake Superior and the site of Fort Saint-Antoine at Lake Pepin, Nicolas Perrot's old headquarters. In the summer of 1695, Le Sueur curried favour with the French colonial government by escorting a Dakota leader named Tiyoskate back to Montreal to conclude an alliance with Governor Frontenac. Tiyoskate made a tearful plea to Frontenac: "All the nations had a father who afforded them protection; all of them have iron. But he [Tiyoskate] was a bastard in quest of a father." Tiyoskate then "spread out a beaver skin on which he arranged twenty-two arrows, and taking them one after another, he named for each a village of his nation and asked the general to take them all under his protection." Tiyoskate's terminology symbolized not only the eagerness of the Dakota for European commerce, but also the prerequisite of creating kinship bonds with the French before commercial exchange could occur. This is the first indication of an official alliance between the French and the Dakota. Unfortunately, Tiyoskate never returned to the Upper Mississippi valley, as he died in Montreal after a month-long illness. In 1700, Le Sueur returned to Sioux Country under the pretext that he was exploring for mines. In 1702, he left Fort L'Huillier and returned to France. The fort was shortly thereafter abandoned, and Le Sueur's garrison fled downriver to the Gulf of Mexico. For Le Sueur among the Dakota, see Anderson, *Kinsmen of Another Kind*, 35–9; For Tiyoskate's plea to Frontenac, see "Narrative of the Most Remarkable Occurrences in Canada," 1694 and 1695, in *DRCNY*, 9:610.
141 Weyhing, "Le Sueur in the Sioux Country," 43.
142 Anderson, *Kinsmen of Another Kind*, 36.
143 ANOM, COL C11A 56/fol.259–60, "Lettre de Dutisné aux membres de la Compagnie des Indes, Fort de Chartres, 14 janvier 1725."
144 Anderson, *Kinsmen of Another Kind*, 40.

145 Skinner, *The Upper Country*, 105–6; Anderson, *Kinsmen of Another Kind*, 39–40.

146 ANOM, COL C11A 38/fol.103–8v, "Lettre de Vaudreuil au Conseil de Marine, Québec, 12 octobre 1717."

147 ANOM, COL C11A 43/fol.99–107, "Résumé d'une lettre de Vaudreuil, 14 janvier 1721."

148 Anderson, *Kinsmen of Another Kind*, 41–2.

149 ANOM, COL C11E 16/fol.112–17v, "Extrait de la lettre écrite à Monsieur le Marquis de Beauharnois par le Révérend Père Guignas, missionnaire de la compagnie de Jésus, datée de la mission de Saint-Michel Archange au fort de Beauharnois, 29 mai 1728."

CHAPTER THREE

1 *DCB*, 2:573.

2 Saint-Thomas, *Les Ursulines de Québec*, 158.

3 Milloy, *The Plains Cree*, 5, 8, 42, 61; Witgen, *An Infinity of Nations*, 163–6.

4 Laut, *Pathfinders of the West*; Burpee, *Pathfinders of the Great Plains*; Rumilly, *La Vérendrye*; Crouse, *La Verendrye, Fur Trader and Explorer*; Kavanagh, *La Vérendrye, His Life and Times*; Champagne, *Les La Vérendrye et Le Poste de l'Ouest*; Champagne, *Nouvelles Études*; Combet, *In Search of the Western Sea*.

5 For the quote, see Frégault, *La civilisation de la Nouvelle-France*, 13.

6 Pritchard, *In Search of Empire*, 240.

7 Ibid.

8 Miquelon, *Dugard of Rouen*, 7–8; Lesueur, *Les troupes coloniales d'Ancien Régime*, 115–16; Wilson, *French Foreign Policy*, 74–5, 79; Campbell, *Power and Politics in Old Regime France*, 142–3.

9 Rule, "Jean-Frédéric Phélypeaux," 370–1.

10 Wilson, *French Foreign Policy*, 35–1.

11 Collins, *The State in Early Modern France*, 267–9.

12 Miquelon, *Dugard of Rouen*, 28–30; Mathieu, *Le commerce entre la Nouvelle-France et les Antilles*, 2–3, 22–31.

13 Banks, *Chasing Empire Across the Sea*, 75–6, 165–6.

14 Rule, "Jean-Frédéric Phélypeaux," 370. For a more extensive survey of the long career of Jean-Frédéric Phélypeaux de Maurepas in service of the French Crown, see Filion, *La Pensée et l'action coloniale de Maurepas*.

15 *DCB*, 3:41–2.

16 Louise Élisabeth de Joybert, the Madame de Vaudreuil, who was purportedly La Vérendrye's patron, had great influence at Versailles. She took up residence in Paris shortly after the death of her husband in 1725, so was never far from metropolitan circles of influence. Crouse, *La Vérendrye, Fur Trader and Explorer*, 30.

17 ANOM, COL C11A 33/fol.257–8v, "Résumé d'une lettre de Pierre Gaultier de La Vérendrye, lieutenant dans le régiment de Bretagne, 15 février 1712"; ANOM, COL C11E 16/fol.314–16v, "Mémoire du Sr de La Vérendrye l'aîné adressé au Ministre évoquant la carrière de son père depuis 1728 et rappelant les services qu'il a rendus, n.d."

18 Lewis, "Misinterpretation of Amerindian Information," 546–7; Lagarde, "Le Passage du Nord-Ouest," 30.

19 For more on the ethos of the ancien régime, and its influence on La Vérendrye in particular, see MacDonell, "Radisson and La Vérendrye," 51–2. See also, Crouch, *Nobility Lost*, 19–23.

20 Combet, "Récits de voyage," 304–6, 309. For an exhaustive study of Pierre de La Vérendrye's family and ancestry, consult Champagne, *Les La Vérendrye et Le Poste de l'Ouest*, 43–80.

21 ANOM, COL C11E 16/fol.119–22, "Lettre de MM. de Beauharnois et Hocquart au Ministre à propos du projet d'établissement sur les bords du lac Ouinipigon du Sr de La Vérendrye, Québec, 15 octobre 1730."

22 Lewis, "Misinterpretation of Amerindian Information," 546–7.

23 ANOM, COL C11A 52/fol.201–2v, "Lettre de Beauharnois au ministre – carte (d'Auchagah?) et mémoire de La Vérendrye concernant la découverte de la mer de l'Ouest; projet de ce dernier de faire un établissement au lac Ouinipigon, Québec, 10 octobre 1730."

24 Lagarde, "Le Passage du Nord-Ouest," 30–1. For the map, see BnF, département Cartes et plans, GE D-11619, Guillaume Delisle, "Carte d'Amérique dressée pour l'usage du Roy," 1722.

25 Havard, *The Great Peace of Montreal*, 4, 120.

26 ANOM, COL C11E 16/fol.119–22, "Lettre de MM. de Beauharnois et Hocquart au Ministre à propos du projet d'établissement sur les bords du lac Ouinipigon du Sr de La Vérendrye, Québec, 15 octobre 1730."

27 Burpee, *Journals and Letters*, 88–9.

28 For a more thorough discussion of the Abenaki and New France, see Miquelon, *New France, 1701–1744*, 25–7; Demos, *Unredeemed Captive*, 15–16, 25; Taylor, *American Colonies*, 290–2. For Beauharnois's suggestion, see Burpee, *Journals and Letters*, 88–9.

29 Champagne, *Les La Vérendrye et Le Poste de l'Ouest*, 109–10.

30 BAnQ Québec, "Greffe de J.-B. Adhémar dit Saint-Martin, Montreal, 28 mars 1731, 28 avril 1731, 30 mai 1731, 4 juin 1731." See also, LAC, MG18-B12, "La formation d'une société de traite entre Jean-Baptiste Gaultier de La Vérendrye, Nicolas Sarrazin et Eustache Gamelin-Châteauvieux, 28 avril 1731."
31 ANOM, COL C11E 16/fol.131–3v, "Articles du règlement qui régira le poste du lac Ouinipigon confié au Sr de La Vérendrye, Montreal, 19 mai 1731." See also, Champagne, *Les La Vérendrye et Le Poste de l'Ouest*, 113–15.
32 Burpee, *Journals and Letters*, 437–8.
33 ANOM, COL C11A 54/fol.385–6v, "Lettre de Beauharnois au ministre, Québec, 1 octobre 1731."
34 Burpee, *Journals and Letters*, 95.
35 Doige, "Warfare Patterns of the Assiniboine to 1809," 79.
36 Witgen, *An Infinity of Nations*, 149.
37 For a discussion of the Monsoni belonging to the Moose doodem, see Lovisek, "The Political Evolution of the Boundary Waters Ojibwa," 280–305.
38 Anderson, "Early Dakota Migration and Intertribal War," 26.
39 Hämäläinen, *Lakota America*, 99–100.
40 Ibid., 55–6, 60–1, 85–7.
41 ANOM, COL C11E 16/fol.282v–3, "Lettre du Sr de La Vérendrye au Ministre, Québec, 31 octobre 1744."
42 HBCA, B.239/a/11, fol.19.
43 Burpee, *Journals and Letters*, 96.
44 Ibid., 106.
45 ANOM, COL C11A 56/fol.336–9v, "Résumé de lettres du Canada, Québec, 18 décembre 1731."
46 Burpee, *Journals and Letters*, 136–7.
47 Ibid., 137–9.
48 *JR*, 54:192–3; *JR*, 66:105–7.
49 Burpee, *Journals and Letters*, 144–5.
50 Aspen parkland is a transitional biome between prairie and boreal forest, which encompasses the entirety of southwestern Manitoba and continues into parts of Minnesota and North Dakota. Carter, *Aboriginal People and Colonizers*, 19.
51 Gohier, *Onontio le médiateur*.
52 White, *The Middle Ground*, 40.
53 Ibid., 84; Belmessous, "Assimilation and Racialism," 332–3; Havard, *Empire et métissages*, 361.

54 White, *The Middle Ground*, 143; Witgen, *An Infinity of Nations*, 50–2; Cohen, "Was There an Amerindian Atlantic?," 404.
55 DuVal, *Native Ground*, 5.
56 Burpee, *Journals and Letters*, 169.
57 Ibid., 175–6.
58 Ibid.
59 Crouch, *Nobility Lost*, 80–1.
60 Burpee, *Journals and Letters*, 175.
61 Ibid., 176.
62 Ibid.
63 Ibid., 181.
64 Ibid., 181–2.
65 Malone, *Skulking Way of War*, 29–30; Starkey, *European and Native American Warfare*, 22.
66 Burpee, *Journals and Letters*, 180–1.
67 Rushforth, *Bonds of Alliance*, 229–37.
68 Burpee, *Journals and Letters*, 211.
69 Jones, *The Aulneau Collection*, 76.
70 Burpee, *Journals and Letters*, 222–3.
71 Champagne, *Nouvelles Études*, 76–7.
72 Jones, *Aulneau Collection*, 76.
73 Milloy, *Plains Cree*, 11–12, 80.
74 Burpee, *Journals and Letters*, 218.
75 ANOM, COL CIIE 16/fol.189–190, "Mémoire intitulé 'Affaire du meurtre de 21 voyageurs arrivé au lac des Bois au mois de juin 1736.' Le Sr de La Vérendrye fils et le père Aulneau, jésuite, périssent aussi lors de cette attaque-surprise menée par des Sioux, ca 1736."
76 Burpee, *Journals and Letters*, 213.
77 Ibid., 216, 219, 221–2.
78 Such war trophies symbolized the acquisition and maintenance of status and prestige for warriors in both Algonquian and Siouan societies. See Reedy-Maschner and Maschner, "Heads, Women, and the Baubles of Prestige," 32–3, 40–1; Starkey, *European and Native American Warfare*, 27, 30–1; Starkey, "Frontier Warfare in North America, 1513–1815," 70–1; Axtell and Sturtevant, "The Unkindest Cut," 451–72; Bishop and Lytwyn, "Barbarism and Ardour of War," 43–4; Havard, *Histoire des coureurs de bois*, 433–5.
79 Burpee, *Journals and Letters*, 263–4.
80 Anderson, *Kinsmen of Another Kind*, 42–3.
81 Burpee, *Journals and Letters*, 220.

82 Ibid., 235.
83 ANOM, COL C11A 67/fol.172v, Relation du sieur de Saint-Pierre, commandant au poste des Sioux, 1737.
84 Ibid.
85 The IHS emblem used by the Jesuits is an abbreviation for the Greek rendering of Jesus's name: "IHSOUS."
86 ANOM, COL C11A 67/fol.172–172v, "Relation du sieur de Saint-Pierre, commandant au poste des Sioux, 1737."
87 ANOM, COL C11A 67/fol.172–3v, "Relation du sieur de Saint-Pierre, commandant au poste des Sioux, 1737."
88 ANOM, COL C11A 67/fol.173, "Relation dù sieur de Saint-Pierre, commandant au poste des Sioux, 1737."
89 ANOM, COL C11A 67/fol.172, "Relation du sieur de Saint-Pierre, commandant au poste des Sioux, 1737."
90 ANOM, COL C11A 67/fol.173, "Relation du sieur de Saint-Pierre, commandant au poste des Sioux, 1737."
91 Anderson, *Kinsmen of Another Kind*, 41.
92 Ibid., 42.
93 Ibid., 45–6.
4 ANOM, COL C11A 67/fol.174v–5, "Relation du sieur de Saint-Pierre, commandant au poste des Sioux, 1737."
95 Foret, "The Failure of Administration," 49–60; Usner, *Indians, Settlers and Slaves*, 81–7.
96 Charlevoix, *Journal of a Voyage*, 1:280–1.
97 Witgen, *An Infinity of Nations*, 165; Rushforth, *Bonds of Alliance*, 222.
98 For the Fox Wars, see Peyser, "The Fate of the Fox Survivors," 83–96; Edmunds and Peyser, *The Fox Wars*; Rushforth, "Slavery, the Fox Wars, and the Limits of Alliance," 53–80.
99 Havard, "Protection and Unequal Alliance," 118–23; White, *The Middle Ground*, 50, 173–4.
100 Berthelette, "Frères et Enfants du même Père," 183–93.
101 Burpee, *Journals and Letters*, 221–2.
102 Ibid.
103 Ibid., 222.
104 Ibid., 220–3.
105 Ibid.
106 Ibid., 295.
107 Ibid., 232.

108 ANOM, COL C11A 69/fol.105–6v, "Extrait de deux lettres écrites à Beauharnois par Denys de La Ronde, juin-juillet 1738."
109 Ibid.
110 ANOM, COL C11E 16/fol.259v–60v, "Lettre de M. de Beauharnois au Ministre, Québec, 12 octobre 1742."
111 ANOM, COL C11A 77/fol.109–109v, "Lettre de Beauharnois au ministre, Québec, 24 septembre 1742."
112 ANOM, COL C11A 77/fol.109, "Lettre de Beauharnois au ministre, Québec, 24 septembre 1742." Brett Rushforth estimates that four arpents represented a "coffle of Sioux [Dakota] slaves" that stretched nearly eight hundred feet. Rushforth, *Bonds of Alliance*, 195.
113 ANOM, COL C11A 77/fol.109, "Lettre de Beauharnois au ministre, Québec, 24 septembre 1742."
114 Burpee, *Journals and Letters*, 384.
115 A 1706 French dictionary defines "Cole, s.f." as follows: "Sorte de composition qui astrient & unit des choses qui étoient séparées" (A kind of composition that draws & joins things together that were separate). The meaning of *colle* in twenty-first-century French remains about the same and translates to English as "glue," "adhesive," or "paste." Richelet, *Dictionnaire françois*, 196.
116 Burpee, *Journals and Letters*, 250.
117 Hackett, "The Monsoni and the Smallpox of 1737–39," 250–1. For Haudenosaunee mourning wars, see Richter, *The Ordeal of the Longhouse*, 58–61.
118 For the debt, see ANOM, COL C11E 16/fol.280–90, "Lettre du Sr de La Vérendrye au Ministre, Québec, 31 octobre 1744."
119 Crouse, *La Vérendrye*, 100, 214–15.
120 Thwaites, *Collections of the State Historical Society of Wisconsin*, 19:29.
121 "July 28, 1754, I, the undersigned, solemnly administered Baptism to an adult slave of Monsieur the Chevalier de la verandrie, about seventeen years old. He was given the name of Joseph." Ibid., 37–8.
122 Saint-Pierre, *Lacorne Saint-Luc*, 177–82.
123 Rushforth, "A Little Flesh We Offer You," 779.
124 Ibid., 785.
125 Ibid., 798, 808.
126 Rushforth, *Bonds of Alliance*, 232, 237.
127 Peyser, *Jacques Legardeur de Saint-Pierre*, 34–5.
128 Burpee, *Journals and Letters*, 451–2.
129 Rushforth, *Bonds of Alliance*, 232.

130 ANOM, COL C11A 117/fol.357, "Certificat de Paul Marin de La Malgue, Montreal, 2 septembre 1744."
131 ANOM, COL C11E, 16/fol.258v, "Lettre de M. de Beauharnois au Ministre, Québec, 12 octobre 1742."
132 ANOM, COL C11A 77/fol.213v, "Paroles des Sioux, Sakis, Renards, Puants de la pointe de Chagouamigon et Folles Avoines à Monsieur le marquis de Beauharnois … des 18, 24, et 25 juillet 1742."
133 Rushforth, *Bonds of Alliance*, 193–6; Hämäläinen, *Lakota America*, 74–5; Rushforth, "Slavery, the Fox Wars, and the Limits of Alliance," 66, 69–70.
134 ANOM, COL C11A 77/fol.111, "Lettre de Beauharnois au ministre, Québec, 24 septembre 1742."
135 ANOM, COL C11A 77/fol.111–111v, "Lettre de Beauharnois au ministre, Québec, 24 septembre 1742."
136 ANOM, COL C11A 67/fol.169, "Lettre de Beauharnois au ministre, Québec, 14 octobre 1737."
137 ANOM, COL C11A 77/fol.235v, "Réponse de Beauharnois 'aux paroles des Sioux, Sakis, Renards, Puants, Sauteux de la Pointe de Chagouamigon et Folles Avoines,' 28 juillet 1742."
138 ANOM, COL C11A 77/fol.111, "Lettre de Beauharnois au ministre, Québec, 24 septembre 1742."
139 ANOM, COL C11A 67/fol.169, "Lettre de Beauharnois au ministre, Québec, 14 octobre 1737."
140 ANOM, COL C11E 16/fol.277–9, "Lettre de M. de Beauharnois au Ministre, Québec, 27 octobre 1744."
141 ANOM, COL C11E 16/fol.280–90, "Lettre du Sr de La Vérendrye au Ministre, Québec, 31 octobre 1744."

CHAPTER FOUR

1 Burpee, *Journals and Letters*, 211–13.
2 While mutual affection may have existed between René Bourassa and his Dakota slave, Bourassa himself does not seem to have considered it a bona fide marital union. Bourassa was legally married to Canadienne Marie-Catherine Leriger de La Plante, with whom he had five children. Like many fur traders, Bourassa may have found comfort and companionship in both free and unfree Indigenous women in the fur trade country while still having a European wife (married in the Catholic Church) back in the Saint Lawrence valley. See DCB, 4:77–8.
3 Ibid.

4 Zoltvany, *Philippe de Rigaud de Vaudreuil*, 208.
5 DCB, 2:403.
6 ANOM, COL C11E 16/fol.189–90, "Mémoire intitulé 'Affaire du meurtre de 21 voyageurs arrivé au lac des Bois au mois de juin 1736.' Le Sr de La Vérendrye fils et le père Aulneau, jésuite, périssent aussi lors de cette attaque-surprise menée par des Sioux, ca 1736."
7 ANOM, COL C11E 16/fol.189–190, "'Affaire du meurtre,' ca 1736.'
8 Burpee, *Journals and Letters*, 210.
9 Ibid., 266.
10 ANOM, COL C11A 67/fol.169, Lettre de Beauharnois au ministre, Québec, 14 octobre 1737.
11 BAnQ Québec, "Greffe de F. Lepailleur de Laferté, Montreal, 28 avril 1738."
12 SHSB, VCD, Galloudek, Louis, 28 April 1738, accessed 6 December 2016, http://archivesshsb.mb.ca/en/permalink/voyageurs54382. In the PRDH database and Voyageur Contracts Database, Galloudek's name appears variously as "Galoudet," "Galoudec," and even "Tallondec." In the fur trade era, the precise spelling of names of illiterate French voyageurs and engagés were in the hands, as it were, of the notaries. See PRDH, Louis Galoudet, Baptism, 27 March 1722, Lévis, Québec, accessed 24 December 2016, http://www.genealogy.umontreal.ca/Membership/en/PRDH/Acte/23079.
13 Burpee, *Journals and Letters*, 309.
14 Ibid., 334.
15 Ibid., 347–8.
16 Ibid., 353.
17 ANOM, COL C11E 16/fol.234–236, "Résumé de l'extrait du journal du Sr de La Vérendryere latif aux Mandanes, ca 1741."
18 Ibid.
19 Binnema, *Common and Contested Ground*, 86–106.
20 The horse was reintroduced into North America in 1519 by the Spanish in mainland Mexico. Feral herds quickly spread throughout the continent and completely changed Indigenous life. Equestrianism revolutionized hunting, warfare, and even the spiritual practices of Great Plains Indigenous peoples. The Comanche, who first and most successfully mastered the horse on the southern plains, completely dominated the American Southwest and northern Mexico because of their facility with horses. Historian Dan Flores has described the horse as "the chief catalyst of an ongoing remaking of the tribal map of western America, as native American groups moved onto the Plains

and incessantly shifted their ranges and alliances in response to a world where accelerating change seemed almost the only constant." Flores, "Bison Ecology and Bison Diplomacy," 467. See also Secoy, *Changing Military Patterns on the Great Plains*, 6–38; Milloy, *The Plains Cree*, 25–6; Hämäläinen, "The Rise and Fall of Plains Indian Horse Cultures"; Hämäläinen, *Comanche Empire*, 240–6. For a discussion of the French use of horses between the Illinois Country and Louisiana, see Kimball Brown, "Allons, Cowboys!"

21 For a good, albeit brief, summary of Pennesha Gegare's career, see Wood and Thiessen, *Early Fur Trade on the Northern Plains*, 24; Fenn, *Encounters at the Heart of the World*, 148–50.

22 Gates, *Five Fur Traders of the Northwest*, 38.

23 Louis-Joseph Gaultier de La Vérendrye and François Gaultier Du Tremblay visited the Mandans as they returned to Fort La Reine in 1743, which was the last recorded visit of French traders to the Mandan before the conquest of New France. There is no evidence that any of La Vérendrye's successors at the Western Posts – Nicolas-Joseph de Noyelles de Fleurimont, Jacques Legardeur de Saint-Pierre, Louis de la Corne, and Charles-René Dejordy de Villebon – made any trips to trade with the Mandans of the Missouri valley.

24 For Central Siouan and Caddoan peoples, see Thorne, *The Many Hands of My Relations*, 13–63.

25 Fenn, *Encounters at the Heart of the World*, 20, 238.

26 Silverman, *Thundersticks*, 236, 265; Hämäläinen, *Comanche Empire*, 130–45.

27 Calloway, *One Vast Winter Count*, 301–3; Milloy, *The Plains Cree*, 49.

28 In the nineteenth century, ethnographers identified Plains Indian Sign Language as a remarkable pidgin language devised by the Indigenous peoples of the Great Plains to allow for inter-tribal communication. In 1885, ethnographers estimated that there were over 110,000 "sign-talking Indians," including Blackfoot, Cheyenne, Dakota, Yankton, Yanktonai, Lakota, Mandan, Hidatsa, Arikara, and Arapahoe. For an anthropological and sociological study of sign language in an Assiniboine community (Fort Belknap Reservation, Montana) see Farnell, *Do You See What I Mean?*

29 Wood, Hunt, and Williams, *Fort Clark and Its Indian Neighbors*, 24. For more on Plains Indian Sign Language, see Wurtzburg and Campbell, "North American Indian Sign Language," 153–67; Davis, *Hand Talk*.

30 Coues, *New Light on the Early History*, 335.
31 Carayon *Eloquence Embodied.*
32 ANOM, COL C13A 13/fol.124, "Salmon au ministre, La Nouvelle-Orléans, 9 décembre 1731."
33 ANOM, COL C11A 31/fol.187–8, "D'Argenteuil au ministre, Montreal, 10 octobre 1710."
34 ANOM C11A 3/fol.239v, "Raudot au Ministre, Québec, 1 novembre 1709."
35 Havard, *Empire et métissages*, 759–60.
36 ANOM, COL C11E 16/fol.259v–60v, "Lettre de M. de Beauharnois au Ministre, Québec, 12 octobre 1742."
37 Bohaker, "Nindoodemag," 23–52; Miller, *Compact, Contract, Covenant*, 7–10; Witgen, *An Infinity of Nations*, 19, 30.
38 Alain Beaulieu has noted that the metaphor of becoming one people was a recurrent feature of Haudenosaunee political overtures to the French in the seventeenth century. The metaphor was congruent with the vocabulary the Haudenosaunee used to describe their own internal relations as living in one house, sharing one heart, and being of one mind. Beaulieu, "Ne faire qu'un seul peuple?" See also Fenton, *The Great Law and the Longhouse*, 70, 102, 122.
39 Burpee, *Journals and Letters*, 101.
40 Lipman, *The Saltwater Frontier*, 105–12.
41 ANOM, C11A 21/fol.74v, "Parolles des sauvages hurons à mr de Vaudreuil, 14 juillet 1703."
42 Lahontan, *New Voyages*, 76.
43 Burpee, *Journals and Letters*, 168–9, 172–4.
44 Ibid., 231–2.
45 La Vérendrye does not indicate the provenance of the slave, but given the patterns of warfare in the 1730s, it is likely that the slave had been a member of the Očhéthi Šakówiŋ, likely from a western oyáte like the Yankton, Yanktonai, or Lakota.
46 Burpee, *Journals and Letters*, 172–3.
47 Ibid., 173.
48 Ibid., 186–7.
49 Ibid., 187–8.
50 Reynolds, "La Verendrye and Manitoba's First Mine."
51 Nish, *François-Étienne Cugnet*; Samson, *Forges du Saint-Maurice.*
52 Dowd, *Groundless*, 25.
53 Ibid., 33.
54 Morris, "How to Prepare Buffalo," 22.

55 JCBL Map Collection, Jacques-Nicolas Bellin, "Carte de L'Amerique Septentrionale Depuis le 28. Degré de Latitude jusqu'au 72. Par M. Bellin," 1755.
56 Dowd, *Groundless*, 17–37.
57 Mapp, *Elusive West*, 25–6.
58 Although Manitoba is home today to several active mines that produce such valuable metals as nickel, copper, zinc, and gold – particularly Flin Flon, Manitoba, where a mine was founded in 1927 by the Hudson Bay Mining and Smelting Company (now known as Hudbay Minerals) – such resources would hardly have been visible to eighteenth-century surveyors, with their relatively antiquated techniques and technology. See Cole, "Mining in Manitoba."
59 Closer to the pays d'en haut, colonial officials wrote that the peace concluded between the Cree and the Zhaagawaamikong-Ojibwes would be advantageous for the success of copper mining west of Lake Superior. ANOM, COL C11A 70/fol.257–259, "Mémoire concernant les Indiens, 1738."
60 Burpee, *Journals and Letters*, 95.
61 Ibid., 140.
62 Ibid., 240.
63 Burpee, *Journals and Letters*, 141; Champagne, *Nouvelles Études*, 60–2.
64 Burpee, *Journals and Letters*, 141.
65 Ibid., 105.
66 Champagne, *Nouvelles Études*, 59–60.
67 *JR*, 48:119–20.
68 Podruchny, *Making the Voyageur World*, 119.
69 Burpee, *Journals and Letters*, 303.
70 Ibid., 251.
71 Champagne, *Les La Vérendrye et Le Poste de l'Ouest*, 453–4.
72 Podruchny, *Making the Voyageur World*, 119–21.
73 ANOM, COL C11A 22/fol.356–93, "'Mémoire historique [de Riverin] à Monseigneur le comte de Pontchartrain sur les mauvais effets de la réunion des castors dans une même main,' Paris, 12 février 1705."
74 SHSB, VCD, Beauvais, Augustin, 24 May 1734, accessed 16 July 2018, http://archivesshsb.mb.ca/en/permalink/voyageurs54037.
75 Podruchny, "Baptizing Novices," 165–95.
76 Balvay, *L'épée et la plume*, 221–4.
77 Burpee, *Journals and Letters*, 149.

78 For more on the hunting and fishing activities of voyageurs and engagés at French posts, see Podruchny, *Making the Voyageur World*, 119–21, 234–40; Havard, *Empire et métissages*, 529–32, 597–601.

79 SHSB, VCD, Le Vallois, Jean, 30 May 1731, accessed 16 July 2018, http://archivesshsb.mb.ca/en/permalink/voyageurs46730.

80 Podruchny, *Making the Voyageur World*, 121–3.

81 Tracking is the act of using long ropes to haul a canoe upstream while walking along the riverbank. By using a rope at both the bow and stern, voyageurs could potentially track their canoes through dangerous upstream currents with minimal risk to themselves or the cargoes.

82 SHSB, VCD, Bissonet, Alexandre, 27 April 1750, accessed 17 July 2018, http://archivesshsb.mb.ca/en/permalink/voyageurs67502.

83 SHSB, VCD, Bissonet, Alexandre, 20 May 1739, accessed 17 July 2018, http://archivesshsb.mb.ca/en/permalink/voyageurs65041; SHSB, VCD, Alexandre Bissonet, Alexandre, 6 June 1749, accessed 17 July 2018, http://archivesshsb.mb.ca/en/permalink/voyageurs67543.

84 Burpee, *Journals and Letters*, 180.

85 Podruchny, *Making the Voyageur World*, 147.

86 Ibid., 149–50.

87 Gratien, "Les engagements pour la traite des fourrures," 12–14; Havard, *Empire et métissages*, 73–5.

88 Englebert and St-Onge, "Paddling into History," 71–104.

89 Havard, *Empire et métissages*, 73–5.

90 ANOM, COL C11A 22/fol.362v.

91 For example, thirty-nine-year-old Jean-Baptiste Pominville contracted to serve as a guide for the Associés de la Mer de l'Ouest in 1738, a relatively old age to engage in fourteen hours of hard labour per day. SHSB, VCD, Pominville, Jean-Baptiste, 27 April 1738, accessed 17 July 2018, http://archivesshsb.mb.ca/en/permalink/voyageurs54799.

92 Combet, "Récits de voyage," 310–11.

93 Podruchny, *Making the Voyageur World*, 34.

94 ANOM, COL C11A 7/fol.193.

95 ANOM, COL C11E 16/fol.131–3v, "Articles du règlement qui régira le poste du lac Ouinipigon confié au Sr de La Vérendrye, 19 mai 1731."

96 BAnQ Vieux-Montreal, "TL4 Fonds Juridiction royale de Montreal, S34 Congés de traite homologués, Enregistrement d'une permission accordée … à De la Veranderie, Juin 1735."

97 St-Onge, "Blue Beads, Vermilion, and Scalpers," 197–8.

98 BAnQ Vieux-Montreal, "TL4 Fonds Juridiction royale de Montreal, S1 Dossiers, Procès entre Charles Nolan Lamarque, négociant, et le sieur de LaVérandrye, pour non respect de son bail concernant l'exploitation des postes de traite de l'Ouest, 19 août 1739."
99 Burpee, *Journals and Letters*, 359.
100 Ibid.
101 BAnQ Vieux-Montreal, "TL4 Fonds Juridiction royale de Montreal, S1 Dossiers, Protestation de Jean-Baptiste Pion ... à l'effet qu'il n'a pas reçu ses gages, 8 septembre 1741."
102 *DCB*, 3:485.
103 BAnQ Québec, "Greffe de J.-B. Adhémar dit Saint-Martin, Montreal, 18 mai 1735." See also Champagne, *Les La Vérendrye et Le Poste de l'Ouest*, 490–1.
104 Burpee, *Journals and Letters*, 437–8.
105 Ibid., 245.
106 Burley, *Servants of the Honourable Company*; Stephen, *Masters and Servants.*
107 Podruchny, *Making the Voyageur World*, 154–6, 160–4.
108 Podruchny, "Unfair Masters and Rascally Servants?," 67. See also Englebert, "Diverging Identities and Converging Interests," 18–24.

CHAPTER FIVE

1 HBCA, B.239/a/43, Joseph Smith, "A Journal on the Most Remarkable Observations and Occurrences on a Journey in Land Performed by Joseph Smith and Joseph Waggoner Who Departed From York Fort August the 23rd 1756 and Returned June the 25th, 1757," 19 May 1757.
2 Ibid.
3 The north end of Lake Winnipegosis is separated from Cedar Lake by a land barrier whose minimum width is six kilometres.
4 HBCA, B.239/a/43, Joseph Smith, "A Journal on the Most Remarkable Observations and Occurrences."
5 Burley, *Servants of the Honourable Company*, 26, 91.
6 Combet, *In Search of the Western Sea*, 85.
7 HBCA, B.239/a/43, Joseph Smith, "A Journal on the Most Remarkable Observations and Occurrences."
8 Ibid.
9 HBCA, B.239/a/42, James Isham, York Factory post journal, 24 June 1757.

10 HBCA, B.239/a/43, Joseph Smith, "A Journal on the Most Remarkable Observations and Occurrences."
11 Morton, *History of the Canadian West*, 254.
12 DuVal, *The Native Ground*, 16.
13 Delâge, "Les Premières Nations et la Guerre de la Conquête (1754–1765)," 2–7.
14 Louise Dechêne eschewed the term "conquest of Canada" in favour of the more accurate "Sixteen Years' War," since the imperial conflict began in earnest in North America in 1744 and ended in 1760 with the British conquest. On the other hand, Denys Delâge posits that the conflict should be called the "Twenty-One Years' War" since he sees Pontiac's War (1763–66) as merely a continuation of the conflict. Dechêne, *Le peuple, l'État et la guerre au Canada*, 293; Delâge, "Les Premières Nations et la Guerre de la Conquête," 7.
15 The Bighorn Mountains, in the modern-day state of Wyoming, form a northwest-trending spur extending northward from the Rocky Mountains onto the Great Plains. There has been some historiographical debate in the United States as to whether Louis-Joseph Gaultier de La Vérendrye and his brother François reached the Rocky Mountains, or merely the Black Hills, in modern-day South Dakota, during their 1742–43 expedition. Based on the length of the journey and the overall distance travelled by the La Vérendrye brothers, the Bighorn Mountains of Wyoming seems the more likely contender. See Libby, "Some Vérendrye Enigmas"; Flandrau, "The Verendrye Expeditions in Quest of the Pacific"; Smurr, "A New La Vérendrye Theory"; Smith, *Explorations of the La Vérendryes*.
16 Burpee, *Journals and Letters*, 417–19.
17 For a recent discussion of the La Vérendrye brothers' possible itinerary for their 1742–43 voyage, as well as a discussion of the identities of the two engagés that accompanied them, see Havard, *L'Amérique fantôme*, 237–76.
18 Mapp, *Elusive West*, 171.
19 *DCB*, 3:253.
20 Only La Vérendrye's servant and the local parish priest attended the funerary rites, since his sons were still out pursuing fame and fortune in the northwestern fur trade. He left a small estate worth perhaps 4,000 livres, much of it consisting of articles of clothing and adornment. See PRDH, Pierre Gauthier Delaverenderie, Sépulture, Montreal, 7 December 1749, accessed 6 December 2017, https://www.genealogie.umontreal.ca/Membership/fr/PRDH/acte/153962.

21 In 1805, the Lewis and Clark Expedition proved that the Missouri River was not a viable all-water route to the Pacific Ocean. A difficult and mountainous 547-kilometre portage separated the Missouri from the Columbia River. Dolin, *Fur, Fortune, and Empire*, 176.

22 ANOM, COL C11A 95/fol.89–91v, Lettre de La Jonquière et Bigot au minister, 20 octobre 1750; ANOM, COL C11A 97/fol.65–68, Lettre de La Jonquière au ministre, 16 septembre 1751. See also, Nute, "Marin versus La Vérendrye," 226–38.

23 Mancall, *Deadly Medicine*, 11–28, 63–79, 170; Ishii, *Bad Fruits of the Civilized Tree*; Derksen, "Colonialism, Consumption, and Control."

24 Deschamps, *Lettres au cher fils*, 306.

25 Anderson, *Crucible of War*, 119.

26 Historian Joseph L. Peyser had equated this enormous amount of brandy to "a full year's supplementary pay for a western fort commandant." Peyser, *Jacques Legardeur de Saint-Pierre*, 237–8, 287–308. Further indirect evidence of La Jonquière's authorization and abetment of Saint-Pierre's large-scale brandy trade at the Western Posts is provided in a lengthy exposé sent to a high official in France in 1754 by Captain Charles de Raymond. Raymond complained that in Canada "the ecclesiastical power and the country's government have from time to time obligingly eased the severity of their prohibition" of the brandy trade. Raymond listed several names of prominent figures in the liquor trade implicating Saint-Pierre and La Jonquière. Peyser, *On the Eve of the Conquest*, 99–100.

27 Peyser, *Jacques Legardeur de Saint-Pierre*, 175.

28 Bougainville, *Ecrits sur le Canada*, 72–3.

29 BAnQ Québec, "Greffe Panet de Méru, Montreal, 12 mai 1758." By the time the French court attempted to convict Villebon as part of *l'Affaire du Canada*, he had already been dead for two years, having perished in the shipwreck of the *Auguste*, which sank off the coast of Cape Breton on 15 November 1761. See "Ordre du roi d'arrêter et d'incarcérer à la Bastille le sieur de Villebon, ancien commandant du poste de la Mer de l'Ouest, Versailles, 16 janvier 1762. Bibliothèque de l'Arsenal vol. 12142/fol.531 sur microfilm, Archives de la Bastille: Prisonniers." For an excellent discussion of *l'Affaire du Canada*, see Crouch, *Nobility Lost*, 131–6. For an excellent primary account of a survivor of the wreck of the *Auguste*, where other notable Canadiens and commandants of the Western Posts Louis-Joseph Gaultier de La Vérendrye and Louis de la Corne, Chevalier de la Corne, also perished, see La Corne, *Journal du voyage*.

30 Burpee, *Journals and Letters*, 487.

31 ANOM, COL C11A 85/fol.85–8v, "Lettre de Beauharnois et Hocquart au ministre, Québec, 17 octobre 1746."

32 ANOM, COL C11A 85/fol.85–8v, "Lettre de Beauharnois au ministre, 03 novembre 1746."

33 For de Noyelles cargo to the Western Posts, see BAnQ Vieux-Montréal, "TL4 Fonds Juridiction royale de Montréal, S34 Congés de traite homologués, Enregistrement d'une permission accordée par Charles de Beauharnois … à Denoyelle, 2 juin 1744." For merchandise that flowed into the Hudson Bay watershed during La Vérendrye's tenure as commandant in 1735, see BAnQ Vieux-Montréal, "TL4 Fonds Juridiction royale de Montréal, S34 Congés de traite homologués, Enregistrement d'une permission accordée par Charles de Beauharnois … à Bourassa, Juin 1735"; "Enregistrement d'une permission accordée par Charles de Beauharnois … au lieutenant De la Veranderie, Juin 1735"; "Enregistrement d'une permission accordée par Charles de Beauharnois … à De la Veranderie, Juin 1735."

34 Miller, *Compact, Contract, Covenant*, 15, 21, 284; Waiser, *A World We Have Lost*, 132–7.

35 "Journal of Occurrences in Canada, 1746, 1747," in *DRCNY*, 10:130.

36 *DCB*, 3:492.

37 Sturtevant, "Jealous Neighbors," 201.

38 The Anglo-American seizure of Louisbourg cost France more than colonial revenue. In 1746, a massive naval expedition led by the Duc d'Anville, which included eleven thousand men and a fleet of sixty-four ships, was designed to recapture Louisbourg and retake Acadia, but instead ended up gouging the Ministry of the Marine's treasury without achieving a single one of its objectives. Many of the French vessels involved did not return and estimates of the dead were as high as eight thousand. Desbarats, "France in North America," 22. James Pritchard's 1995 monograph *Anatomy of a Naval Disaster* sheds new light on the extent of the tragedy and raises questions about the role and effectiveness of naval power during the intercolonial wars of the mid-eighteenth century. Pritchard's book explores the limits of empire and naval power in the eighteenth century.

39 Delâge, "Les Premières Nations et la Guerre de la Conquête," 31.

40 White, *The Middle Ground*, 117–19.

41 Ibid., 199–200.

42 For the War of the Austrian Succession (1740–48) in the pays d'en haut and Ohio Valley, see MacLeod, "Une Conspiration Générale";

White, *The Middle Ground*, 187, 193; Warren, *The Worlds the Shawnees Made*, 197–204; Delâge, "Les Premières Nations et la Guerre de la Conquête," 2–8; Anderson, *Crucible of War*, 24–65; McDonnell, *Masters of Empire*, 122–3, 134–97; Sturtevant, "Jealous Neighbors," 175–217; Skinner, *The Upper Country*, 163–72.

43 Innis, *The Fur Trade in Canada*, 138.

44 Carlos and Lewis, "Indians, the Beaver, and the Bay," 474.

45 Ray and Freeman, *"Gives Us Good Measure,"* 166.

46 Carlos and Lewis, "Indians, the Beaver, and the Bay," 480–1.

47 MacLeod, "Une Conspiration Générale," 40.

48 ANOM, COL C11A 81/fol.145, "Lettre de Beauharnois au ministre, Québec, 8 octobre 1744."

49 MacLeod, "Une Conspiration Générale," 41.

50 ANOM, COL C11A 85/fol.85–85v, "Lettre de Beauharnois et Hocquart au ministre, Québec, 17 octobre 1746."

51 MacLeod, "Une Conspiration Générale," 41–2, 174.

52 Innis, *The Fur Trade in Canada*, 110–11.

53 Hall, "Ocean Crossings," 16–20; Pritchard, *In Search of Empire*, 161.

54 Peyser, *Jacques Legardeur de Saint-Pierre*, 185.

55 Ibid., 180–1.

56 Ibid., 182.

57 Ibid., 182–3.

58 LAC, R11599-1-8-F, Fonds Viger-Verreau, carton 5, fol.2v, "Lettre de M. de S. Pierre à Beauharnois," 25 March 1734.

59 Havard, *Histoire des coureurs de bois*, 426–33.

60 Peyser, *Jacques Legardeur de Saint-Pierre*, 170.

61 Milloy, *The Plains Cree*, 75–7.

62 Peyser, *Jacques Legardeur de Saint-Pierre*, 186–7.

63 Ibid.

64 Ibid, 187.

65 Ibid.

66 White, *The Middle Ground*, 90.

67 Most historians, following an uncritical reading of Saint-Pierre's journal, have portrayed Saint-Pierre as brave and cunning and the Nakoda as treacherous and cowardly. For example, Elizabeth Losey wrote that "Saint-Pierre, certainly not deficient in courage, grabbed a blazing brand and, standing in front of the open door to the powder magazine, threatened to throw it inside, blowing them all up, including himself. The bluff worked and the frightened Assiniboines fled the fort." Losey, *Let Them Be Remembered*, 55.

68 Peyser, *Jacques Legardeur de Saint-Pierre*, 187.
69 Ibid., 187–8.
70 ANOM, COL C11A 99/fol.114–127, "Lettre de Duquesne au ministre, Québec, 31 octobre 1753."
71 Foster, "Wintering, the Outsider Adult Male and the Ethnogenesis of the Western Plains Métis."
72 ANOM, COL C11A 34/fol.228–61v, "Lettre de Vaudreuil et Bégon au ministre, Québec, 20 septembre 1714."
73 ANOM, COL C11A 34/fol.354–61, "Lettre de Ramezay, gouverneur de Montréal, au ministre, 18 septembre 1714."
74 ANOM, COL C11A 124/fol.512, "Extrait de quelques lettres des missionnaires de Canada au père d'Avaugour, leur procureur en France, depuis la fin d'août jusqu'au commencement de novembre 1721."
75 ANOM, COL C11A 67/fol.180–4, "Lettre de Beauharnois au ministre, Québec, 16 octobre 1737."
76 ANOM, COL C11A 87/fol.254–5v, "Lettre de La Galissonière au ministre – le 'désordre' des coureurs de bois a augmenté cette année, Québec, 21 octobre 1747"; ANOM, COL C11A 91/fol.121v–2, "Lettre de La Galissonière au ministre concernant le pays des Illinois, Québec, 1 septembre 1748"; ANOM, COL C11A 95/fol.260–5, "Lettre de La Jonquière au ministre, Québec, 29 septembre 1750."
77 Pénicaut, *Fleur de Lys and Calumet*, 46–9.
78 HBCA, B.239/a/11, Thomas McCliesh, York Factory post journal, 12 June 1729.
79 Champagne, *Les La Vérendrye et Le Poste de l'Ouest*, 125–8; Champagne, *Nouvelles Études*, 72–3, 200.
80 LAC, R11599-1-8-F, "Fonds Viger-Verreau, Instructions du gouverneur La Jonquière au capitaine Jacques Legardeur, Montreal, 27 mai 1750."
81 ANOM, COL B 81/fol.39, "Le Président du Conseil de Marine à M. de Beauharnois, Versailles, 28 avril 1745."
82 HBCA, B.239/b/18, Humphrey Marten, York Factory correspondence book, 6 August 1759.
83 HBCA, B.3/b/20, Joseph Isbister, Fort Albany correspondence books, 9 May 1743.
84 HBCA, B.239/b/5, James Isham, York Factory post journal, 12 July 1747.
85 HBCA B.239/b/5, John Potts, Moose Factory post journal, 22 September 1747.

86 HBCA, B.239/b/5, James Isham, York Factory post journal, 4 July 1748.
87 Ellis, *A Voyage to Hudson's-Bay*, 212.
88 HBCA, B.239/b/8, George Spence, Fort Albany post journal, 23 May 1752.
89 HBCA, B.239/b/11, James Isham, York Factory post journal, 16 August 1754.
90 For more on the Blackfoot, especially in the late eighteenth and early nineteenth centuries, when HBC, NWC, and American traders were fully engaged in the buffalo trade on the northern Great Plains, see Binnema, "Allegiances and Interests"; Binnema and Dobak, "Like the Greedy Wolf."
91 Belyea, *A Year Inland*, 41.
92 HBCA, B.239/a/11, John Newton, York Factory post journal, 17 May 1749.
93 Ibid.
94 Champagne, *Les La Vérendrye et Le Poste de l'Ouest*, 453–4.
95 Robson, *An Account of Six Years Residence in Hudson's-Bay*, 62–3.
96 Ibid., 62.
97 Belyea, *A Year Inland*, 190.
98 Champagne, *Nouvelles Études*, 78. See also, Morton, *A History of the Canadian West*, 254.
99 Champagne, *Nouvelles Études*, 63–82; Losey, *Let Them Be Remembered*, 176–8.
100 Kavanagh, *The Assiniboine Basin*, 14–15; Champagne, *Nouvelles Études*, 64–5; Losey, *Let Them Be Remembered*, 200–10.
101 HBCA, B.64/a/1, James Sutherland, Eschabitchewan House post journal, 18 December 1792; Lytwyn, *The Fur Trade of the Little North*, 6.
102 Champagne, *Nouvelles Études*, 78–9.
103 HBCA, B.239/b/18, Humphrey Marten, York Factory correspondence book, 6 August 1759.
104 Belyea, *A Year Inland*, 189.
105 Shannon, "Dressing for Success," 3–42; White, *Wild Frenchmen and Frenchified Indians*, 1–20.
106 White, *The Middle Ground*, 181.
107 White, *Wild Frenchmen and Frenchified Indians*, 98–101, 232.
108 Havard, *The Great Peace of Montreal*, 138.
109 Quaife, *The Western Country*, 16.

110 Kalm, *The America of 1750*, 473–5, 534–5. See also Vigeant, Ribot, and Hélie, "Dietary Habits in New France," 560.

111 *JR*, 67:134.

112 Kalm, *The America of 1750*, 560.

113 Sleeper-Smith, *Indigenous Prosperity*, 163–74. See also Anderson, "The Flow of European Trade Goods," 402–4, 407.

114 Hennepin, *A New Discovery*, 294.

115 ANOM, COL C11A 11/fol.262, "Lettre de Champigny au ministre, Québec, 10 mai 1691."

116 *JR*, 65:220.

117 Thwaites, *Collections of the State Historical Society of Wisconsin*, 19:22.

118 Ibid., 32.

119 Ibid., 66.

120 Ibid., 22, 32.

121 Sleeper-Smith, "Women, Kin, and Catholicism," 432.

122 Pigeon, "Au nom du Bon Dieu," 6.

123 Ibid., 52, 56, 61, 94–5, 116–18, 120.

124 Kenyon and Turnbull, *The Battle for James Bay*, 53.

125 Podruchny, "Baptizing Novices," 172–4, 190. For more on "Oiseau Rock" and "Pointe aux Baptêmes," see Havard, *Empire et métissages*, 724.

126 Blair, *Indian Tribes of the Upper Mississippi Valley*, 287–8.

127 Pigeon, "Au nom du Bon Dieu," 61; Sleeper-Smith, "Women, Kin, and Catholicism," 425–6, 444.

128 Burpee, *Journals and Letters*, 226–7.

129 Campbell, "Out of the Grave," 21.

130 In the New Testament, Jesus says to Peter: "I will give you the keys of the kingdom of heaven, and whatever you bind on Earth shall be bound in heaven, and whatever you loose on Earth shall be loosed in heaven" (Matt. 16:19).

131 Podruchny, *Making the Voyageur World*, 83–5, 194.

132 Jones, *Aulneau Collection*, 110–11.

133 Ibid.

134 Moreau, *The Writings of David Thompson*, 1:178.

135 Charlevoix, *Journal of a Voyage*, 2:97.

136 Havard, *Empire et métissages*, 722–3.

137 Podruchny, *Making the Voyageur World*, 52–3, 55; Pigeon, "Au nom du Bon Dieu," 38.

138 *JR*, 64:260.

139 Cliche, *Les Pratiques de Dévotion En Nouvelle-France*, 59.
140 *JR*, 67:45–7.
141 Moreau, *The Writings of David Thompson*, 2:130.
142 Podruchny, *Making the Voyageur World*, 52; Pigeon, "Au nom du Bon Dieu," 298–9.
143 Prud'homme, *L'élément français au nord-ouest*, 8; Kavanagh, *Assiniboine Basin*, 12.
144 Balvay, *L'épée et la plume*, 221–8.
145 Belyea, *A Year Inland*, 186.
146 Kalm, *The America of 1750*, 462–75.
147 Desloges, *À table en Nouvelle-France*, 39–40.
148 Kellogg, *Early Narratives of the Northwest*, 174.
149 Havard, *Empire et métissages*, 598.
150 Hennepin, *A New Discovery*, 650.
151 Burpee, *Journals and Letters*, 253–4.
152 Ibid., 343.
153 Ibid., 130, 149, 182.
154 Lytwyn, *Muskekowuck Athinuwick*, 139, 142.
155 Ellis, *A Voyage to Hudson's-Bay*, 30–1.
156 Pigeon, "Au nom du Bon Dieu," 58–61.
157 Kalm, *The America of 1750*, 534.
158 Belyea, *A Year Inland*, 63.
159 Ibid., 204.
160 Ibid., 63.
161 HBCA, B.239/a/44, James Isham, York Factory post journal, 4 July 1758.
162 For more on the HBC exploration of the interior, particularly the Saskatchewan River route, see Waiser, *A World We Have Lost*, 157–74.
163 Robson, *An Account of Six Years Residence in Hudson's-Bay*, 6.
164 Belyea, *A Year Inland*, 58.
165 Ibid., 186–7.
166 Ibid., 190.
167 Ibid., 189.
168 Robson, *An Account of Six Years Residence in Hudson's-Bay*, 53–4.
169 Anderson, *Kinsmen of Another Kind*, 30.
170 Sleeper-Smith, *Indian Women and French Men*, 42.
171 Van Kirk, *Many Tender Ties*; Brown, *Strangers in Blood*; Sleeper-Smith, "Women, Kin, and Catholicism," 423–52; Van Kirk, "The Custom of the Country," 481–518.

172 Van Kirk, *Many Tender Ties*, 51.
173 Balvay, *L'épée et la plume*, 203.
174 ANOM, COL C11A 30/fol.10, "Vaudreuil et Raudot au ministre, Québec, 13 septembre 1709."
175 ANOM, COL C13A 3/fol.819–24, "Duclos au ministre, Nouvelle-Orléans, 25 décembre 1715."
176 ANOM, COL C13A 20/fol.20, "Bienville et Salmon au ministre, Nouvelle-Orléans, 13 octobre 1709."
177 Belmessous, "Assimilation and Racialism," 340–1, 347–8; Aubert, "The Blood of France," 445–6, 451–3.
178 Balvay, *L'épée et la plume*, 203; Brown, *Strangers in Blood*, 3–6, 62–80; Van Kirk, *Many Tender Ties*, 28–52.
179 *JR*, 16:161.
180 For French-Dakota marital unions and strategic marriages à la façon du pays, see St-Onge, "Familial Foes?," 308–16. For French-Nakoda marriages à la façon du pays, see Denig, *Five Indian Tribes of the Upper Missouri*, 231; Rodnick, *The Fort Belknap Assiniboine of Montana*, 58–61.
181 Kathleen DuVal argues that the patrilineal Quapwas of the lower Arkansas valley rebuked Canadien traders' attempt to marry à la façon du pays because exogamous marriage alliances with foreign traders were neither politically or commercially necessary nor socially appealing. Similarly, DuVal posits that Apalachee refugees at Mobile, already greatly weakened and reduced from disease epidemics, warfare, and relocation, feared that marriage with alien peoples, like the French, would further undermine Apalachee cultural identity. The Apalachee resolve not to marry into the French community was probably an indication of their determination to preserve their cultural and social distinctiveness. Recognizing their precarious position on the "Native ground" in Louisiana, the French wisely chose to respect Quapaw and Apalachee gender relations and guidelines for interactions. In other words, métissage and marriages à la façon du pays were not a foregone conclusion of all French-Indigenous interactions in North America. DuVal, "Indian Intermarriage and Métissage," 285–96; DuVal, *Native Ground*, 84–5.
182 DuVal, "Indian Intermarriage and Métissage," 304.
183 Anderson, *Kinsmen of Another Kind*, 31.
184 Van Kirk, *Many Tender Ties*, 24.

185 "*Johnstone et al. vs. Connolly*, Appeal Court, 7 Sept. 1869," *La Revue Legale* 1:280. Quoted in Van Kirk, *Many Tender Ties*, 40.
186 Warren, *History of the Ojibway People*, 195.
187 Witgen, *An Infinity of Nations*, 19, 30, 75–6.
188 Bohaker, "Nindoodemag," 25–6, 31, 43–4, 47; Simpson, "Looking after Gdoo-naaganinaa," 32; Bohaker, "Anishinaabe Toodaims," 94, 96, 98–103, 112; Bohaker, "Reading Anishinaabe Identities," 13–14; Miller, *Ogimaag*, 16–19.
189 Bohaker, "Nindoodemag," 26; Bohaker, "Reading Anishinaabe Identities," 13.
190 Bohaker, "Anishinaabe Toodaims," 97–8.
191 St-Onge, "Le poste de La Pointe sur l'île Madeline," 41–2.
192 LaBounty, "This Countries Ladies"; White, *Grand Portage as a Trading Post*, 46, 74, 149–50.
193 Bohaker, "Anishinaabe Toodaims," 99–100, 102; Bohaker, "Nindoodemag," 48, 51.
194 Burpee, *Journals and Letters*, 211–12.
195 Rushforth, *Bonds of Alliance*, 264.
196 DuVal, "Indian Intermarriage and Métissage," 276.
197 Rushforth, *Bonds of Alliance*, 264.
198 For treatments of Indian slavery and captivity elsewhere in colonial North America, see Gallay, *The Indian Slave Trade*; Ekberg, *Stealing Indian Women*; Ethridge and Shuck-Hall, *Mapping the Mississippian Shatter Zone*; Steele, *Setting All the Captives Free*; Trudel, *Canada's Forgotten Slaves*.
199 Brown, *Ethnohistorian in Rupert's Land*, 106.
200 Warkentin, "Make It Last Forever as It Is," 149–78; Brown, *Ethnohistorian in Rupert's Land*, 103–22, 164–70; Brown, *Strangers in Blood*, 81–96; Burley, *Servants of the Honourable Company*, 123–7.
201 Brown, *Ethnohistorian in Rupert's Land*, 106.

CHAPTER SIX

1 Elite Troupes de la Marine officers Jacques Legardeur de Saint-Pierre, Louis de la Corne, Charles-René Dejordy de Villebon, and Louis-Joseph Gaultier de La Vérendrye all fought and perished either during or immediately after the Seven Years' War. Saint-Pierre died in combat at the Battle of Lake George in 1755, where he served under the command of the Baron de Dieskau. La Corne and La Vérendrye

drowned at sea when the ship *Auguste* sank off the coast of Cape Breton Island in 1761. For the Battle of Lake George, see Anderson, *Crucible of War*, 119. For the wreck of the *Auguste*, which sank on 15 November 1761, see Saint-Pierre, *Lacorne Saint-Luc*, 149–212.

2 Morton, *Manitoba: A History*, 36; Innis, *Fur Trade in Canada*, 139; Rich, *The History of the Hudson's Bay Company*, 647; Ray and Freeman, *"Give Us Good Measure,"* 36; Lytwyn, *The Fur Trade of the Little North*, 8; Thistle, *Indian-European Trade Relations*, 24.

3 Giraud, *Métis in the Canadian West*, 379–464; Stanley, *The Birth of Western Canada*; Bumsted, *Fur Trade Wars*; Bumsted, *Lord Selkirk*, 303–16; Ens, "The Battle of Seven Oaks," 93–119; Ens and Sawchuk, *From New Peoples to New Nations*, 71–91; Teillet, *The North-West Is Our Mother*, 63–80, 121–6.

4 Literature on Métis history, particularly the ethnogenesis of the Métis people and the Métis Nation, is indeed voluminous. For the key texts, see Peterson and Brown, *The New Peoples*; Brown, "Woman as Centre and Symbol in the Emergence of Metis Communities," 39–46; Payment, *The Free People*; St-Onge, Podruchny, and Macdougall, *Contours of a People*; Macdougall, *One of the Family*.

5 Nicks and Morgan, "Grande Cache," 167.

6 Pannekoek, "Metis Studies," 111–12.

7 Miller, "From Riel to the Métis," 14.

8 Devine, "Les Desjarlais," 129–58; St-Onge, "Early Forefathers to the Athabasca Métis," 109–61; Devine, *The People Who Own Themselves*; Hogue, *Metis and the Medicine Line*; Macdougall, *One of the Family*.

9 Macdougall and St-Onge, "Rooted in Mobility," 26.

10 HBCA, B.239/a/47, James Isham, York Factory post journal, 13 September 1759.

11 Calloway, *The Scratch of a Pen*, 138–49, 165–8.

12 For Pontiac's War, see White, *Middle Ground*, 269–314; Widder, *Beyond Pontiac's Shadow*, 95–188; McDonnell, *Masters of Empire*, 198–239; Dowd, *War under Heaven*; Delâge, "Pontiac, une guerre d'indépendance," 313–34. For the slow mobilization of British capital, see Miquelon, "The Baby Family in the Trade of Canada," 37–40. Dale Miquelon argues that Canadien merchants continued to control the trade after the conquest of Canada until 1774, after which British merchants began to dominate the fur trade.

13 Englebert, "Merchant Representatives," 63–4, 81–2.

14 Marrero, "Women at the Crossroads," 159–85; Hatter, *Citizens of Convenience*, 8, 22–5; Teasdale, *Fruits of Perseverance*, 3–5, 7. See also Gitlin, *Bourgeois Frontier*, 15–16, 26–7; Waiser, *A World We Have Lost*, 175; Calloway, *The Scratch of a Pen*, 112–13.

15 The Nassauaketon Odawa doodem often appears in French colonial documents, such as the Great Peace of Montreal Treaty, as the "nation de la fourche." Havard, *Great Peace of Montreal*, 279.

16 McDonnell, *Masters of Empire*, 249–50.

17 White, *The Middle Ground*, 230–1, 235; Crouch, *Nobility Lost*, 42–6; Widder, *Beyond Pontiac's Shadow*, xxv, xxvi, 22–3, 147–50.

18 Carleton to Shelburne, 2 March 1768, *Wisconsin Historical Collections*, 18:288–92. Quoted in McDonnell, *Masters of Empire*, 268.

19 Reid, "Quebec Fur-Traders and Western Policy," 26–7.

20 Sleeper-Smith, *Indian Women and French Men*, 62–4; Gitlin, *Bourgeois Frontier*, 43, 45, 67, 81, 120, 154–5, 190; Saler, *The Settlers' Empire*, 42–5, 50–2, 121–8, 133–9; Murphy, *Great Lakes Creoles*.

21 HBCA, B.239/a/64, William Tomison, "A Journal of the most remarkable Transactions and Occurrences of a Journey In Land Commencing 15th July 1769 and Ending 18th July 1770 kept by William Tomison," 25 October 1769.

22 Cocking, *Journal of Matthew Cocking*, 105.

23 SHSB, VCD, Hanot dit Bouguignon, Henry, 12 May 1758, accessed 5 November 2019, https://archivesshsb.mb.ca/en/permalink/voyageurs50400.

24 Champagne, *Nouvelles Études*, 78–9; Lytwyn, *The Fur Trade of the Little North*, 6.

25 HBCA, B.64/a/1, James Sutherland, Eschabitchewan House post journal, 18 December 1792.

26 PRDH, Henri Janot Bourguignon, Baptism, 28 February 1717, Chateau-Chinon, Nievre, France, accessed 5 November 2019, https://www.prdh-igd.com/Membership/en/PRDH/Individu/150513.

27 Fromhold, *The Western Cree*, 71; Giraud, *Métis in the Canadian West*, 124; Havard, *Histoire des coureurs de bois*, 319.

28 Wallace, *Pedlars from Quebec*, 6; Giraud, *Métis in the Canadian West*, 151, 155–7. For voyageurs engaged to work for Blondeau in 1767, see SHSB, VCD, Lebeau, Albert, 27 April 1767, accessed 8 November 2019, https://archivesshsb.mb.ca/en/permalink/voyageurs50715; SHSB, VCD, Lasonde, Louis, 21 May 1767, accessed 8 November 2019, https://archivesshsb.mb.ca/en/permalink/voyageurs50717.

29 Kavanagh, *Assiniboine Basin*, 14–15; Champagne, *Nouvelles études*, 64–5; Losey, *Let Them Be Remembered*, 200–10.
30 For evidence of Charles Boyer trading in the Rainy Lake district, see SHSB, VCD, Roy Dit dejardins, Joseph Pierre, 25 May 1744, accessed 6 November 2019, https://archivesshsb.mb.ca/en/permalink/voyageurs66698; SHSB, VCD, Cargré Dit malouin, Claude (fils), 4 May 1744, accessed 6 November 2019, https://archivesshsb.mb.ca/en/permalink/voyageurs65200.
31 Morton, "Forrest Oakes," 87–100. See also Kavanagh, *Assiniboine Basin*, 15–16; Giraud, *Métis in the Canadian West*, 156–7, 177.
32 Cocking, *Journal of Matthew Cocking*, 199.
33 HBCA, B.239/a/58, William Pink, "William Pink's In Land Journal 1767 & 8."
34 Wallace, *The Pedlars from Quebec*, 3.
35 Morton, *History of the Canadian West*, 288.
36 HBCA, B.239/a/58, William Pink, "William Pink's In Land Journal 1767 & 8."
37 Swan and Jerome, "Indigenous Knowledge," 31–54.
38 Havard, *Histoire des coureurs de bois*, 590–1. Perhaps most famously, Anishinaabeg bestowed the name "Metaminens" upon Nicolas Perrot, which meant "homme aux jambes de fer," or "the man with the iron legs," to signify the important role that he played as a peacemaker and diplomat between the various Indigenous peoples of the pays d'en haut and the Upper Mississippi valley. *DCB*, 2:518.
39 Carson, "Brébeuf Was Never Martyred," 230–1.
40 Lacombe, *Dictionnaire de la langue des Cris*, 588.
41 Léonard, *Mémoire des noms de lieux*, 538–9.
42 HBCA, B.198/a/10, Tomison, "Observations of a Journey Inland."
43 Cocking, *Journal of Matthew Cocking*, 118.
44 SHSB, VCD, Jérôme dit Latour, François, 3 July 1756, accessed 20 March 2019, https://archivesshsb.mb.ca/en/permalink/voyageurs67940.
45 SHSB, VCD, Saint-Michel, Gabriel, 7 June 1757, accessed 20 March 2019 https://archivesshsb.mb.ca/en/permalink/voyageurs56477; SHSB, VCD, Beaunoyer, Joseph, 9 June 1757, accessed 20 March 2019, https://archivesshsb.mb.ca/en/permalink/voyageurs56479.
46 Englebert and St-Onge, "Paddling into History," 79–85.
47 Lart, "Fur-Trade Returns," 353.
48 Carver, *The Journals of Jonathan Carver and Related Documents*, 132.
49 Ibid., 197–8.

50 Ibid., 197.

51 Wallace, *Pedlars from Quebec*, 5–8, 11; Thistle, *Indian-European Trade Relations*, 26; Campbell, *The North West Company*, 7; Rumilly, *La compagnie du Nord-Ouest*, 65–6, 71; Wallace, *Documents Relating to the North West Company*, 3.

52 HBCA, B.239/a/61, William Pink, "William Pink's In Land Journal 1768 & 9."

53 HBCA, B.239/b/29, Moses Norton, York Factory correspondence book, 1767–68.

54 Kehoe, "Aboriginal Pottery from Site Fhna-3," 18–21; Kehoe, "Ethnicity at a Pedlar's Post in Saskatchewan," 52–60; Kehoe and Meyer, *François' House*.

55 Thistle, *Indian-European Trade Relations*, 26–7; Innis, *Fur Trade in Canada*, 189; Morton, *History of the Canadian West*, 280–1.

56 For Jérôme's nephew Pierre, see Swan and Jerome, "Indigenous Knowledge," 51–2. For the voyageur contract, see SHSB, VCD, Jerome, Pierre, 21 March 1769, accessed 20 March 2019, https://archivesshsb.mb.ca/en/permalink/voyageurs55308.

57 No further contracts for Pierre Jérôme exist, but the kinship and parish-based organization of the fur trade suggests that he would have joined his uncle. Pierre Jérôme ended his career as an interpreter at Fort Edmonton (Fort-des-Prairies) and then Fort Carlton, both on the North Saskatchewan River, which suggests that he did achieve some success in the fur trade in the Saskatchewan region. Swan and Jerome, "Indigenous Knowledge," 52.

58 Ibid.

59 Brown, *An Ethnohistorian in Rupert's Land*, 137–8; Thistle, "The Twatt Family," 83.

60 Greer, *Peasant, Lord, and Merchant*, 193, 227; Englebert and St-Onge, "Paddling into History," 85–92.

61 HBCA, B.49/a/1, fol.10, Samuel Hearne, Cumberland House post journal, 9 October 1774.

62 HBCA, B.49/a/1, fol.10v, Samuel Hearne, Cumberland House post journal, 11 October 1774.

63 HBCA, B.49/a/1, fol.10, Samuel Hearne, Cumberland House post journal, 9 October 1774.

64 I describe the encounter between Matthew Cocking and François Jérôme in the introduction.

65 DuVal, *Native Ground*, 70, 72, 90.

66 HBCA, B.49/a/1, fol.10, Samuel Hearne, Cumberland House post journal, 9 October 1774.

67 Wallace, *Documents Relating to the North West Company*, 44–5.

68 HBCA, B.3/a/71, Thomas Hutchins, Fort Albany post journal, 5 July 1776.

69 Ibid.

70 Van Kirk, *Many Tender Ties*, 11; Brown, *Strangers in Blood*, 24–5, 30–1; Carlos and Nicholas, "Agency Problems in Early Chartered Companies," 855–6.

71 The average number of voyageurs engaged to work in the Hudson Bay watershed per year when La Vérendrye was commandant (1731–43) was calculated using the Voyageur Contracts Database to find the sum of contracts for the Western Posts between 1731 and 1742 and then dividing that number by twelve. Nicole St-Onge and Robert Englebert, "Voyageur Contracts Database," Société historique de Saint-Boniface, accessed 2 November 2021, https://archivesshsb.mb.ca/en.

72 LAC, MG21–Add.MSS.–21759/fol.13, Haldimand papers, letters and drafts relating to the Upper Posts, 1778–82, "Memorial of the merchants and traders from Montreal to the Great Carrying Place on Lake Superior and the Interior Country commonly named the North or Mer de l'Ouest," 11 May 1780.

73 HBCA, A.11/74, fol.175, William Tomison, York Factory, 24 August 1786.

74 HBCA, B.198/a/10, William Tomison, "Observations of a Journey Inland to the Great Lake Performed by William Tomison Steward at Severn House Mr. Andrew Graham Master from June 16th, 1767 to June 30th, 1768," 3 September 1767.

75 HBCA, B.239/a/57, Ferdinand Jacobs, York Factory post journal, 21 June 1768.

76 HBCA, B.239/a/57, Ferdinand Jacobs, York Factory post journal, 26 June 1768.

77 HBCA, B.239/a/57, Ferdinand Jacobs, York Factory post journal, 27 June 1768.

78 HBCA, B.49/a/7, Joseph Hanson, Cumberland House post journal, 2 July 1778.

79 HBCA, B.49/a/1, Samuel Hearne, Cumberland House post journal, 23 June 1775.

80 Morse, *Fur Trade Canoe Routes of Canada*, 75–9.

81 For the founding of the North West Company in 1779 and its subsequent reorganizations in 1783 and 1787, see Rumilly, *La compagnie*

du Nord-Ouest, 90–3, 100–5; Wallace, *Pedlars from Quebec*, 29–30; Wallace, *Documents Relating to the North West Company*, 15–29.

82 St-Onge and Podruchny, "Scuttling along a Spider's Web," 61–2, 68–9.

83 Englebert, "Merchant Representatives," 63. See also Englebert, "Beyond Borders."

84 St-Onge and Podruchny, "Scuttling along a Spider's Web," 64–70; Murphy, "Women, Networks, and Colonization," 230–64.

85 For a good historiographical discussion of French change and continuity in western North America following the 1763 Treaty of Paris, see Englebert, "Beyond Borders," 12–19.

86 HBCA, B.49/a/4, William Walker, Cumberland House post journal, 15 July 1776.

87 HBCA, B.49/a/7, Humphrey Martin, York Factory post journal, 4 August 1778.

88 Henry the Elder, *Alexander Henry's Travels and Adventures*, 245.

89 HBCA, B.239/b/38, fol.22–22v, Humphrey Marten, York Factory correspondence book, 1778–79.

90 HBCA, B.87/a/1, fol.7v–8, Robert Longmoor, Hudson House post journal, 18 December 1778.

91 Thistle, *Indian-European Trade Relations*, 25.

92 Rich, *The History of the Hudson's Bay Company*, 2:37.

93 For a historical outline of the "Plains Métis," see Ens and Sawchuk, *From New Peoples to New Nations*, 51–5.

94 HBCA B.198/b/1, Humphrey Marten, Severn House correspondence book, 26 October 1759; HBCA, B.239/a/46, Humphrey Marten, York Factory post journal, 21–29 June 1759; HBCA, B.239/b/18, Ferdinand Jacobs, Prince of Wales Fort, 16 July 1759; HBCA, B.239/b/18, Humphrey Marten, York Factory correspondence book, 6 August 1759; HBCA, A.11/3.fol.43, Robert Temple and Council to London Committee, Fort Albany, 8 September 1760. For secondary sources discussing Jean-Baptiste Desjarlais's employment with the HBC, see Rich, *History of the Hudson's Bay Company*, 2:1–2; Brown, *Strangers in Blood*, xii; Stephen, "A Puzzle Revisited," 39; Stephen, "Masters and Servants," 190.

95 *DCB*, 4:647; Thistle, *Indian-European Trade Relations*, 26.

96 SHSB, VCD, Primot, Louis, 20 May 1749, https://archivesshsb.mb.ca/en/permalink/voyageurs48638 (accessed 5 November 2019).

97 HBCA, B.239/a/53, Ferdinand Jacobs, York Factory post journal, 22 June 1766.

98 Havard, *Histoire des coureurs de bois*, 590–1.

99 HBCA, B.239/a/53, Ferdinand Jacobs, York Factory post journal, 22 June 1766.
100 Ibid.
101 White, "To Ensure that He Not Give Himself Over to the Indians," 111–12, 134–5, 145, 148.
102 However, some HBC factors and officers harboured Native women in their private quarters in contradiction of official company policy. See Brown, *Strangers in Blood*, 21–2; Van Kirk, *Many Tender Ties*, 37–8; Stephen, "Masters and Servants," 96, 157–61.
103 White, "To Ensure that He Not Give Himself Over to the Indians," 120, 145.
104 HBCA, B.239/a/53, Ferdinand Jacobs, York Factory post journal, 22 June 1766.
105 Stephen, "Masters and Servants," 248–9.
106 HBCA, B.239/a/54, Andrew Graham, York Factory post journal, 2 July 1766.
107 HBCA, B.239/a/54, Andrew Graham, York Factory post journal, 6 July 1766.
108 HBCA, B.239/a/65, Ferdinand Jacobs, York Factory post journal, 7 July 1771.
109 HBCA, B.239/a/57, Ferdinand Jacobs, York Factory post journal, 3 July 1768.
110 Cocking, *Journal of Matthew Cocking*, 115.
111 Rich, *History of the Hudson's Bay Company*, 2:30.
112 Ibid., 37.
113 Cocking, *Journal of Matthew Cocking*, 119.
114 HBCA, B.239/a/68, Andrew Graham, York Factory post journal, 18 June 1773.
115 HBCA, B.49/a/1, fol.11–11v, Andrew Graham, York Factory post journal, 11 September 1774.
116 The year 1815 marked the first time the HBC hired Canadien voyageurs out of Montreal en masse, which differed significantly with the HBC's earlier practices of hiring Scottish Orkneymen as the company's primary source of labour. The HBC's decision to hire Canadiens out of Montreal for expeditions to the Athabasca Country to compete against the NWC stemmed from the recommendation of Colin Robertson, a company official, in 1810. Englebert, "Diverging Identities and Converging Interests," 18–19, 23.
117 HBCA, B.239/b/34, Ferdinand Jacobs, York Factory correspondence book, 1773–74.

118 HBCA, B.239/b/34, Matthew Cocking, York Factory correspondence book, 1773–74.

119 Tyrrell, *Journals of Samuel Hearne and Philip Turnor*, 252.

120 HBCA, B.49/a/1, fol.10, Samuel Hearne, Cumberland House post journal, 9 October 1774.

121 HBCA, B.42/a/87, fol.61v, Moses Norton, Churchill post journal, 12 July 1773.

122 HBCA, B.239/b/35, fol.13, Andrew Graham, York Factory correspondence book, 1773–74.

123 Louis Primeau was not the first company employee to desert the HBC and go into the service of the Montreal pedlars. Numerous company employees, both British and French, such as Isaac Batt, David Thompson, and Edward Umfreville, would join the ranks of Montreal-based traders. Giraud, *Métis in the Canadian West*, 169.

124 HBCA, G.2/32, Philip Turnor, "Map of Hudson's Bay and the Rivers and Lakes Between the Atlantick and Pacifick Oceans," 1794.

125 Tyrrell, *Journals of Samuel Hearne and Philip Turnor*, 353–4.

126 Tyrrell, *Journals of Samuel Hearne and Philip Turnor*, 106; Giraud, *Métis in the Canadian West*, 188; Wallace, *Pedlars from Quebec*, 13; Rumilly, *La compagnie du Nord-Ouest*, 70–1, 74, 86.

127 Fenn, *Pox Americana*; Hackett, *A Very Remarkable Sickness*, 93–118.

128 HBCA, B.239/b/42, Matthew Cocking, York Factory correspondence book, August 1782.

129 HBCA, B.78/a/7, John Kipling, Gloucester House post journal, 22 June 1782.

130 HBCA, B.198/a/28, William Falconer, Severn House post journal, 14 April 1783.

131 HBCA, B.239/b/42, Matthew Cocking, York Factory correspondence book, August 1782.

132 HBCA, B.239/b/42, William Falconer, York Factory correspondence book, 12 August 1782.

133 For a discussion of the effects of the 1775–82 smallpox epidemic on the Hudson Bay watershed and the northern Great Plains, see Peers, *Ojibwa of Western Canada*, 14–21; Sundstrom, "Smallpox Used Them Up"; Lytwyn, "God Was Angry with Their Country"; Fenn, *Pox Americana*, 167–223; Hackett, *A Very Remarkable Sickness*, 93–118; Calloway, *One Vast Winter Count*, 415–25; Fenn, *Encounters at the Heart of the World*, 154–73; Havard, *Histoire des coureurs de bois*, 732; Waiser, *A World We Have Lost*, 218–21.

134 Meyer and Thistle, "Saskatchewan River Rendezvous," 421, 426.
135 Moreau, *Writings of David Thompson*, 1:119.
136 Franklin, *Narrative of a Journey*, 50–1.
137 Meyer and Russell, "Through the Woods Whare Thare Ware Now Track Ways," 169.
138 Meyer and Russell, "The Pegogamaw Crees," 307.
139 Donald Gunn, "Peguis Vindicated," *Nor'Wester*, 28 April 1860. Quoted in Peers, *Ojibwa of Western Canada*, 21.
140 For Ojibwe movement following the smallpox epidemic, see Peers, *Ojibwa of Western Canada*, 18–21.
141 Ens and Sawchuk, *From New Peoples to New Nations*, 42.
142 Waiser, *A World We Have Lost*, 197.
143 On a personal note, my own Métis family traces one of its branches to the marriage between a Canadien voyageur named Toussaint Berthelet *dit* Savoyard (1780–1866) and an Ojibwe woman named Marguerite Sauteuse. Similarly, Métis historian Heather Devine's extensively studied Desjarlais family also originates with a marriage between Joseph Desjarlais (1754–1833) and an influential (possibly widowed) Ojibwe woman named Okimaskwew in 1783. For the Berthelet (or Berthelette) family, see "Toussaint Berthelet dit Savoyard (1780–1866), Marguerite Sauteuse (1776–?)," Red River Ancestry.ca, last modified 26 June 2017, https://www.redriverancestry.ca/BERTHELET-TOUSSAINT-1780.php. For the Desjarlais family, see Devine, *The People Who Own Themselves*, 3, 76–81; Devine, "Les Desjarlais," 157.
144 The Métis community of Île-à-la-Crosse is tied to one of the most important and influential families in Métis history, the Riels. Île-à-la-Crosse was also the birthplace of Louis Riel Sr. (1817–1864) and is the burial place of Marguerite Riel (sister of Louis Riel). See Longpré, *Ile-a-la-Crosse*.
145 Waiser, *A World We Have Lost*, 241–2; Devine, *The People Who Own Themselves*, 131–3.
146 DCB, 4:647.
147 Friesen, *The Canadian Prairies*, 59, 81.
148 Macdougall, *One of the Family*, 4, 34, 37.
149 Franklin, *Narrative of a Journey to the Shores of the Polar Sea*, 43, 47, 59–60, 76–7, 104–5, 115–16, 144.
150 Sprague and Frye, *The Genealogy of the First Metis Nation*, table 1, no. 3980.

151 Brown, *Strangers in Blood*, 62–3; Mandelbaum, *The Plains Cree*, 146–8, 294; Morantz, "Economic and Social Accommodations," 68–9.

152 Morice, *Dictionnaire historique des canadiens et des métis français de l'ouest*, 234.

153 Binnema and Ens, *The Hudson's Bay Company Edmonton House Journals*, 67.

154 MacLeod and Morton, *Cuthbert Grant of Grantown*; Sawchuk, *The Métis of Manitoba*; Giraud, *Métis in the Canadian West*, 477–81, 594–6; Friesen, *Canadian Prairies*, 77–9; Dick, "The Seven Oaks Incident," 91–113; Coutts and Stuart, *The Forks and the Battle of Seven Oaks*; Barkwell, *The Battle of Seven Oaks*; Bumsted, *Fur Trade Wars*, 133–52; Havard, *Histoire des coureurs de bois*, 738–43; Ens and Sawchuk, *From New Peoples to New Nations*, 71–91.

155 Macdougall, *One of the Family*, 17–20.

156 Swan, "Crucible," 173–4, 204, 219, 329, 334, 338.

157 For the formation of the Comité national des Métis (whose members elected Louis Riel as their secretary) and the prevention of Canadian land-survey parties from Ontario from entering the Red River Colony, see Ens and Sawchuk, *From New Peoples to New Nations*, 100–1. For Primeau's biography and likely participation at "La Barrière" in St Norbert parish in October 1869, see Lawrence J. Barkwell, "Primeau (Primot), Jean-Baptiste (1841–c. 1899)," Virtual Museum of Métis History and Culture, Gabriel Dumont Institute of Native Studies and Applied Research, accessed 20 June 2019, http://www.metismuseum.ca/resource.php/149213.

158 For Jacqueline Peterson's changing position, see Peterson, "Many Roads to Red River," 39, 64; Peterson, "Red River Redux," 26–7, 30.

EPILOGUE

1 HBCA, B.27/a/11, John Peter Pruden, Carlton House post journal, 28 November 1821.

2 Masson, *Les Bourgeois de la Compagnie du Nord-Ouest*, 63, 397.

3 Swan and Jerome, "Indigenous Knowledge," 52.

4 *St Ann's Centennial: 100 Years of Faith, Turtle Mountain Indian Reservation, Belcourt, North Dakota, 1885–1985* (Belcourt, ND: St Ann's Church, 1985), 385.

5 Coues, *New Light on the Early History*, 545, 554, 584, 587, 599.

6 Ibid., 555, 603.

7 Rich and Fleming, *Colin Robertson's Correspondence Book*, 194.
8 Swan and Jerome, "Indigenous Knowledge," 52.
9 Mapp, "Atlantic History from Imperial, Continental, and Pacific Perspectives."
10 Anderson, *Crucible of War*, 407. For the end of the Seven Years' War, see Crouch, *Nobility Lost*, 38–125; Dechêne, *Le peuple, l'État et la guerre au Canada*, 397–428; McDonnell, *Masters of Empire*, 160–97; White, *Middle Ground*, 223–68.
11 Crouch, *Nobility Lost*, 124–8.
12 DCB, 6:398; Swan, "The Crucible," 78–9, 321–2; Swan and Jerome, "Indigenous Knowledge," 52–3.
13 For a description of the Red River Colony in the 1820s, see Friesen, *Canadian Prairies*, 89–90; Macdougall and St-Onge, "Rooted in Mobility," 23, 25, 35.

APPENDIX

1 For a historical outline of the "Plains Métis," see Ens and Sawchuk, *From New Peoples to New Nations*, 51–5.
2 Teillet, *The North-West Is Our Mother*, 109, 134, 183; Ens and Sawchuk, *From New Peoples to New Nations*, 58–9.
3 Brown, *Strangers in Blood*, 52–8.
4 Ibid., 21–2, 52–7, 60–1; Van Kirk, *Many Tender Ties*, 37–8, 41–6; Ens and Sawchuk, *From New Peoples to New Nations*, 55–9; Stephen, *Masters and Servants*, 127, 255–7, 263.
5 For a fur trade lexicon, including the meaning of *en dérouine*, see Podruchny, *Making the Voyageur World*, 201–3.
6 Devine, *The People Who Own Themselves*, 136–8; Devine, "Les Desjarlais," 136, 139, 149–50; Thistle, "The Twatt Family," 77–80.
7 Brown, *Strangers in Blood*, 163–8, 204–5.
8 Brown, "Woman as Centre and Symbol in the Emergence of Metis Communities," 40–1; Brown, *Strangers in Blood*, 73–4, 77–8, 151.
9 McLean, *Home from the Hill*, 48; Coates and Morrison, *The Forgotten North*, 28; Waiser, *A World We Have Lost*, 335–6.
10 Brown, *Strangers in Blood*, 77, 109.
11 Pannekoek, *A Snug Little Flock*, 18, 33; Macdougall and St-Onge, "Rooted in Mobility," 27–8; Pigeon, "Au nom du Bon Dieu," 27–8; Brown, *Strangers in Blood*, 173; Spry, "The Métis and Mixed-Bloods," 95–118.

Bibliography

ARCHIVAL SOURCES

Archives nationales d'outre-mer, Aix-en-Provence, France (ANOM)

Série B: Correspondance générale: dépêches du roi, du ministre de la Marine et du Conseil d'État aux administrateurs des colonies

Série C11A: Correspondance générale: lettres, mémoires, etc., envoyés en France par les administrateurs du Canada et autres personnes

Série C13A: Correspondance à l'arrivée en provenance de la Louisiane

Série C11E: Correspondance générale, des limites et des postes

Série C11G: Canada et divers

Série F3: Collection Moreau de Saint-Méry

Bibliothèque et Archives nationales du Québec (BAnQ)

Archives des notaires du Québec des origines à 1934

Fonds Archives de la marine (France)

TP1, Fonds Conseil souverain

TL4, Fonds Juridiction royale de Montréal

Bibliothèque nationale de France (BnF), Paris, France

Département des cartes et plans

Hudson's Bay Company Archives (HBCA), Provincial Archives of Manitoba, Winnipeg, MB

Albany, B.3
Carlton House, B.27
Churchill, B.42
Cumberland House, B.49
Gloucester House, B.78
Hudson's Bay Company Manuscript Maps Collection
Moose Factory, B.135
Red River Settlement census returns sent to the governor and Committee, 1827–43, E.5/1–11
Severn, B.198
Upper Hudson House, B.87
York Factory, B.239

John Carter Brown Library, Providence, RI

John Carter Brown Library Map Collection

Library and Archives Canada, Ottawa

Collection Pierre Gaultier de La Vérendrye
Haldimand papers
Fonds Viger-Verreau

Newberry Library, Chicago, IL

Edward E. Ayer Collection

Société historique de Saint-Boniface, Winnipeg, MB

Voyageur Contracts Database

Université de Montréal, Montreal, QC

Programme de recherche en démographie historique (PRDH)

University of Manitoba, Winnipeg, MB

Elizabeth Dafoe Library and Archives and Special Collections

Western Michigan University, Archives and Regional History Collections, Kalamazoo, MI

French Michilimackinac Research Project Collection

PRINTED SOURCES

Allain, Mathé. *"Not Worth a Straw": French Colonial Policy and the Early Years of Louisiana*. Lafayette: Center for Louisiana Studies, University of Southwestern Louisiana, 1988.

Allaire, Bernard. "The Occupation of Quebec by the Kirke Brothers." In *Champlain: The Birth of French America*, edited by Raymonde Litalien and Denis Vaugeois, translated by Kathe Roth, 245–57. Montreal and Kingston: McGill-Queen's University Press, 2004.

– *La rumeur dorée, Roberval et l'Amérique*. Montreal: Les Éditions La Presse, 2013.

Allaire, Gratien. "Les engagements pour la traite des fourrures." *Revue d'histoire de l'Amérique française* 34, no. 1 (1980): 3–26.

– "Fur Trade Engagés, 1701–1745." In *Rendezvous: Selected Papers of the Fourth North American Fur Trade Conference, 1981*, edited by Thomas C. Buckley, 15–26. St Paul, MN: North American Fur Trade Conference, 1984.

– "Officiers et marchands: Les sociétés de commerce des fourrures, 1715–1760." *Revue d'histoire de l'Amérique française* 40, no. 3 (1987): 409–28.

Andersen, Chris. "From Nation to Population: The Racialisation of 'Métis' in the Canadian Census." *Nations and Nationalism* 14, no. 2 (2008): 347–68.

– *"Métis": Race, Recognition, and the Struggle for Indigenous Peoplehood*. Vancouver: UBC Press, 2014.

– "*Moya 'Tipimsook* ('The People Who Aren't Their Own Bosses'): Racialization and the Misrecognition of 'Métis' in Upper Great Lakes Ethnohistory." *Ethnohistory* 58, no. 1 (2011): 37–63.

Anderson, Dean L. "The Flow of European Trade Goods into the Western Great Lakes Region, 1715–1760." In *Rethinking the Fur Trade:*

Cultures of Exchange in an Atlantic World, edited by Susan Sleeper-Smith, 385–410. Lincoln: University of Nebraska Press, 2009.

Anderson, Fred. *Crucible of War: The Seven Years' War and the Fate of Empire in British North America, 1754–1766*. New York: Vintage, 2000.

Anderson, Gary Clayton. "French-Indian Relations in the Far West: The Sioux Trade: 1650–1755." *Proceedings of the Meeting of the French Colonial Historical Society* 8 (1985): 104–12.

– *Kinsmen of Another Kind: Dakota-White Relations in the Upper Mississippi Valley, 1650–1862*. Lincoln: University of Nebraska Press, 1984.

Anderson, Karen L. *Chain Her by One Foot: The Subjugation of Women in Seventeenth-Century New France*. London: Routledge, 1991.

Aubert, Guillaume. "'The Blood of France': Race and Purity of Blood in the French Atlantic World." *William and Mary Quarterly* 61, no. 3 (2004): 439–78.

Augeron, Mickaël, John de Bry, and Annick Notter. *Floride, un rêve français (1562–1565)*. La Rochelle: Musée du Nouveau Monde, 2012.

Axtell, James. *The European and the Indian: Essays in the Ethnohistory of Colonial North America*. New York: Oxford University Press, 1981.

– *The Invasion Within: The Contest of Cultures in Colonial North America*. New York: Oxford University Press, 1985.

Axtell, James, and William C. Sturtevant. "The Unkindest Cut, or Who Invented Scalping?" *William and Mary Quarterly* 37, no. 3 (1980): 451–72.

Balvay, Arnaud. *L'épée et la plume: Amérindiens et soldats des Troupes de la Marine en Louisiane et au Pays d'en haut (1683–1763)*. Quebec: Presses Université Laval, 2006.

– "Tattooing and Its Role in French–Native American Relations in the Eighteenth Century." *French Colonial History* 9, no. 1 (2008): 1–14.

Banks, Kenneth J. *Chasing Empire across the Sea: Communications and the State in the French Atlantic, 1713–1763*. Montreal and Kingston: McGill-Queen's University Press, 2002.

– "Communications and 'Imperial Overstretch': Lessons from the Eighteenth-Century French Atlantic." *French Colonial History* 6 (2005): 17–32.

Barbiche, Bernard. "Henri IV and the World Overseas: A Decisive Time in the History of New France." In *Champlain: The Birth of French America*, edited by Raymonde Litalien and Denis Vaugeois, translated by Kathe Roth, 24–32. Montreal and Kingston: McGill-Queen's University Press, 2004.

Barkwell, Lawrence J. *The Battle of Seven Oaks: A Metis Perspective.* 2nd ed. Winnipeg: Louis Riel Institute, 2015.

Barman, Jean. *French Canadians, Furs, and Indigenous Women in the Making of the Pacific Northwest.* Vancouver: UBC Press, 2014.

– *Iroquois in the West.* Montreal and Kingston: McGill-Queen's University Press, 2019.

Barr, Juliana. *Peace Came in the Form of a Woman: Indians and Spaniards in the Texas Borderlands.* Chapel Hill: University of North Carolina Press, 2007.

Barr, Juliana, and Edward Countryman. *Contested Spaces of Early America.* Philadelphia: University of Pennsylvania Press, 2014.

Beaulieu, Alain. "The Birth of the Franco-American Alliance." In *Champlain: The Birth of French America*, edited by Raymonde Litalien and Denis Vaugeois, translated by Kathe Roth, 153–62. Montreal and Kingston: McGill-Queen's University Press, 2004.

– *Convertir les fils de Caïn: Jésuites et amérindiens nomades en Nouvelle-France, 1632–1642.* Quebec: Nuit Blanche, 1994.

– "Ne faire qu'un seul peuple?: Iroquois et Français à 'l'âge héroïque' de la Nouvelle-France (1600–1660)." PhD dissertation, Université Laval, 1993.

Beik, William. *Absolutism and Society in Seventeenth-Century France: State Power and Provincial Aristocracy in Languedoc.* Cambridge: Cambridge University Press, 1985.

– "Review Article: The Absolutism of Louis XIV as Social Collaboration." *Past and Present* 188 (2005): 195–224.

Bellfy, Phil. *Three Fires Unity: The Anishnaabeg of the Lake Huron Borderlands.* Lincoln: University of Nebraska Press, 2011.

Belmessous, Saliha. *Assimilation and Empire: Uniformity in French and British Colonies, 1541–1954.* Oxford: Oxford University Press, 2013.

– "Assimilation and Racialism in Seventeenth and Eighteen-Century French Colonial Policy." *American Historical Review* 110, no. 2 (2005): 322–49.

Belyea, Barbara, ed. *A Year Inland: The Journal of a Hudson's Bay Company Winterer.* Waterloo, ON: Wilfrid Laurier University Press, 2000.

Berlin, Ira. *Many Thousands Gone: The First Two Centuries of Slavery in North America.* Cambridge, MA: Belknap Press of Harvard University Press, 1998.

Berthelette, Scott. "'*Frères et Enfants du même Père*': The French Illusion of Empire West of the Great Lakes, 1731–1743." *Early American Studies* 14, no. 1 (2016): 174–98.

– "New France and the Hudson Bay Watershed: Transatlantic Networks, Backcountry Specialists, and French Imperial Projects in post-Utrecht North America, 1713–1729." *Canadian Historical Review* 101, no. 1 (2020): 1–26.

Biggar, H.P. *The Works of Samuel de Champlain: 1599–1632*. 7 vols. Toronto: Champlain Society, 1922–36.

Binnema, Ted. "Allegiances and Interests: Niitsitapi (Blackfoot) Trade, Diplomacy, and Warfare, 1806–1831." *Western Historical Quarterly* 37, no. 3 (2006): 327–49.

– *Common and Contested Ground: A Human and Environmental History of the Northwestern Plains*. Norman: University of Oklahoma Press, 2001.

– "A Fur Trade Historian's View of Seasonal Bison Movements on the Northern Plains." In *Bison and People on the North American Great Plains: A Deep Environmental History*, edited by Geoff Cunfer and Bill Waiser, 157–77. Texas A&M University Press, 2016.

Binnema, Ted, and William A. Dobak. "'Like the Greedy Wolf': The Blackfeet, the St Louis Fur Trade, and War Fever, 1807–1831." *Journal of the Early Republic* 29, no. 3 (2009): 411–40.

Binnema, Ted, and Gerhard J. Ens. *The Hudson's Bay Company Edmonton House Journals, Correspondence, and Reports, 1806–1821*. Calgary: Alberta Records Publication Board, Historical Society of Alberta, 2012.

Bird, Louis. *Telling Our Stories: Omushkego Legends and Histories from Hudson Bay*. Peterborough, ON: Broadview Press, 2005.

Bishop, Charles A. "Northern Algonquians, 1550–1760." In *Aboriginal Ontario: Historical Perspectives on the First Nations*, edited by Edward S. Rogers and Donald B. Smith, 275–88. Toronto: Dundurn Press, 1994.

– *The Northern Ojibwa and the Fur Trade: An Historical and Ecological Study*. Toronto: Holt, Rinehart and Winston, 1974.

Bishop, Charles A., and Victor P. Lytwyn. "Barbarism and Ardour of War from the Tenderest Years: Cree-Inuit Warfare in the Hudson Bay Region." In *North American Indigenous Warfare and Ritual Violence*, edited by Richard J. Chacon and Rubén G. Mendoza, 30–57. Tucson: University of Arizona Press, 2007.

Blackburn, Carole. *Harvest of Souls: The Jesuit Missions and Colonialism in North America, 1632–1650*. Montreal and Kingston: McGill-Queen's University Press, 2000.

Blair, Emma Helen. *The Indian Tribes of the Upper Mississippi Valley and Region of the Great Lakes as Described by Nicolas Perrot,*

French Commandant in the Northwest; Bacqueville de la Potherie, French Royal Commissioner to Canada; Morrell Marston, American Army Officer; and Thomas Forsyth, United States Agent at Fort Armstrong. 2 vols. Cleveland, OH: Arthur H. Clark, 1911.

Bohaker, Heidi. "Anishinaabe Toodaims: Contexts for Politics, Kinship, and Identity in the Eastern Great Lakes." In *Gathering Places: Aboriginal and Fur Trade Histories*, edited by Carolyn Podruchny and Laura Peers, 93–118. Vancouver: UBC Press, 2010.

– *Doodem and Council Fire: Anishinaabe Governance through Alliance*. Toronto: University of Toronto Press, 2020.

– "Nindoodemag: The Significance of Algonquian Kinship Networks in the Eastern Great Lakes Region, 1600–1701." *William and Mary Quarterly* 63, no. 1 (2006): 23–52.

– "Reading Anishinaabe Identities: Meaning and Metaphor in Nindoodem Pictographs." *Ethnohistory* 57, no. 1 (2010): 11–33.

Bohr, Roland. *Gifts from the Thunder Beings: Indigenous Archery and European Firearms in the Northern Plains and Central Subarctic, 1670–1870*. Lincoln: University of Nebraska Press, 2014.

Borins, Edward H. "La Compagnie du Nord, 1682–1700." Master's thesis, McGill University, 1968.

Bosher, J.F. *The Canada Merchants, 1713–1763*. New York: Oxford University Press, 1987.

Boucher, Philip P. *France and the American Tropics to 1700: Tropics of Discontent?* Baltimore: Johns Hopkins University Press, 2008.

– *Les Nouvelles Frances: France in America, 1500–1815: An Imperial Perspective*. Providence, RI: John Carter Brown Library, 1989.

Bougainville, Louis Antoine de. *Ecrits sur le Canada: Mémoire – Journal – Lettres*. Sillery, QC: Les éditions du Septentrion, 2003.

Bourrie, Mark. *Bush Runner: The Adventures of Pierre-Esprit Radisson*. Windsor, ON: Biblioasis, 2019.

Branch, Jordan. *The Cartographic State: Maps, Territory, and the Origins of Sovereignty*. Cambridge: Cambridge University Press, 2013.

Brandão, José António. *Your Fyre Shall Burn No More: Iroquois Policy toward New France and Its Native Allies to 1701*. Lincoln: University of Nebraska Press, 2000.

Brewer, John. *The Sinews of Power: War, Money, and the English State, 1688–1783*. Cambridge, MA: Harvard University Press, 1990.

Brooks, James F. *Captives and Cousins: Slavery, Kinship, and Community in the Southwest Borderlands*. Chapel Hill: University of North Carolina Press, 2002.

Brown, George W., Marcel Trudel, André Vachon, and David Hayne, eds. *Dictionary of Canadian Biography/Dictionnaire biographique du Canada*. Vols. 1–6. Toronto: University of Toronto Press; Quebec: Presses de l'Université Laval, 1966–87.

Brown, Jennifer S.H. *An Ethnohistorian in Rupert's Land: Unfinished Conversations*. Edmonton: Athabasca University Press, 2017.

– *Strangers in Blood: Fur Trade Company Families in Indian Country*. Vancouver: UBC Press, 1980.

– "Woman as Centre and Symbol in the Emergence of Metis Communities," *Canadian Journal of Native Studies* 3, no. 1 (1983): 39–46.

Brown, Jennifer S.H., and John S. Long. *Together We Survive: Ethnographic Intuitions, Friendships, and Conversations*. Montreal and Kingston: McGill-Queen's University Press, 2016.

Brown, Jennifer S.H., and Elizabeth Vibert. *Reading Beyond Words: Contexts for Native History*. Peterborough, ON: Broadview Press, 2003.

Brown, Margaret Kimball. "Allons, Cowboys!" *Journal of the Illinois State Historical Society* 76, no. 4 (1983): 273–82.

Buache, Philippe. *Considérations geographiques et physiques sur les nouvelles decouvertes au nord de la Grande Mer*. Paris: de l'Imprimerie de Ballard, 1753, 1755.

Bumsted, J.M. *Fur Trade Wars: The Founding of Western Canada*. Winnipeg: Great Plains, 1999.

– *Lord Selkirk: A Life*. Winnipeg: University of Manitoba Press, 2008.

Burkholder, Mark A., and Lyman L. Johnson. *Colonial Latin America*. 6th ed. New York: Oxford University Press, 2008.

Burley, Edith I. *Servants of the Honourable Company: Work, Discipline, and Conflict in the Hudson's Bay Company, 1770–1879*. New York: Oxford University Press, 1997.

Burpee, Lawrence J., ed. and trans. *Journals and Letters of Pierre Gaultier De Varennes De La Vérendrye and His Sons: With Correspondence between the Governors of Canada and the French Court, Touching the Search for the Western Sea*. Toronto: Champlain Society, 1927.

– *Pathfinders of the Great Plains: A Chronicle of La Vérendrye and His Sons*. Toronto: Glasgow, Brook, 1915.

Calloway, Colin G. *One Vast Winter Count: The Native American West before Lewis and Clark*. Lincoln: University of Nebraska Press, 2003.

– *The Scratch of a Pen: 1763 and the Transformation of North America*. New York: Oxford University Press, 2006.

Campbell, Marjorie Wilkins. *The North West Company*. Toronto: MacMillan, 1957.

Campbell, Peter R. *Power and Politics in Old Regime France*. London: Routledge, 1996.

Campbell, T.J. "Out of the Grave: The Discovery of Fort St Charles in 1908." *Bulletin of the Historical Society of St Boniface* 5, no. 3 (1915): 1–22.

Campeau, Lucien. *La mission des jésuites chez les Hurons, 1634–1650*. Montreal: Éditions Bellarmin, 1987.

Carayon, Céline. *Eloquence Embodied: Nonverbal Communication among French and Indigenous Peoples in the Americas*. Chapel Hill: University of North Carolina Press, 2019.

Carlos, Ann M., and Frank D. Lewis. *Commerce by a Frozen Sea: Native Americans and the European Fur Trade*. Philadelphia: University of Pennsylvania Press, 2010.

– "Indians, the Beaver, and the Bay: The Economics of Depletion in the Lands of the Hudson's Bay Company, 1700–1763." *Journal of Economic History* 53, no. 3 (1993): 465–94.

Carlos, Ann M., and Stephen Nicholas. "Agency Problems in Early Chartered Companies: The Case of the Hudson's Bay Company." *Journal of Economic History* 50, no. 4 (1990): 853–75.

Carpin, Gervais. "Migrations to New France in Champlain's Time." In *Champlain: The Birth of French America*, edited by Raymonde Litalien and Denis Vaugeois, translated by Kathe Roth, 163–79. Montreal and Kingston: McGill-Queen's University Press, 2004.

Carson, James Taylor. "Brébeuf Was Never Martyred: Reimagining the Life and Death of Canada's First Saint." *Canadian Historical Review* 97, no. 2 (2016): 222–43.

Carter, Sarah. *Aboriginal People and Colonizers of Western Canada to 1900*. Toronto: University of Toronto Press, 1999.

Carver, Jonathan. *The Journals of Jonathan Carver and Related Documents, 1766–1770*. Edited by John Parker. St Paul: Minnesota Historical Society Press, 1976.

Chalmers, George. *A Collection of Treaties between Great Britain and Other Powers*. London: J. Stockdale, 1790.

Champagne, Antoine. *Les La Vérendrye et Le Poste de l'Ouest*. Quebec: Les Presses de l'Université Laval, 1968.

– *Nouvelles Études sur Les La Vérendrye et le Poste de l'Ouest*. Quebec: Les Presses de l'Université Laval, 1971.

Charlevoix, Pierre François-Xavier de. *Journal of a Voyage to North-America.* 2 vols. London: Printed for R. and J. Dodsley, in Pall-Mall, 1761.

Clark, Emily. *Masterless Mistresses: The New Orleans Ursulines and the Development of a New World Society, 1727–1834.* Chapel Hill: University of North Carolina Press, 2007.

Cliche, Marie-Aimée. *Les Pratiques de Dévotion En Nouvelle-France: Comportements Populaires et Encadrement Ecclésial Dans Le Gouvernement de Québec.* Quebec: Les Presses de l'Université Laval, 1988.

Choquette, Leslie. *Frenchmen into Peasants: Modernity and Tradition in the Peopling of French Canada.* Cambridge, MA: Harvard University Press, 1997.

– "Proprietorships in French North America." In *Constructing Early Modern Empires: Proprietary Ventures in the Atlantic World, 1500–1750*, edited by Louis H. Roper and Bertrand Van Ruymbeke, 117–32. Leiden: Brill, 2007.

Coates, Colin M. *The Metamorphoses of Landscape and Community in Early Quebec.* Montreal and Kingston: McGill-Queen's University Press, 2000.

– "La mise en scène du pouvoir: La préséance en Nouvelle-France." *Bulletin d'histoire politique* 14, no. 1 (2005): 109–18.

Coates, Ken, and William R. Morrison. *The Forgotten North: A History of Canada's Provincial Norths.* Toronto: James Lorimer and Company, 1992.

Cocking, Matthew. *Journal of Matthew Cocking from York Factory to the Blackfeet Country, 1772–1773.* Edited by Lawrence J. Burpee. Ottawa: Royal Society of Canada, 1908.

Codignola, Luca. "Competing Networks: Roman Catholic Ecclesiastics in French North America, 1610–58." *Canadian Historical Review* 80, no. 4 (1999): 539–84.

Cohen, Paul. "Was There an Amerindian Atlantic? Reflections on the Limits of a Historiographical Concept." *History of European Ideas* 34, no. 4 (2008): 388–410.

Cole, George E. "Mining in Manitoba." *MHS Transactions* Series 3 (1948–49 season).

Collins, James B. *Classes, Estates, and Order in Early Modern Brittany.* Cambridge: Cambridge University Press, 1994.

– *The State in Early Modern France.* 2nd ed. Cambridge: Cambridge University Press, 2009.

Colpitts, George. *Pemmican Empire: Food, Trade, and the Last Bison Hunts in the North American Plains, 1780–1882*. New York: Cambridge University Press, 2014.

Combet, Denis. *In Search of the Western Sea: Selected Journals of La Vérendrye/À la recherche de la mer de l'Ouest: Mémoires choisis de La Vérendrye*. Winnipeg: Great Plains, 2001.

– "Récits de voyage du père Gonnor et de Le Gardeur de Saint-Pierre." *Cahiers franco-canadiens de l'Ouest* 10, no. 2 (1998): 301–32.

Conrad, Glenn R. "Administration of the Illinois Country: The French Debate." *Louisiana History: Journal of the Louisiana Historical Association* 36, no. 1 (1995): 31–53.

Cook, Peter. "Onontio Gives Birth: How the French in Canada Became Fathers to Their Indigenous Allies, 1645–73." *Canadian Historical Review* 96, no. 2 (2015): 165–93.

Cook, Ramsay. *The Voyages of Jacques Cartier*. Toronto: University of32799_MCGILL_BertheletteToronto Press, 1993.

Corbiere, Alan Ojiig. "Anishinaabe Treaty-Making in the 18th-and-19th-Century Northern Great Lakes: From Shared Meanings to Epistemological Chasms." PhD dissertation, York University, 2020.

Cosandey, Fanny, and Robert Descimon. *L'Absolutisme en France: histoire et historiographie*. Paris: Le Seuil, 2002.

Coues, Elliott, editor. *New Light on the Early History of the Greater Northwest: The Manuscript Journals of Alexander Henry, Fur Trader of the Northwest Company, and of David Thompson, Official Geographer and Explorer of the Same Company, 1799–1814*. New York: Francis P. Harper, 1897.

Courville, Serge. *Quebec: A Historical Geography*. Translated by Richard Howard. Vancouver: UBC Press, 2008.

Coutts, Robert and Richard Stuart. *The Forks and the Battle of Seven Oaks in Manitoba History, Part II: Reflections on the Battle of Seven Oaks*. Winnipeg: Manitoba Historical Society, 1994.

Crouch, Christian Ayne. *Nobility Lost: French and Canadian Martial Cultures, Indians and the End of New France*. Ithaca, NY: Cornell University Press, 2014.

Crouse, Nellis M. *La Verendrye, Fur Trader and Explorer*. Toronto: Ryerson Press, 1956.

Cunfer, Geoff, and Bill Waiser. *Bison and People on the North American Great Plains: A Deep Environmental History*. College Station: Texas A&M University Press, 2016.

Dangeau, Philippe de Courcillon, Marquis de. *Mémoire Du Marquis de Dangeau sur ce qui s'est passé dans la chambre du roi pendant sa maladie*. Paris: impr. de Firmin Didot frères, fils et cie, 1858.

Daschuk, James. *Clearing the Plains: Disease, Politics of Starvation, and the Loss of Aboriginal Life*. Regina: University of Regina Press, 2013.

Davies, K.G., and A.M. Johnson, eds. *Letters from Hudson Bay 1703–40*. London: Hudson's Bay Record Society, 1965.

D'Avignon, Mathieu. *Champlain et les fondateurs oubliés: Les figures du père et le mythe de la fondation*. Quebec: Presses de l'Université Laval, 2008.

Davis, Jeffrey E. *Hand Talk: Sign Language among American Indian Nations*. Cambridge: Cambridge University Press, 2010.

Dawdy, Shannon Lee. *Building the Devil's Empire: French Colonial New Orleans*. Chicago: University of Chicago Press, 2008.

Dawson, Nelson-Martin, and Charles Vincent. *L'atelier Delisle: l'Amerique du Nord sur la table à dessin*. Sillery, QC: Les éditions du Septentrion, 2000.

Dechêne, Louise. *Habitants and Merchants in Seventeenth Century Montreal*. Translated by Liana Vardi. Montreal and Kingston: McGill-Queen's University Press, 2007.

– *Le peuple, l'ètat et la guerre au Canada sous le régime français*. Montreal: Boréal, 2008.

Delâge, Denys. "L'alliance franco-amérindienne, 1660–1701." *Recherches amérindiennes au Québec* 19, no. 1 (1989): 3–15.

– *Bitter Feast: Amerindians and Europeans in Northeastern North America, 1600–64*. Translated by Jane Brierley. Vancouver: UBC Press, 1993.

– "Modèles coloniaux, métaphores familiales et changements de régime en Amérique du Nord, XVIIe–XIXe siècles." *Les Cahiers des dix* 60 (2006): 19–78.

– "Pontiac, une guerre d'indépendance." In *La fin de la Nouvelle-France*, edited by Bertrand Fonck and Laurent Veyssière, 313–34. Paris: Armand Colin, 2013.

– "Les Premières Nations et la Guerre de la Conquête (1754–1765)." *Les Cahiers des dix* 63 (2009): 1–67.

– "La religion dans l'alliance franco-amérindienne." *Anthropologie et Sociétés* 15, no. 1 (1991): 55–87.

Delanglez, Jean. "A Mirage: The Sea of the West (part II)." *Revue d'histoire de l'Amérique française* 1, no. 4 (1948): 541–68.

Demos, John. *The Unredeemed Captive: A Family Story from Early America*. New York: Alfred Knopf, 1994.
Denig, Edwin Thompson. *The Assiniboine*. Regina: Canadian Plains Research Centre, 2000.
– *Five Indian Tribes of the Upper Missouri*. Norman: University of Oklahoma Press, 1961.
Dépatie, Sylvie, Christian Dessureault, and Mario Lalancette. *Contributions à l'étude du régime seigneurial Canadien*. Montreal: Hurtubise HMH, 1987.
Derksen, Samuel. "Colonialism, Consumption, and Control: The Illinois Country Liquor Trade, 1750–1803." Master's thesis, University of Saskatchewan, 2017.
Desbarats, Catherine. "Following the 'Middle Ground.'" *William and Mary Quarterly* 63, no. 1 (2006): 81–96.
– "France in North America: The Net Burden of Empire during the First Half of the Eighteenth Century." *French History* 11, no. 1 (1997): 1–28.
Desbarats, Catherine, and Allan Greer. "Où est la Nouvelle-France." *Revue d'histoire de l'Amérique française* 64, nos. 3–4 (2011): 31–62.
Deschamps, Nicole. *Lettres au cher fils: Correspondance d'Elisabeth Bégon avec son gendre, 1748–1753*. Montreal: Les Éditions Hurtubise, 1972.
Deslandres, Dominique. *Croire et faire croire: Les missions françaises au XVIIe siècle, 1600–1650*. Paris: Fayard, 2003.
– "'Et loing de France, en l'une & l'autre mer, Les Fleurs de Liz, tu as fait renommer': Quelques hypothèses touchant la religion, le genre et l'expansion de la souveraineté française en Amérique aux xvie–xviiie siècles." *Revue d'histoire de l'Amérique française* 64, nos. 3–4 (2011): 93–117.
Desloges, Yvon. *À table en Nouvelle-France Alimentation populaire, gastronomie et traditions alimentaires dans la vallée laurentienne avant l'avènement des restaurants*. Sillery, QC: Les éditions du Septentrion, 2009.
Devine, Heather. "Les Desjarlais: The Development and Dispersion of a Proto-Métis Hunting Band." In *From Rupert's Land to Canada: Essays in Honour of John E. Foster*, edited by Theodore Binnema, Gerhard J. Ens, and Rod Macleod, 129–58. Edmonton: University of Alberta Press, 2001.
– *The People Who Own Themselves: Aboriginal Ethnogenesis in a Canadian Family, 1660–1900*. Calgary: University of Calgary Press, 2004.

DeVoto, Bernard. *The Course of Empire*. Boston: Houghton, Mifflin and Company, 1952.

Dewar, Helen. "Souveraineté dans les colonies, souveraineté en métropole: Le rôle de la Nouvelle-France dans la consolidation de l'autorité maritime en France, 1620–1628." *Revue d'Histoire de L'Amerique Française* 64, nos. 3–4 (2011): 63–92.

– "'Y establir nostre auctorité': Assertions of Imperial Sovereignty through Proprietorships and Chartered Companies in New France, 1598–1663." PhD dissertation, University of Toronto, 2012.

Dick, Lyle. "The Seven Oaks Incident and the Construction of a Historical Tradition, 1816 to 1970." *Canadian Historical Association/La Société historique du Canada* 2, no. 1 (1991): 91–113.

Doige, Gary Blake. "Warfare Patterns of the Assiniboine to 1809." Master's thesis, University of Manitoba, 1989.

Dolin, Eric Jay. *Fur, Fortune, and Empire: The Epic History of the Fur Trade in America*. New York: W.W. Norton and Company, 2010.

Dowd, Gregory Evans. *Groundless: Rumors, Legends, and Hoaxes on the Early American Frontier*. Baltimore: Johns Hopkins University Press, 2015.

– *War under Heaven: Pontiac, the Indian Nations, and the British Empire*. Baltimore: Johns Hopkins University Press, 2004.

Dubois, Laurent. *Avengers of the New World: The Story of the Haitian Revolution*. Cambridge, MA: Harvard University Press, 2004.

– *A Colony of Citizens: Revolution and Slave Emancipation in the French Caribbean, 1787–1804*. Chapel Hill: University of North Carolina Press, 2004.

– "The French Atlantic." In *Atlantic History: A Critical Appraisal*, edited by Jack P. Greene and Philip D. Morgan, 137–61. New York: Oxford University Press, 2009.

Dupilet, Alexandre, and Thierry Sarmant. "Polysynodie et gouvernement par conseil en France et en Europe du XVIIe au XIXe siècle." *Revue Histoire, économie et société* 26, no. 4 (2007): 51–65.

DuVal, Kathleen. "Indian Intermarriage and Métissage in Colonial Louisiana." *William and Mary Quarterly* 65, no. 2 (2008): 267–304.

– *The Native Ground: Indians and Colonists in the Heart of the Continent*. Philadelphia: University of Pennsylvania Press, 2006.

Eccles, W.J. *Canada under Louis XIV, 1663–1701*. Toronto: McClelland and Stewart, 1964.

– *The French in North America*. Rev. ed. Markham, ON: Fitzhenry and Whiteside, 1998.

– *Frontenac: The Courtier Governor*. Toronto: McClelland and Stewart, 1959.

– "The Social, Economic, and Political Significance of the Military Establishment in New France." *Canadian Historical Review* 52, no. 1 (1971): 1–22.

Edelson, S. Max. *The New Map of Empire: How Britain Imagined America before Independence*. Cambridge, MA: Harvard University Press, 2017.

Edmunds, David, and Joseph L. Peyser. *The Fox Wars: The Mesquakie Challenge to New France*. Norman: University of Oklahoma Press, 1993.

Ekberg, Carl J. *French Roots in the Illinois Country: The Mississippi Frontier in Colonial Times*. Urbana: University of Illinois Press, 1998.

– *Stealing Indian Women: Native Slavery in the Illinois Country*. Urbana: University of Illinois Press, 2007.

Elisabeth, Léo. *La Société Martiniquaise Aux XVIIe et XVIIIe Siècles, 1664–1789*. Paris: Éditions Kathala et SHM, 2003.

Elliott, J.H. *Empires of the Atlantic World: Britain and Spain in America, 1492–1830*. New Haven, CT: Yale University Press, 2006.

Ellis, Henry. *A Voyage to Hudson's-Bay by the "Dobbs Galley" and "California" in the Years 1746 and 1747 for Discovering a North West Passage*. Dublin: George and Alexander Ewing, 1749.

Englebert, Robert. "Beyond Borders: Mental Mapping and the French River World in North America, 1763–1805." PhD dissertation, University of Ottawa, 2010.

– "Colonial Encounters and the Changing Contours of Ethnicity: Pierre-Louis de Lorimier and *Métissage* at the Edges of Empire." *Ohio Valley History* 18, no. 2 (2018): 45–69.

– "Diverging Identities and Converging Interests: Corporate Competition, Desertion, and Voyageur Agency, 1815–1818." *Manitoba History* 55 (2007): 18–24.

– "Merchant Representatives and the French River World, 1763–1803." *Michigan Historical Review* 34, no. 1 (2008): 63–82.

Englebert, Robert, and Nicole St-Onge. "Paddling into History: French-Canadian Voyageurs and the Creation of a Fur Trade World, 1730–1804." In *De Pierre-Esprit Radisson à Louis Riel: Voyageurs et Métis*, edited by Denis Combet, Luc Côté, and Gilles Lesage, 71–104. Winnipeg: Les Presses universitaires de Saint-Boniface, 2013.

Englebert, Robert, and Guillaume Teasdale, eds. *French and Indians in the Heart of North America, 1630–1815*. East Lansing: Michigan State University Press, 2013.

Ens, Gerhard J. "The Battle of Seven Oaks and the Articulation of a Metis National Tradition, 1811–1849." In *Contours of a People: Métis Family, Mobility, and History*, edited by Nicole St-Onge, Carolyn Podruchny, and Brenda Macdougall, 93–119. Norman: University of Oklahoma Press, 2012.

– *Homeland to Hinterland: The Changing Worlds of the Red River Métis in the Nineteenth Century*. Toronto: University of Toronto Press, 1996.

Ens, Gerhard J., and Joe Sawchuk. *From New Peoples to New Nations: Aspects of Metis History and Identity from the Eighteenth to the Twenty-First Centuries*. Toronto: University of Toronto Press, 2016.

Ethridge, Robbie. *From Chicaza to Chickasaw: The European Invasion and the Transformation of the Mississippian World, 1540–1715*. Chapel Hill: University of North Carolina Press, 2010.

Ethridge, Robbie, and Sheri M. Shuck-Hall, eds. *Mapping the Mississippian Shatter Zone: The Colonial Indian Slave Trade and Regional Instability in the American South*. Lincoln: University of Nebraska Press, 2009.

Farnell, Brenda M. *Do You See What I Mean? Plains Indian Sign Talk and the Embodiment of Action*. Austin: University of Texas Press, 1995.

Fausz, J. Frederick. "Middlemen in Peace and War: Virginia's Earliest Indian Interpreters, 1608–1632." *Virginia Magazine of History and Biography* 95 (1988): 41–64.

Fenn, Elizabeth. *Encounters at the Heart of the World: A History of the Mandan People*. New York: Hill and Wang, 2014.

– *Pox Americana: The Great Smallpox Epidemic of 1775–82*. New York: Hill and Wang, 2001.

Fenton, William N. *The Great Law and the Longhouse: A Political History of the Iroquois Confederacy*. Norman: University of Oklahoma Press, 1998.

Filion, Maurice. *La Pensée et l'action coloniale de Maurepas vis-à-vis du Canada, 1723–1749: L'âge d'or de la colonie*. Ottawa: Leaméac, 1972.

Flandrau, Grace. "The Verendrye Expeditions in Quest of the Pacific." *Quarterly of the Oregon Historical Society* 26, no. 2 (1925): 64–82.

Flores, Dan. "Bison Ecology and Bison Diplomacy: The Southern Plains from 1800 to 1850." *Journal of American History* 78, no. 2 (1991): 465–85.

Foran, Timothy P. *Defining Métis: Catholic Missionaries and the Idea of Civilization in Northwestern Saskatchewan, 1845–1898*. Winnipeg: University of Manitoba Press, 2017.

Ford, Franklin L. *Robe and Sword: The Regrouping of the French Aristocracy After Louis XIV*. Cambridge, MA: Harvard University Press, 1953.

Foret, Michael J. "The Failure of Administration: The Chickasaw Campaign of 1739–1749." *Revue de Louisiane/Louisiana Review* 11 (1982): 49–60.

Foster, John E. "Wintering, the Outsider Adult Male and the Ethnogenesis of the Western Plains Métis." *Prairie Forum* 19 (1994): 1–13.

Fournier, Martin. *Les officiers des Troupes de la Marine au Canada: 1683–1760*. Sillery, QC: Les éditions du Septentrion, 2017.

– *Pierre-Esprit Radisson, 1636–1710: Merchant Adventurer*. Translated by Mary E. Brennan-Ricard. Sillery, QC: Les éditions du Septentrion, 2002.

Francis, Daniel, and Toby Morantz. *Partners in Furs: A History of the Fur Trade in Eastern James Bay, 1600–1870*. Montreal and Kingston: McGill-Queen's University Press, 1983.

Franklin, John. *Narrative of a Journey to the Shores of the Polar Sea, in the Years 1819, 20, 21, and 22*. London: J. Murray, 1823.

Frégault, Guy. *Canada: The War of the Conquest*. Translated by Margaret M. Cameron. Toronto: Oxford University Press, 1969.

– *La civilisation de la Nouvelle-France, 1713–1744*. Montreal: Éditions Fides, 1969.

– "Politique et politiciens au début du XVIIIe siècle." *Écrits du Canada français* 11 (1961): 90–208.

Friesen, Gerald. *The Canadian Prairies: A History*. Toronto: University of Toronto Press, 1987.

Fromhold, Joachim. *The Western Cree (Pakisimotan Wi Iniwak) – the Canoe Cree 1650–1770*. Morrisville, NC: Lulu Press, 2010.

Furstenberg, Francois. "The Significance of the Trans-Appalachian Frontier in Atlantic History." *American Historical Review* 113, no. 3 (2008): 647–77.

Gagné, Joseph. *Inconquis: Deux retraites françaises vers la Louisiane après 1760*. Sillery, QC: Les éditions du Septentrion, 2016.

Gallay, Alan. *The Indian Slave Trade: The Rise of the English Empire in the American South, 1670–1717*. New Haven, CT: Yale University Press, 2003.

Garrigus, John D. *Before Haiti: Race and Citizenship in French Saint-Domingue*. New York: Palgrave Macmillan, 2006.

Gates, Charles M. *Five Fur Traders of the Northwest: Being the Narrative of Peter Pond and the Diaries of John Macdonell, Archibald N. McLeod,*

Hugh Faries, and Thomas Connor. St Paul: Minnesota Historical Society, 1965.

Gaudry, Adam. "Communing with the Dead: The 'New Métis,' Métis Identity Appropriation, and the Displacement of Living Métis Culture." *American Indian Quarterly* 41, no. 3 (2017): 162–90.

Gaudry, Adam, and Darryl Leroux. "White Settler Revisionism and Making Métis Everywhere: The Evocation of Métissage in Quebec and Nova Scotia." *Critical Ethnic Studies* 3, no. 1 (2017): 116–42.

Gibbon, Guy. *The Sioux: The Dakota and Lakota Nations.* Malden, UK: Blackwell, 2003.

Giraud, Marcel. *The Métis in the Canadian West.* 2 vols. Translated by George Woodcook. Edmonton: The University of Alberta Press, 1986.

Gitlin, Jay. *The Bourgeois Frontier: French Towns, French Traders, and American Expansion.* New Haven, CT: Yale University Press, 2009.

Glover, Jeffrey. *Paper Sovereigns: Anglo-Native Treaties and the Law of Nations, 1604–1664.* Philadelphia: University of Pennsylvania Press, 2014.

Gohier, Maxime. *Onontio le médiateur: Le gestion des conflits amérindiens en Nouvelle-France 1603–1717.* Sillery, QC: Septentrion, 2008.

Grabowski, Jan. "French Criminal Justice and Indians in Montreal, 1670–1760." *Ethnohistory* 43, no. 3 (1996): 405–29.

Grandin, Greg. *The Blood of Guatemala: A History of Race and Nation.* Durham, NC: Duke University Press, 2000.

Gray, Colleen. *The Congrégation de Notre-Dame, Superiors, and the Paradox of Power, 1693–1796.* Montreal and Kingston: McGill-Queen's University Press, 2007.

Greene, Candace S., and Russell Thornton. *The Year the Stars Fell: Lakota Winter Counts at the Smithsonian.* Lincoln: University of Nebraska Press, 2007.

Greene, Jack P., and Philip D. Morgan. *Atlantic History: A Critical Appraisal.* Oxford: Oxford University Press, 2008.

Greer, Allan. *The Jesuit Relations: Natives and Missionaries in Seventeenth-Century North America.* Boston: Bedford/St Martin's, 2000.

– *Mohawk Saint: Catherine Tekakwitha and the Jesuits.* New York: Oxford University Press, 2005.

– *Peasant, Lord, and Merchant: Rural Society in Three Quebec Parishes, 1740–1840.* Toronto: University of Toronto Press, 1985.

– *The People of New France.* Toronto: University of Toronto Press, 1997.

– *Property and Dispossession: Natives, Empires and Land in Early Modern North America.* Cambridge: Cambridge University Press, 2018.

Grenier, Benoît. *Brève histoire du régime seigneurial*. Montreal: Boréal, 2012.

Griffiths, N.E.S. *From Migrant to Acadian: A North American Border People, 1604–1755*. Montreal and Kingston: McGill-Queen's University Press, 2005.

Groulx, Lionel. *Histoire du Canada français depuis la découverte*. Tome I. 4th ed. Montreal: Éditions Fides, 1960.

– *Notre grande aventure: L'Empire français en Amérique du Nord (1535–1760)*. Montreal: Éditions Fides, 1976.

Hackett, Paul. "Historical Mourning Practices Observed among the Cree and Ojibway Indians of the Central Subarctic." *Ethnohistory* 52, no. 3 (2005): 503–33.

– "The Monsoni and the Smallpox of 1737–39." In *Pushing the Margins: Native and Northern Studies*, edited by Jill E. Oakes, Roderick R Riewe, Marlyn Bennett, and Brenda Chisholm, 244–57. Winnipeg: University of Manitoba Press, 2001.

– *A Very Remarkable Sickness: Epidemics in the Petit Nord, 1670 to 1846*. Winnipeg: University of Manitoba Press, 2002.

Hall, Gwendolyn Midlo. *Africans in Colonial Louisiana: The Development of Afro-Creole Culture in the Eighteenth Century*. Baton Rouge: Louisiana State University Press, 1992.

Hall, Norma J. "Ocean Crossings: Hudson's Bay Company Seafaring in a Northern North Atlantic World." *Manitoba History* 71 (2013): 16–20.

Hämäläinen, Pekka. *The Comanche Empire*. New Haven, CT: Yale University Press, 2008.

– *Lakota America: A New History of Indigenous Power*. New Haven, CT: Yale University Press, 2019.

– "The Politics of Grass: European Expansion, Ecological Change, and Indigenous Power in the Southwest Borderlands." *William and Mary Quarterly* 67, no. 2 (2010): 173–208.

– "The Rise and Fall of Plains Indian Horse Cultures." *Journal of American History* 90, no. 3 (2003): 833–62.

Hämäläinen, Pekka, and Samuel Truett. "On Borderlands." *Journal of American History* 98, no. 2 (2011): 338–61.

Hamon, M. Max. *The Audacity of His Enterprise: Louis Riel and the Métis Nation that Canada Never Was, 1840–1875*. Montreal and Kingston: McGill-Queen's University Press, 2020.

Harris, Richard Colebrook. *The Seigneurial System in Early Canada: A Geographical Study*. Montreal and Kingston: McGill-Queen's University Press, 1984.

Hatter, Lawrence B.A. *Citizens of Convenience: The Imperial Origins of American Nationhood on the U.S.-Canadian Border*. Charlottesville: University of Virginia Press, 2017.

Havard, Gilles. *L'Amérique fantôme: Les aventuriers francophones du Nouveau Monde*. Paris: Flammarion, 2019.

– *Empire et métissages: Indiens et Français dans le Pays d'en haut 1660–1715*. Sillery, QC: Septentrion, 2003.

– *The Great Peace of Montreal of 1701: French-Native Diplomacy in the Seventeenth Century*. Translated by Phyllis Aronoff and Howard Scott. Montreal and Kingston: McGill-Queen's University Press, 2001.

– *Histoire des coureurs de bois: Amérique du Nord, 1600–1840*. Paris: Les Indes Savantes, 2016.

– "'Nous ne ferons plus qu'un peuple': Le métissage en Nouvelle France à l'époque de Champlain." In *Le nouveau monde et Champlain*, edited by Guy Martinière and Didier Poton, 85–107. Paris: Les Indes Savantes, 2008.

Havard, Gilles, and Cécile Vidal. *Histoire de l'Amérique Française*. Paris: Flammarion, 2003.

Hennepin, Louis. *A New Discovery of a Vast Country in America*. 2 vols. Edited by Reuben Gold Thwaites. Chicago: A.C. McClurg and Company, 1903.

Henry, Alexander (the elder). *Alexander Henry's Travels and Adventures in the Years 1760–1776*. Edited by Milo Milton Quaife. Chicago: Lakeside Press, R.R. Donnelley and Sons, 1921.

Hickerson, Harold. *The Chippewa and Their Neighbors: A Study in Ethnohistory*. Toronto: Holt, Rinehart and Winston, 1970.

Hinderaker, Eric. *Elusive Empires: Constructing Colonialism in the Ohio Valley, 1673–1800*. Cambridge: Cambridge University Press, 1997.

Hodson, Christopher, and Brett Rushforth. "Absolutely Atlantic: Colonialism and the Early Modern French Sate in Recent Historiography." *History Compass* 8, no. 1 (2010): 101–17.

Hofstra, Warren R., ed. *Cultures in Conflict: The Seven Years' War in North America*. Lanham, MD: Rowman and Littlefield, 2007.

Hogue, Michel. *Metis and the Medicine Line: Creating a Border and Dividing a People*. Regina: University of Regina Press, 2015.

Houllemare, Marie. "Seeing the Empire Through Lists and Charts: French Colonial Records in the Eighteenth Century." *Journal of Early Modern History* 22, no. 5 (2018): 371–91.

Howard, James H. "Yanktonai Ethnohistory and the John K. Bear Winter Count." *Plains Anthropologist* 21, 73 (1976): 1–78.

Hunt, George T. *Wars of the Iroquois: A Study in Intertribal Trade Relations*. Madison: University of Wisconsin Press, 1940.

Hurt. John J. *Louis XIV and the Parlements: The Assertion of Royal Authority*. Manchester: Manchester University Press, 2002.

Innis, Harold Adams. *The Fur Trade in Canada: An Introduction to Canadian Economic History*. New Haven, CT: Yale University Press, 1930.

Isham, James. *James Isham's Observations on Hudsons Bay, 1743 and Notes and Observations on a Book Entitled A Voyage to Hudson's Bay in the Dobbs Galley, 1749*. Edited by E.E. Rich and A.M. Johnson. London: Hudson's Bay Record Society, 1949.

Ishii, Izumi. *Bad Fruits of the Civilized Tree: Alcohol and the Sovereignty of the Cherokee Nation*. Lincoln: University of Nebraska Press, 2008.

Jaenen, Cornelius J. *Friend and Foe: Aspects of French-Amerindian Cultural Contact in the Sixteenth and Seventeenth Centuries*. New York: Columbia University Press, 1976.

Jennings, Francis. *The Ambiguous Iroquois Empire. The Covenant Chain Confederation of Indian Tribes with English Colonies from its Beginnings to the Lancaster Treaty of 1744*. New York: W.W. Norton and Company, 1984.

– *The Invasion of America: Indians, Colonialism, and the Cant of Conquest*. Chapel Hill: University of North Carolina Press, 1978.

Jérémie *dit* Lamontagne, Nicolas. "Description du Détroit & de la Baye d'Hudson, avec la maniere dont ces Pays ont esté découverts." In *Le Nouveau Mercure: Janvier 1719*. Paris: Chez Guillaume Cavalier, 1719.

– *Twenty Years of York Factory, 1694–1714*. Edited and translated by Robert Douglas and J.N. Wallace. Ottawa: Thorburn and Abbott, 1926.

Jones, Arthur E. *The Aulneau Collection, 1734–1745*. Montreal: Archives of St Mary's College, 1893.

Jones, Elizabeth. *Gentlemen and Jesuits: Quests for Glory and Adventure in the Early Days of New France*. Toronto: University of Toronto Press, 1986.

Kalm, Pehr. *The America of 1750: Peter Kalm's Travels in North America*. 2 vols. Adolph B. Benson. New York: Dover, 1966.

Kavanagh, Martin. *The Assiniboine Basin: A Social Study of the Discovery, Exploration, and Settlement of Manitoba*. Winnipeg: Public Press, 1946.

– *La Vérendrye, His Life and Times*. Brandon, MB: Fletcher and Son, 1967.

Kehoe, Alice B. "Aboriginal Pottery From Site Fhna-3, The François Le Blanc Trading Post." *Plains Anthropologist* 9, no. 23 (1964): 18–21.

– "Ethnicity at a Pedlar's Post in Saskatchewan." *Western Canadian Journal of Anthropology* 6, no. 1 (1976): 52–60.

Kehoe, Alice B., and David A. Meyer. *François' House: An Early Fur Trade Post on the Saskatchewan River.* Regina: Saskatchewan Culture and Youth, 1978.

Kellogg, Louise Phelps. *Early Narratives of the Northwest, 1634–1699.* New York: Barnes and Noble, 1945.

– *French Régime in Wisconsin and the Northwest.* Madison: State Historical Society of Wisconsin, 1925.

Kennedy, Gregory M.W. *Something of a Peasant Paradise? Comparing Rural Societies in Acadie and the Loudunais, 1604–1755.* Montreal and Kingston: McGill-Queen's University Press, 2014.

Kenyon, Walter Andrew, and John Reid Turnbull. *The Battle for James Bay, 1686.* Toronto: Macmillan of Canada, 1971.

Klooster, Wim. *The Dutch Moment: War, Trade, and Settlement in the Seventeenth-Century Atlantic World.* Ithaca, NY: Cornell University Press, 2016.

– *Illicit Riches: The Dutch Trade in the Caribbean, 1648–1795.* Leiden: KITLV Press, 1995.

Labelle, Kathryn Magee. *Dispersed But Not Destroyed: A History of the Seventeenth-Century Wendat People.* Vancouver: UBC Press, 2013.

– "Faire La Chaudière: The Wendat Feast of Souls, 1636." In *French and Indians in the Heart of North America, 1630–1815*, edited by Robert Englebert and Guillaume Teasdale, 1–20. East Lansing: Michigan State University Press, 2013.

LaBounty, Andrew E. "'This Countries Ladies': Gender Negotiations at the Northwest Company, Grand Portage." *Nebraska Anthropologist* 24 (2009): 36–45.

Lachance, André. *Juger et punir en Nouvelle-France: Chroniques de la vie quotidienne au XVIIIe siècle.* Montreal: Libre expression, 2000.

Lacombe, Albert. *Dictionnaire de la langue des Cris.* Montreal: C.O. Beauchemin & Valois, 1874.

La Corne, Luc de. *Journal du voyage de M. Saint-Luc de La Corne, écuyer, dans le navire l'Auguste, en l'an 1761.* Montreeal: Chez Fleury Mesplet, 1778.

Lacoursière, Jacques. *Canada-Québec synthèse historique, 1534–2010.* Sillery, QC: Septentrion, 2005.

Lagarde, Lucie. "Le passage du Nord-Ouest et la Mer de l'Ouest dans la Cartographie française du 18e siècle, contribution à l'étude de l'oeuvre des Delisle et Buache." *Imago Mundi* 41, no. 1 (1989): 19–43.

Lahontan, Louis Armand de Lom d'Arce, Baron de. *New Voyages to North America*. 2 vols. Edited by Reuben Gold Thwaites. Chicago: A.C. McClurg and Company, 1905.

Lalancette, Louis. "Les capitaines des troupes de la Marine de 1683 à 1739: La carrière militaire en Nouvelle-France." Master's thesis, Université de Montréal, 2015.

Lanctôt, Gustave. *A History of Canada*. Vol. 2: *From the Royal Régime to the Treaty of Utrecht, 1663–1713*. Translated by Margaret M. Cameron. Toronto: Clarke, Irwin and Company, 1964.

Larouche, Leonidas. *Le second registre de Tadoussac, 1668–1700*. Montreal: Presses de l'Université du Québec, 1972.

Lart, Charles. "Fur-Trade Returns, 1767." *Canadian Historical Review* 3, no. 4 (1922): 351–8.

Latimer, Jon. *Buccaneers of the Caribbean: How Piracy Forged an Empire*. Cambridge, MA: Harvard University Press, 2009.

Laut, Agnes. *Pathfinders of the West; Being the Thrilling Story of the Adventures of the Men Who Discovered the Great Northwest: Radisson, La Vérendrye, Lewis and Clark*. Toronto: W. Briggs, 1904.

Leavelle, Tracy Neal. *The Catholic Calumet: Colonial Conversions in French and Indian North America*. Philadelphia: University of Pennsylvania Press, 2011.

Le Clercq, Christian. *First Establishment of the Faith in New France*. 2 vols. Edited by John G. Shea. New York: J.G. Shea, 1881.

Lee, Jacob F. *Masters of the Middle Waters: Indian Nations and Colonial Ambitions along the Mississippi*. Cambridge, MA: Belknap Press of Harvard University Press, 2019.

Lennox, Jeffers. *Homelands and Empires: Indigenous Spaces, Imperial Fictions, and Competition for Territory in Northeastern North America, 1690–1763*. Toronto: University of Toronto Press, 2017.

Léonard, Carol Jean. *Mémoire des noms de lieux d'origine et d'influence françaises en Saskatchewan*. Quebec: Éditions Gid, 2010.

Lesueur, Boris. *Les troupes coloniales d'Ancien Régime: Fidelitate per Mare et Terras*. Paris: Éditions SPM, 2014.

Lewis, G. Malcolm. "La grande rivière et fleuve de l'Ouest/The Realities and Reasons behind a Major Mistake in the 18th-Century Geography of North America." *Cartographica* 28, no. 1 (1991): 54–87.

– "Misinterpretation of Amerindian Information as a Source of Error on Euro-American Maps." *Annals of the Association of American Geographers* 77, no. 4 (1987): 542–63.

Libby, Orin G. "Some Vérendrye Enigmas." *Mississippi Valley Historical Review* 3, no. 2 (1916): 143–60.

Lipman, Andrew. "No More Middle Grounds?" *Reviews in American History* 44, no. 1 (2016): 24–30.

– *The Saltwater Frontier: Indians and the Contest for the American Coast*. New Haven, CT: Yale University Press, 2015.

Litalien, Raymonde. *Explorateurs de l'Amérique du Nord, 1492–1795*. Quebec: Les éditions du Septentrion, 1993.

Litalien, Raymonde, Jean-François Palomino, and Denis Vaugeois. *Mapping a Continent: Historical Atlas of North America, 1492–1814*. Montreal and Kingston: McGill Queen's University Press, 2007.

Longpré, Robert. *Ile-a-la-Crosse, 1776–1976: Sakitawak Bi-centennial*. Ile-a-la-Crosse, SK: Ile-a-la-Crosse Bi-centennial Committee, 1977.

Losey, Elizabeth Browne. *Let Them Be Remembered: The Story of the Fur Trade Forts*. New York: Vantage Press, 1999.

Lovisek, J.A. "The Political Evolution of the Boundary Waters Ojibwa." In *Papers of the Twenty-Fourth Algonquian Conference*, edited by William Cowan, 280–305. Ottawa: Carleton University, 1993.

Lozier, Jean-François. *Flesh Reborn: The Saint Lawrence Valley Mission Settlements through the Seventeenth Century*. Montreal and Kingston: McGill Queen's University Press, 2018.

– "Les origines huronnes-wendates de Kanesatake." *Recherches amérindiennes au Québec* 44, nos. 2–3 (2014): 103–16.

Lynn, John A. *Giant of the Grand Siècle: The French Army, 1610–1715*. Cambridge: Cambridge University Press, 1997.

– *The Wars of Louis XIV, 1667–1714*. London: Longman, 1999.

Lytwyn, Victor P. *The Fur Trade of the Little North: Indians, Pedlars, and Englishmen East of Lake Winnipeg, 1760–1821*. Winnipeg: Rupert's Land Research Centre, 1986.

– "'God Was Angry with Their Country': The Smallpox Epidemic of 1782–83 among the Hudson Bay Lowland Cree." In *Papers of the Thirtieth Algonkian Conference*, edited by David H. Pentland, 142–64. Winnipeg: University of Manitoba Press, 1999.

– *Muskekowuck Athinuwick: Original People of the Great Swampy Land*. Winnipeg: University of Manitoba Press, 2002.

MacDonell, Alan. "Radisson and La Vérendrye: Two Frontiersmen, Two Frontiers." *Western Humanities Review* 60, no. 2 (2006): 51–9.

Macdougall, Brenda. *One of the Family: Métis Culture in Nineteenth-Century Northwestern Saskatchewan*. Vancouver: UBC Press, 2010.

Macdougall, Brenda, and Nicole St-Onge. "Rooted in Mobility: Métis Buffalo-Hunting Brigades." *Manitoba History* 71 (2013): 21–32.

MacLeod, D. Peter. "The Anishinabeg Point of View: The History of the Great Lakes Region to 1800 in Nineteenth-Century Mississauga, Odawa, and Ojibwa Historiography." *Canadian Historical* 73, no. 2 (1992): 194–210.

– "'Une Conspiration Générale': The Exercise of Power by the Amerindians during the War of the Austrian Secession, 1744–1748." PhD dissertation, University of Ottawa, 1992.

MacLeod, Margaret, and W.L. Morton. *Cuthbert Grant of Grantown.* Toronto: McClelland and Stewart, 1974.

MacMillan, Ken. *Sovereignty and Possession in the English New World: The Legal Foundations of Empire, 1576–1640.* Cambridge: Cambridge University Press, 2006.

Malone, Patrick M. *The Skulking Way of War: Technology and Tactics among the New England Indians.* Lanham, MD: Madison Books, 1991.

Mancall, Peter C. *Deadly Medicine: Indians and Alcohol in Early America.* Ithaca, NY: Cornell University Press, 1995.

Mancke, Elizabeth. "Negotiating An Empire: Britain and Its Overseas Peripheries, ca. 1550–1780." In *Negotiated Empires: Centers and Peripheries in the Americas, 1500–1820*, edited by Christine Daniels and Michael V. Kennedy, 235–82. New York: Routledge, 2002.

Mandelbaum, David G. *The Plains Cree: An Ethnographic, Historical, and Comparative Study.* Regina: Canadian Plains Research Centre, 1979.

Mapp, Paul W. "Atlantic History from Imperial, Continental, and Pacific Perspectives." *William and Mary Quarterly* 63, no. 4 (2006): 713–24.

– *The Elusive West and the Contest for Empire, 1713–1763.* Chapel Hill: University of North Carolina Press, 2011.

– "French Reactions to the British Search for a Northwest Passage from Hudson Bay and the Origins of the Seven Years' War." *Terrae Incognitae* 33, no. 1 (2001): 13–32.

Marrero, Karen L. *Detroit's Hidden Channels: The Power of French-Indigenous Families in the Eighteenth Century.* Winnipeg: University of Manitoba Press, 2020.

– "Women at the Crossroads: Trade, Mobility, and Power in Early French America and Detroit." In *Women in Early America: Transnational Histories, Rethinking Master Narratives*, edited by Thomas Foster, 159–85. New York: New York University Press, 2015.

Masson, L.R. *Les Bourgeois de la Compagnie du Nord-Ouest: Récits de voyage, lettres et rapports inédits relatifs au Nord-Ouest Canadien.* 2 vols. New York: Antiquarian Press, 1960.

Mathieu, Jacques. *Le commerce entre la Nouvelle-France et les Antilles au XVIIIe siecle.* Montreal: Fides, 1984.

Mathieu, Jacques, Pauline Therrien-Fortier, and Rénald Lessard. "Mobilité et sédentarité: Stratégies familiales en Nouvelle-France." *Recherches sociographiques* 28 (1987): 211–27.

McDonnell, Michael A. "Maintaining a Balance of Power: Michilimackinac, the Anishinaabe Odawas, and the Anglo-Indian War of 1763." *Early American Studies* 13, no. 1 (2015): 38–79.

– *Masters of Empire: Great Lakes Indians and the Making of America.* New York: Hill and Wang, 2015.

McLean, Don. *Home from the Hill: A History of the Metis in Western.* Regina: Gabriel Dumont Institute of Native Studies and Applied Research, 1987.

McNab, David T., and Ute Lischke. *The Long Journey of Canada's Forgotten People: Studies in Métis History and Identities.* Waterloo, ON: Wilfrid Laurier University Press, 2007.

McShea, Bronwen. *Apostles of Empire: The Jesuits and New France.* Lincoln: University of Nebraska Press, 2019.

Merrell, James. *Into The American Woods: Negotiators on the Pennsylvania Frontier.* New York: W.W. Norton and Company, 1999.

Metcalf, Alida. *Go-Betweens and the Colonization of Brazil: 1500–1600.* Austin: University of Texas Press, 2005.

Meyer, David, and Dale Russell. "The Pegogamaw Crees and Their Ancestors: History and Archaeology in the Saskatchewan Forks Region." *Plains Anthropologist* 51, no. 199 (2006): 303–24.

– "'Through the Woods Whare Thare Ware Now Track Ways': Kelsey, Henday and Trails in East Central Saskatchewan." *Canadian Journal of Archaeology/Journal Canadien d'Archéologie* 31, no. 3 (2007): 163–97.

Meyer, David, and Paul C. Thistle. "Saskatchewan River Rendezvous Centers and Trading Posts: Continuity in a Cree Social Geography." *Ethnohistory* 42, no. 3 (1995): 403–44.

Miller, Cary. *Ogimaag: Anishinaabeg Leadership, 1760–1845.* Lincoln: University of Nebraska Press, 2010.

Miller, J.R. *Compact, Contract, Covenant: Aboriginal Treaty-Making in Canada.* Toronto: University of Toronto Press, 2009.

– "From Riel to the Métis." *Canadian Historical Review* 69, no. 1 (1988): 1–20.

Milloy, John S. *The Plains Cree: Trade, Diplomacy and War, 1790 to 1870*. Winnipeg: University of Manitoba Press, 1988.

Miquelon, Dale. "Ambiguous Concession: What Diplomatic Archives Reveal about Article 15 of the Treaty of Utrecht and France's North American Policy." *William and Mary Quarterly* 67, no. 3 (2010): 459–86.

– "The Baby Family in the Trade of Canada, 1750–1820." Master's thesis, Carleton University, 1966.

– *Dugard of Rouen: French Trade to Canada and the West Indies, 1729–1770*. Montreal and Kingston: McGill-Queen's University Press, 1978.

– "Envisioning the French Empire: Utrecht, 1711–1713." *French Historical Studies* 24, no. 4 (2001): 653–77.

– *New France, 1701-1744: A Supplement to Europe*. Toronto: McClelland and Stewart, 1987.

Mitchell, Barbara. *Mapmaker: Philip Turnor in Rupert's Land in the Age of Enlightenment*. Regina: University of Regina Press, 2017.

Mniyo, Samuel, and Robert Goodvoice. *The Red Road and Other Narratives of the Dakota Sioux*. Edited by Daniel Beveridge. Lincoln: University of Nebraska Press, 2020.

Moogk, Peter N. *La Nouvelle France: The Making of French Canada – A Cultural History*. East Lansing: Michigan State University Press, 2000.

– "Reluctant Exiles: Emigrants from France in Canada before 1760." *William and Mary Quarterly* 46, no. 3 (1989): 463–505.

Moote, A. Lloyd. *The Revolt of the Judges: The Parlement of Paris and the Fronde, 1643–1652*. Princeton, NJ: Princeton University Press, 1971.

Morantz, Toby. "Economic and Social Accommodations of the James Bay Inlanders to the Fur Trade." In *The Subarctic Fur Trade: Native Social and Economic Adaptations*, edited by Shepard Krech III, 55–79. Vancouver: UBC Press, 1984.

Moreau, William E. *The Writings of David Thompson*. Vol. 1, *The Travels, 1850 Version*. Montreal and Kingston: McGill-Queen's University Press, 2009.

Morice, Adrien Gabriel. *Dictionnaire historique des canadiens et des métis français de l'ouest*. Saint-Boniface, MB: l'Archevêché, 1908.

Morris, Christopher. "How to Prepare Buffalo, and Other Things the French Taught Indians about Nature." In *French Colonial Louisiana and the Atlantic World*, edited by Bradley G. Bond, 22–42. Baton Rouge: Louisiana State University Press, 2005.

Morrison, Kenneth M. "Baptism and Alliance: The Symbolic Mediations of Religious Syncretism." *Ethnohistory* 37, no. 4 (1990): 416–37.

Morrissey, Robert Michael. *Empire by Collaboration: Indians, Colonists, and Governments in Colonial Illinois Country*. Philadelphia: University of Pennsylvania Press, 2015.

– "Kaskaskia Social Network: Kinship and Assimilation in the French-Illinois Borderlands, 1695–1735." *William and Mary Quarterly* 70, no. 1 (2013): 103–46.

Morse, Eric W. *Fur Trade Canoe Routes of Canada/Then and Now*. Ottawa: Roger Duhamel, Queen's Printer, 1969.

Morton, Arthur Silver. "Forrest Oakes, Charles Boyer, Joseph Fulton, and Peter Pangman in the North-West, 1765–1793." *Transactions of the Royal Society of Canada* 3, no. 31 (1937): 87–100.

– *A History of the Canadian West to 1870–71: Being a History of Rupert's Land (the Hudson's Bay Company's Territory) and of the North-West Territory (Including the Pacific Slope)*. London: T. Nelson and Sons, 1939.

– *Manitoba: A History*. Toronto: University of Toronto Press, 1957.

Murphy, Lucy Eldersveld. *A Gathering of Rivers: Indians, Métis and Mining in the Western Great Lakes, 1737–1832*. Lincoln: University of Nebraska Press, 2000.

– *Great Lakes Creoles: A French-Indian Community on the Northern Borderlands, Prairie Du Chien, 1750–1860*. Cambridge: Cambridge University Press, 2014.

– "Women, Networks, and Colonization in Nineteenth-Century Wisconsin." In *Contours of a People: Métis Family, Mobility, and History*, edited by Nicole St-Onge, Carolyn Podruchny, and Brenda Macdougall, 230–64. Norman: University of Oklahoma Press, 2012.

Nicholls, Andrew. *Fleeting Empire: Early Stuart Britain and the Merchant Adventurers to Canada*. Montreal and Kingston: McGill-Queen's University Press, 2010.

Nicks, Trudy, and Kenneth Morgan. "Grande Cache: The Historic Development of an Indigenous Alberta Métis." In *The New Peoples: Being and Becoming Métis in North America*, edited by Jacqueline Peterson and Jennifer S.H. Brown, 163–81. Winnipeg: University of Manitoba Press, 1985.

Nish, Cameron. *Canadian Historical Documents Series*. Vol. 1, *The French Régime*. Scarborough, ON: Prentice Hall of Canada, 1965.

– *François-Étienne Cugnet 1719–1751: Entrepreneur et entreprises en Nouvelle-France*. Montreal: Fides, 1975.

Noel, Jan. *Along a River: The First French-Canadian Women*. Toronto: University of Toronto Press, 2011.

Norall, Frank. *Bourgmont, Explorer of the Missouri, 1698–1725*. Lincoln: University of Nebraska Press, 1988.

Nute, Grace Lee. "Marin versus La Vérendrye." *Minnesota History* 32, no. 4 (1951): 226–38.

O'Callaghan, Edmund Bailey. *Documents Relative to the Colonial History of the State of New York*. 15 vols. Albany, NY: Weed, Parsons and Company, 1853–87.

Ouellet, Réal, and Alain Beaulieu. *Lahontan: Œuvres complètes*. Montreal: Les Presses de l'Université de Montréal, 1990.

Pagden, Anthony. *European Encounters with the New World: From Renaissance to Romanticism*. New Haven, CT: Yale University Press, 1993.

Palmer, Jennifer. *Intimate Bonds: Family and Slavery in the French Atlantic*. Philadelphia: University of Pennsylvania Press, 2016.

Palomino, Jean-François. "Pratiques cartographiques en Nouvelle-France: La prise en charge de l'État dans la description de son espace colonial à l'orée du xviiie siècle." *Canadian Society for Eighteenth-Century Studies/Société Canadienne d'étude du dix-huitième siècle* 31 (2012): 21–39.

Pannekoek, Frits. "Metis Studies: The Development of a Field and New Directions." In *From Rupert's Land to Canada: Essays in Honour of John E. Foster*, edited by Ted Binnema, Gerhard Ens, and Rod Macleod, 111–28. Edmonton: University of Alberta Press, 2001.

– *A Snug Little Flock: The Social Origins of the Riel Resistance of 1869–70*. Winnipeg: Watson and Dwyer, 1991.

Parker, David. *Class and State in Ancien Régime France: The Road to Modernity?* London: Routledge, 1996.

– *The Making of French Absolutism*. New York: St Martin's Press, 1983.

Parmenter, Jon. *The Edge of the Woods: Iroquoia, 1534, 1701*. East Lansing: Michigan State University Press, 2010.

Payment, Diane P. *The Free People – Li Gens Libres: A History of the Métis Community of Batoche, Saskatchewan*. Calgary: University of Calgary Press, 2009.

Pedley, Mary Sponberg. *The Commerce of Cartography: Making and Marketing Maps in Eighteenth-Century France and England*. Chicago: University of Chicago Press, 2005.

Peers, Laura. *The Ojibwa of Western Canada, 1780 to 1870*. St Paul: Minnesota Historical Society Press, 1994.

Pénicaut, André. *Fleur de Lys and Calumet: Being the Penicaut Narrative of French Adventure in Louisiana*. Edited and translated by Richebourg McWilliams. Tuscaloosa, AL: University of Alabama Press, 1988.

Peterson, Jacqueline. "Many Roads to Red River: Métis Genesis in the Great Lakes Region, 1680–1815." In *The New Peoples: Being and Becoming Métis in North America*, edited by Jacqueline Peterson and Jennifer S.H. Brown, 35–71. Winnipeg: University of Manitoba Press, 1985.

– "Red River Redux: Métis Ethnogenesis and the Great Lakes Region." In *Contours of a People: Métis Family, Mobility, and History*, edited by Nicole St-Onge, Carolyn Podruchney, and Brenda Macdougall, 3–22. Norman: University of Oklahoma Press, 2012.

Peterson, Jacqueline, and Jennifer S.H. Brown, eds. *The New Peoples: Being and Becoming Métis in North America*. Winnipeg: University of Manitoba Press, 1985.

Petitfils, Jean-Christian. *Le régent*. Paris: Fayard, 1986.

Petto, Christine M. "From L'état, c'est moi to c'est l'état: Mapping in Early Modern France." *Cartographica* 40, no. 3 (2005): 53–78.

Pevitt, Christine. *Philippe, Duc D'Orleans: Regent of France*. New York: Atlantic Monthly Press, 1997.

Peyser, Joseph L. "The Fate of the Fox Survivors: A Dark Chapter in the History of the French in the Upper Country, 1726–1737." *State Historical Society of Wisconsin* 73 (1990): 82–110.

– *Jacques Legardeur de Saint-Pierre: Officer, Gentleman, Entrepreneur*. East Lansing: Michigan State University Press, 1996.

– *On the Eve of the Conquest: The Chevalier de Raymond's Critique of New France in 1754*. East Lansing: Michigan State University Press, 1998.

Pigeon, Émilie. "Au nom du Bon Dieu et du Buffalo: Metis Lived Catholicism on the Northern Plains." PhD dissertation, York University, 2017.

Podruchny, Carolyn. "Baptizing Novices: Ritual Moments among French Canadian Voyageurs in the Montreal Fur Trade, 1780–1821." *Canadian Historical Review* 83, no. 2 (2002): 165–95.

– *Making the Voyageur World: Travelers and Traders in the North American Fur Trade*. Lincoln: University of Nebraska Press, 2006.

– "Unfair Masters and Rascally Servants? Labour Relations among Bourgeois, Clerks and Voyageurs in the Montréal Fur Trade, 1780–1821." *Labour/Le Travail* 43 (1999): 43–70.

Pratt, Mary Louise. *Imperial Eyes: Travel Writing and Transculturation.* London: Routledge, 1992.

Pritchard, James. *Anatomy of a Naval Disaster: The 1746 French Expedition to North America.* Montreal and Kingston: McGill-Queen's University Press, 1995.

– *In Search of Empire: The French in the Americas, 1670–1730.* Cambridge: Cambridge University Press, 2004.

Prud'homme, Louis Arthur. *L'élément français au nord-ouest: Voyageurs canadiens-français et Métis, 1763–1870.* Montreal: Compagnie de pub. de la Revue canadienne, 1904.

Quaife, Milo Milton, ed. and trans. *The Western Country in the 17th Century: The Memoirs of Lamothe Cadillac and Pierre Liette.* Chicago: Lakeside Press, 1947.

Ray, Arthur J. *Indians in the Fur Trade: Their Role as Hunters, Trappers and Middlemen in the Lands Southwest of Hudson Bay 1660–1870.* Toronto: University of Toronto Press, 1974.

Ray, Arthur J., and Donald Freeman. *"Give Us Good Measure": An Economic Analysis of Relations between the Indians and the Hudson's Bay Company before 1763.* Toronto: University of Toronto Press, 1978.

Reedy-Maschner, Katherine L., and Herbert D.G. Maschner. "Heads, Women, and the Baubles of Prestige: Trophies of War in the Artic and Subarctic." In *The Taking and Displaying of Human Body Parts as Trophies by Amerindians*, edited by Richard J. Chacon and David H. Dye, 32–41. New York: Springer, 2007.

– "Marauding Middlemen: Western Expansion and Violent Conflict in the Subarctic." *Ethnohistory* 46, no. 4 (1999): 703–43.

Regourd, François. "Kourou 1763: Succès d'une enquête, échec d'un project colonial." In *Connaissances et pouvoirs: Les espaces impériaux (XVIe–XVIIIe siècles), France, Espagne, Portugal*, edited by Charlotte de Castelnau-L'Estoile and François Regourd, 233–52. Pessac, FR: Presses Universitaires de Bordeaux, 2005.

Reid, Marjorie G. "The Quebec Fur-Traders and Western Policy, 1763–1774." *Canadian Historical Review* 6, no. 1 (1925): 15–32.

Reynolds, George F. "La Verendrye and Manitoba's First Mine." *Manitoba Pageant* 16, no. 3 (Spring 1971). http://www.mhs.mb.ca/docs/pageant/16/firstmine.shtml.

Rich, E.E. *The History of the Hudson's Bay Company.* 2 vols. Toronto: McClelland and Stewart, 1960.

Rich, E.E., and H. Fleming. *Colin Robertson's Correspondence Book, 1817–1822.* Toronto: Champlain Society, 1939.

Richelet, Pierre. *Dictionnaire françois, contenant généralement tous les mots tant vieux que nouveaux et plusieurs remarques sur la langue françoise*. Amsterdam: J. Elzevir, 1706.

Richter, Daniel K. *Before the Revolution: America's Ancient Pasts*. Cambridge, MA: Harvard University Press, 2011.

– *Facing East from Indian Country: A Native History of Early America*. Harvard University Press, 2003.

– *The Ordeal of the Longhouse*. Chapel Hill: University of North Carolina Press, 1992.

Robson, Joseph. *An Account of Six Years Residence in Hudson's-Bay from 1733 to 1736, and 1744 to 1747*. London: Printed for J. Payne and J. Bouquet, 1752.

Rodnick, David. *The Fort Belknap Assiniboine of Montana: A Study in Cultural Change*. New Haven, CT: Bureau of Indian Affairs, 1938.

Røge, Pernille. "'La Clef de Commerce': The Changing Role of Africa in France's Atlantic Empire ca. 1760–1797." *History of European Ideas* 34, no. 4 (2008): 431–43.

– *Economistes and the Reinvention of Empire: France in the Americas and Africa, c. 1750–1802*. Cambridge: Cambridge University Press, 2019.

Roper, L.H., and Bertrand Van Ruymbeke, eds. *Constructing Early Modern Empires: Proprietary Ventures in the Atlantic World, 1500–1750*. Leiden: Brill, 2007.

Rule, John C. "Jean-Frédéric Phélypeaux, Comte de Pontchartrain et Maurepas: Reflections on His Life and His Papers." *Louisiana History: The Journal of the Louisiana Historical Association* 6, no. 4 (1965): 365–77.

Rule, John C., and Ben S. Trotter. *A World of Paper: Louis XIV, Colbert de Torcy, and the Rise of the Information State*. Montreal and Kingston: McGill-Queen's University Press, 2014.

Rumilly, Robert. *La compagnie du Nord-Ouest: Une épopée montréalaise, tome 1*. Montreal: Fides, 1980.

– *La Vérendrye: Découvreur canadien*. Montreal: A. Lévesque, 1933.

Rushforth, Brett. *Bonds of Alliance: Indigenous and Atlantic Slaveries in New France*. Chapel Hill: University of North Carolina Press, 2012.

– "Insinuating Empire: Indians, Smugglers, and the Imperial Geography of Eighteenth-Century Montreal." In *Frontier Cities: Encounters at the Crossroads of Empire*, edited by Jay Gitlin, Barbara Berglund, and Adam Arenson, 49–65. Philadelphia: University of Pennsylvania Press, 2013.

– "A Little Flesh We Offer You." *William and Mary Quarterly* 60, no. 4 (2003): 777–808.
– "Slavery, the Fox Wars, and the Limits of Alliance." *William and Mary Quarterly* 63, no. 1 (2006): 53–80.
Russell, Dale. *Eighteenth-Century Western Cree and Their Neighbours.* Ottawa: Canadian Museum of Civilization, 1991.
Saint-Pierre, Marjolaine. *Lacorne Saint-Luc: L'Odyssée d'un noble, 1711–1784.* Sillery, QC: Éditions du Septentrion, 2013.
Saint-Thomas, Catherine Burke. *Les Ursulines de Québec depuis leur établissement jusqu'à nos jours, Volume 2.* Quebec: Des Presses de C. Darveau, 1878.
Sale, Kirkpatrick. *The Conquest of Paradise: Christopher Columbus and the Columbian Legacy.* New York: Alfred A. Knopf, 1990.
Saler, Bethel. *The Settlers' Empire: Colonialism and State Formation in America's Old Northwest.* Philadelphia: University of Pennsylvania Press, 2015.
Salisbury, Neal. *Manitou and Providence: Indians, Europeans, and the Making of New England, 1500–1643.* New York: Oxford University Press, 1984.
Samson, Roch. *The Forges du Saint-Maurice: Beginnings of the Iron and Steel Industry in Canada, 1730–1883.* Quebec: Presses de l'Université Laval, 1998.
Sawchuk, Joe. *The Métis of Manitoba: Reformulation of an Ethnic Identity.* Toronto: Peter Martin Associates Press, 1978.
Sayre, Gordon M. *Les Sauvages Américans: Representations of Native Americans in French and English Colonial Literature.* Chapel Hill: University of North Carolina Press, 1997.
Scott, James C. *The Art of Not Being Governed: An Anarchist History of Upland Southeast Asia.* New Haven, CT: Yale University Press, 2009.
– *Seeing Like a State: How Certain Schemes to Improve the Human Condition Have Failed.* New Haven, CT: Yale University Press, 1998.
Secoy, Frank Raymond. *Changing Military Patterns on the Great Plains.* Seattle: University of Washington Press, 1953.
Seed, Patricia. *Ceremonies of Possession in Europe's Conquest of the New World, 1492–1640.* Cambridge: Cambridge University Press, 1995.
Seeman, Erik R. *The Huron-Wendat Feast of the Dead: Indian-European Encounters in Early North America.* Baltimore: Johns Hopkins University Press, 2011.

Shannon, Timothy J. "Dressing for Success on the Mohawk Frontier: Hendrick, William Johnson, and the Indian Fashion." *William and Mary Quarterly* 53, no. 1 (1996): 13–42.

Shennan, J.H. *Philippe, Duke of Orleans: Regent of France, 1715–1723*. London: Thames and Hudson, 1979.

Silverman, David J. *Thundersticks: Firearms and the Violent Transformation of Native America*. Cambridge, MA: Belknap Press of Harvard University Press, 2016.

Simpson, Leanne. "Looking after Gdoo-naaganinaa: Precolonial Nishnaabeg Diplomatic and Treaty Relationships." *Wicazo Sa Review* 23, no. 2 (2008): 29–42.

Skinner, Claiborne A. *The Upper Country: French Enterprise in the Colonial Great Lakes*. Baltimore: Johns Hopkins University Press, 2008.

Sleeper-Smith, Susan. *Indian Women and French Men: Rethinking Cultural Encounter in the Western Great Lakes*. Amherst: University of Massachusetts Press, 2001.

– *Indigenous Prosperity and American Conquest: Indian Women of the Ohio River Valley, 1690–1792*. Chapel Hill: University of North Carolina Press, 2018.

– "Introduction: The Middle Ground Revisited." *William and Mary Quarterly* 63, no. 1 (2006): 3–8.

– ed. *Rethinking the Fur Trade: Cultures of Exchange in an Atlantic World*. Lincoln: University of Nebraska Press, 2009.

– "Women, Kin, and Catholicism: New Perspectives on the Fur Trade." *Ethnohistory* 47, no. 2 (2000): 423–52.

Smith, G. Hubert. *The Explorations of the La Vérendryes in the Northern Plains, 1738–43*. Lincoln: University of Nebraska Press, 1980.

Smith, James G.E. "The Western Woods Cree: Anthropological Myth and Historical Reality." *American Ethnologist* 14, no. 3 (1987): 434–48.

Smurr, John W. "A New La Vérendrye Theory." *Pacific Northwest Quarterly* 43 (1952): 51–64.

Soll, Jacob. *The Information Master: Jean-Baptiste Colbert's Secret State Intelligence System*. Ann Arbor: University of Michigan Press, 2009.

– *The Reckoning: Financial Accountability and the Rise and Fall of Nations*. New York: Basic Books, 2014.

Sprague, D.N., and R.P. Frye. *The Genealogy of the First Metis Nation: The Development and Dispersal of the Red River Settlement, 1820–1900*. Winnipeg: Pemmican Publications, 1983.

Spry, Irene M. "The Métis and Mixed-Bloods of Rupert's Land before 1870." In *The New Peoples: Being and Becoming Métis in North*

America, edited by Jacqueline Peterson and Jennifer S.H. Brown, 95–118. Winnipeg: University of Manitoba Press, 1985.

Stanley, George F.G. *The Birth of Western Canada: A History of the Riel Rebellions*. Toronto: University of Toronto Press, 1961.

Starkey, Armstrong. *European and Native American Warfare, 1675–1815*. Norman: University of Oklahoma Press, 1998.

– "Frontier Warfare in North America, 1513–1815." In *Technology, Disease and Colonial Conquests, Sixteenth to Eighteenth Centuries: Essays Reappraising the Guns and Germs Theories*, edited by George Raudzens, 59–84. Leiden: Brill, 2001.

– *War in the Age of Enlightenment, 1700–1789*. London: Praeger, 2003.

Starna, William A., and José António Brandão. "From the Mohawk-Mahican War to the Beaver Wars: Questioning the Pattern." *Ethnohistory* 51, no. 4 (2004): 725–50.

Steele, Ian K. *Setting All the Captives Free: Capture, Adjustment, and Recollection in Allegheny Country*. Montreal and Kingston: McGill-Queen's University Press, 2013.

Stephen, Scott. *Masters and Servants: The Hudson's Bay Company and Its North American Workforce, 1668–1786*. Edmonton: University of Alberta Press, 2019.

– "Masters and Servants: The Hudson's Bay Company and its Personnel, 1668–1782." PhD dissertation, University of Manitoba, 2006.

– "A Puzzle Revisited: Historiographic and Documentary Problems in the Journals of Anthony Henday." Master's thesis, University of Winnipeg/University of Manitoba, 1997.

Stern, Philip J. *The Company-State: Corporate Sovereignty and the Early Modern Foundations of the British Empire in India*. Oxford: Oxford University Press, 2011.

St-Onge, Nicole. "Blue Beads, Vermilion, and Scalpers: The Social Economy of the 1810–1812 Astorian Overland Expedition's French-Canadian Voyageurs." In *French and Indians in the Heart of North America, 1630–1815*, edited by Robert Englebert and Guillaume Teasdale, 183–216. East Lansing: Michigan State University Press, 2013.

– "The Dissolution of a Métis Community: Pointe à Grouette, 1860–1885." *Studies in Political Economy* 18 (1985): 149–72.

– "Early Forefathers to the Athabasca Métis: Long-Term North West Company Employees." In *The Long Journey of a Forgotten People: Métis Identities and Family Histories*, edited by David T. McNab and Ute Lischke, 109–61. Waterloo, ON: Wilfrid Laurier University Press, 2007.

– "Familial Foes? French-Sioux Families and Plains Métis Brigades in the Nineteenth Century." *American Indian Quarterly* 39, no. 3 (2015): 302–37.

– "'He Was Neither a Soldier nor a Slave: He Was under the Control of No Man': Kahnawake Mohawks in the Northwest Fur Trade, 1790–1850." *Canadian Journal of History* 51, no. 1 (2016): 1–32.

– "Le poste de La Pointe sur l'île Madeline, tremplin vers le monde franco-anichinabé de la traite des fourrures." *Revue d'histoire de l'Amérique française* 73, nos. 1–2 (2019): 13–43.

– *Saint-Laurent, Manitoba: Evolving Métis Identities, 1850–1914*. Regina: Canadian Plains Research Centre, 2004.

St-Onge, Nicole, Carolyn Podruchny, and Brenda Macdougall, eds. *Contours of a People: Métis Family, Mobility, and History*. Norman: University of Oklahoma Press, 2012.

Sturtevant, Andrew. "'Inseparable Companions' and Irreconcilable Enemies: the Hurons and Odawas of French Détroit, 1701–38." *Ethnohistory* 60, no. 2 (2013): 219–43.

– "Jealous Neighbors: Rivalry and Alliance among the Native Communities of Detroit, 1701–1766." PhD dissertation, College of William and Mary, 2011.

Sundstrom, Linea. "Smallpox Used Them Up: References to Epidemic Disease in Northern Plains Winter Counts, 1714–1920." *Ethnohistory* 44, no. 2 (1997): 305–43.

Swan, Ruth. "The Crucible: Pembina and the Origins of the Red River Valley Metis." PhD dissertation, University of Manitoba, 2009.

Swan, Ruth, and Edward A. Jerome. "Indigenous Knowledge, Literacy and Research on Métissage and Métis Origins on the Saskatchewan River: The Case of the Jerome Family." In *The Western Métis: Profile of a People*, edited by Patrick C. Douaud, 31–54. Regina: University of Regina Press, 2007.

Taylor, Alan. *American Colonies: The Settling of North America*. London: Penguin, 2001.

– *The Divided Ground: Indians, Settlers, and the Northern Borderland of the American Revolution*. New York: Alfred A. Knopf, 2006.

Teasdale, Guillaume. *Fruits of Perseverance: The French Presence in the Detroit River Region, 1701–1815*. Montreal and Kingston: McGill-Queen's University Press, 2019.

Teillet, Jean. *The North-West Is Our Mother: The Story of Louis Riel's People, the Metis Nation*. Toronto: HarperCollins Canada, 2019.

Thierry, Éric. *La France de Henri IV en Amérique du nord: De la création de l'Acadie à la fondation de Québec*. Paris: Honoré Champion, 2008.

Thistle, Paul C. *Indian-European Trade Relations in the Lower Saskatchewan River Region to 1840*. Winnipeg: University of Manitoba Press, 1986.

– "The Twatt Family, 1780–1840: Amerindian, Ethnic Category, or Ethnic Group Identity?" In *The Western Métis: Profile of a People*, edited by Patrick C. Douaud, 73–89. Regina: University of Regina Press, 2007.

Thomson, Janice E. *Mercenaries, Pirates, and Sovereigns: State-Building and Extraterritorial Violence in Early Modern Europe*. Princeton, NJ: Princeton University Press, 1994.

Thorne, Tanis C. *The Many Hands of My Relations: French and Indians on the Lower Missouri*. Columbia: University of Missouri Press, 1996.

Thwaites, Reuben Gold. *Collections of the State Historical Society of Wisconsin*. 20 vols. Madison: State Historical Society of Wisconsin, 1855–1915.

– *Father Marquette*. New York: D. Appleton and Company, 1902.

– *The Jesuit Relations and Allied Documents: Travels and Exploration of the Jesuit Missionaries in New France, 1610–1791; the Original French, Latin, and Italian Texts, with English Translations and Notes*. 73 vols. Cleveland, OH: Burrows, 1896–1901.

Townsend, Camilla. *Malintzin's Choices: An Indian Woman in the Conquest of Mexico*. Albuquerque: University of New Mexico Press, 2006.

Townsend, Joan B. "Firearms against Native Arms: A Study in Comparative Efficiencies with an Alaskan Example." *Arctic Anthropology* 20, no. 2 (1983): 1–33.

Trémaudan, August-Henri de. *Histoire de la nation métisse dans l'ouest Canadien*. Montreal: Éditions Albert Lévesque, 1935.

Trigger, Bruce G. *The Children of Aataentsic: A History of the Huron People to 1660*. Montreal and Kingston: McGill-Queen's University Press, 1976.

– *Natives and Newcomers: Canada's "Heroic Age" Reconsidered*. Montreal and Kingston: McGill-Queen's University Press, 1985.

Trudel, Marcel. *Canada's Forgotten Slaves: Two Hundred Years of Bondage*. Translated by George Tombs. Montreal: Véhicule Press, 2013.

– *Les Débuts du régime seigneurial au Canada*. Montreal: Fides, 1974.

– *Dictionnaire des esclaves et de leurs propriétaires au Canada français*. Montreal: Hurtubise, 1990.

True, Micah. *Masters and Students: Jesuit Mission Ethnography in Seventeenth-Century New France*. Montreal and Kingston: McGill-Queen's University Press, 2015.

Tyrrell, J. B. *Journals of Samuel Hearne and Philip Turnor between the Years 1774 and 1792*. New York: Greenwood Press, 1968.

Usner, Daniel H. *Indians, Settlers, and Slaves in a Frontier Exchange Economy: The Lower Mississippi Valley before 1783*. Chapel Hill: North Carolina University Press, 1992.

Van Kirk, Sylvia. "'The Custom of the Country': An Examination of Fur Trade Marriage Practices." In *Rethinking the Fur Trade: Cultures of Exchange in an Atlantic World*, edited by Susan Sleeper-Smith, 481–518. Lincoln: University of Nebraska Press, 2009.

– *Many Tender Ties: Women in Fur-Trade Society, 1670–1870*. Norman: University of Oklahoma Press, 1980.

Verney, Jack. *The Good Regiment: The Carignan-Salières Regiment in Canada, 1665–1668*. Montreal and Kingston: McGill-Queen's University Press, 1991.

Vézina, Robert. "Le Lexique des voyageurs francophones et les contacts interlinguistiques dans le milieu de la traite des pelleteries: Approche sociohistorique, philologique et lexicologique." PhD dissertation, Université Laval, 2010.

Vidal, Cécile. "French Louisiana in the Age of the Companies, 1712–1731." In *Constructing Early Modern Empires: Proprietary Ventures in the Atlantic World, 1500–1750*, edited by Louis H. Roper and Bertrand Van Ruymbeke, 133–62. Leiden: Brill, 2007.

Vigeant, J., I. Ribot, and J.-F. Hélie. "Dietary Habits in New France during the 17th and 18th Centuries: An Isotopic Perspective." *American Journal of Physical Anthropology* 162, no. 3 (2017): 462–75.

Waiser, Bill. *A World We Have Lost: Saskatchewan before 1905*. Markham, ON: Fifth House, 2016.

Wallace, W. Stewart. *Documents Relating to the North West Company*. Toronto: Champlain Society, 1934.

– *The Pedlars from Quebec and Other Papers on the Nor'Westers*. Toronto: Ryerson Press, 1954.

Warkentin, Germaine. "'Make It Last Forever as It Is': John McDonald of Garth's Vision of a Native Kingdom in the Northwest." In *Gathering Places: Aboriginal and Fur Trade Histories*, edited by Carolyn Podruchny and Laura Peers, 149–78. Vancouver: UBC Press, 2010.

– ed. *Pierre-Esprit Radisson: The Collected Writings*. 2 vols. Montreal and Kingston: McGill-Queen's University Press, 2012 and 2014.

Warkentin, Germaine, and Carolyn Podruchny. *Decentring the Renaissance: Canada and Europe in Multidisciplinary Perspective, 1500–1700*. Toronto: University of Toronto Press, 2001.

Warren, Stephen. *The Worlds the Shawnees Made: Migration and Violence in Early America*. Chapel Hill: University of North Carolina Press, 2014.

Warren, William Whipple. *History of the Ojibway People*. St Paul: Minnesota Historical Society, 1885.

Weyhing, Richard. "'Gascon Exaggerations': The Rise of Antoine Laumet dit de Lamothe, Sieur de Cadillac, the Foundation of Colonial Detroit, and the Origins of the Fox Wars." In *French and Indians in the Heart of North America, 1630–1815*, edited by Robert Englebert and Guillaume Teasdale, 77–112. East Lansing: Michigan State University Press, 2013.

– "'LeSueur in the Sioux Country': Rethinking France's Indian alliance in the Pays d'en Haut." *Atlantic Studies* 10, no. 1 (2013): 9–14.

White, Bruce M. "Encounters with Spirits: Ojibwa and Dakota Theories about the French and Their Merchandise." *Ethnohistory* 41, no. 3 (1994): 369–405.

– *Grand Portage as a Trading Post: Patterns of Trade at "the Great Carrying Place."* Grand Marais, MN: Grand Portage National Monument, National Park Service, 2005.

White, Richard. "Creative Misunderstandings and New Understandings." *William and Mary Quarterly* 63, no. 1 (2006): 9–14.

– *The Middle Ground: Indians, Empires, and Republics in the Great Lakes Region, 1600–1815*. Cambridge: Cambridge University Press, 1991.

White, Sophie. "'To Ensure that He Not Give Himself Over to the Indians': Cleanliness, Frenchification, and Whiteness." *Journal of Early American History* 2, no. 2 (2012): 111–49.

– *Wild Frenchmen and Frenchified Indians: Material Culture and Race in Colonial Louisiana*. Philadelphia: University of Pennsylvania Press, 2013.

Wicken, Bill. "Encounters with Tall Sails and Tall Tales: Mi'kmaq Society, 1500–1760." PhD dissertation, McGill University, 1994.

Widder, Keith R. *Beyond Pontiac's Shadow: Michilimackinac and the Anglo-Indian War of 1763*. East Lansing: Michigan State University Press, 2013.

Wien, Thomas. "Familles paysannes et marché de l'engagement pour le commerce des fourrures au Canada au XVIIIE siècle." In *Famille et marché. XVIe–XXe siècles*, edited by Christian Dessureault, Joseph

Goy, and John A. Dickinson, 167–80. Sillery, QC: Les éditions du Septentrion, 2003.
– "Le Pérou éphémère, termes d'échange et éclatement du commerce franco-amérindien, 1645–1670." In *Vingt ans après, Habitants et marchands: Lectures de l'histoire des XVIIe et XVIIIe siècles Canadiens*, edited by Sylvie Dépatie, Catherine Desbarats, Danielle Gauvreau, Mario Lalancette, and Thomas Wien, 160–88. Montreal and Kingston: McGill-Queen's University Press, 1998.
– "Selling Beaver Skins in North America and Europe, 1720–1760: The Uses of Fur-Trade Imperialism." *Journal of the Canadian Historical Association/Revue de la Société historique du Canada* 1, no. 1 (1990): 293–317.
Wilson, Arthur McCandless. *French Foreign Policy during the Administration of Cardinal Fleury, 1726–1743: A Study in Diplomacy and Commercial Development*. Westport, CT: Greenwood Press, 1972.
Wingerd, Mary Lethert. *North Country: The Making of Minnesota*. Minneapolis: University of Minnesota Press, 2010.
Witgen, Michael. *An Infinity of Nations: How the Native New World Shaped Early North America*. Philadelphia: University of Pennsylvania Press, 2012.
– "The Rituals of Possession: Native Identity and the Invention of Empire in Seventeenth-Century Western North America." *Ethnohistory* 54, no. 4 (2007): 639–68.
Wolf, John B. *Louis XIV: A Profile*. London: Palgrave Macmillan, 1968.
Wood, W. Raymond, William J. Hunt, and Randy H. Williams. *Fort Clark and Its Indian Neighbors: A Trading Post on the Upper Missouri*. Norman: Oklahoma University Press, 2011.
Wood, W. Raymond, and Thomas D. Thiessen. *Early Fur Trade on the Northern Plains: Canadian Traders among the Mandan and Hidatsa Indians, 1738–1818*. Norman: University of Oklahoma Press, 1985.
Wurtzburg, Susan, and Lyle Campbell. "North American Indian Sign Language: Evidence for Its Existence before European Contact." *International Journal of American Linguistics* 61, no. 2 (1995): 153–67.
Yannakakis, Yanna. *The Art of Being In-between: Native Intermediaries, Indian Identity, and Local Rule in Colonial Oaxaca*. Durham, NC: Duke University Press, 2008.
Zoltvany, Yves F. *The Government of New France: Royal, Clerical or Class Rule?* Scarborough, ON: Prentice-Hall, 1971.
– *Philippe de Rigaud de Vaudreuil: Governor of New France, 1703–1725*. Toronto: McClelland and Stewart, 1974.

Index